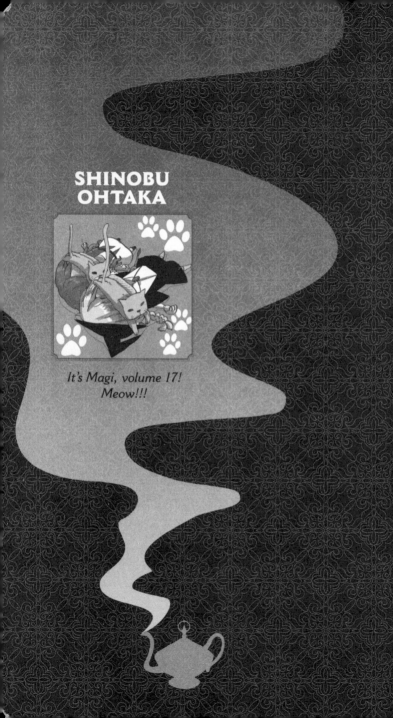

SHINOBU OHTAKA

*It's Magi, volume 17!
Meow!!!*

MAGI

Volume 17

Shonen Sunday Edition

Story and Art by
SHINOBU OHTAKA

MAGI Vol.17
by Shinobu OHTAKA
© 2009 Shinobu OHTAKA
All rights reserved.
Original Japanese edition published by SHOGAKUKAN.
English translation rights in the United States of America, Canada, the United Kingdom,
Ireland, Australia and New Zealand arranged with SHOGAKUKAN.

Translation & English Adaptation ◆ John Werry

Touch-up Art & Lettering ◆ Stephen Dutro

Editor ◆ Mike Montesa

Printed in the U.S.A.

Published by VIZ Media, LLC
P.O. Box 77010
San Francisco, CA 94107

10 9 8 7 6 5 4 3 2 1
First printing, April 2016

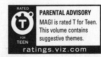

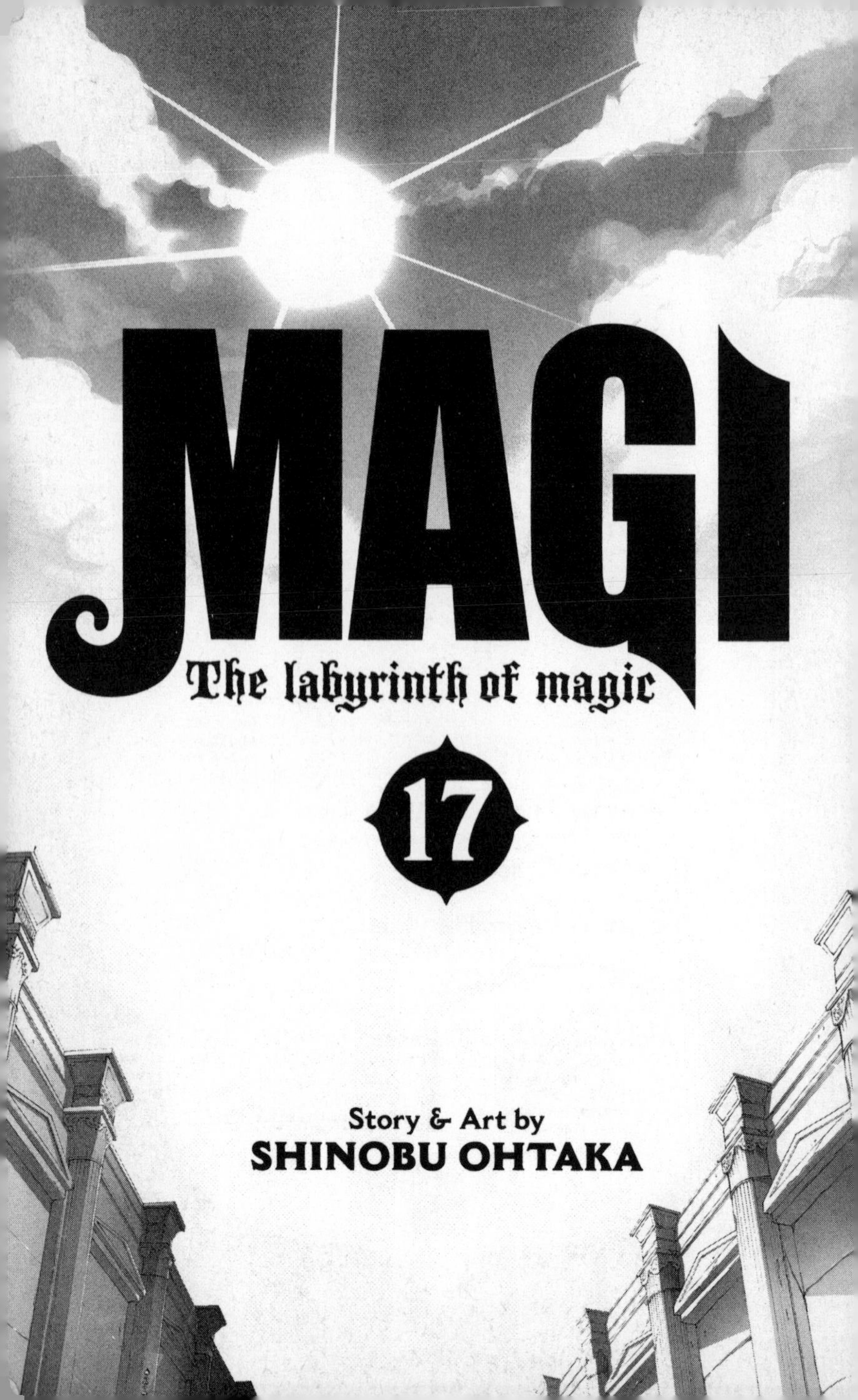

MAGI

The labyrinth of magic

17

Story & Art by

SHINOBU OHTAKA

MAGI
The labyrinth of magic
17

CONTENTS

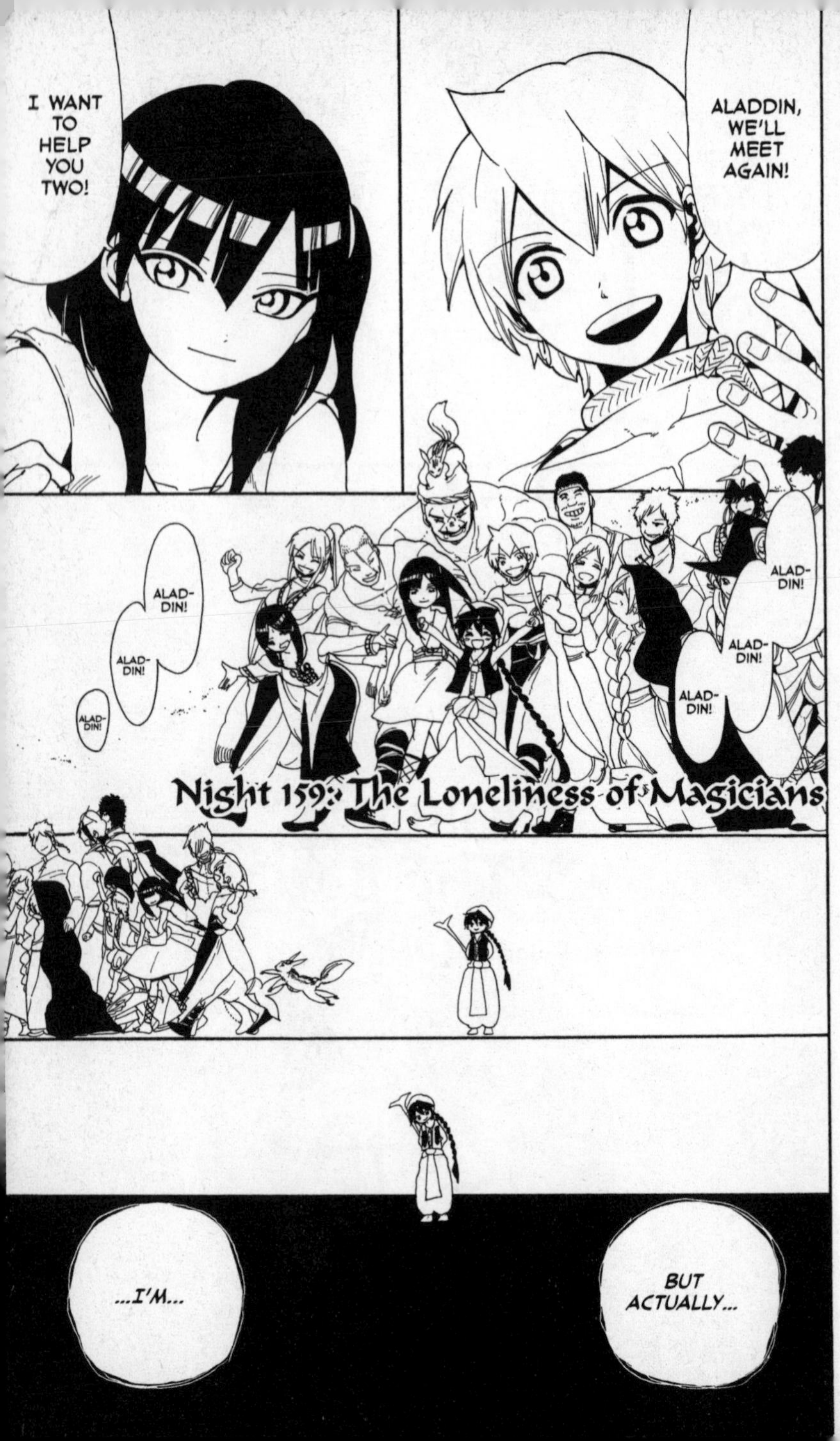
ALADDIN, WE'LL MEET AGAIN!
I WANT TO HELP YOU TWO!
ALAD-DIN!
ALAD-DIN!
ALAD-DIN!
ALAD-DIN!
ALAD-DIN!
ALAD-DIN!
Night 159: The Loneliness of Magicians
BUT ACTUALLY...
...I'M...

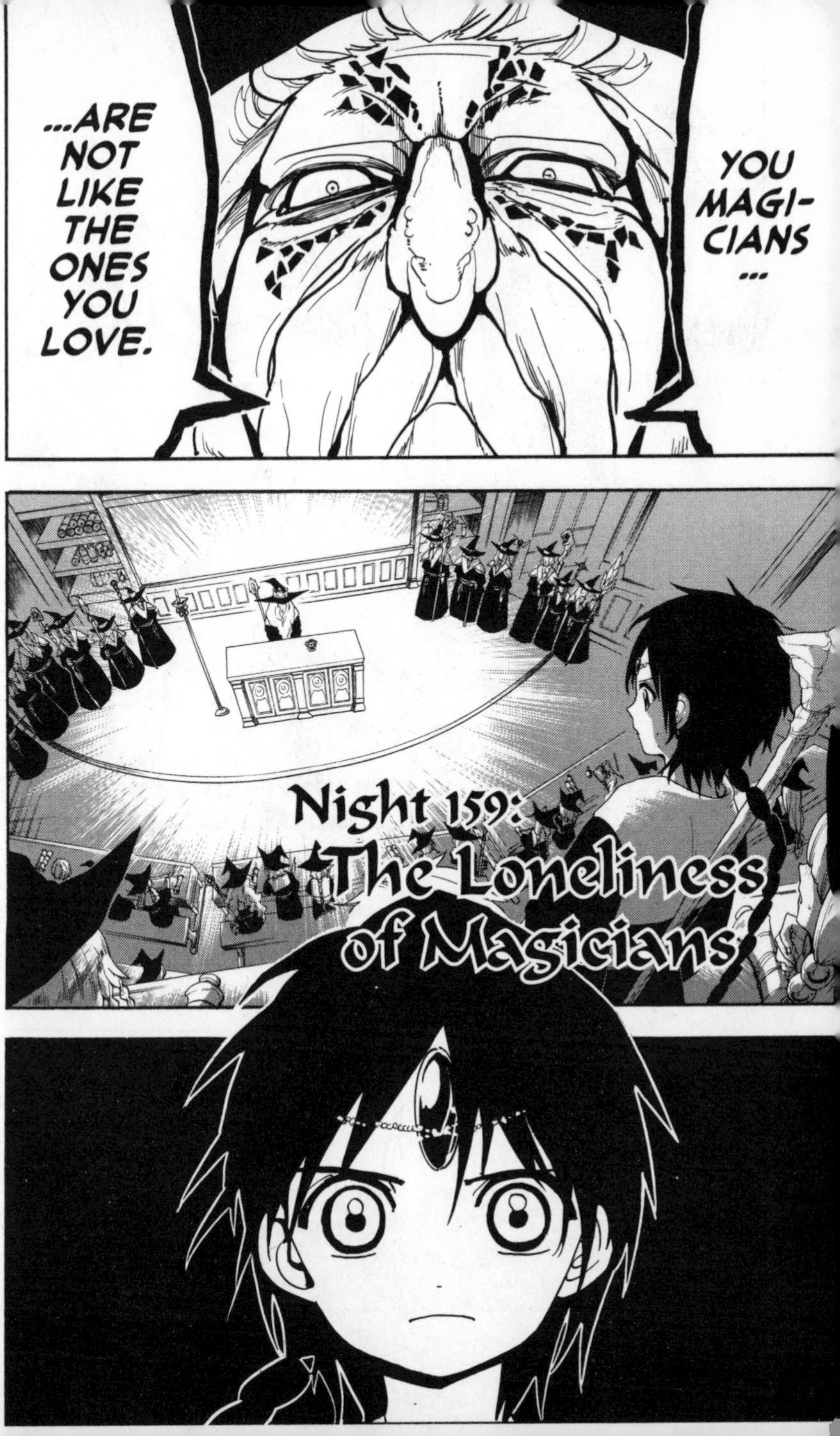
YOU MAGICIANS...
...ARE NOT LIKE THE ONES YOU LOVE.
Night 159: The Loneliness of Magicians

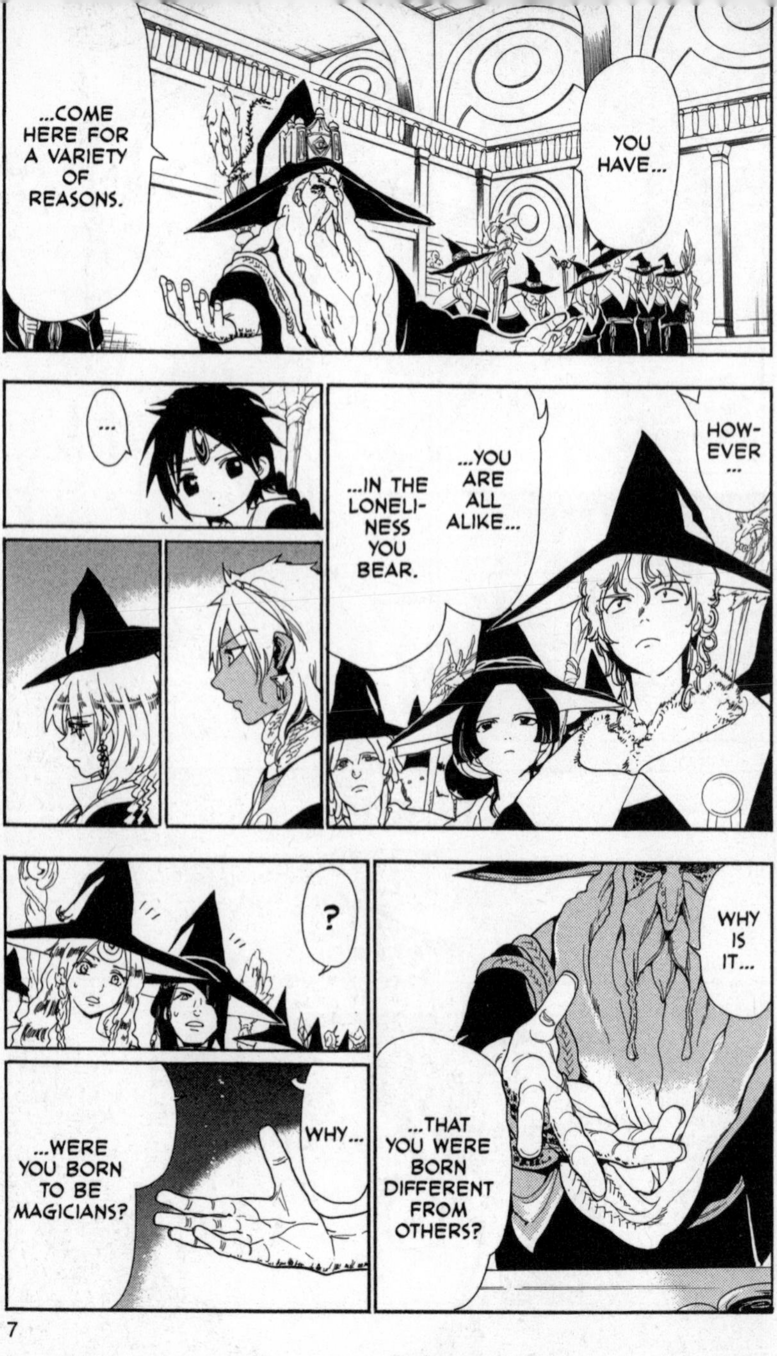
YOU HAVE...
...COME HERE FOR A VARIETY OF REASONS.
HOW-EVER...
...YOU ARE ALL ALIKE...
...IN THE LONELI-NESS YOU BEAR.
...
WHY IS IT...
...THAT YOU WERE BORN DIFFERENT FROM OTHERS?
?
WHY...
...WERE YOU BORN TO BE MAGICIANS?

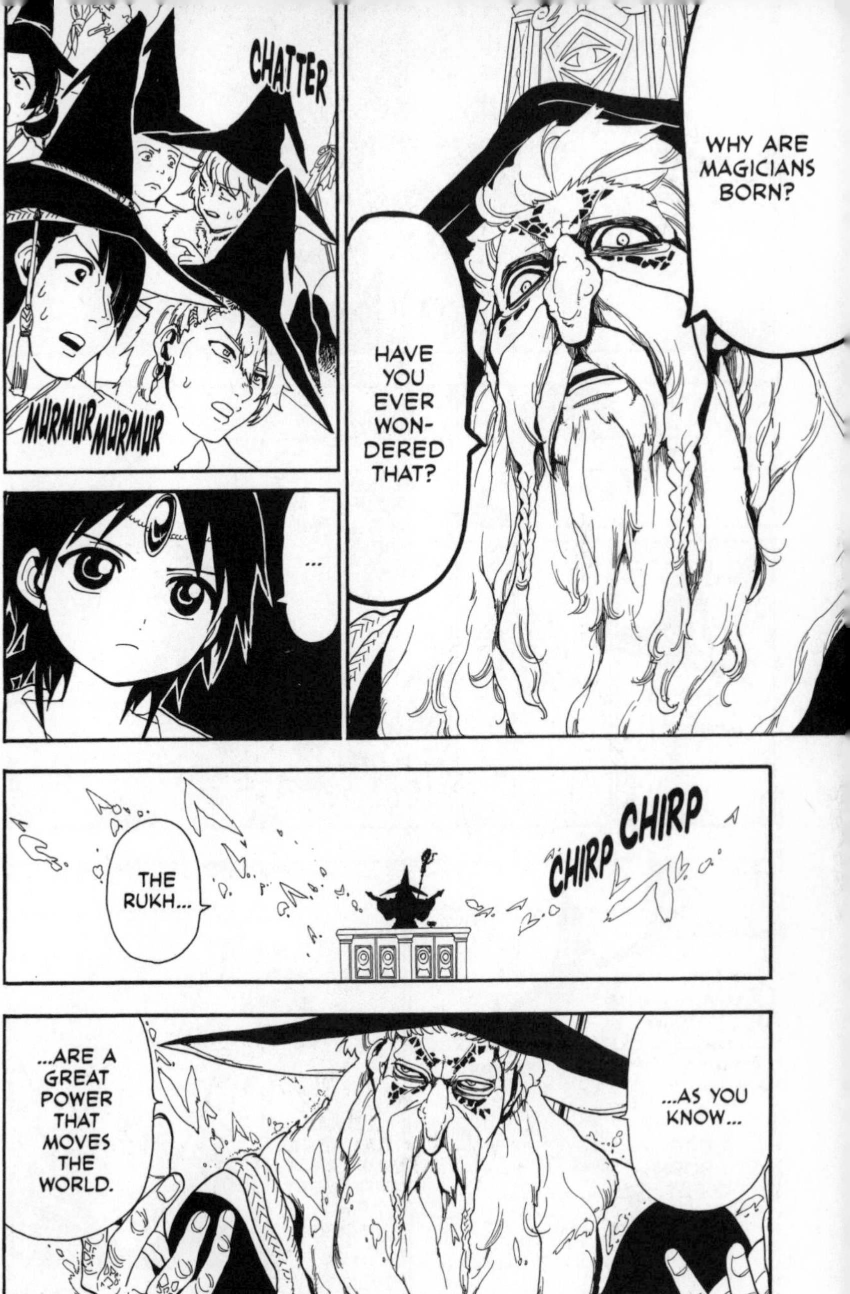
WHY ARE MAGICIANS BORN?
HAVE YOU EVER WON-DERED THAT?
CHATTER
MURMUR MURMUR
...
CHIRP CHIRP
THE RUKH...
...AS YOU KNOW...
...ARE A GREAT POWER THAT MOVES THE WORLD.

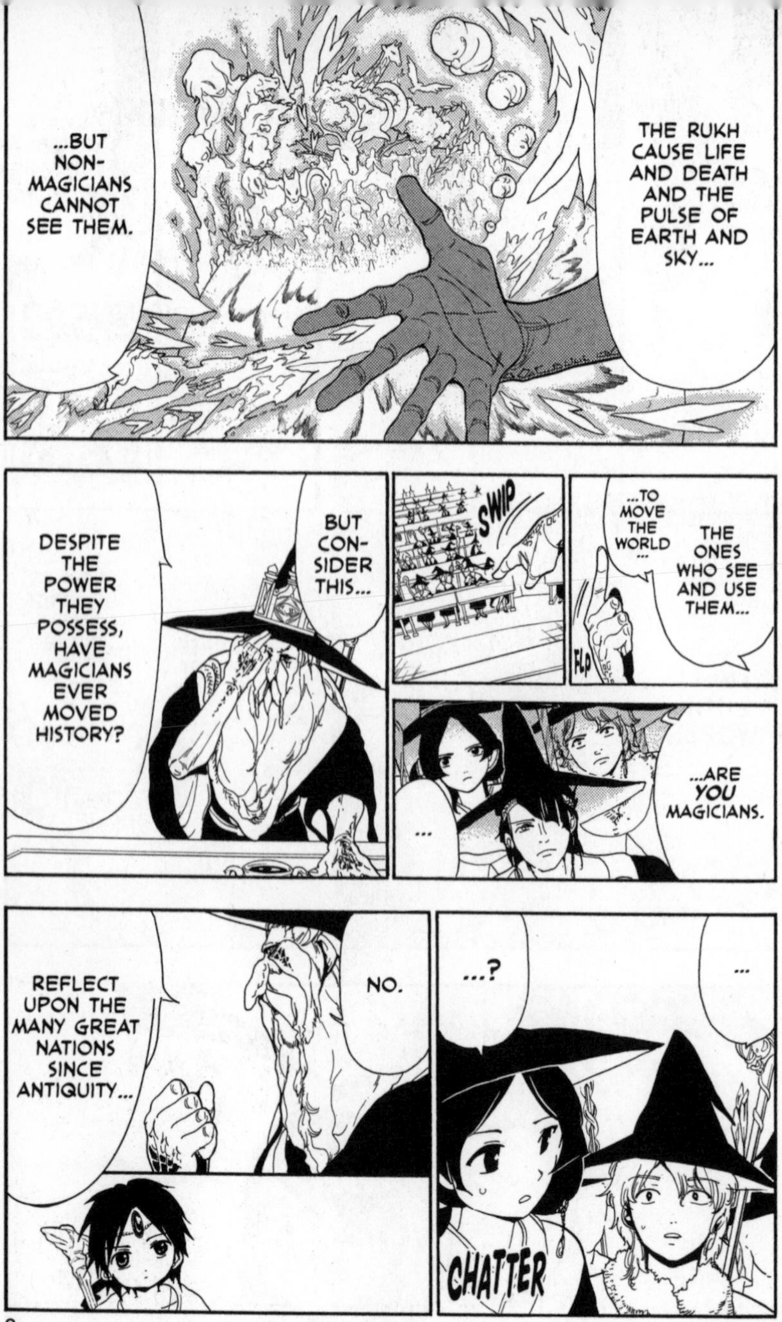
THE RUKH CAUSE LIFE AND DEATH AND THE PULSE OF EARTH AND SKY...
...BUT NON-MAGICIANS CANNOT SEE THEM.
THE ONES WHO SEE AND USE THEM...
...TO MOVE THE WORLD...
FLP
SWIP
...ARE YOU MAGICIANS.
...
BUT CON-SIDER THIS...
DESPITE THE POWER THEY POSSESS, HAVE MAGICIANS EVER MOVED HISTORY?
...
...?
CHATTER
NO.
REFLECT UPON THE MANY GREAT NATIONS SINCE ANTIQUITY...

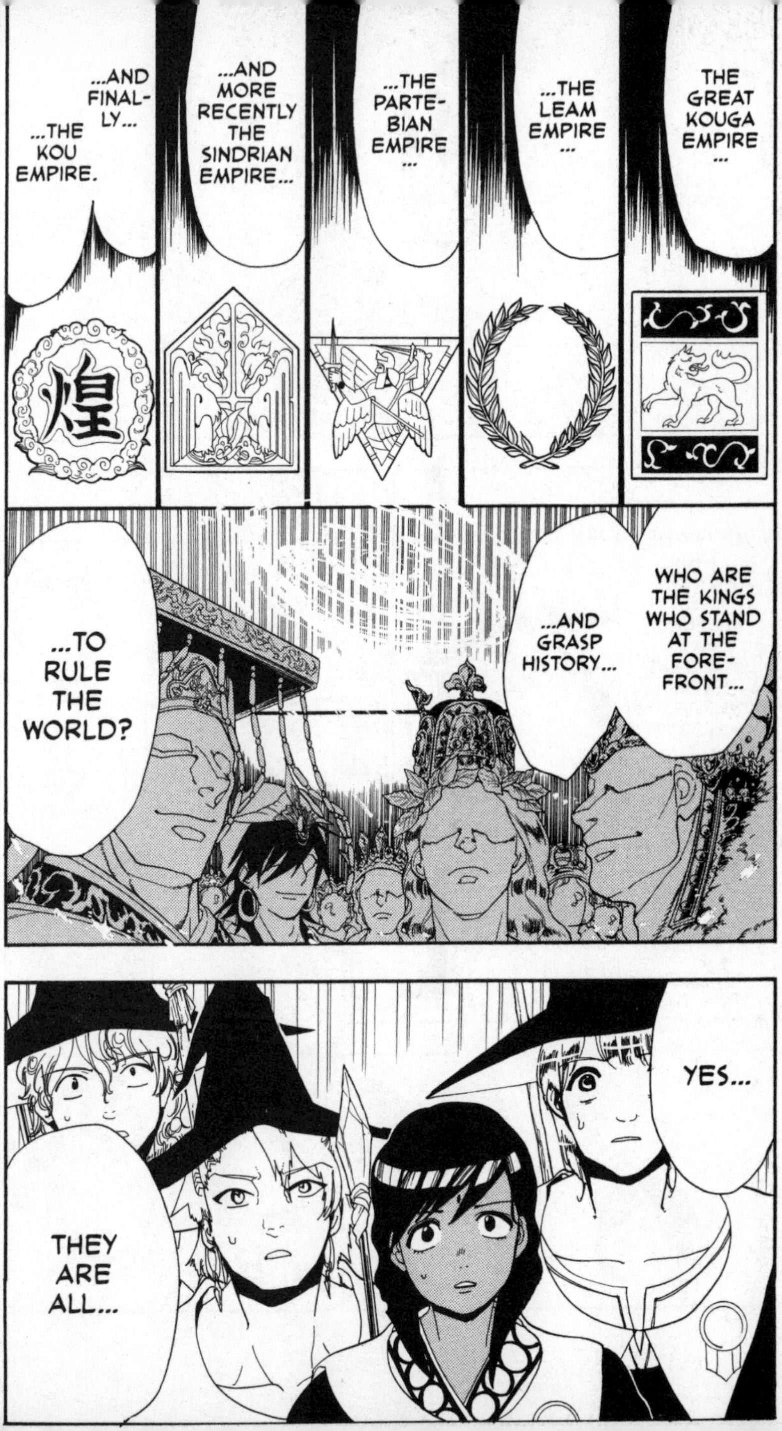
THE GREAT KOUGA EMPIRE...
...THE LEAM EMPIRE...
...THE PARTE-BIAN EMPIRE...
...AND MORE RECENTLY THE SINDRIAN EMPIRE...
...AND FINAL-LY...
...THE KOU EMPIRE.
煌
WHO ARE THE KINGS WHO STAND AT THE FORE-FRONT...
...AND GRASP HISTORY...
...TO RULE THE WORLD?
YES...
THEY ARE ALL...

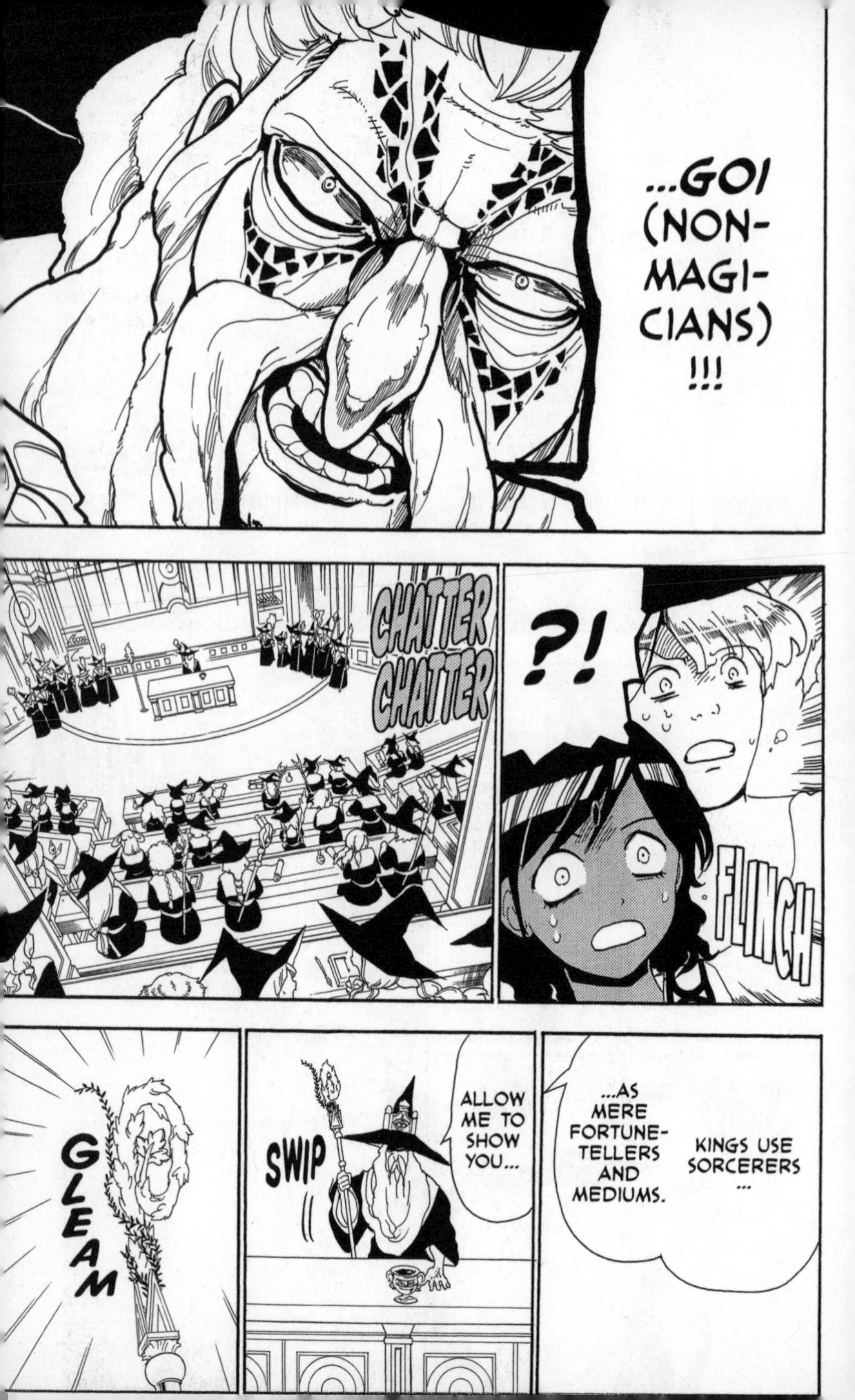
...GOI (NON-MAGICIANS) !!!
?!
FLINCH
CHATTER CHATTER
KINGS USE SORCERERS ...
...AS MERE FORTUNE-TELLERS AND MEDIUMS.
ALLOW ME TO SHOW YOU...
SWIP
GLEAM

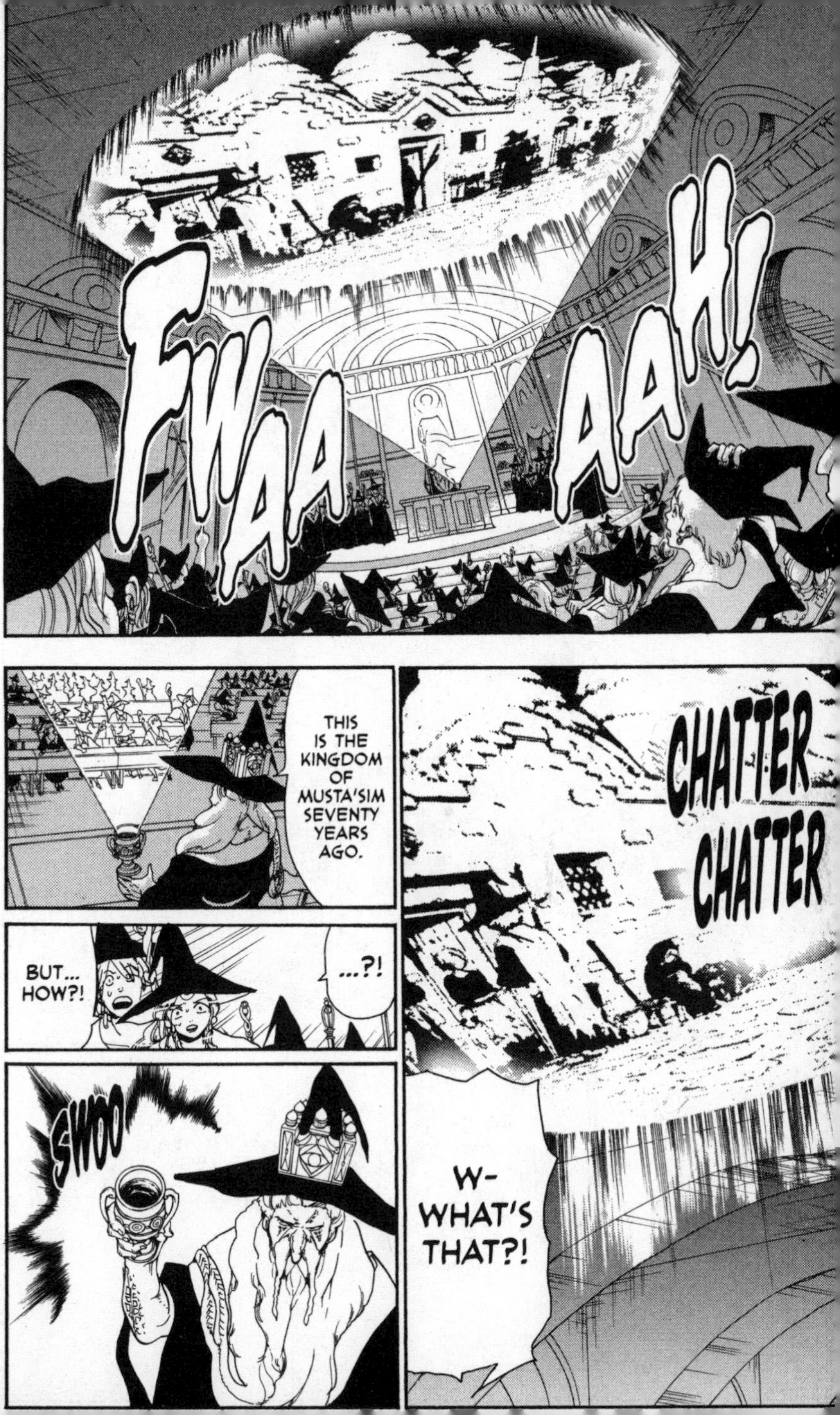
FWAA AAH!
CHATTER CHATTER
W-WHAT'S THAT?!
THIS IS THE KINGDOM OF MUSTA'SIM SEVENTY YEARS AGO.
...?!
BUT... HOW?!
SWOO

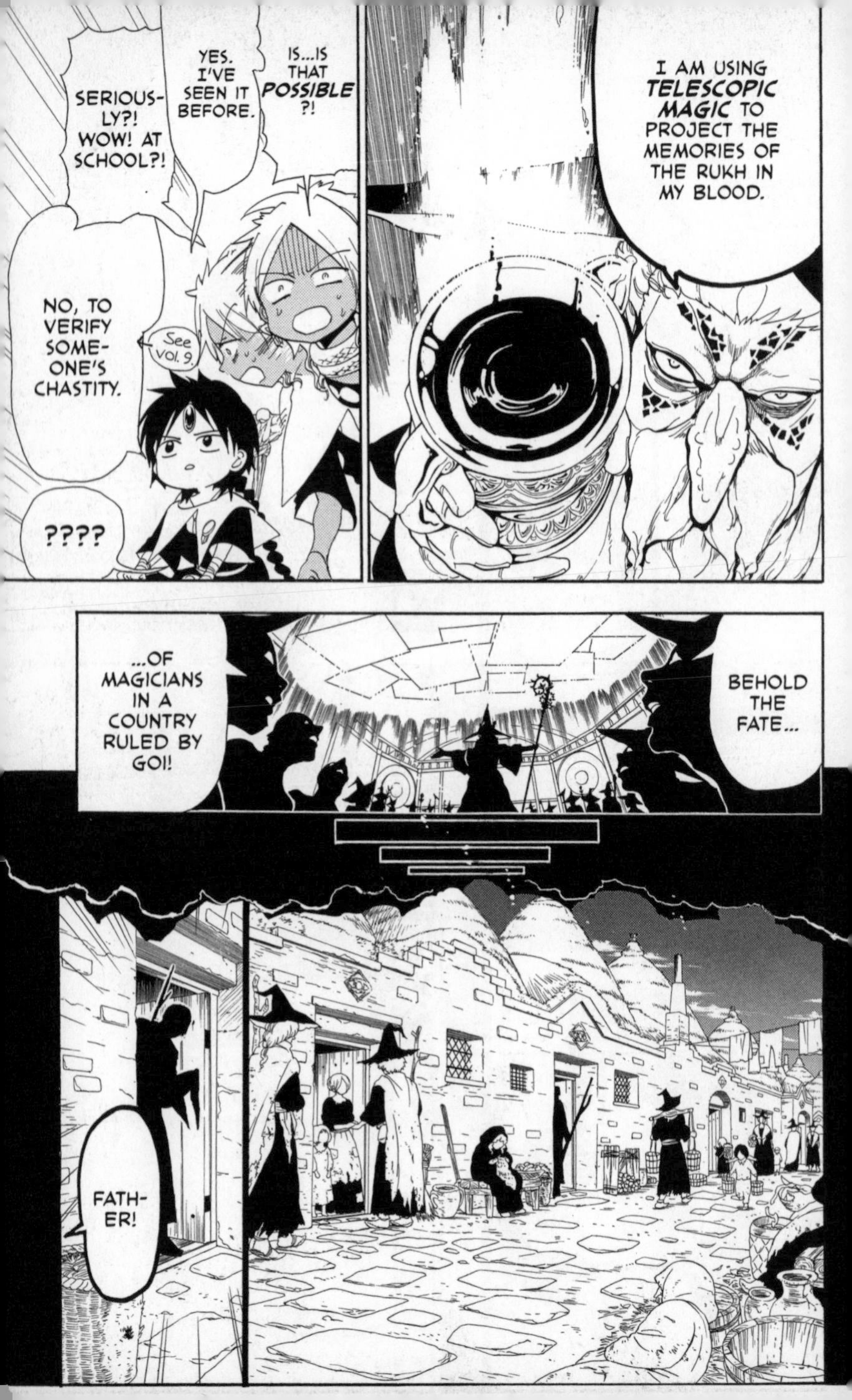
I AM USING *TELESCOPIC MAGIC* TO PROJECT THE MEMORIES OF THE RUKH IN MY BLOOD.
IS...IS THAT *POSSIBLE*?!
YES. I'VE SEEN IT BEFORE.
SERIOUS-LY?! WOW! AT SCHOOL?!
NO, TO VERIFY SOME-ONE'S CHASTITY.
See vol. 9.
????
BEHOLD THE FATE...
...OF MAGICIANS IN A COUNTRY RULED BY GOI!
FATH-ER!

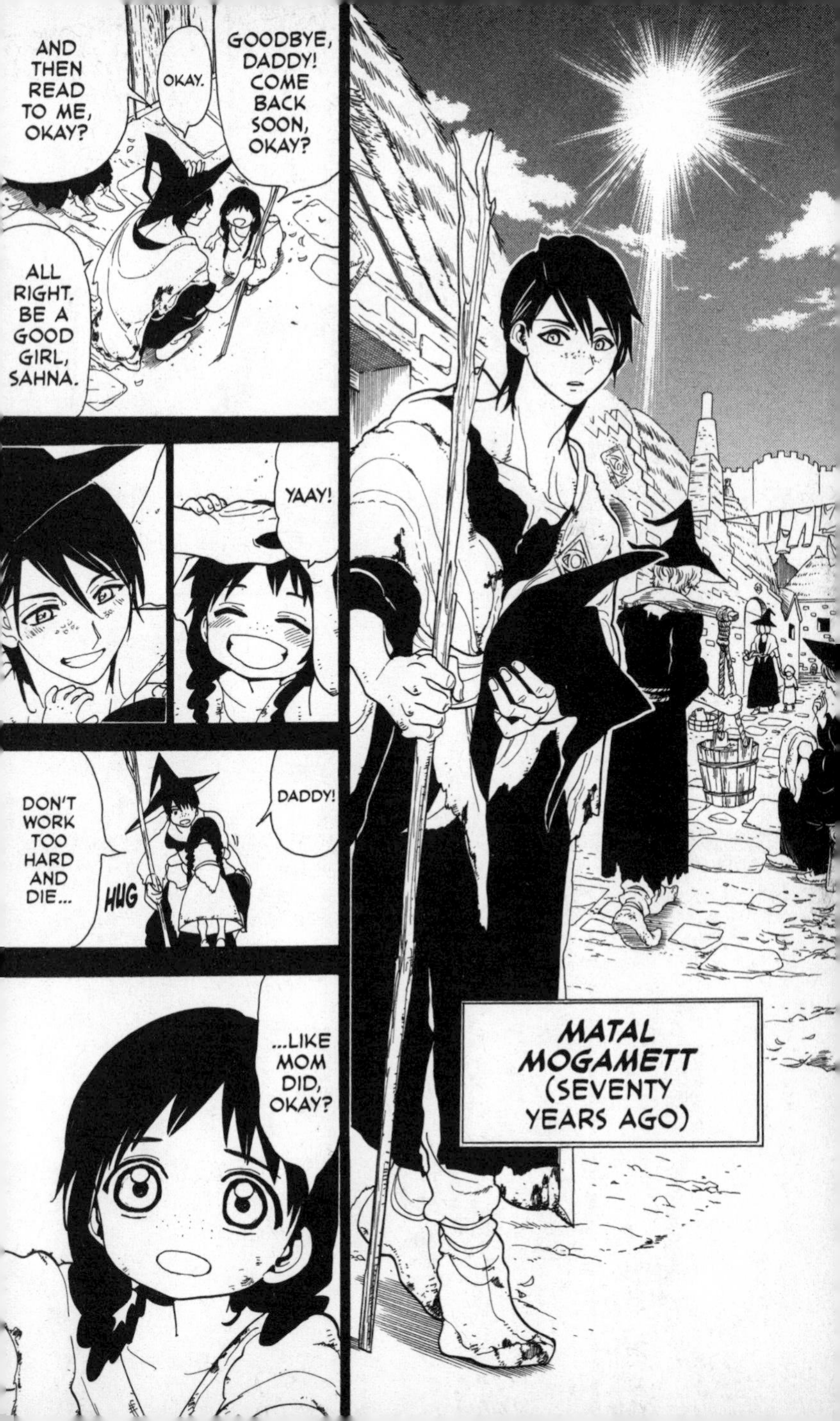
MATAL MOGAMETT (SEVENTY YEARS AGO)
GOODBYE, DADDY! COME BACK SOON, OKAY?
OKAY.
AND THEN READ TO ME, OKAY?
ALL RIGHT. BE A GOOD GIRL, SAHNA.
YAAY!
DADDY!
HUG
DON'T WORK TOO HARD AND DIE...
...LIKE MOM DID, OKAY?

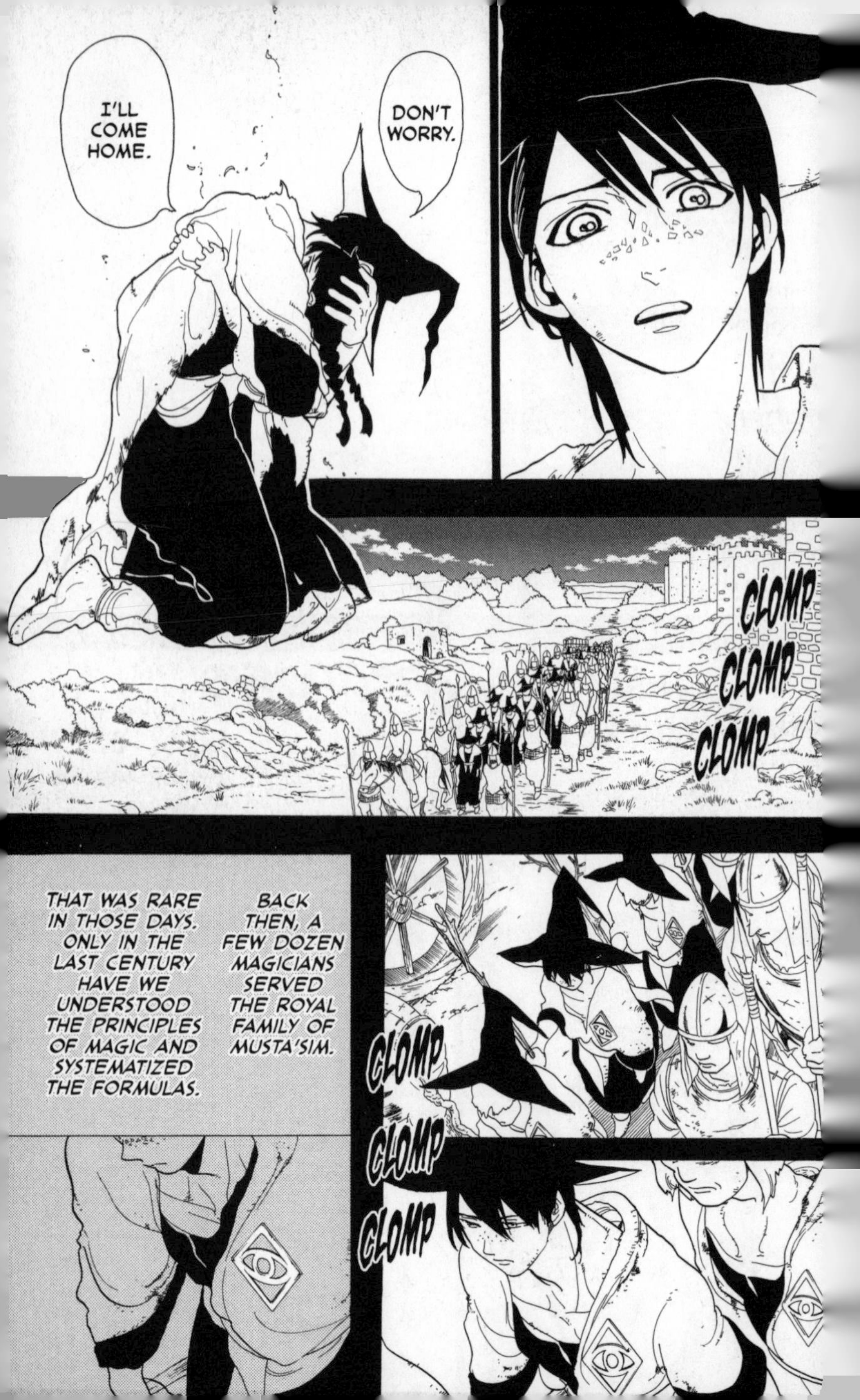
DON'T WORRY.
I'LL COME HOME.
CLOMP
CLOMP
CLOMP
CLOMP
BACK THEN, A FEW DOZEN MAGICIANS SERVED THE ROYAL FAMILY OF MUSTA'SIM.
THAT WAS RARE IN THOSE DAYS. ONLY IN THE LAST CENTURY HAVE WE UNDERSTOOD THE PRINCIPLES OF MAGIC AND SYSTEMATIZED THE FORMULAS.
CLOMP
CLOMP

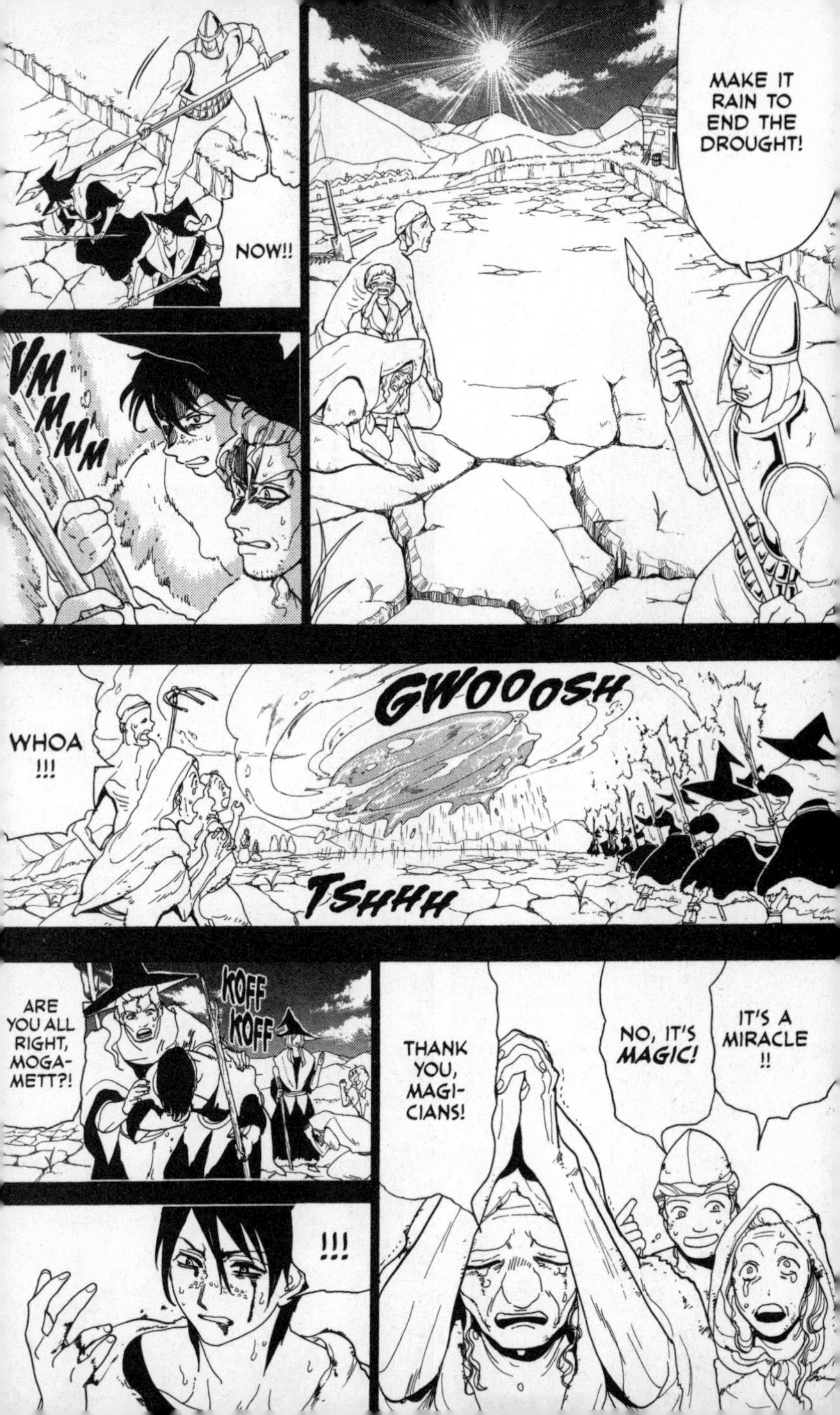
MAKE IT RAIN TO END THE DROUGHT!
NOW!!
VMMMMM
GWOOOSH
WHOA!!!
TSHHH
IT'S A MIRACLE!!
NO, IT'S *MAGIC!*
THANK YOU, MAGICIANS!
KOFF KOFF
ARE YOU ALL RIGHT, MOGAMETT?!
!!!

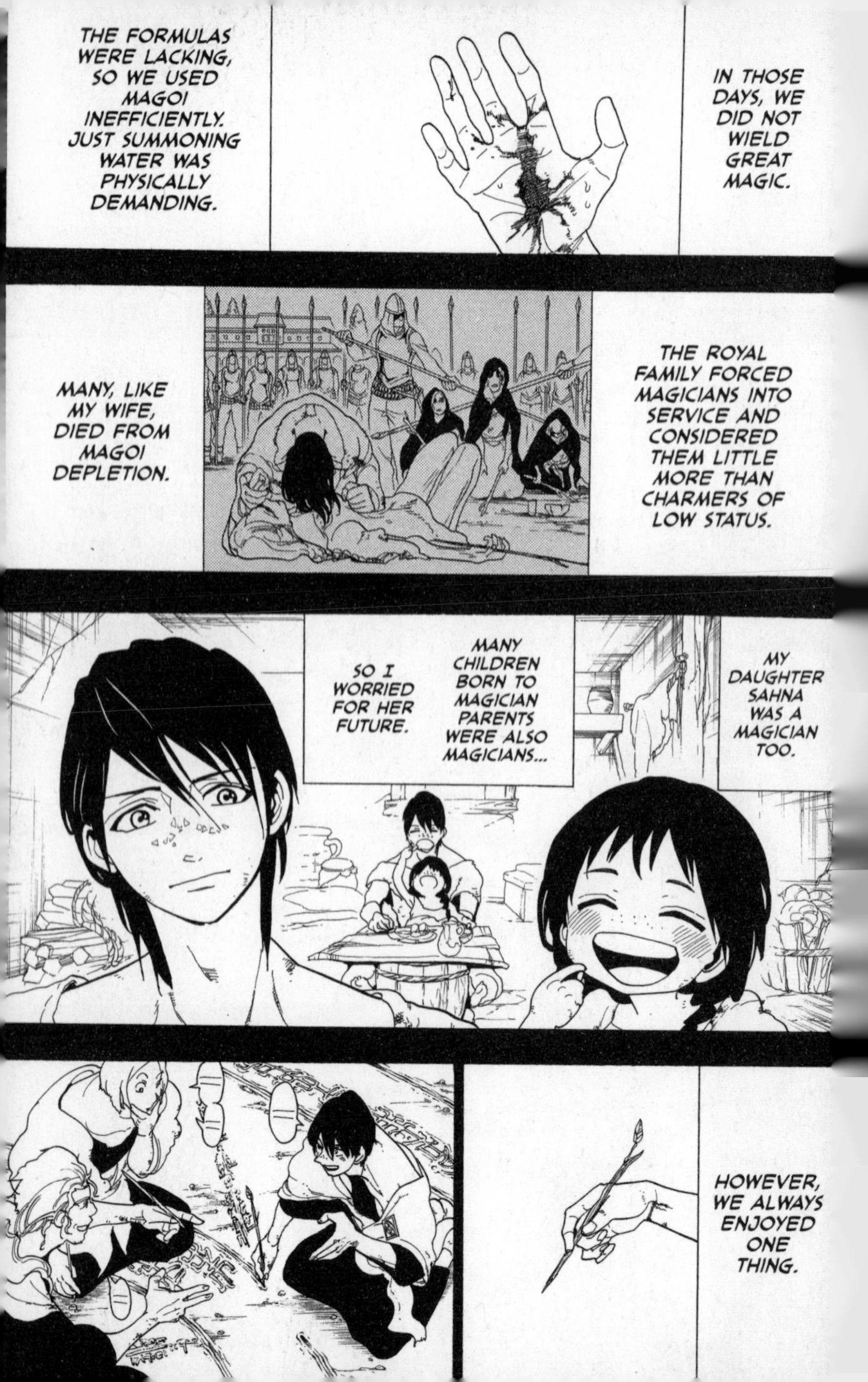
IN THOSE DAYS, WE DID NOT WIELD GREAT MAGIC.
THE FORMULAS WERE LACKING, SO WE USED MAGOI INEFFICIENTLY. JUST SUMMONING WATER WAS PHYSICALLY DEMANDING.
THE ROYAL FAMILY FORCED MAGICIANS INTO SERVICE AND CONSIDERED THEM LITTLE MORE THAN CHARMERS OF LOW STATUS.
MANY, LIKE MY WIFE, DIED FROM MAGOI DEPLETION.
MY DAUGHTER SAHNA WAS A MAGICIAN TOO.
MANY CHILDREN BORN TO MAGICIAN PARENTS WERE ALSO MAGICIANS...
SO I WORRIED FOR HER FUTURE.
HOWEVER, WE ALWAYS ENJOYED ONE THING.

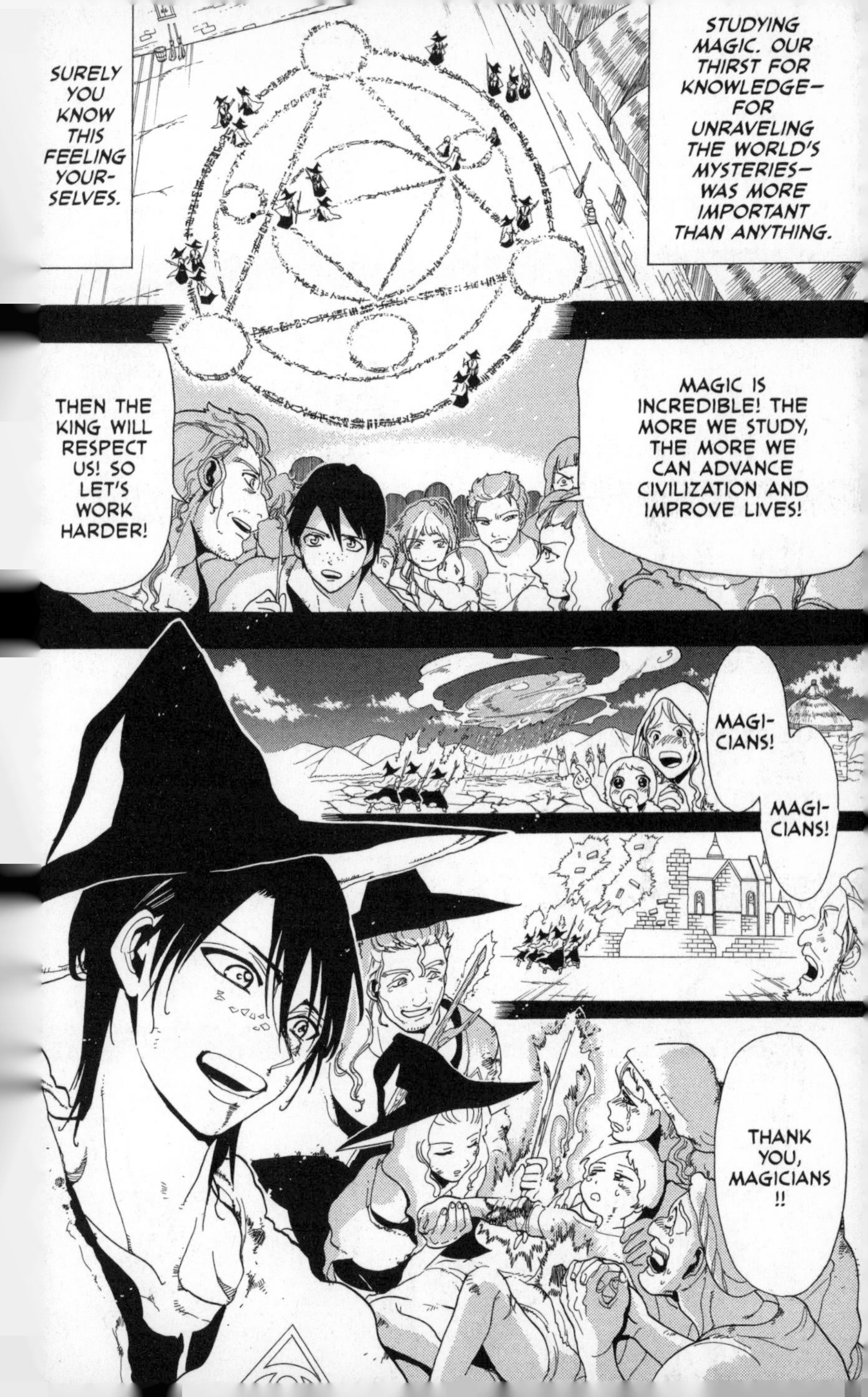
STUDYING MAGIC. OUR THIRST FOR KNOWLEDGE—FOR UNRAVELING THE WORLD'S MYSTERIES—WAS MORE IMPORTANT THAN ANYTHING.
SURELY YOU KNOW THIS FEELING YOURSELVES.
MAGIC IS INCREDIBLE! THE MORE WE STUDY, THE MORE WE CAN ADVANCE CIVILIZATION AND IMPROVE LIVES!
THEN THE KING WILL RESPECT US! SO LET'S WORK HARDER!
MAGICIANS!
MAGICIANS!
THANK YOU, MAGICIANS!!

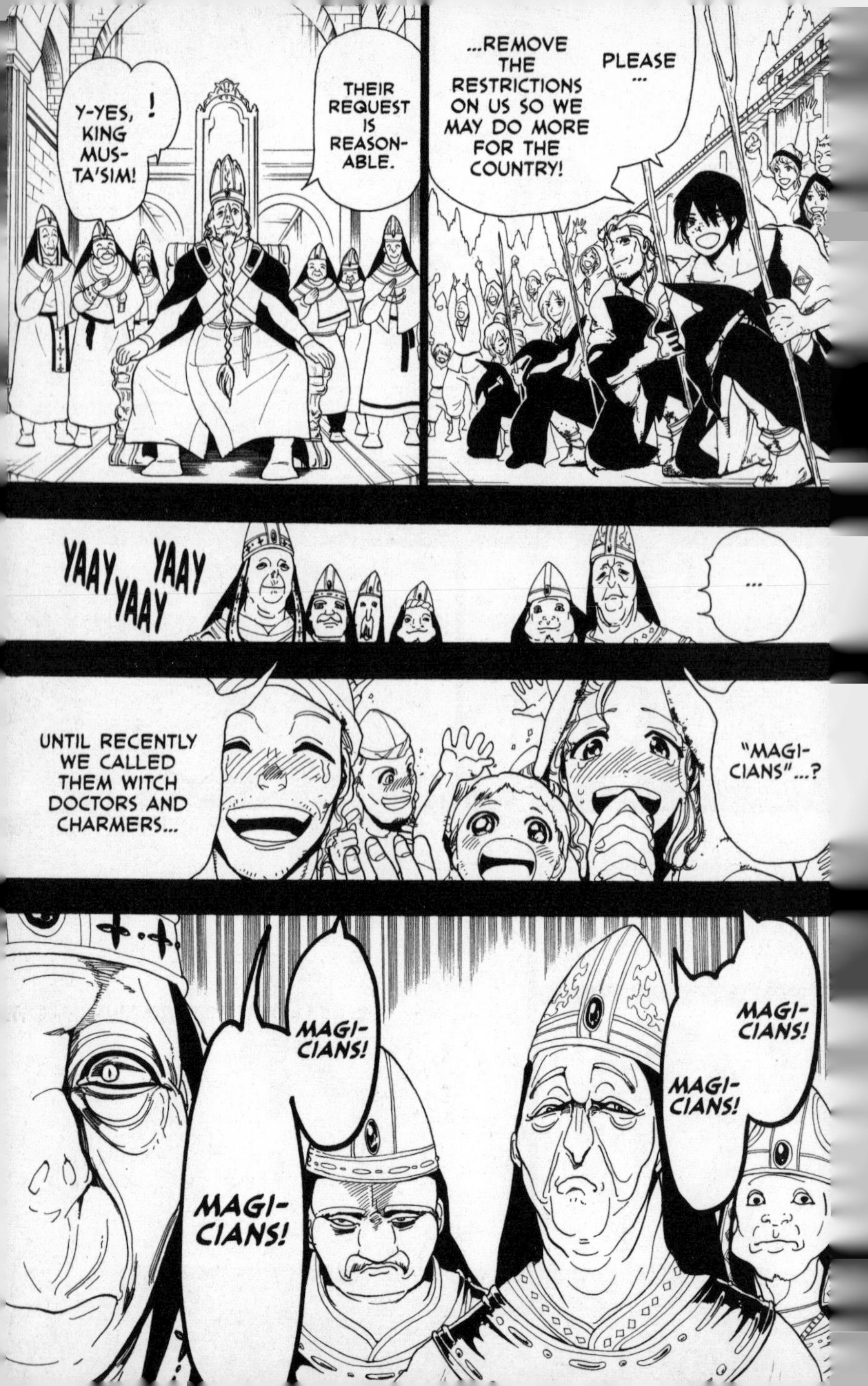
PLEASE ...
...REMOVE THE RESTRICTIONS ON US SO WE MAY DO MORE FOR THE COUNTRY!
THEIR REQUEST IS REASONABLE.
Y-YES, KING MUSTA'SIM!
!
...
YAAY YAAY YAAY
"MAGICIANS"...?
UNTIL RECENTLY WE CALLED THEM WITCH DOCTORS AND CHARMERS...
MAGICIANS!
MAGICIANS!
MAGICIANS!
MAGICIANS!

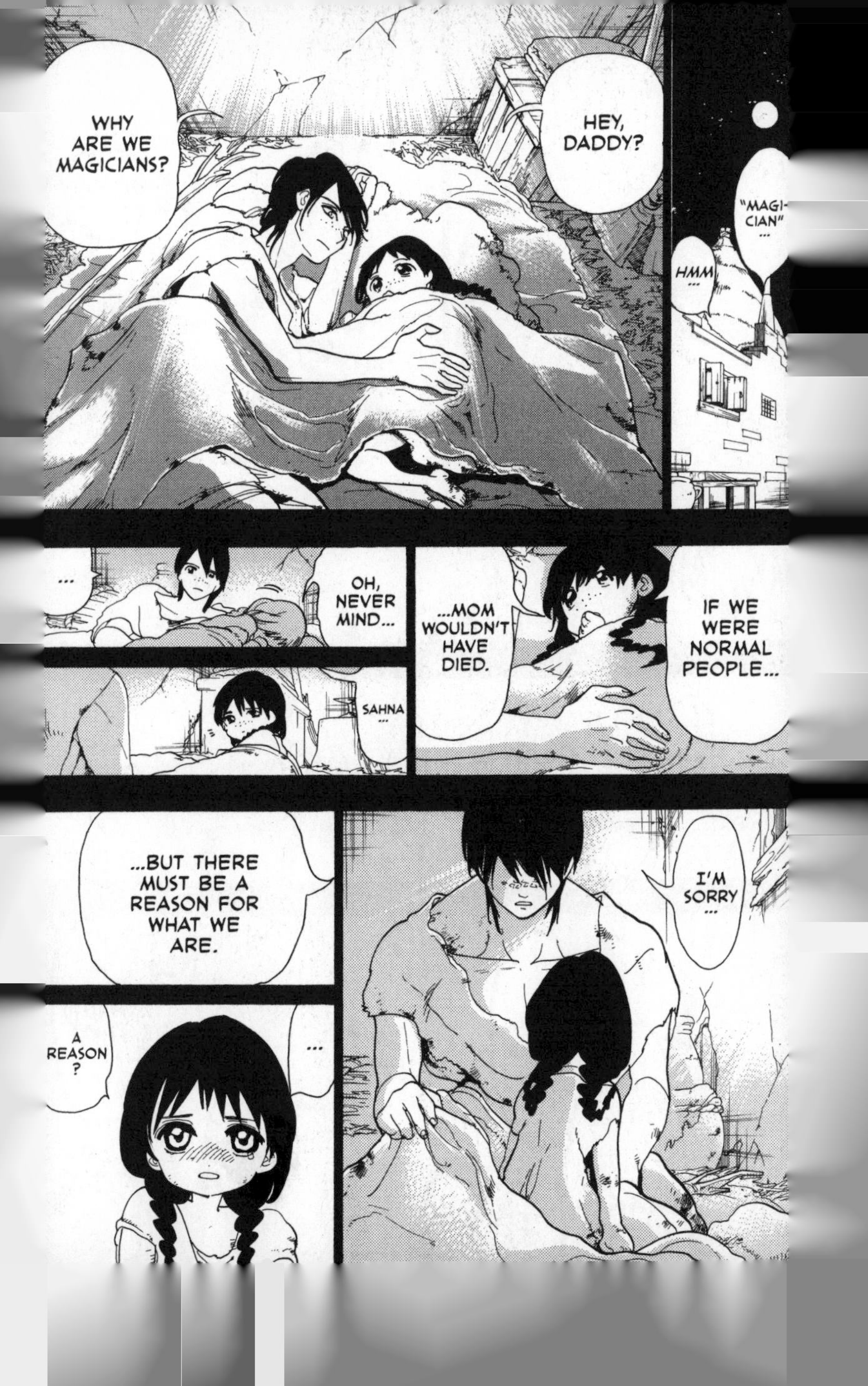
"MAGICIAN"...
HMM...
HEY, DADDY?
WHY ARE WE MAGICIANS?
IF WE WERE NORMAL PEOPLE...
...MOM WOULDN'T HAVE DIED.
OH, NEVER MIND...
...
SAHNA...
I'M SORRY...
...BUT THERE MUST BE A REASON FOR WHAT WE ARE.
...
A REASON?

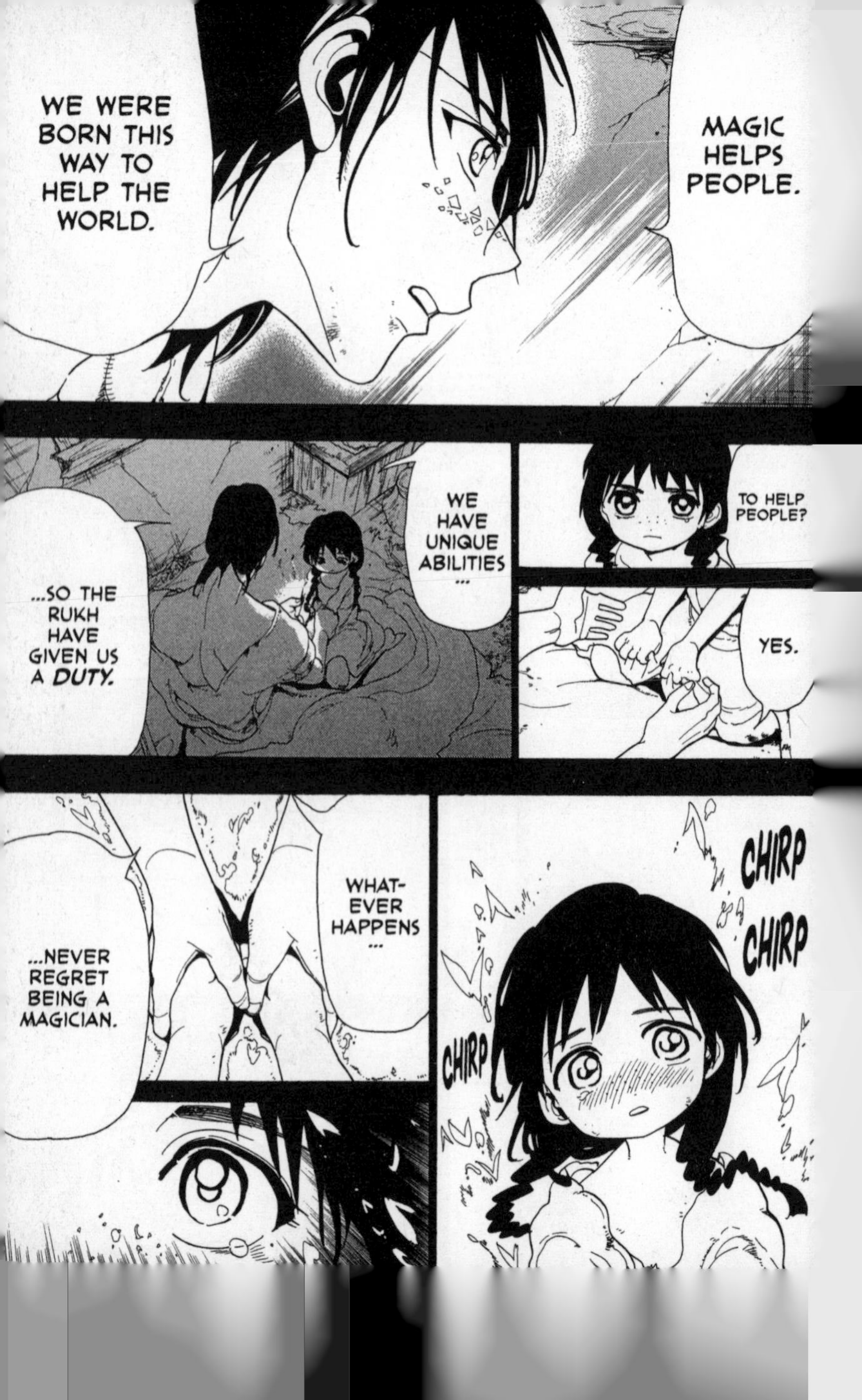
MAGIC HELPS PEOPLE.
WE WERE BORN THIS WAY TO HELP THE WORLD.
TO HELP PEOPLE?
YES.
WE HAVE UNIQUE ABILITIES ...
...SO THE RUKH HAVE GIVEN US A *DUTY.*
CHIRP
CHIRP
CHIRP
WHAT-EVER HAPPENS ...
...NEVER REGRET BEING A MAGICIAN.

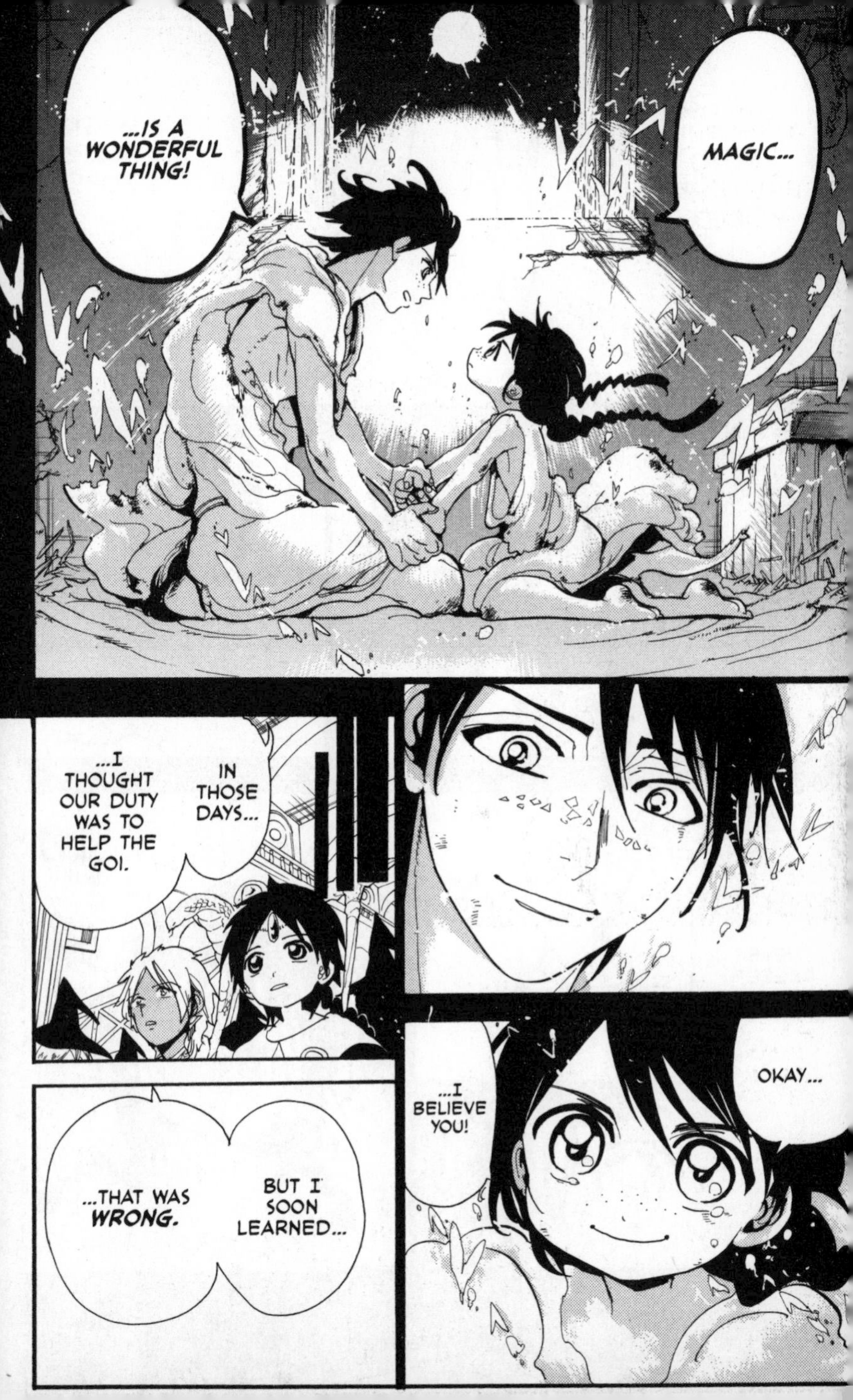
MAGIC...
...IS A WONDERFUL THING!
IN THOSE DAYS...
...I THOUGHT OUR DUTY WAS TO HELP THE GOI.
OKAY...
...I BELIEVE YOU!
BUT I SOON LEARNED...
...THAT WAS WRONG.

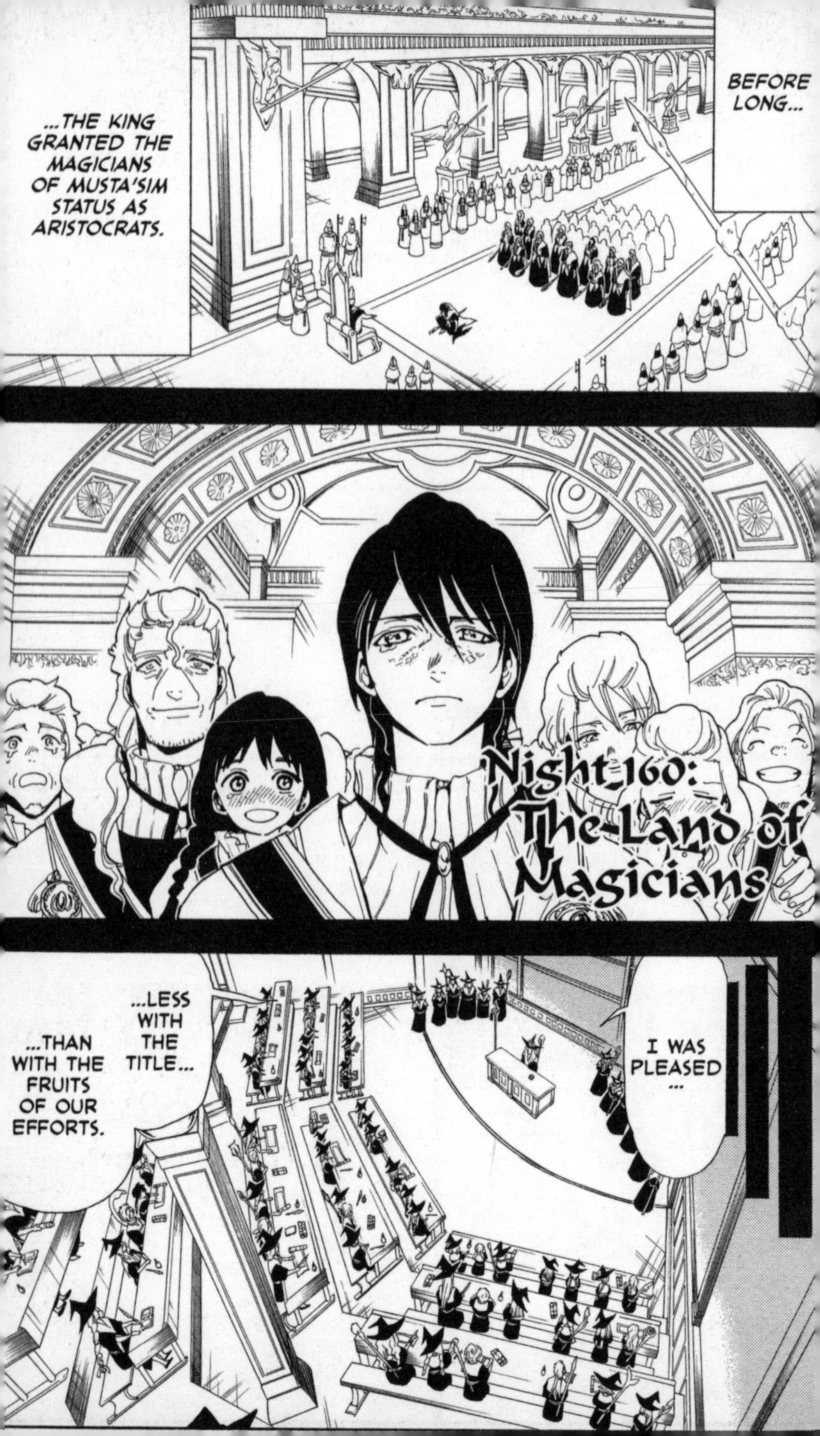

BEFORE LONG...
...THE KING GRANTED THE MAGICIANS OF MUSTA'SIM STATUS AS ARISTOCRATS.
Night 160: The Land of Magicians
I WAS PLEASED...
...LESS WITH THE TITLE...
...THAN WITH THE FRUITS OF OUR EFFORTS.

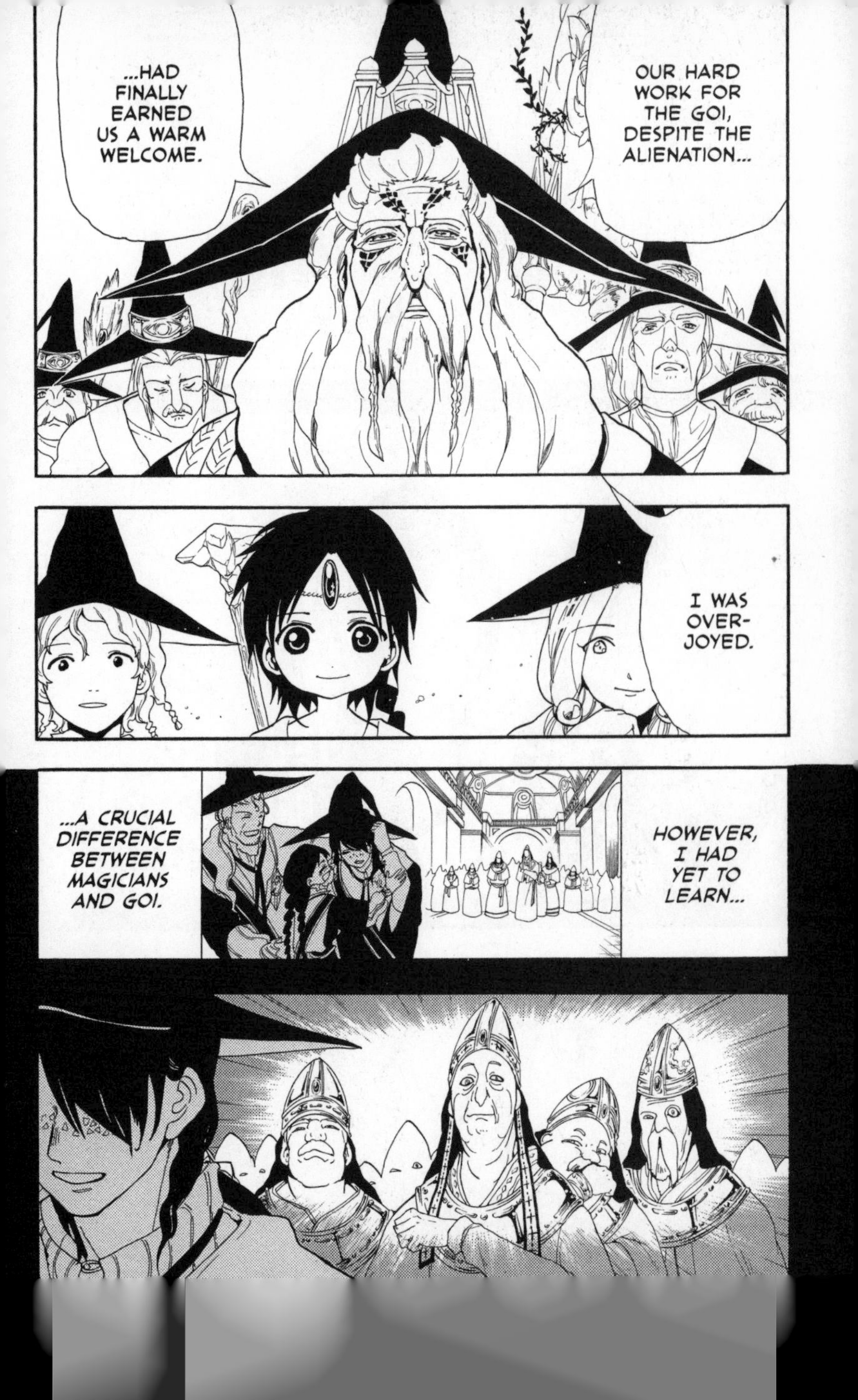
OUR HARD WORK FOR THE GOI, DESPITE THE ALIENATION...
...HAD FINALLY EARNED US A WARM WELCOME.
I WAS OVER-JOYED.
HOWEVER, I HAD YET TO LEARN...
...A CRUCIAL DIFFERENCE BETWEEN MAGICIANS AND GOI.

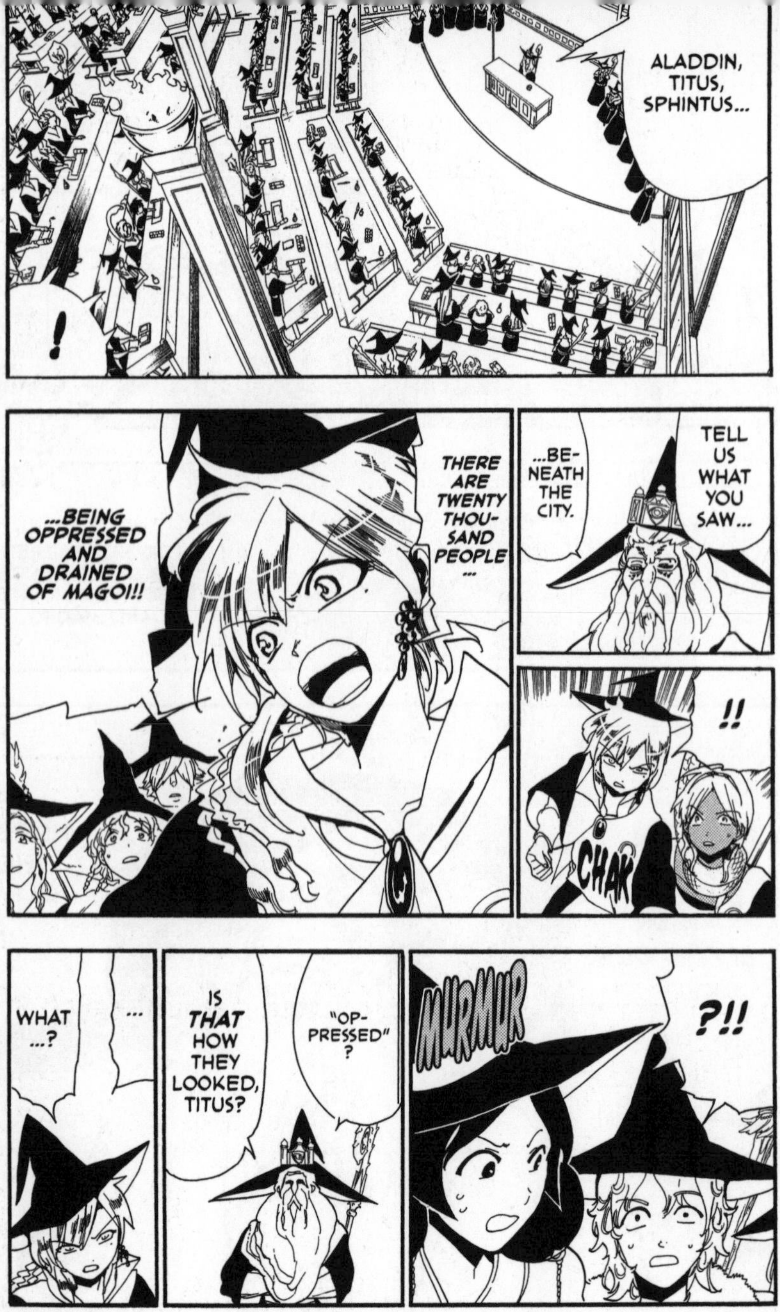
ALADDIN, TITUS, SPHINTUS...
!
TELL US WHAT YOU SAW...
...BENEATH THE CITY.
!!
THERE ARE TWENTY THOUSAND PEOPLE...
...BEING OPPRESSED AND DRAINED OF MAGOI!!
?!!
MURMUR
"OPPRESSED"?
IS *THAT* HOW THEY LOOKED, TITUS?
...
WHAT...?

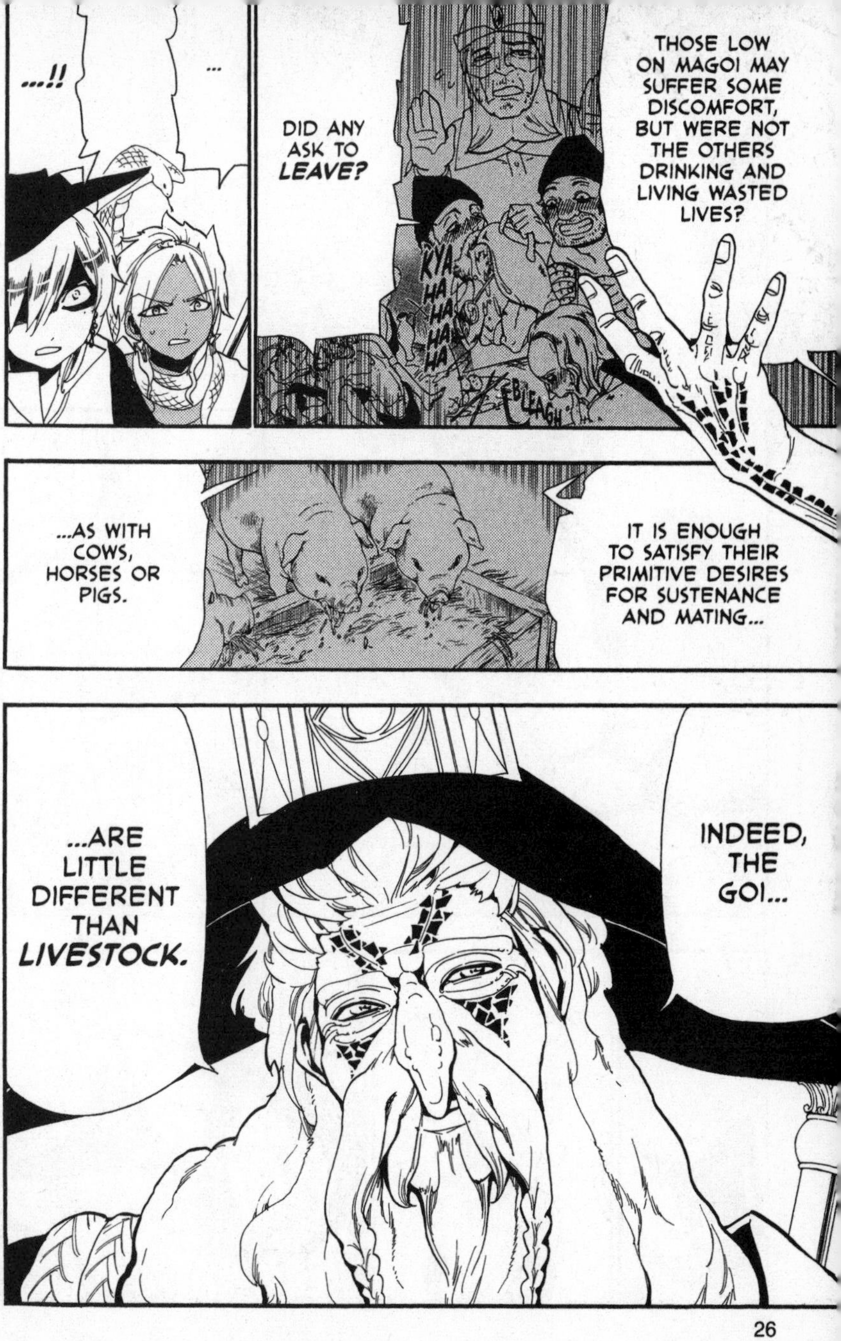
THOSE LOW ON MAGOI MAY SUFFER SOME DISCOMFORT, BUT WERE NOT THE OTHERS DRINKING AND LIVING WASTED LIVES?
DID ANY ASK TO *LEAVE?*
KYA HA HA HA HA
BLEAGH
...
...!!
IT IS ENOUGH TO SATISFY THEIR PRIMITIVE DESIRES FOR SUSTENANCE AND MATING...
...AS WITH COWS, HORSES OR PIGS.
INDEED, THE GOI...
...ARE LITTLE DIFFERENT THAN *LIVESTOCK.*

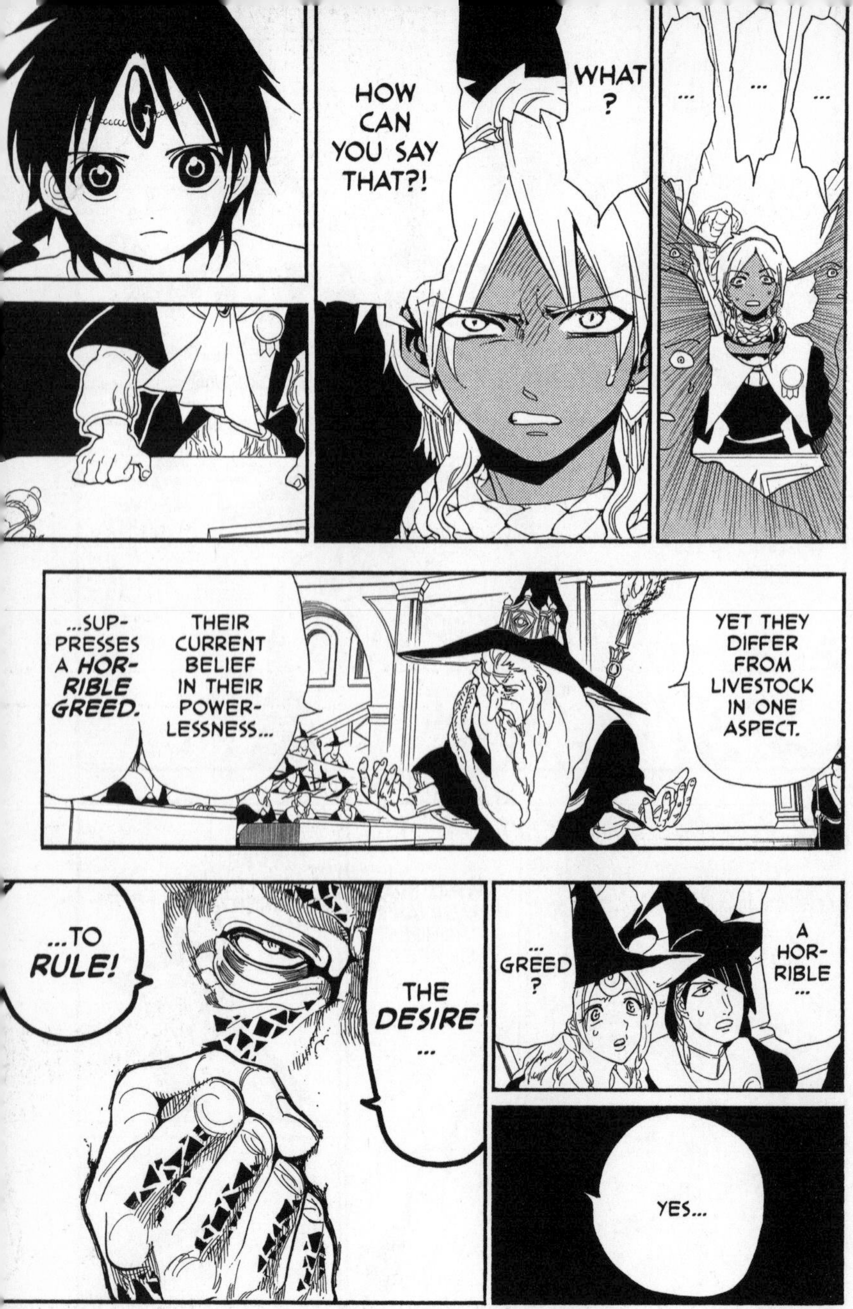
... ...
WHAT?
HOW CAN YOU SAY THAT?!
YET THEY DIFFER FROM LIVESTOCK IN ONE ASPECT.
THEIR CURRENT BELIEF IN THEIR POWERLESSNESS...
...SUPPRESSES A *HORRIBLE GREED.*
A HORRIBLE...
...GREED?
YES...
THE *DESIRE*...
...TO *RULE!*

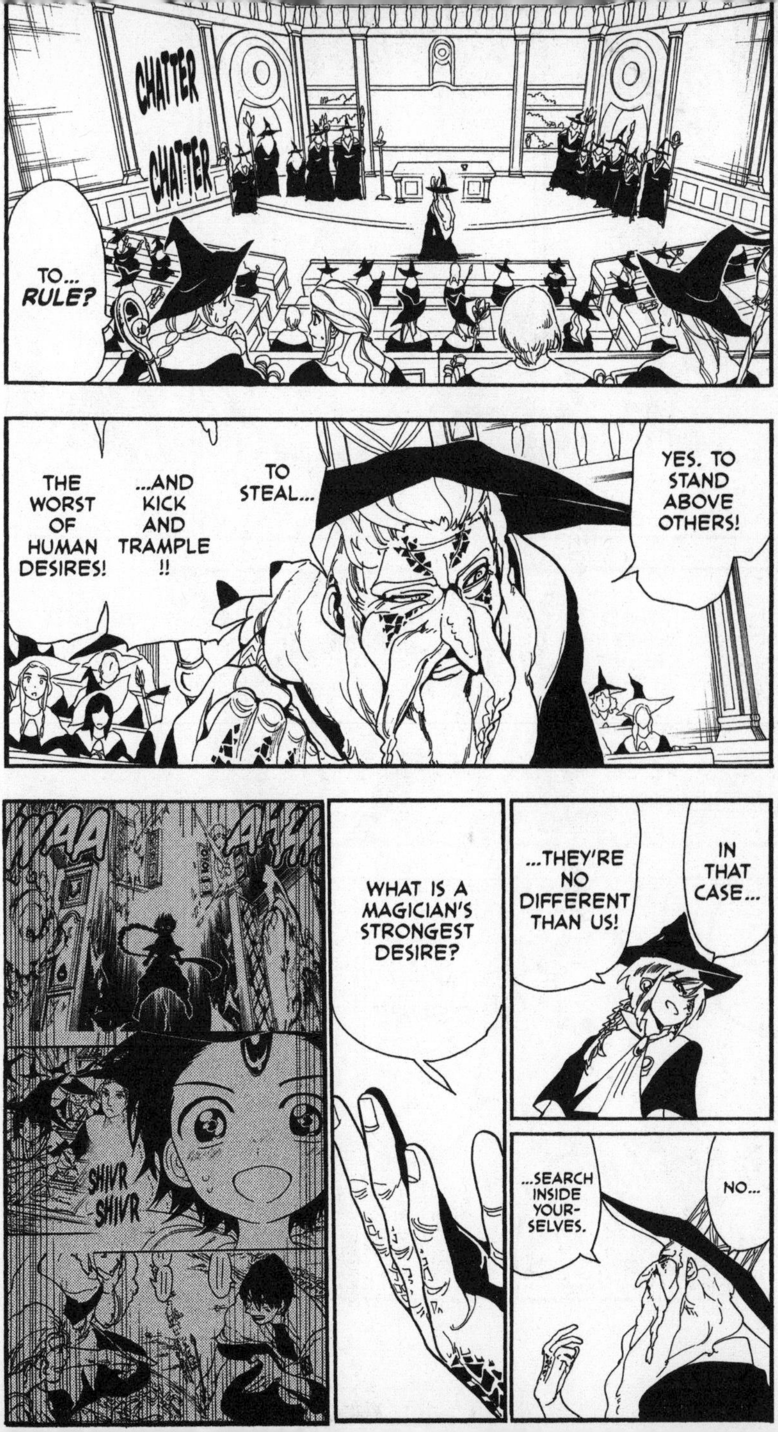
CHATTER
CHATTER
TO... RULE?
YES. TO STAND ABOVE OTHERS!
TO STEAL...
...AND KICK AND TRAMPLE !!
THE WORST OF HUMAN DESIRES!
IN THAT CASE...
...THEY'RE NO DIFFERENT THAN US!
NO...
...SEARCH INSIDE YOURSELVES.
WHAT IS A MAGICIAN'S STRONGEST DESIRE?
WAA
SHIVR SHIVR

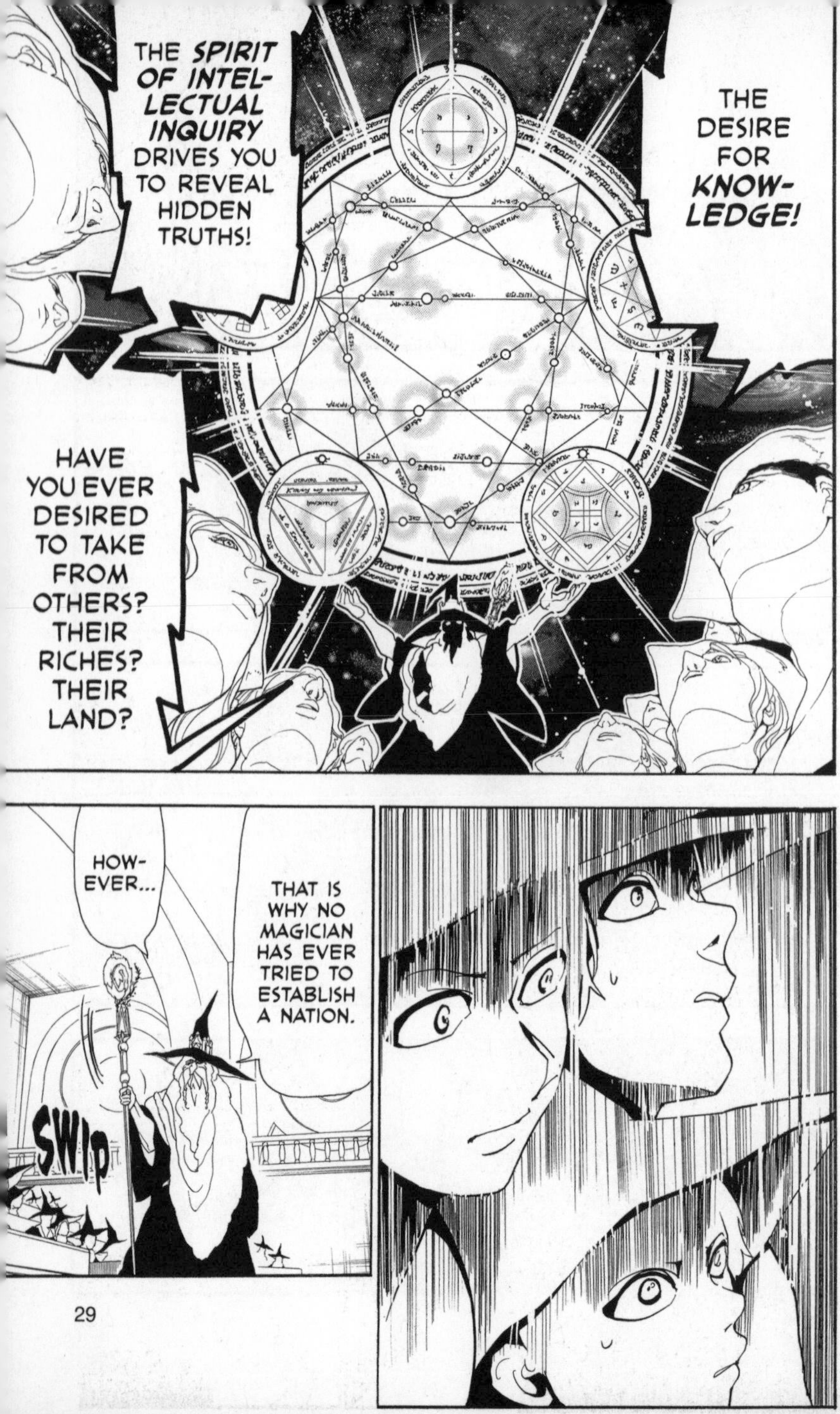
THE DESIRE FOR KNOW-LEDGE!
THE SPIRIT OF INTEL-LECTUAL INQUIRY DRIVES YOU TO REVEAL HIDDEN TRUTHS!
HAVE YOU EVER DESIRED TO TAKE FROM OTHERS? THEIR RICHES? THEIR LAND?
THAT IS WHY NO MAGICIAN HAS EVER TRIED TO ESTABLISH A NATION.
HOW-EVER...
SWIP

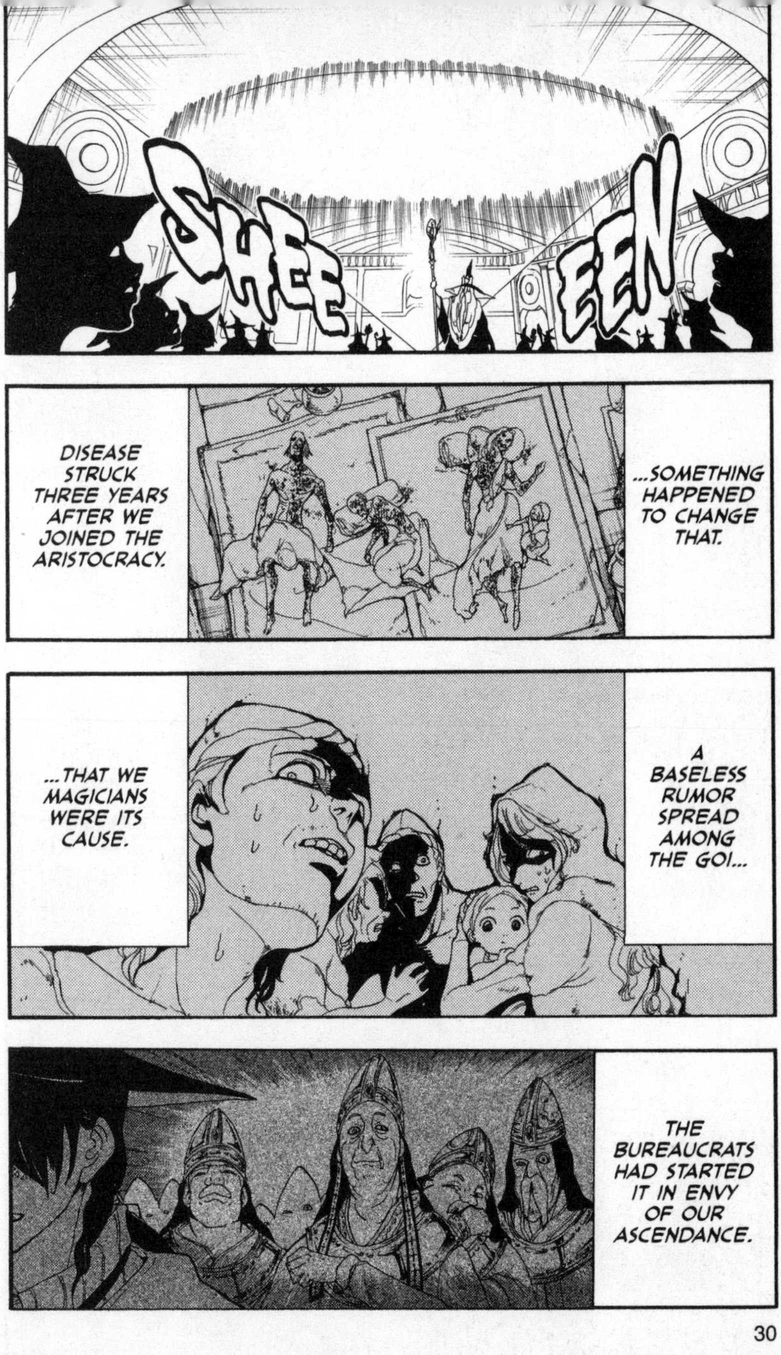
SHEE
EEN
...SOMETHING HAPPENED TO CHANGE THAT.
DISEASE STRUCK THREE YEARS AFTER WE JOINED THE ARISTOCRACY.
A BASELESS RUMOR SPREAD AMONG THE GOI...
...THAT WE MAGICIANS WERE ITS CAUSE.
THE BUREAUCRATS HAD STARTED IT IN ENVY OF OUR ASCENDANCE.

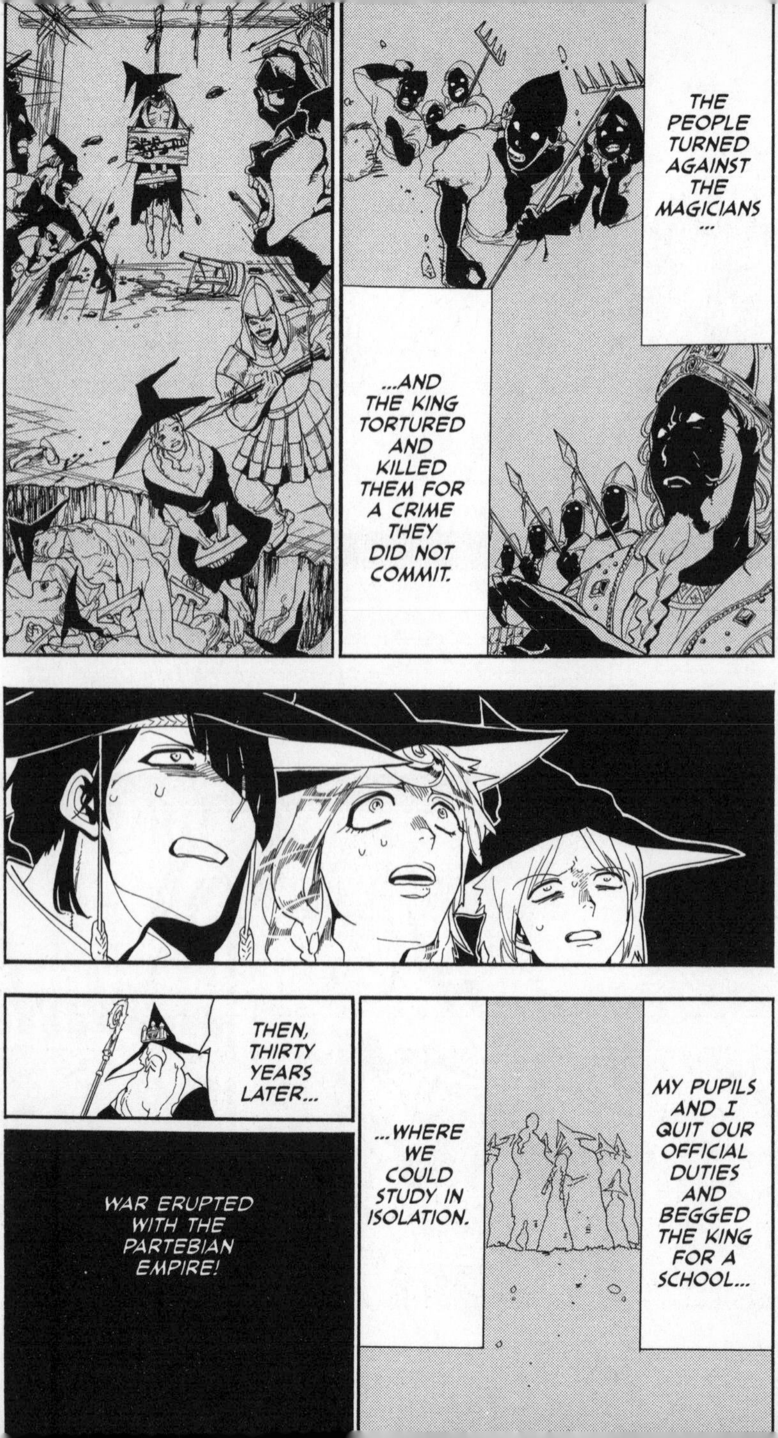
THE PEOPLE TURNED AGAINST THE MAGICIANS...
...AND THE KING TORTURED AND KILLED THEM FOR A CRIME THEY DID NOT COMMIT.
MY PUPILS AND I QUIT OUR OFFICIAL DUTIES AND BEGGED THE KING FOR A SCHOOL...
...WHERE WE COULD STUDY IN ISOLATION.
THEN, THIRTY YEARS LATER...
WAR ERUPTED WITH THE PARTEBIAN EMPIRE!

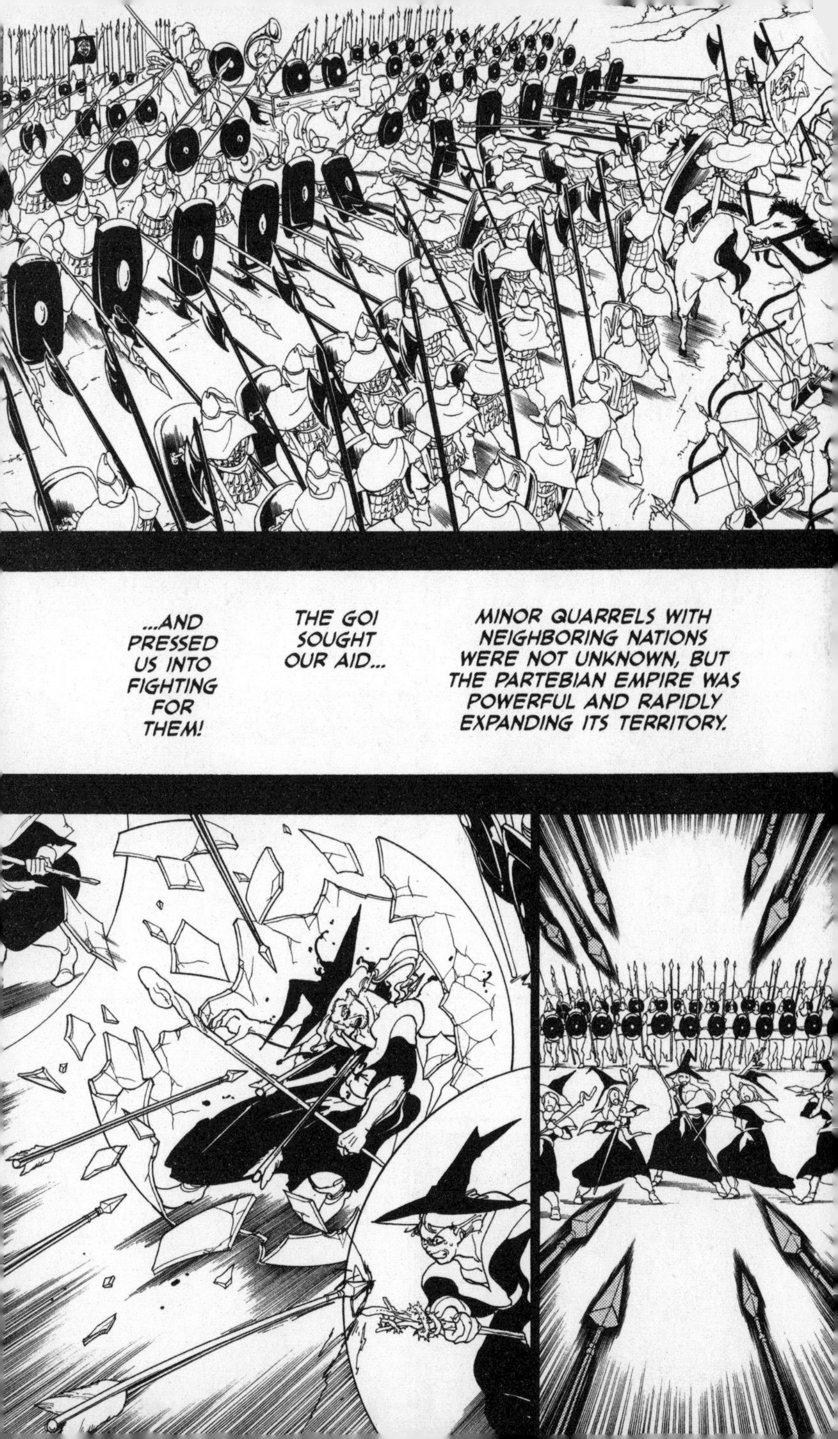
MINOR QUARRELS WITH NEIGHBORING NATIONS WERE NOT UNKNOWN, BUT THE PARTEBIAN EMPIRE WAS POWERFUL AND RAPIDLY EXPANDING ITS TERRITORY.
THE GOI SOUGHT OUR AID...
...AND PRESSED US INTO FIGHTING FOR THEM!

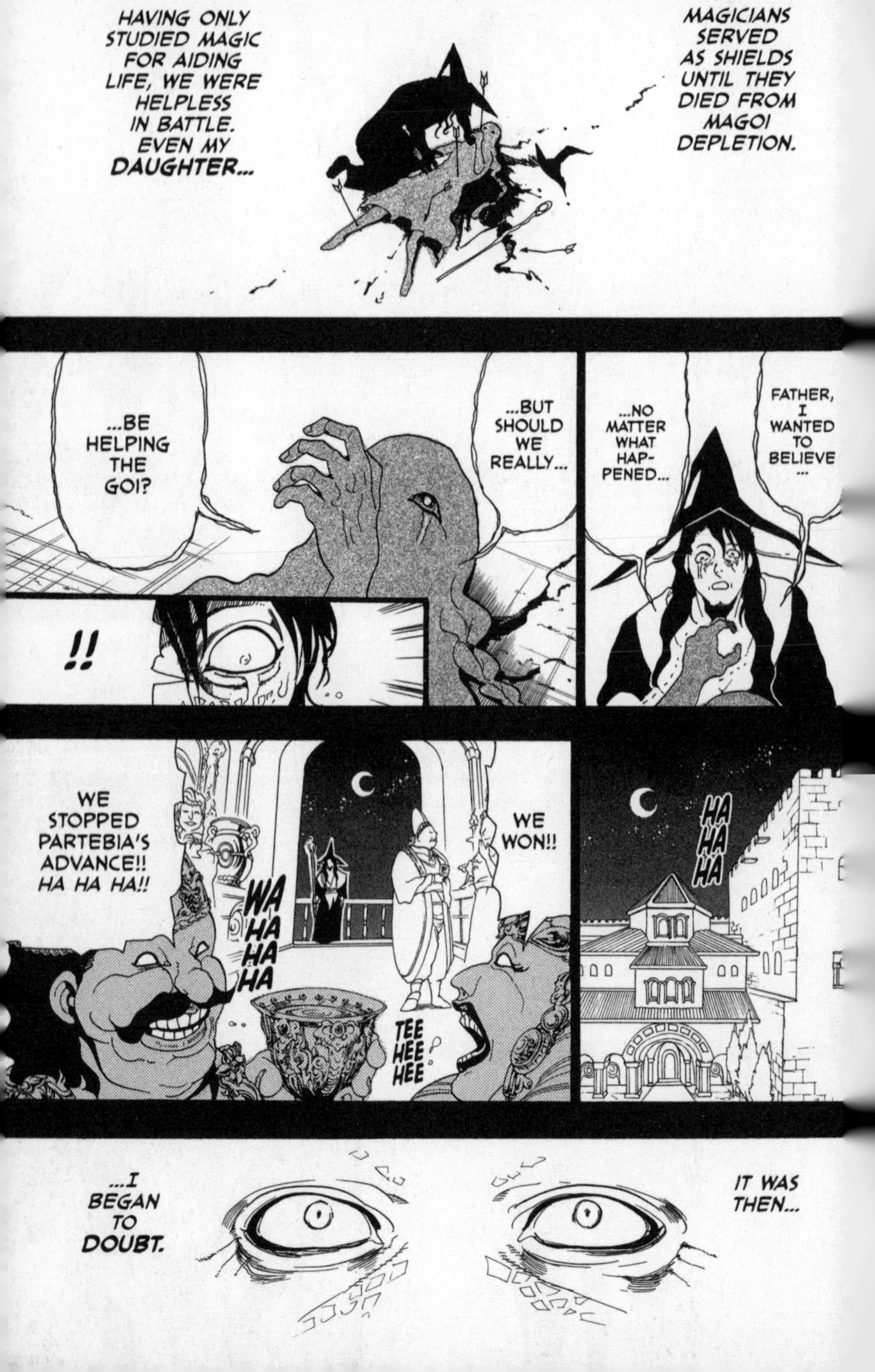
MAGICIANS SERVED AS SHIELDS UNTIL THEY DIED FROM MAGOI DEPLETION.
HAVING ONLY STUDIED MAGIC FOR AIDING LIFE, WE WERE HELPLESS IN BATTLE. EVEN MY DAUGHTER...
FATHER, I WANTED TO BELIEVE ...
...NO MATTER WHAT HAP-PENED...
...BUT SHOULD WE REALLY...
...BE HELPING THE GOI?
!!
HA HA HA
WE WON!!
WE STOPPED PARTEBIA'S ADVANCE!! HA HA HA!!
WA HA HA HA
TEE HEE HEE
IT WAS THEN...
...I BEGAN TO DOUBT.

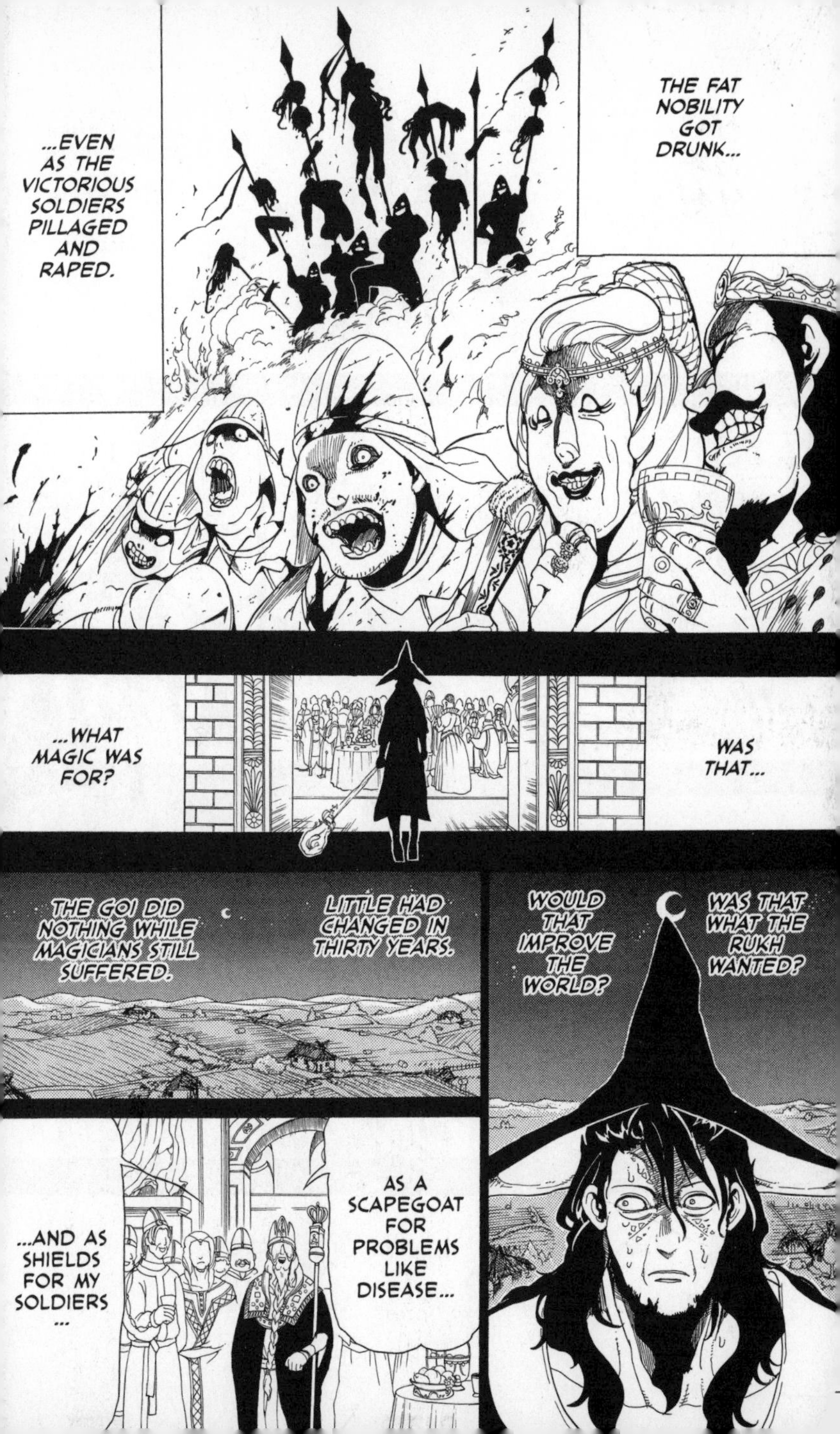
THE FAT NOBILITY GOT DRUNK...
...EVEN AS THE VICTORIOUS SOLDIERS PILLAGED AND RAPED.
WAS THAT...
...WHAT MAGIC WAS FOR?
WAS THAT WHAT THE RUKH WANTED?
WOULD THAT IMPROVE THE WORLD?
LITTLE HAD CHANGED IN THIRTY YEARS.
THE GOI DID NOTHING WHILE MAGICIANS STILL SUFFERED.
AS A SCAPEGOAT FOR PROBLEMS LIKE DISEASE...
...AND AS SHIELDS FOR MY SOLDIERS ...

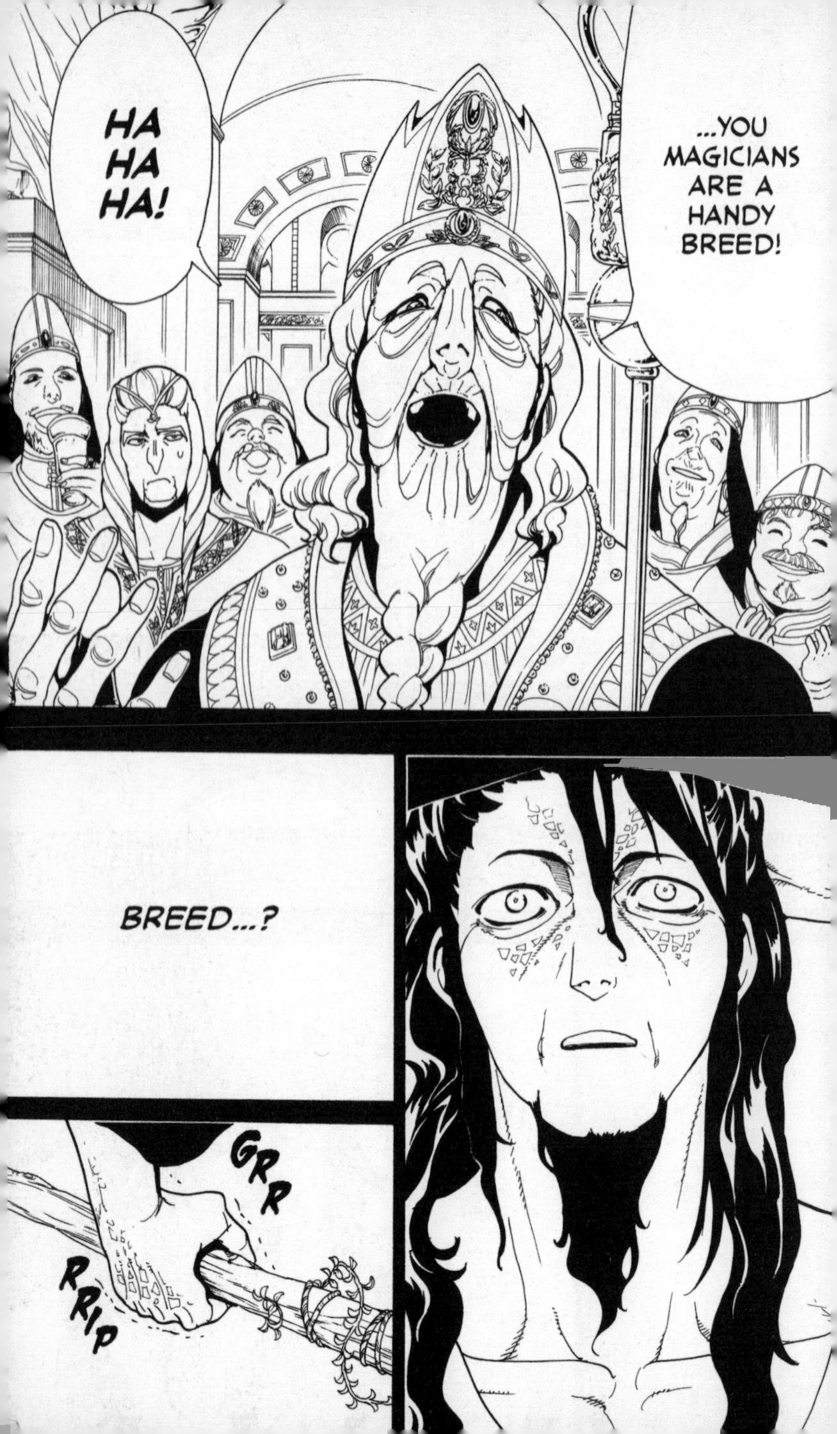
...YOU MAGICIANS ARE A HANDY BREED!
HA HA HA!
BREED...?
GRR
RRIP

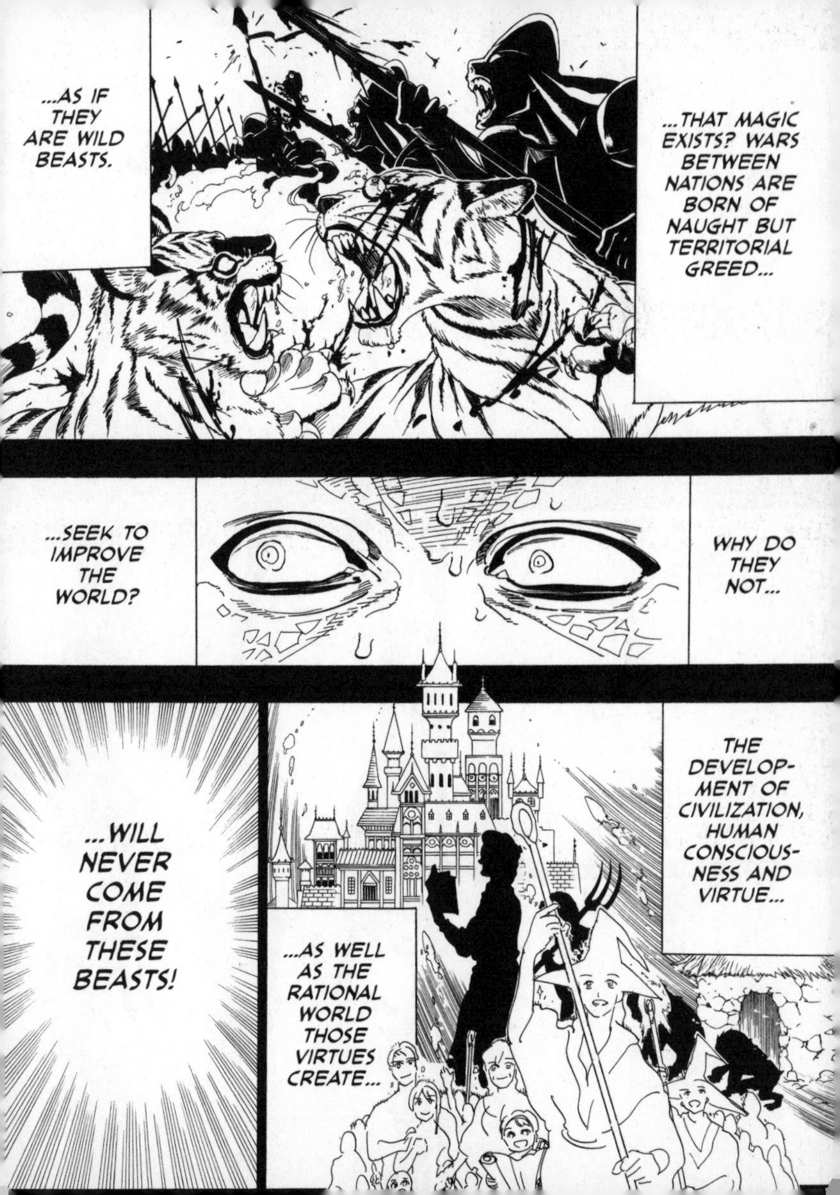
...THAT MAGIC EXISTS? WARS BETWEEN NATIONS ARE BORN OF NAUGHT BUT TERRITORIAL GREED...
...AS IF THEY ARE WILD BEASTS.
WHY DO THEY NOT...
...SEEK TO IMPROVE THE WORLD?
THE DEVELOPMENT OF CIVILIZATION, HUMAN CONSCIOUSNESS AND VIRTUE...
...AS WELL AS THE RATIONAL WORLD THOSE VIRTUES CREATE...
...WILL NEVER COME FROM THESE BEASTS!

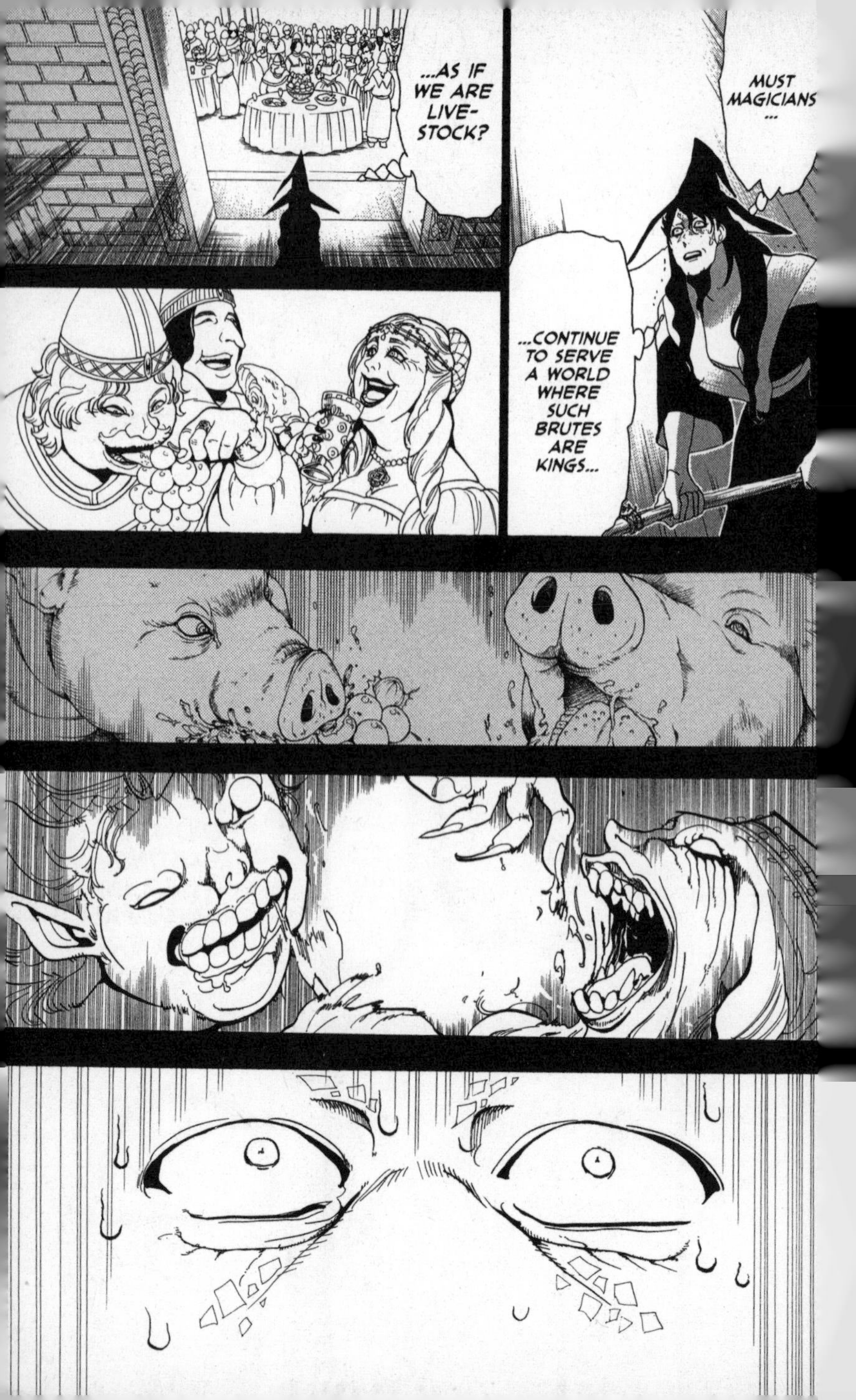
MUST MAGICIANS ...
...CONTINUE TO SERVE A WORLD WHERE SUCH BRUTES ARE KINGS...
...AS IF WE ARE LIVE-STOCK?

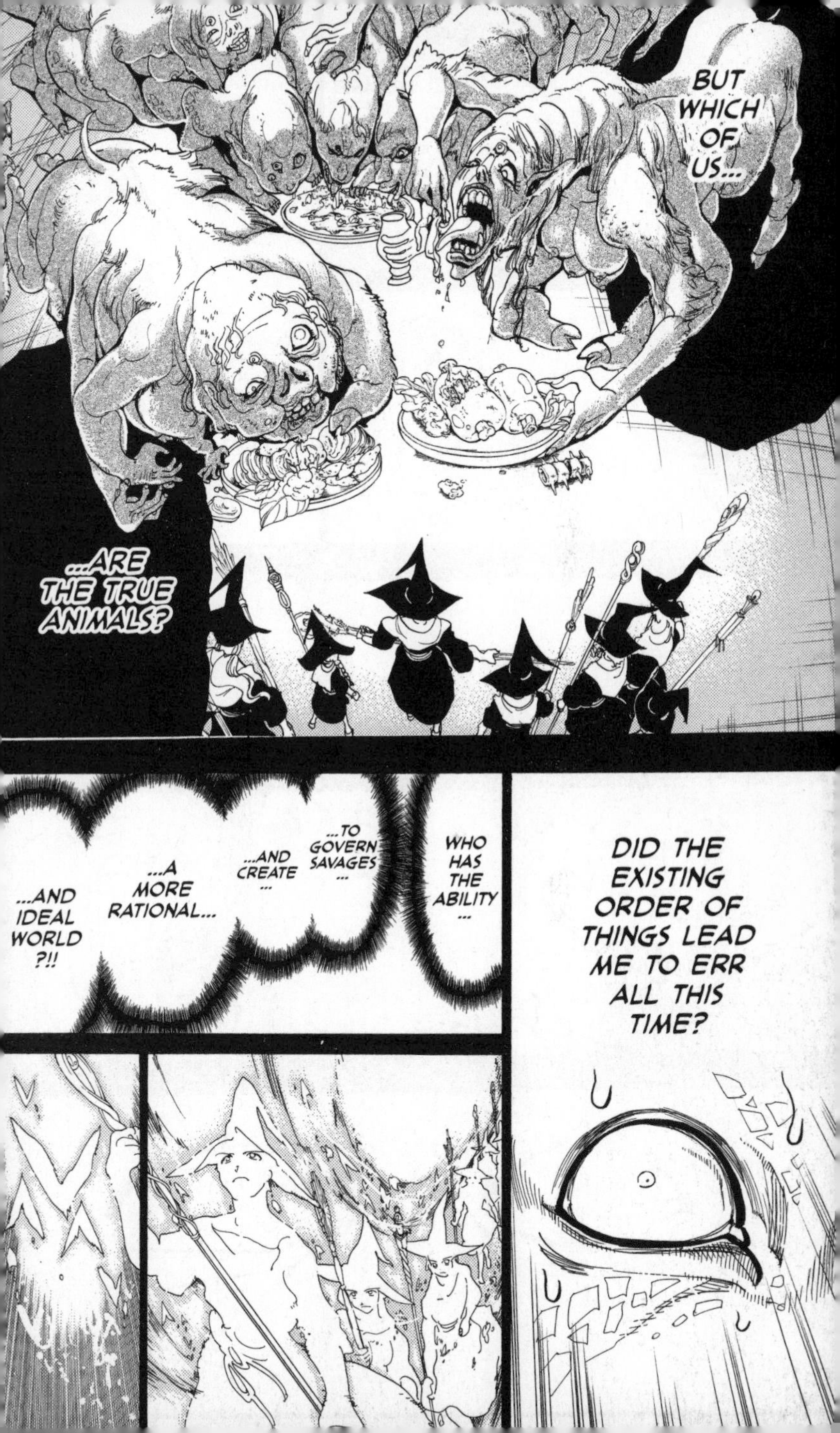
BUT WHICH OF US...
...ARE THE TRUE ANIMALS?
DID THE EXISTING ORDER OF THINGS LEAD ME TO ERR ALL THIS TIME?
WHO HAS THE ABILITY ...
...TO GOVERN SAVAGES ...
...AND CREATE ...
...A MORE RATIONAL...
...AND IDEAL WORLD ?!!

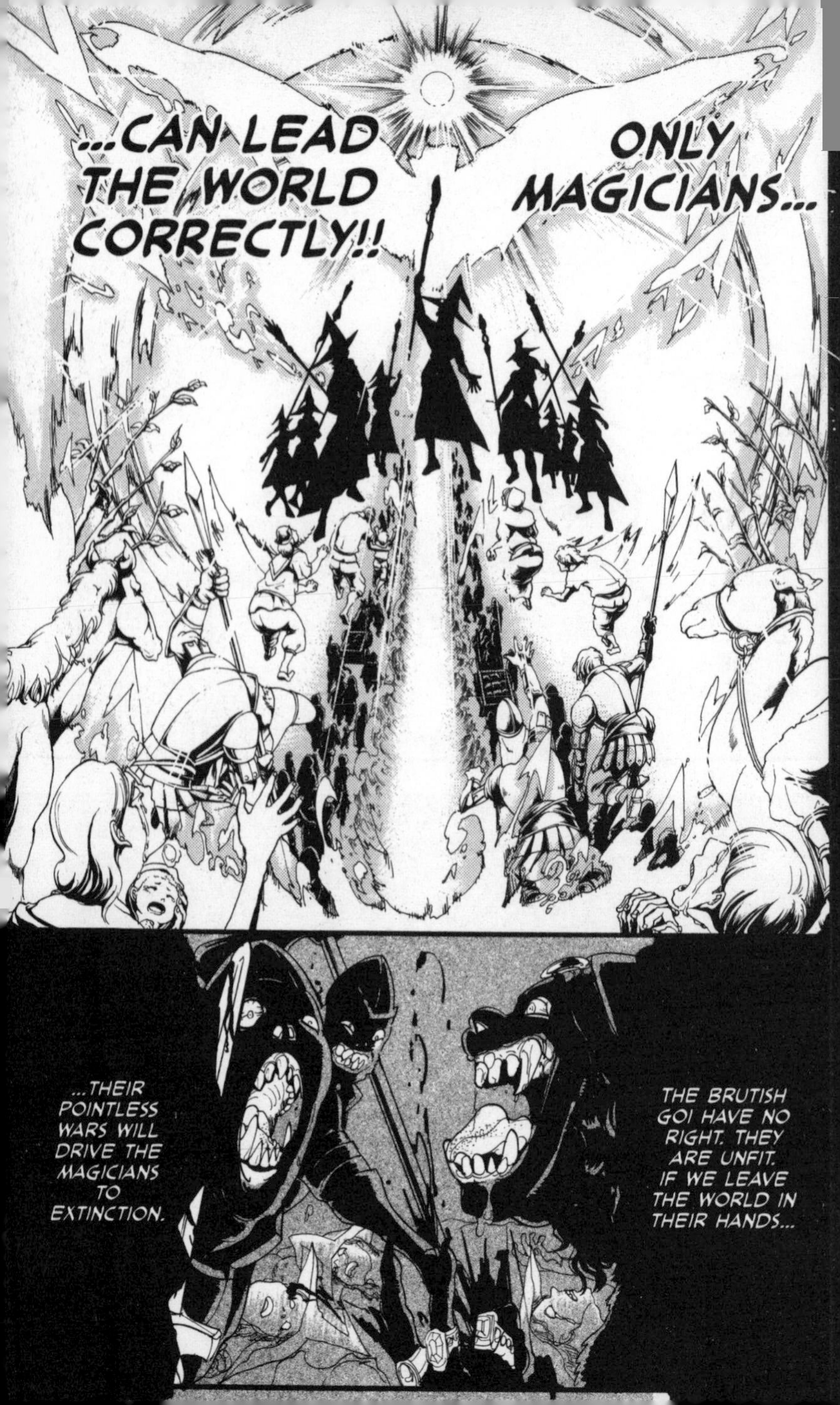
ONLY MAGICIANS...
...CAN LEAD THE WORLD CORRECTLY!!
THE BRUTISH GOI HAVE NO RIGHT. THEY ARE UNFIT. IF WE LEAVE THE WORLD IN THEIR HANDS...
...THEIR POINTLESS WARS WILL DRIVE THE MAGICIANS TO EXTINCTION.

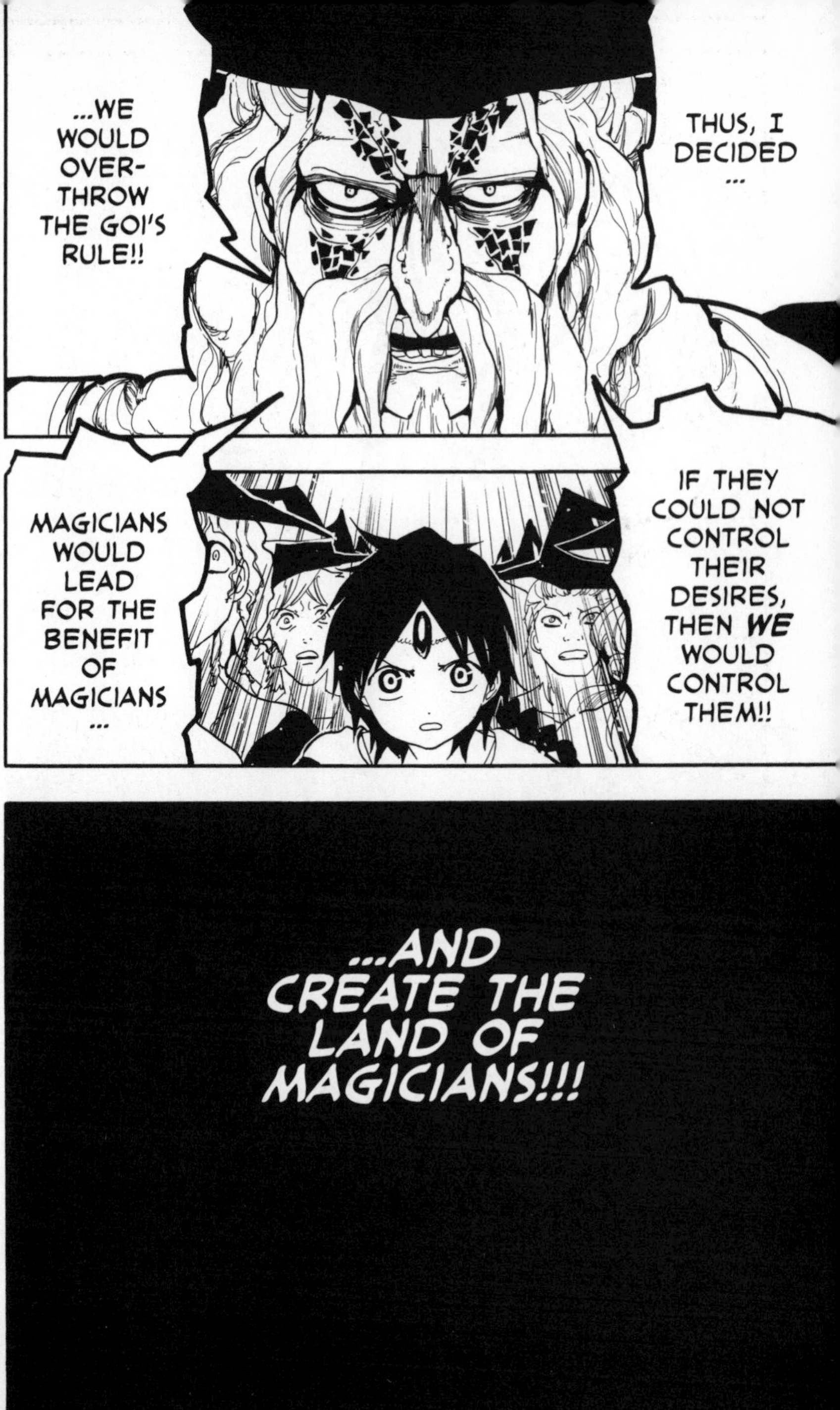
THUS, I DECIDED ...
...WE WOULD OVER-THROW THE GOI'S RULE!!
IF THEY COULD NOT CONTROL THEIR DESIRES, THEN *WE* WOULD CONTROL THEM!!
MAGICIANS WOULD LEAD FOR THE BENEFIT OF MAGICIANS ...
...AND CREATE THE LAND OF MAGICIANS!!!

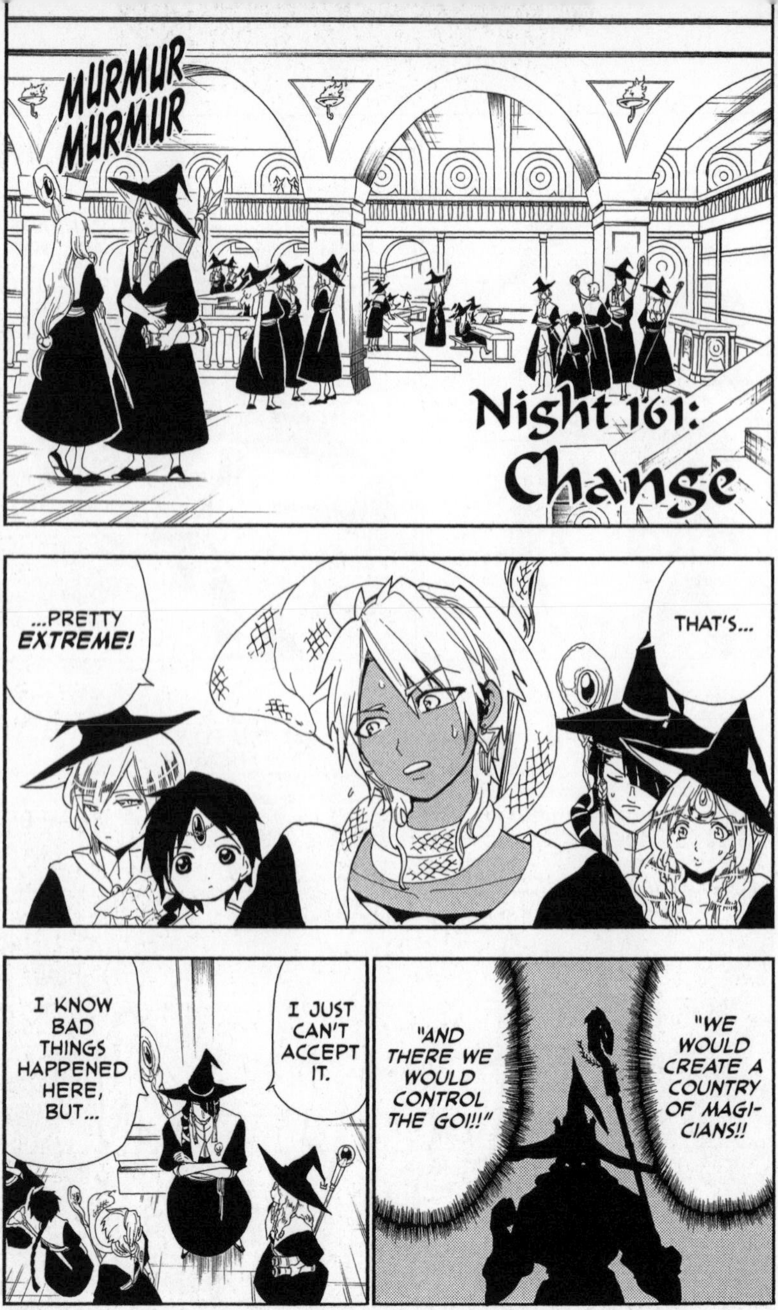
MURMUR MURMUR
Night 161: Change
THAT'S...
...PRETTY EXTREME!
"WE WOULD CREATE A COUNTRY OF MAGICIANS!!
"AND THERE WE WOULD CONTROL THE GOI!!"
I JUST CAN'T ACCEPT IT.
I KNOW BAD THINGS HAPPENED HERE, BUT...

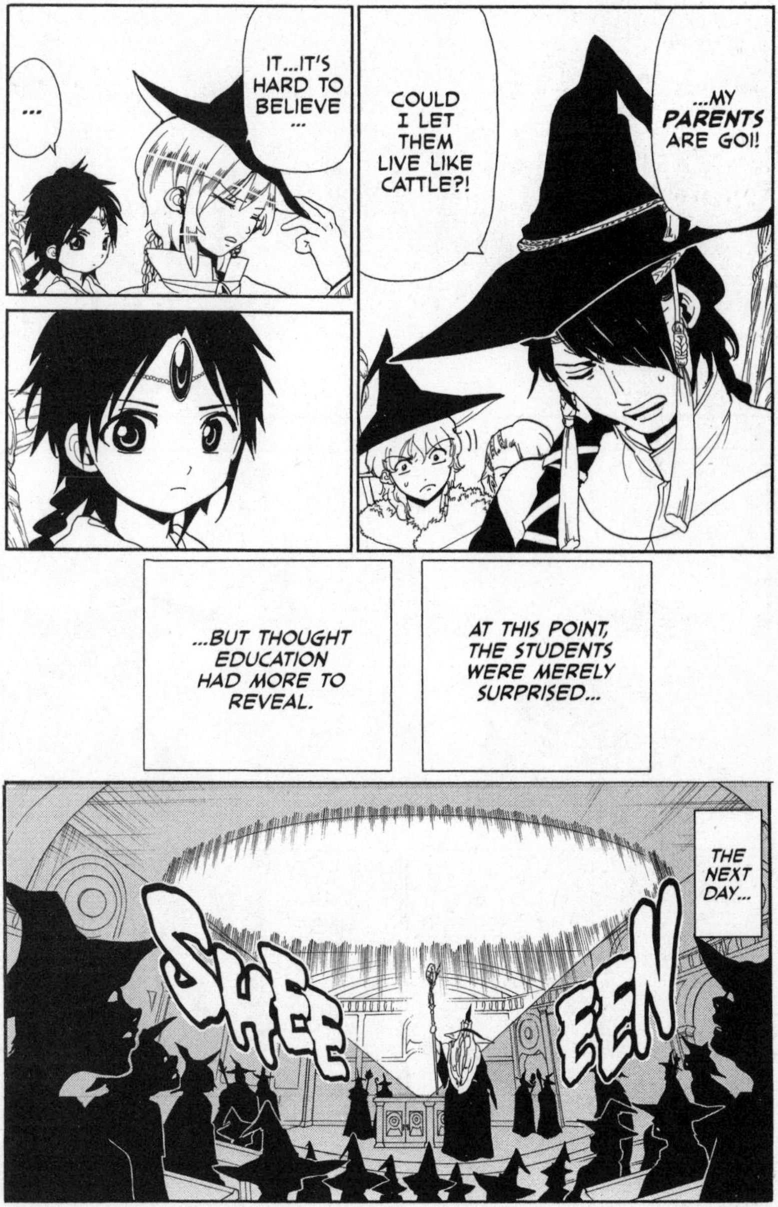
...MY PARENTS ARE GOI!
COULD I LET THEM LIVE LIKE CATTLE?!
IT...IT'S HARD TO BELIEVE ...
...
AT THIS POINT, THE STUDENTS WERE MERELY SURPRISED...
...BUT THOUGHT EDUCATION HAD MORE TO REVEAL.
THE NEXT DAY...
SHEE
EEN

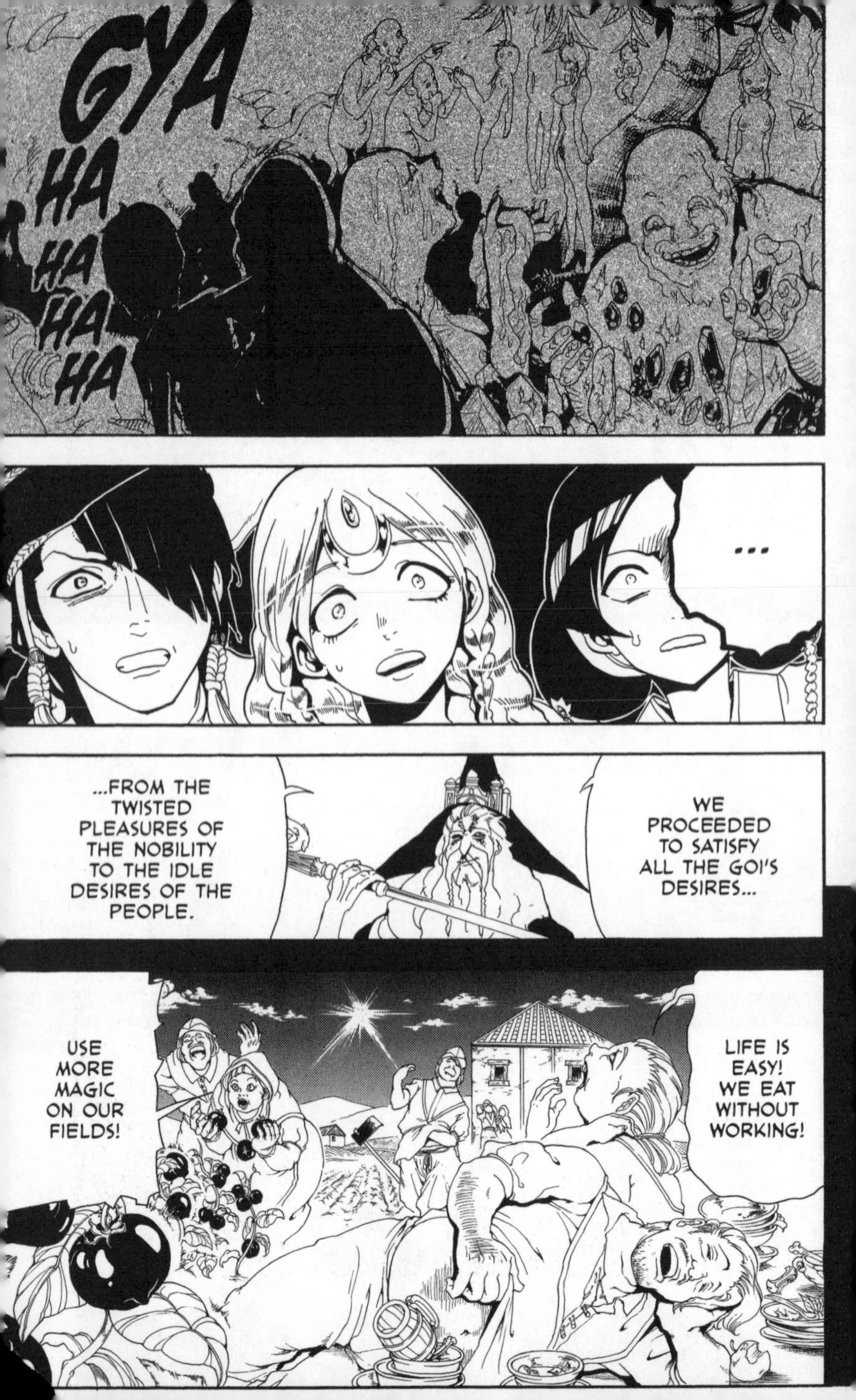
GYA HA HA HA HA
...
WE PROCEEDED TO SATISFY ALL THE GOI'S DESIRES...
...FROM THE TWISTED PLEASURES OF THE NOBILITY TO THE IDLE DESIRES OF THE PEOPLE.
LIFE IS EASY! WE EAT WITHOUT WORKING!
USE MORE MAGIC ON OUR FIELDS!

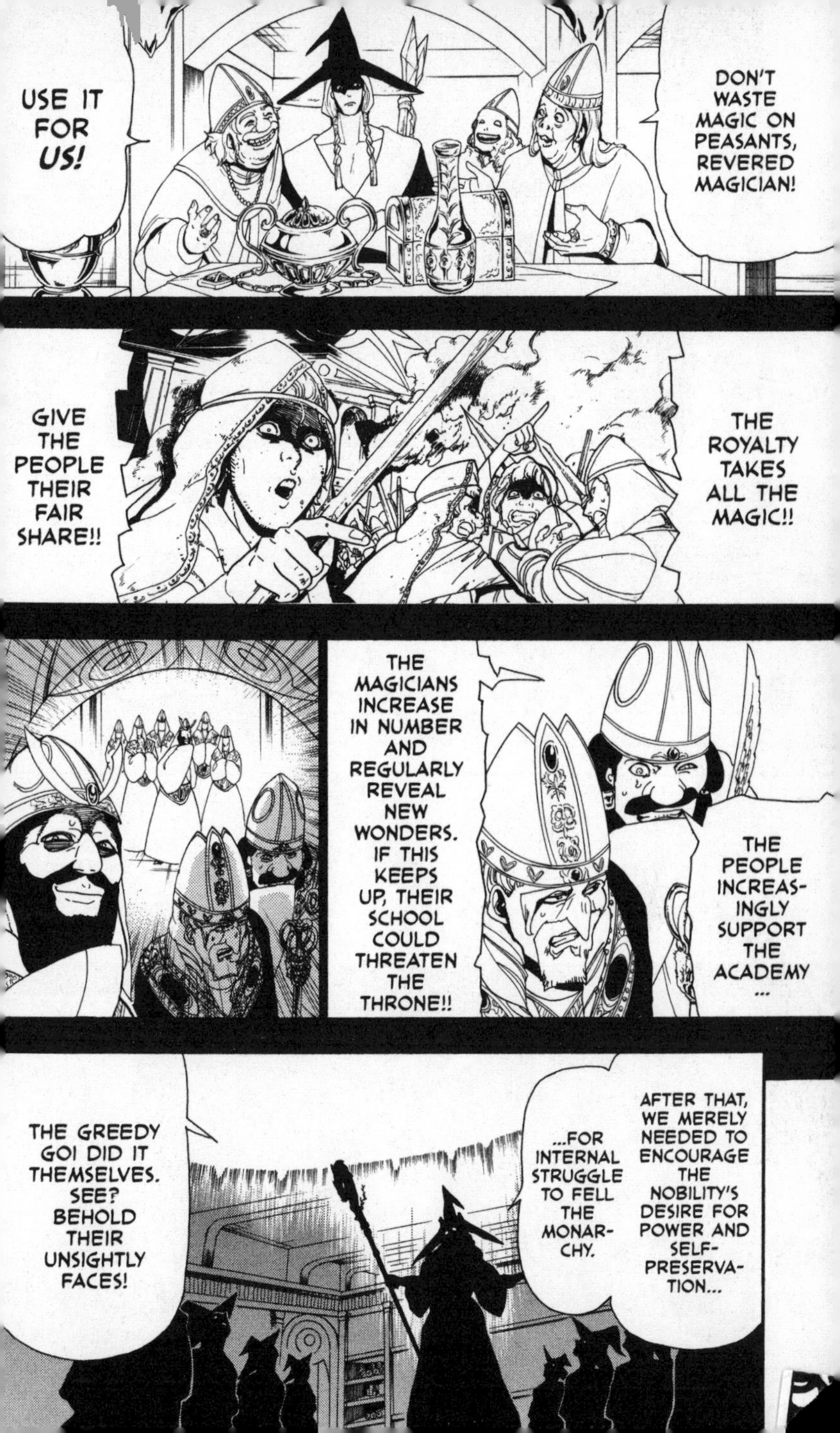
DON'T WASTE MAGIC ON PEASANTS, REVERED MAGICIAN!
USE IT FOR *US!*
THE ROYALTY TAKES ALL THE MAGIC!!
GIVE THE PEOPLE THEIR FAIR SHARE!!
THE PEOPLE INCREAS-INGLY SUPPORT THE ACADEMY ...
THE MAGICIANS INCREASE IN NUMBER AND REGULARLY REVEAL NEW WONDERS. IF THIS KEEPS UP, THEIR SCHOOL COULD THREATEN THE THRONE!!
AFTER THAT, WE MERELY NEEDED TO ENCOURAGE THE NOBILITY'S DESIRE FOR POWER AND SELF-PRESERVA-TION...
...FOR INTERNAL STRUGGLE TO FELL THE MONAR-CHY.
THE GREEDY GOI DID IT THEMSELVES. SEE? BEHOLD THEIR UNSIGHTLY FACES!

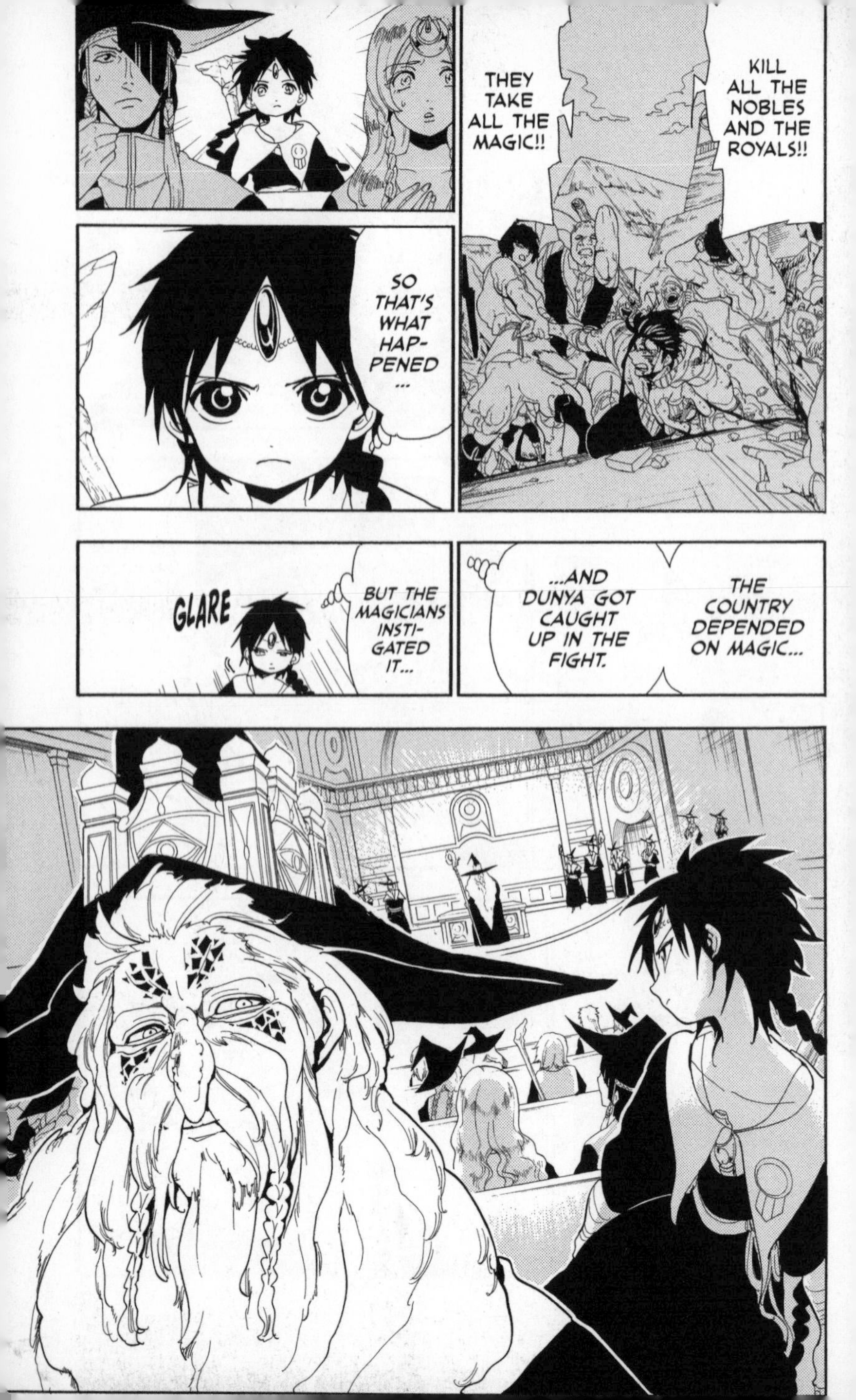
KILL ALL THE NOBLES AND THE ROYALS!!
THEY TAKE ALL THE MAGIC!!
SO THAT'S WHAT HAP-PENED...
THE COUNTRY DEPENDED ON MAGIC...
...AND DUNYA GOT CAUGHT UP IN THE FIGHT.
BUT THE MAGICIANS INSTI-GATED IT...
GLARE

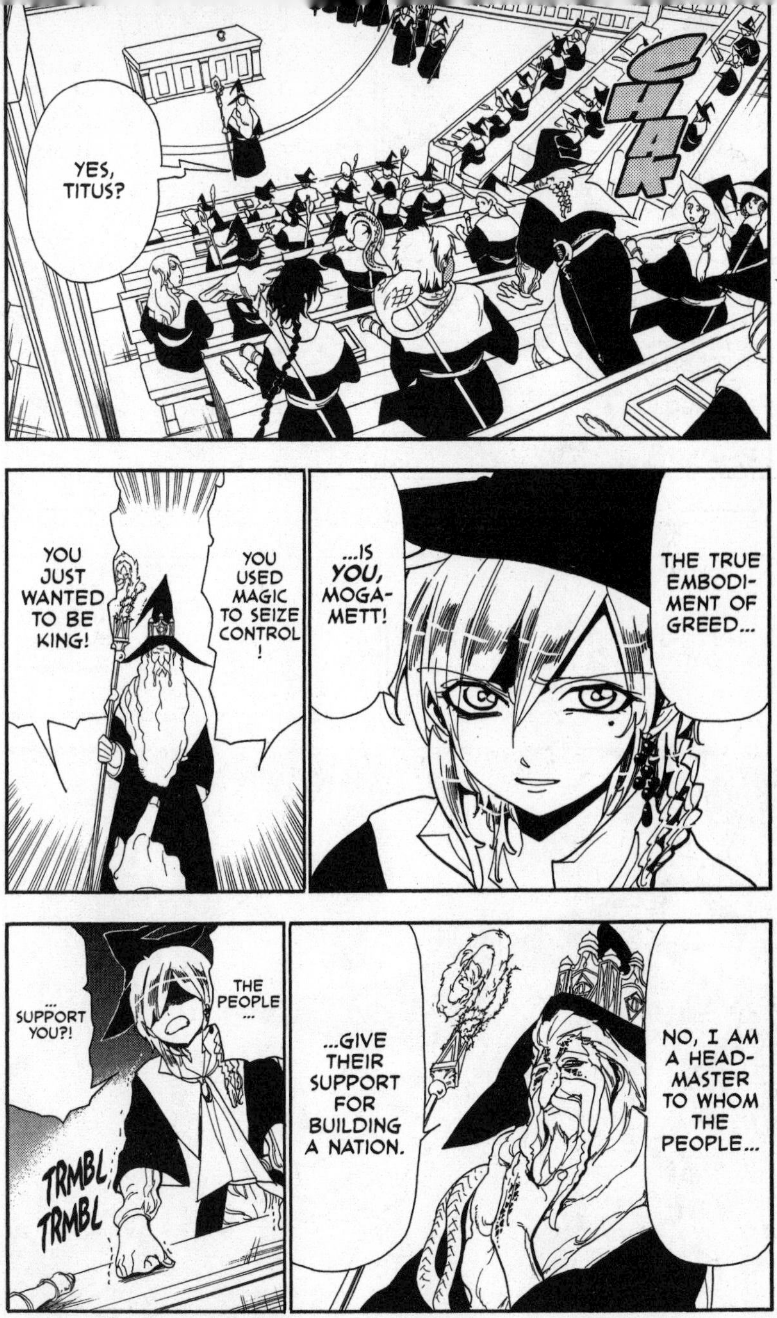
CHAK
YES, TITUS?
THE TRUE EMBODIMENT OF GREED...
...IS *YOU*, MOGAMETT!
YOU USED MAGIC TO SEIZE CONTROL!
YOU JUST WANTED TO BE KING!
NO, I AM A HEADMASTER TO WHOM THE PEOPLE...
...GIVE THEIR SUPPORT FOR BUILDING A NATION.
THE PEOPLE...
...SUPPORT YOU?!
TRMBL TRMBL

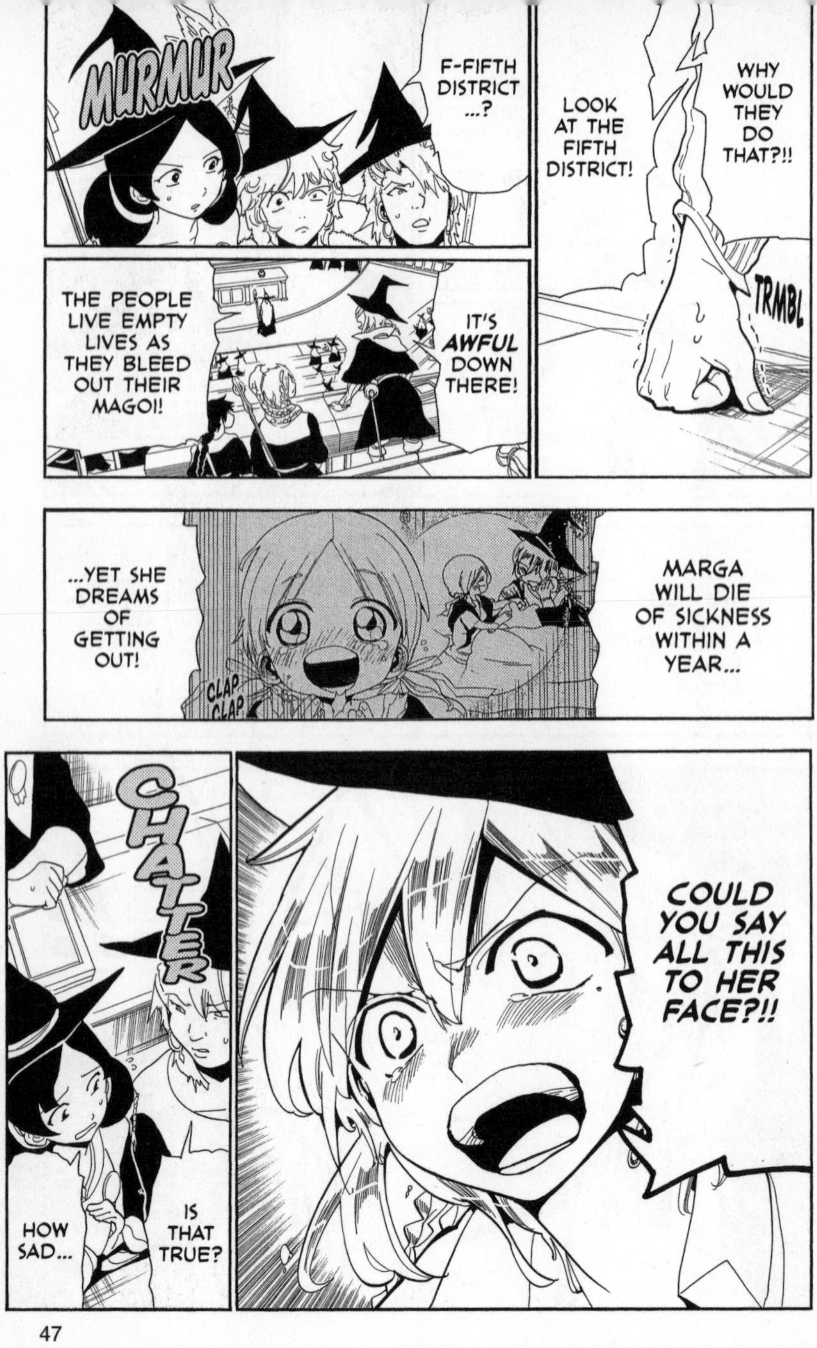
WHY WOULD THEY DO THAT?!!
LOOK AT THE FIFTH DISTRICT!
TRMBL
F-FIFTH DISTRICT ...?
MURMUR
IT'S *AWFUL* DOWN THERE!
THE PEOPLE LIVE EMPTY LIVES AS THEY BLEED OUT THEIR MAGOI!
MARGA WILL DIE OF SICKNESS WITHIN A YEAR...
...YET SHE DREAMS OF GETTING OUT!
CLAP CLAP
COULD YOU SAY ALL THIS TO HER FACE?!!
CHATTER
IS THAT TRUE?
HOW SAD...

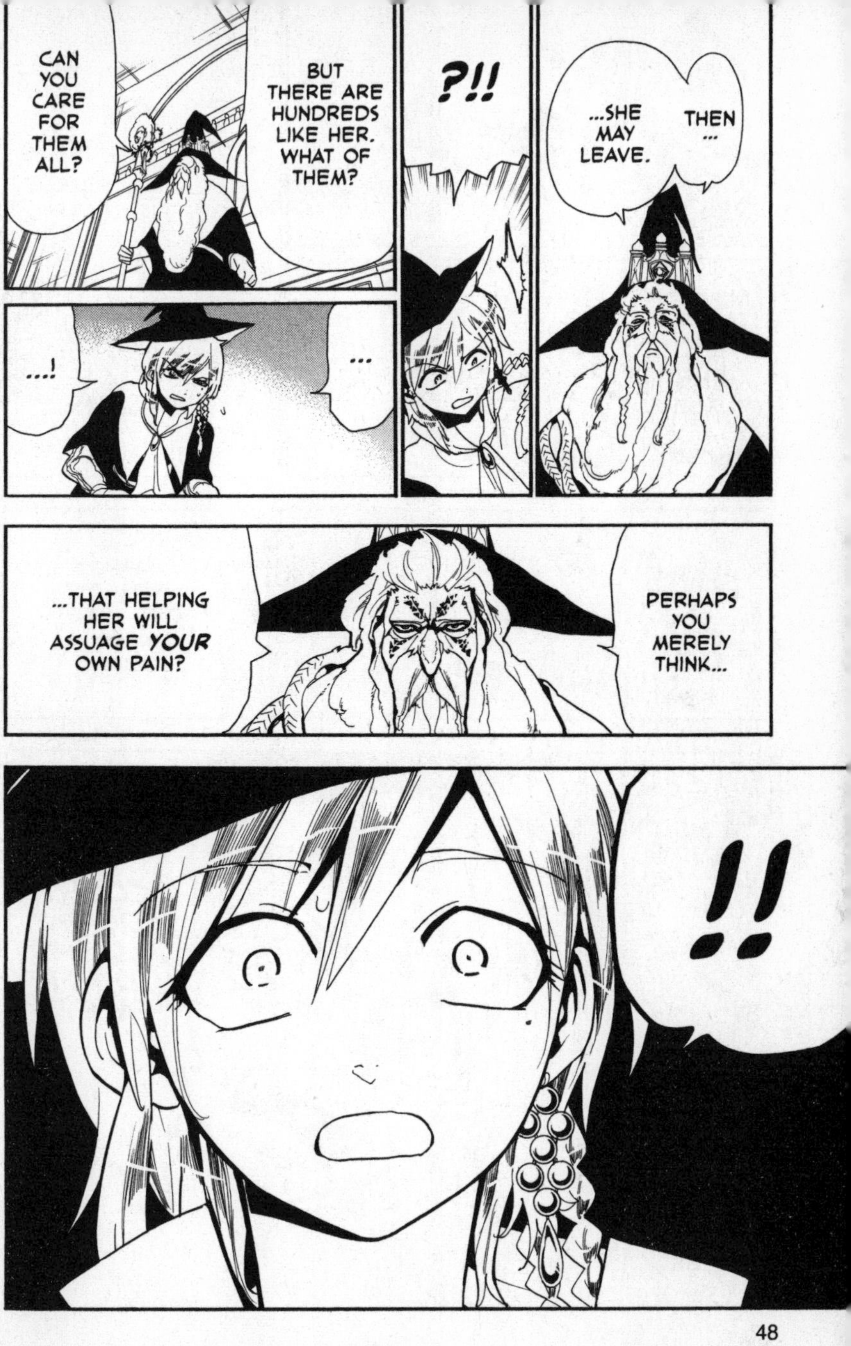
THEN ...
...SHE MAY LEAVE.
?!!
BUT THERE ARE HUNDREDS LIKE HER. WHAT OF THEM?
CAN YOU CARE FOR THEM ALL?
...
...!
PERHAPS YOU MERELY THINK...
...THAT HELPING HER WILL ASSUAGE *YOUR* OWN PAIN?
!!

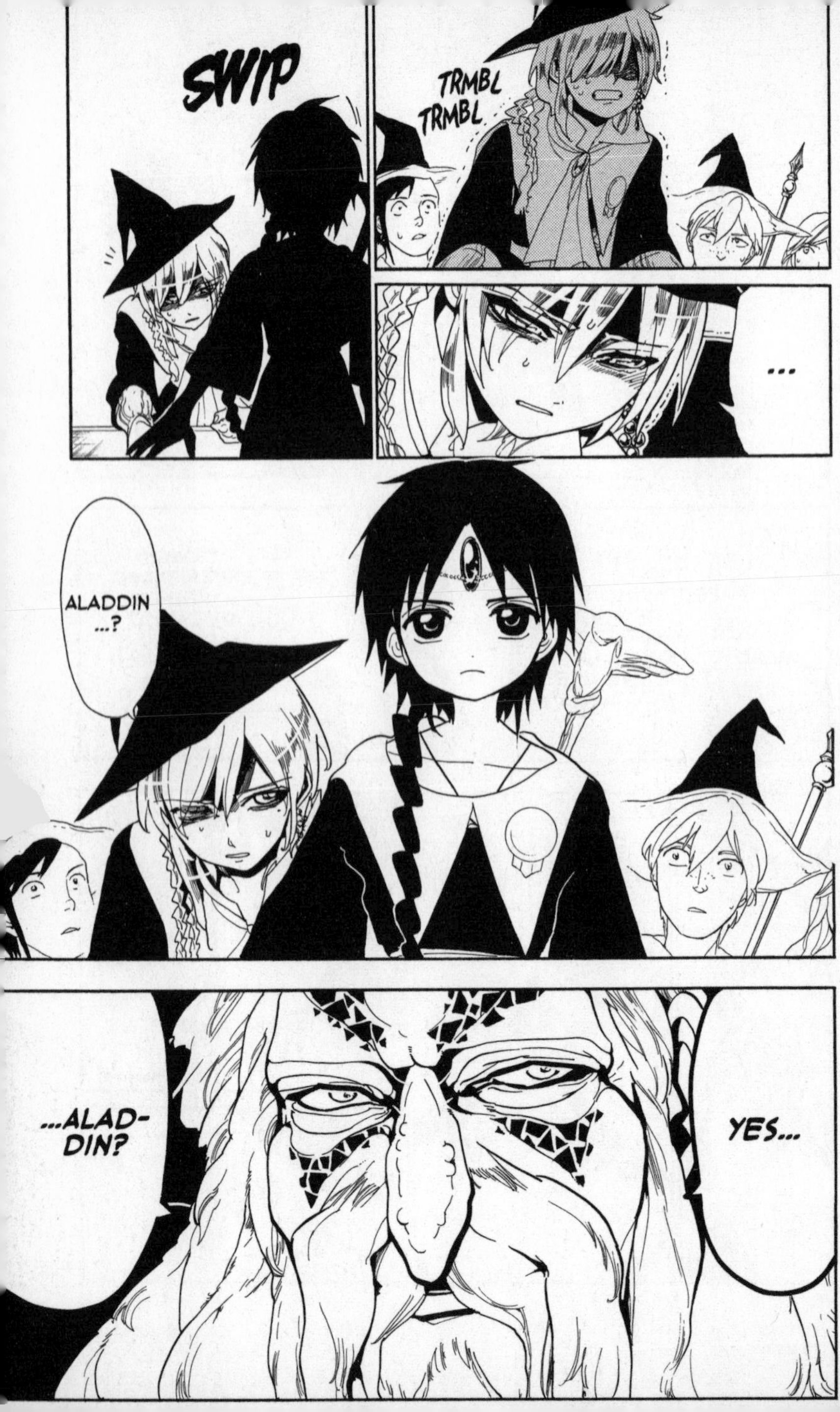
TRMBL TRMBL
...
SWIP
ALADDIN ...?
YES...
...ALAD-DIN?

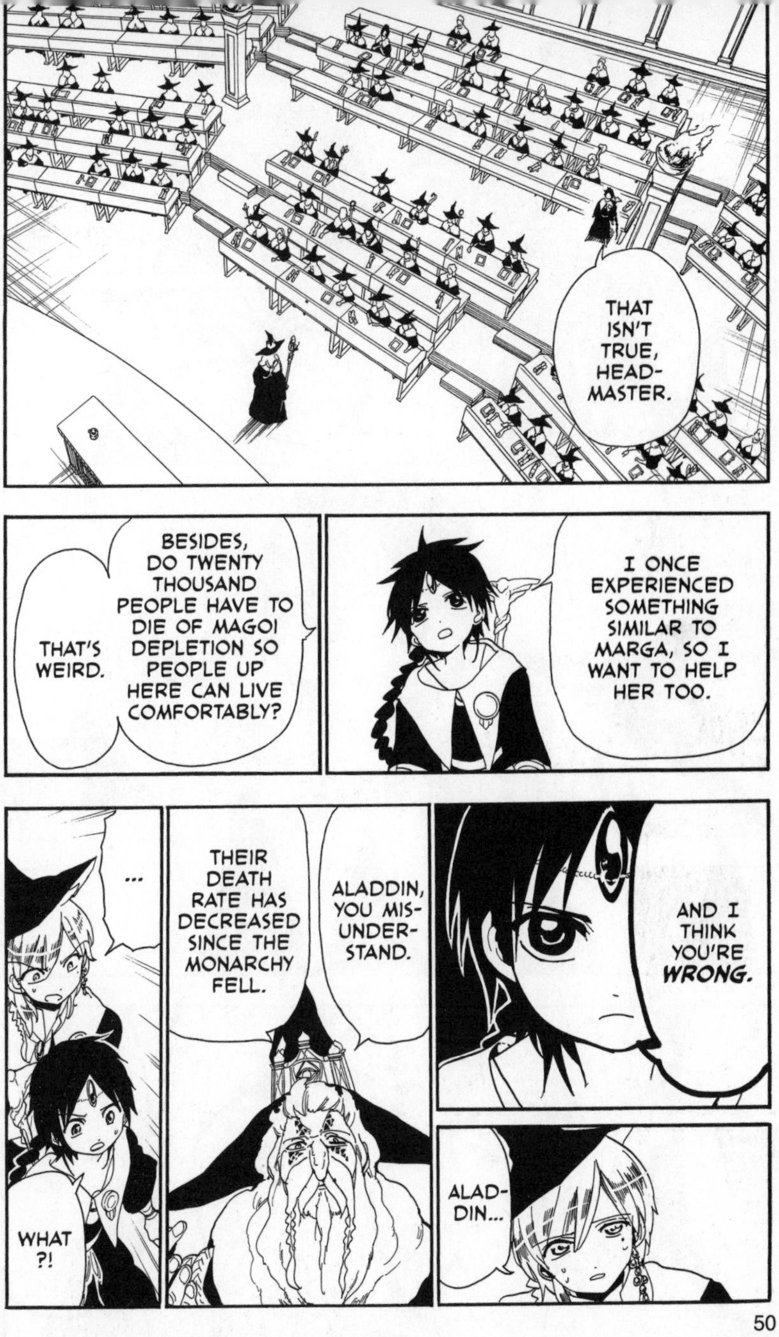
THAT ISN'T TRUE, HEAD-MASTER.
I ONCE EXPERIENCED SOMETHING SIMILAR TO MARGA, SO I WANT TO HELP HER TOO.
BESIDES, DO TWENTY THOUSAND PEOPLE HAVE TO DIE OF MAGOI DEPLETION SO PEOPLE UP HERE CAN LIVE COMFORTABLY?
THAT'S WEIRD.
AND I THINK YOU'RE ***WRONG.***
ALAD-DIN...
ALADDIN, YOU MIS-UNDER-STAND.
THEIR DEATH RATE HAS DECREASED SINCE THE MONARCHY FELL.
...
WHAT ?!

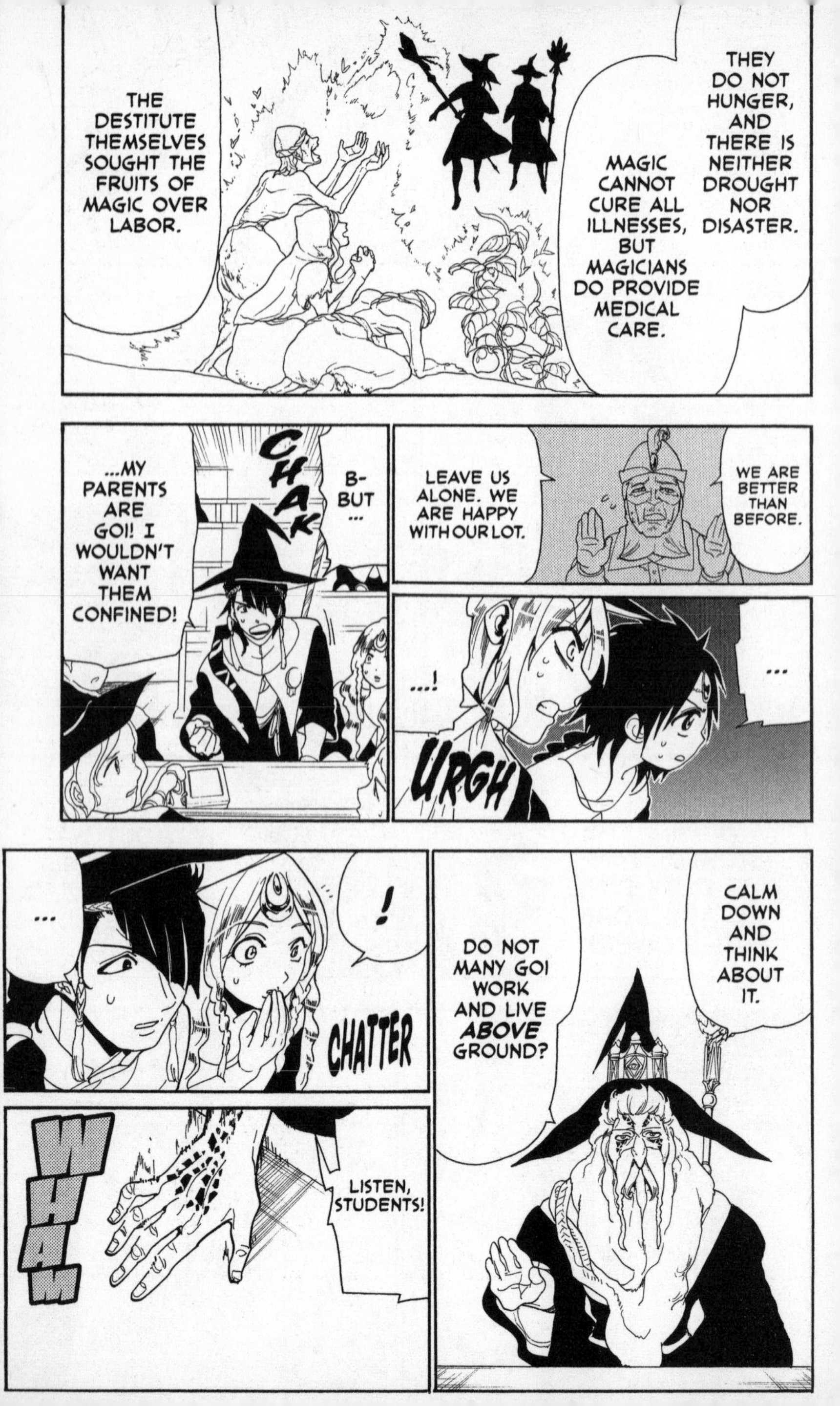
THEY DO NOT HUNGER, AND THERE IS NEITHER DROUGHT NOR DISASTER.
MAGIC CANNOT CURE ALL ILLNESSES, BUT MAGICIANS DO PROVIDE MEDICAL CARE.
THE DESTITUTE THEMSELVES SOUGHT THE FRUITS OF MAGIC OVER LABOR.
WE ARE BETTER THAN BEFORE.
LEAVE US ALONE. WE ARE HAPPY WITH OUR LOT.
...
...!
URGH
CHAK
B-BUT ...
...MY PARENTS ARE GOI! I WOULDN'T WANT THEM CONFINED!
CALM DOWN AND THINK ABOUT IT.
DO NOT MANY GOI WORK AND LIVE *ABOVE* GROUND?
!
...
CHATTER
LISTEN, STUDENTS!
WHAM

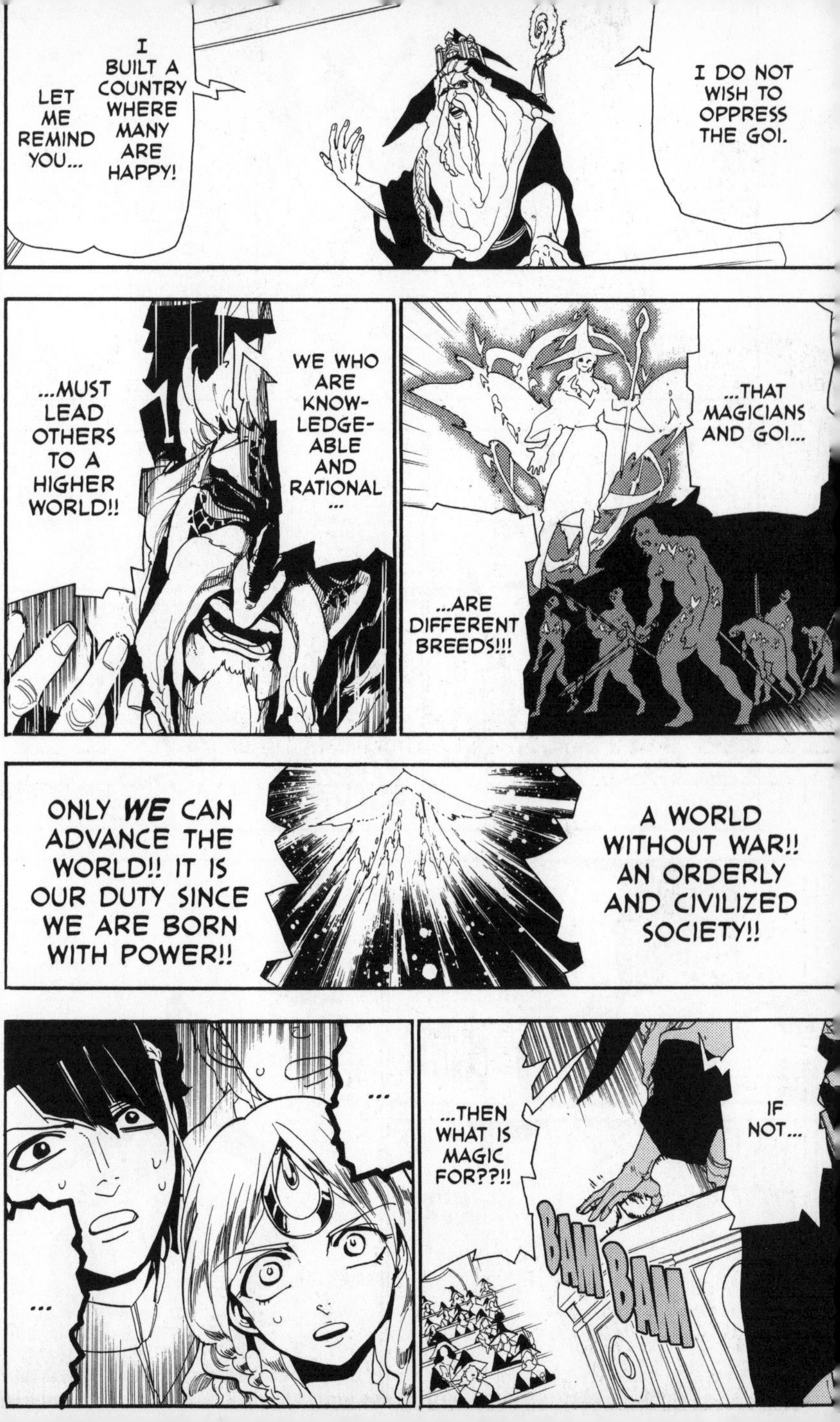
I DO NOT WISH TO OPPRESS THE GOI.
I BUILT A COUNTRY WHERE MANY ARE HAPPY!
LET ME REMIND YOU...
...THAT MAGICIANS AND GOI...
...ARE DIFFERENT BREEDS!!!
WE WHO ARE KNOWLEDGEABLE AND RATIONAL...
...MUST LEAD OTHERS TO A HIGHER WORLD!!
A WORLD WITHOUT WAR!! AN ORDERLY AND CIVILIZED SOCIETY!!
ONLY *WE* CAN ADVANCE THE WORLD!! IT IS OUR DUTY SINCE WE ARE BORN WITH POWER!!
IF NOT...
...THEN WHAT IS MAGIC FOR??!!
BAM BAM
...
...

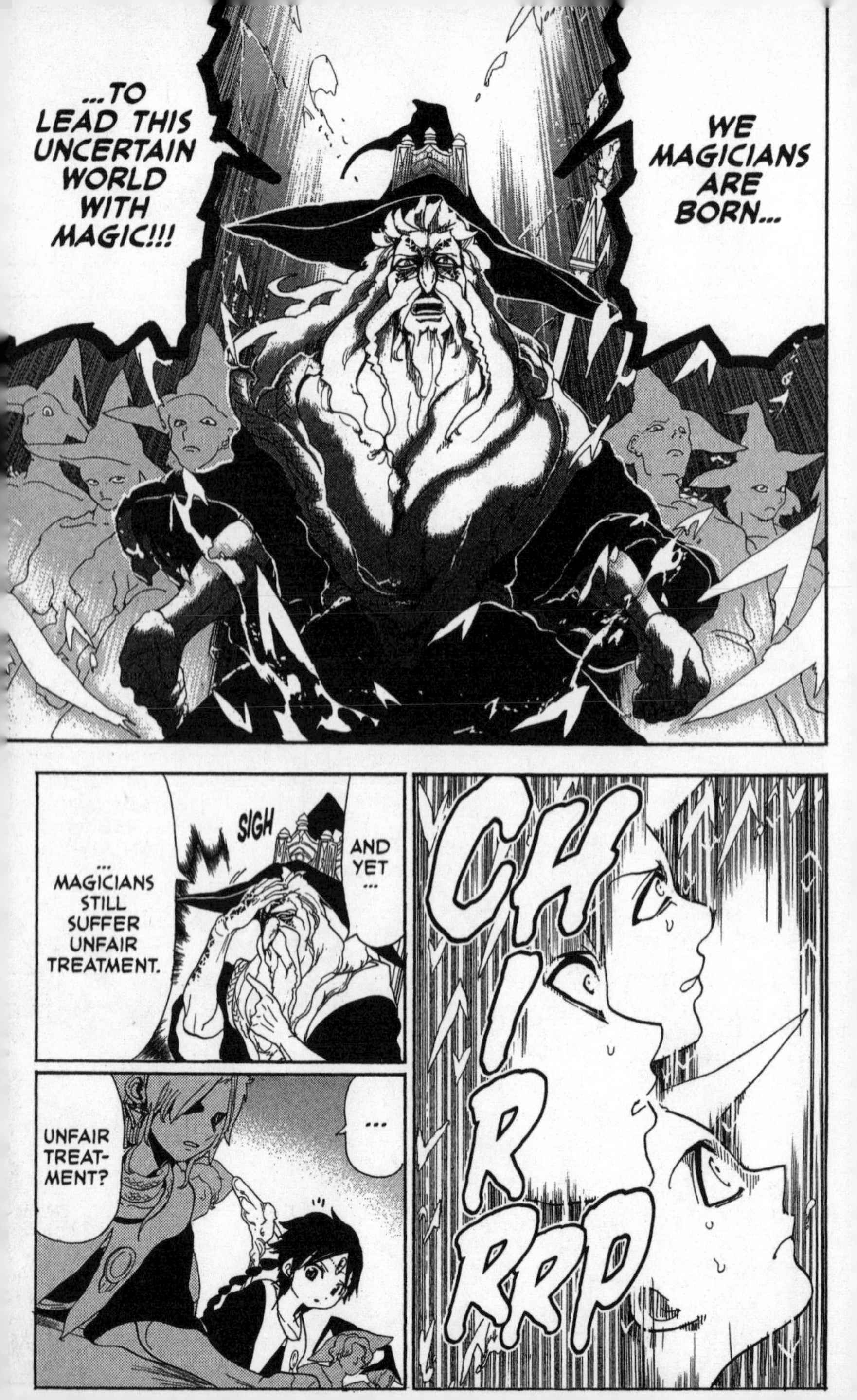
WE MAGICIANS ARE BORN...
...TO LEAD THIS UNCERTAIN WORLD WITH MAGIC!!!
CHIRRRP
SIGH
AND YET ...
... MAGICIANS STILL SUFFER UNFAIR TREATMENT.
...
UNFAIR TREAT-MENT?

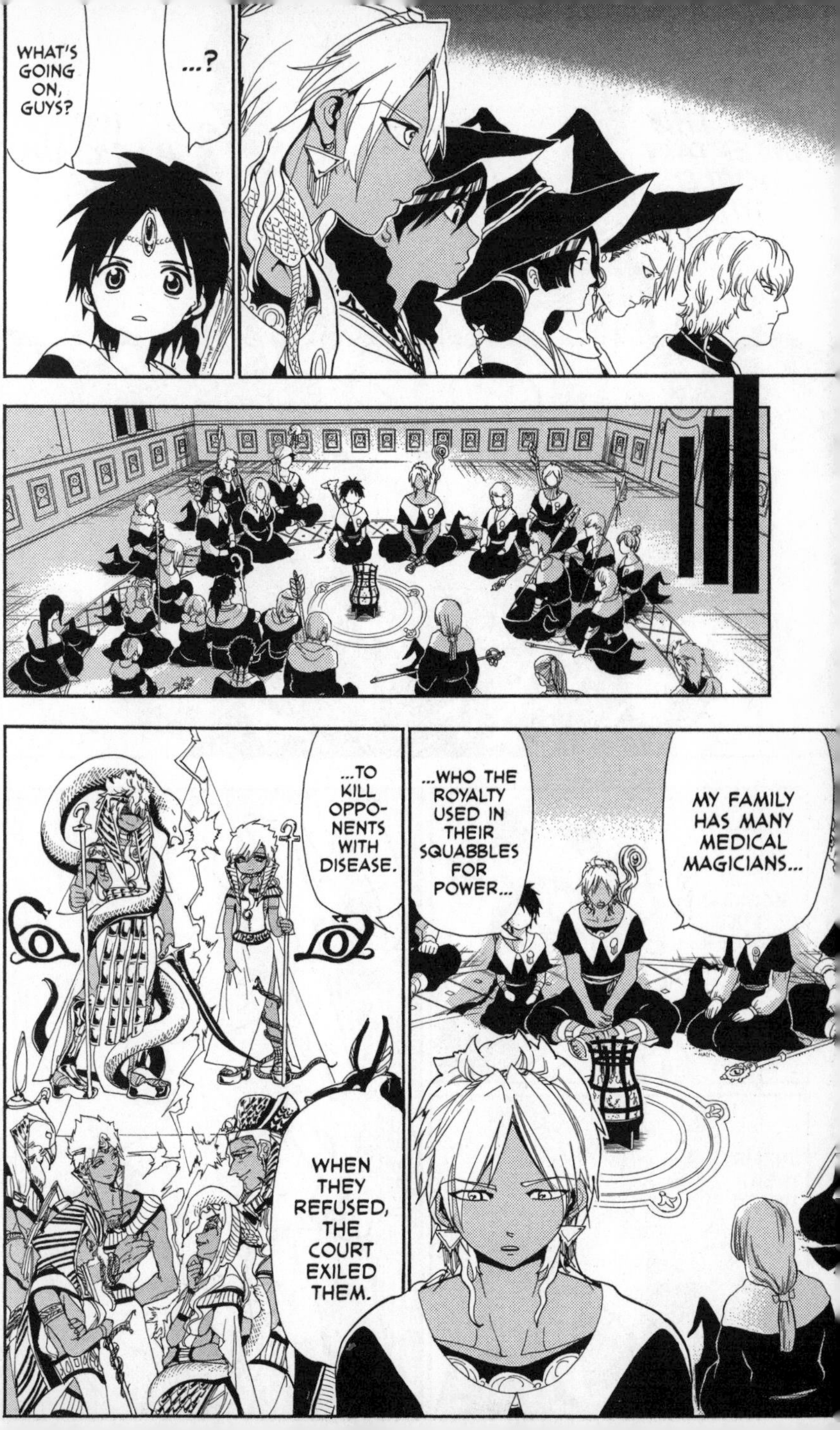
...?
WHAT'S GOING ON, GUYS?
MY FAMILY HAS MANY MEDICAL MAGICIANS...
...WHO THE ROYALTY USED IN THEIR SQUABBLES FOR POWER...
...TO KILL OPPO-NENTS WITH DISEASE.
WHEN THEY REFUSED, THE COURT EXILED THEM.

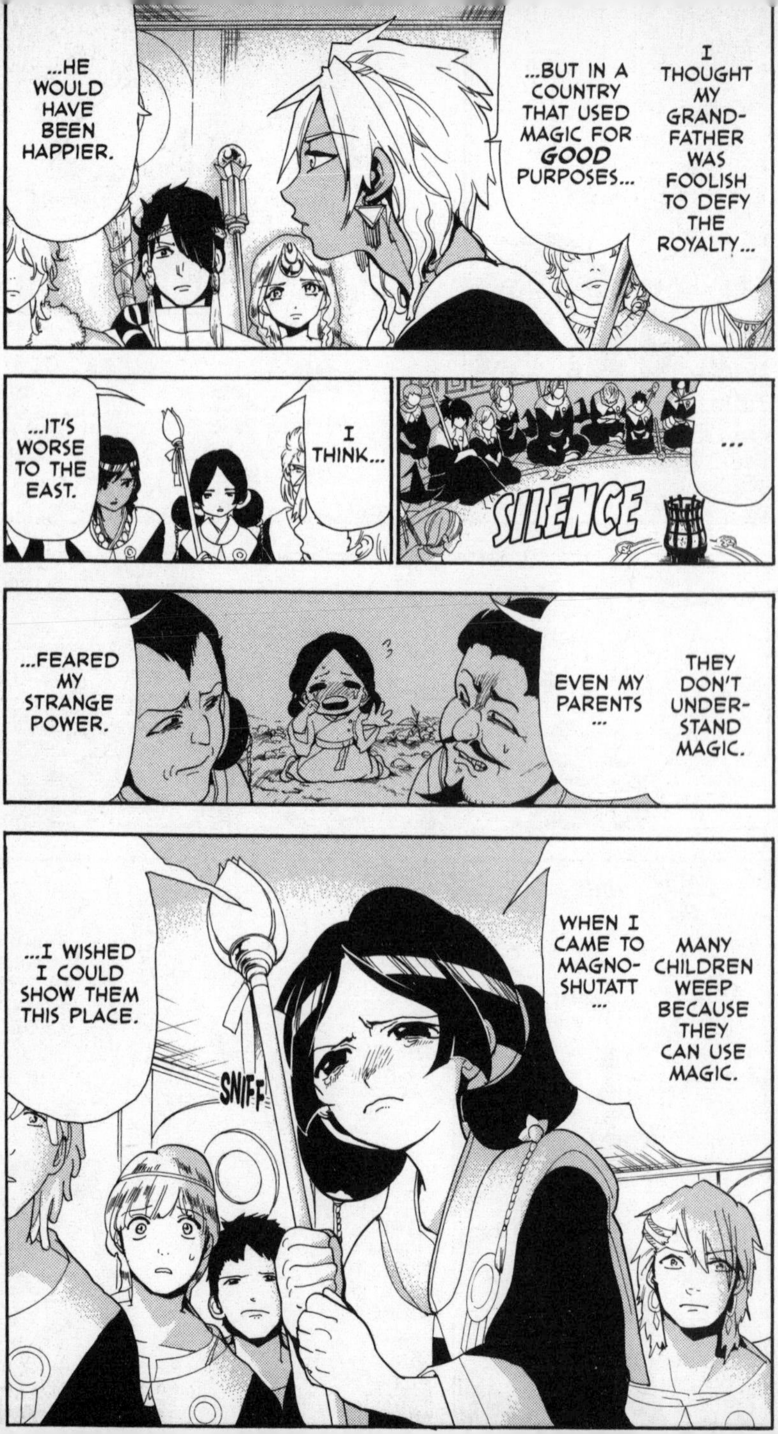
I THOUGHT MY GRANDFATHER WAS FOOLISH TO DEFY THE ROYALTY...
...BUT IN A COUNTRY THAT USED MAGIC FOR GOOD PURPOSES...
...HE WOULD HAVE BEEN HAPPIER.
...
SILENCE
I THINK...
...IT'S WORSE TO THE EAST.
THEY DON'T UNDERSTAND MAGIC.
EVEN MY PARENTS...
...FEARED MY STRANGE POWER.
MANY CHILDREN WEEP BECAUSE THEY CAN USE MAGIC.
WHEN I CAME TO MAGNOSHUTATT...
SNIFF
...I WISHED I COULD SHOW THEM THIS PLACE.

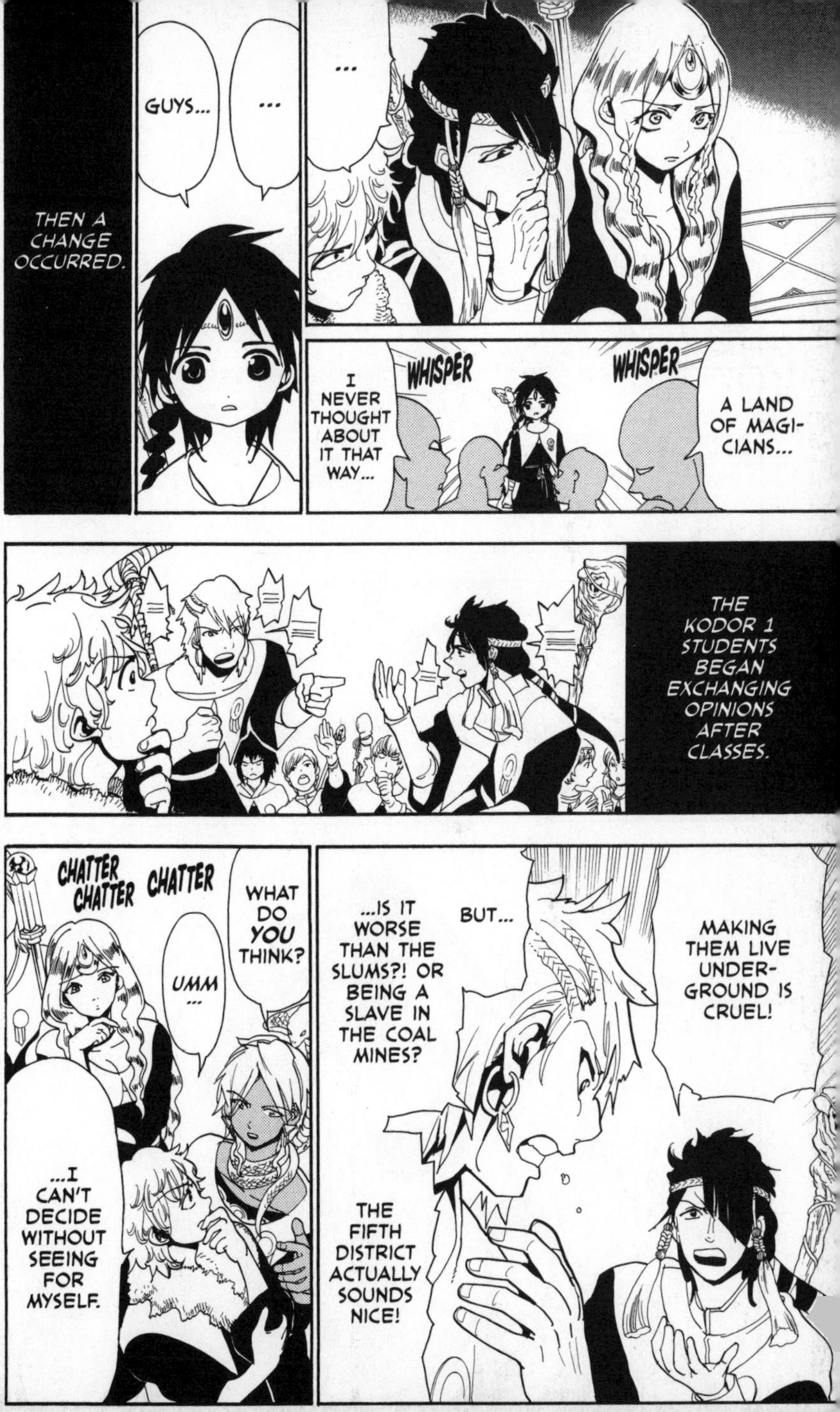
...
WHISPER
A LAND OF MAGI-CIANS...
WHISPER
I NEVER THOUGHT ABOUT IT THAT WAY...
GUYS...
...
THEN A CHANGE OCCURRED.
THE KODOR 1 STUDENTS BEGAN EXCHANGING OPINIONS AFTER CLASSES.
MAKING THEM LIVE UNDER-GROUND IS CRUEL!
BUT...
...IS IT WORSE THAN THE SLUMS?! OR BEING A SLAVE IN THE COAL MINES?
THE FIFTH DISTRICT ACTUALLY SOUNDS NICE!
WHAT DO *YOU* THINK?
CHATTER CHATTER
CHATTER
UMM ...
...I CAN'T DECIDE WITHOUT SEEING FOR MYSELF.

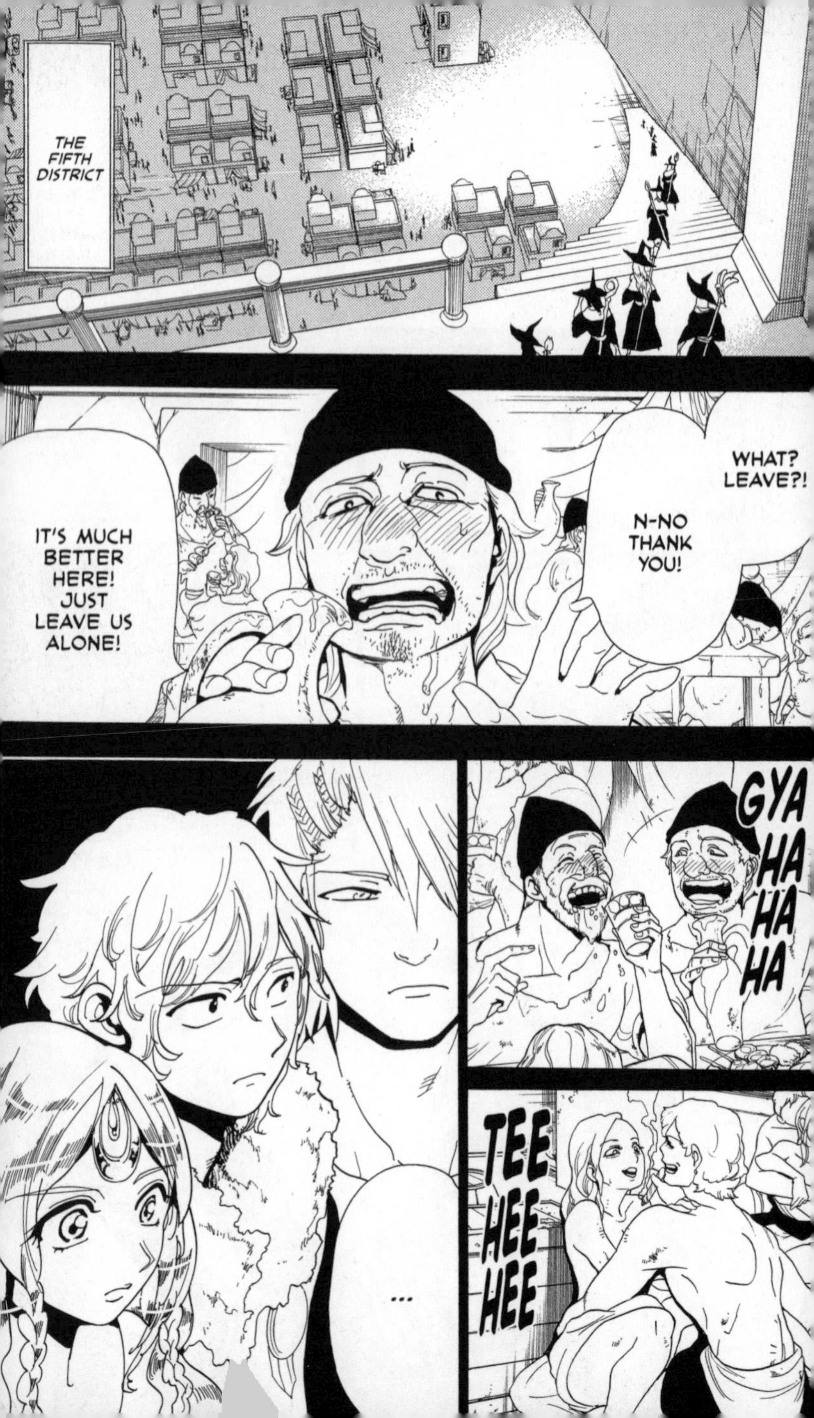
THE FIFTH DISTRICT
WHAT? LEAVE?!
N-NO THANK YOU!
IT'S MUCH BETTER HERE! JUST LEAVE US ALONE!
GYA HA HA HA HA
TEE HEE HEE HEE
...

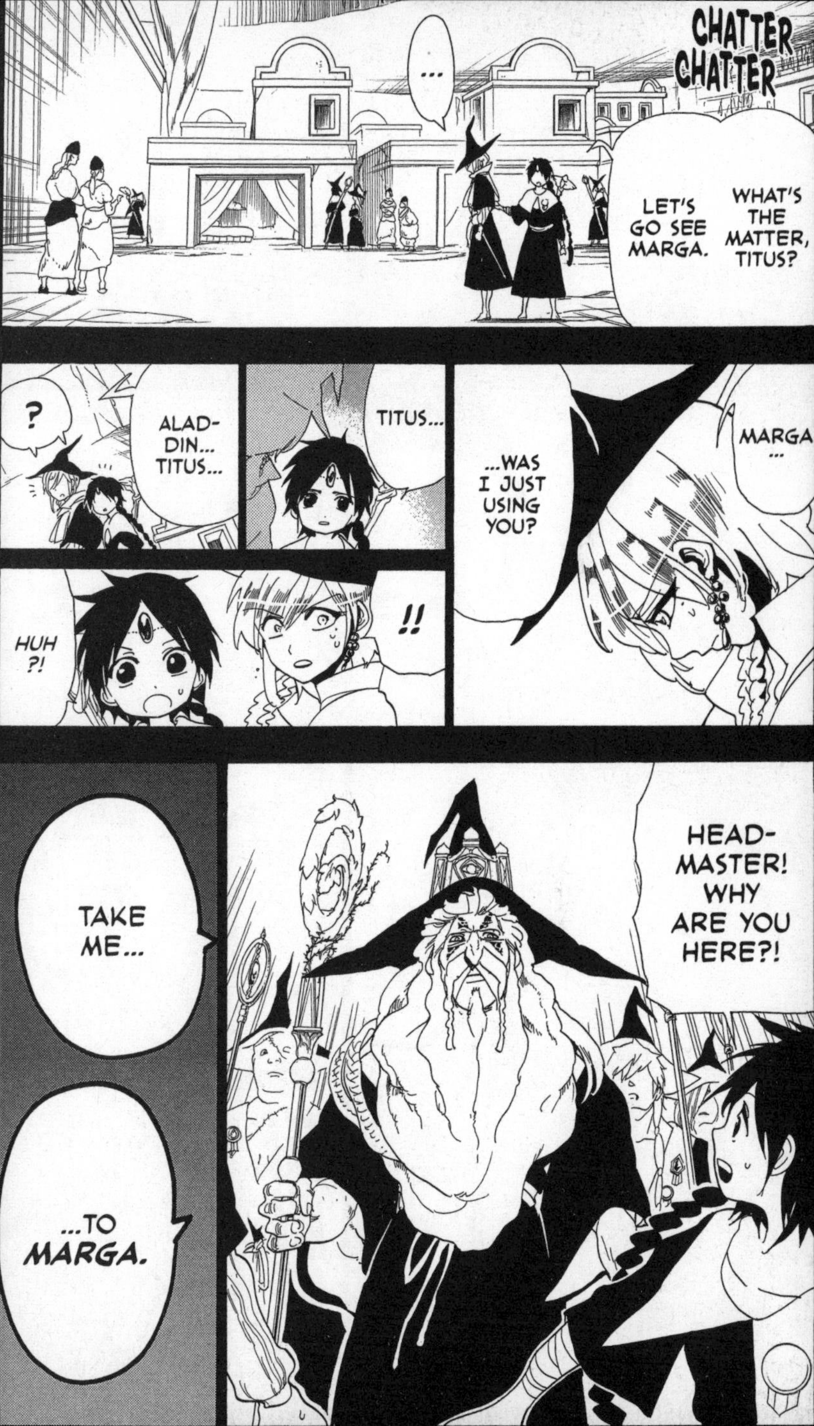
CHATTER CHATTER
WHAT'S THE MATTER, TITUS?
LET'S GO SEE MARGA.
...
MARGA...
...WAS I JUST USING YOU?
TITUS...
ALAD-DIN... TITUS...
?
!!
HUH?!
HEAD-MASTER! WHY ARE YOU HERE?!
TAKE ME...
...TO MARGA.

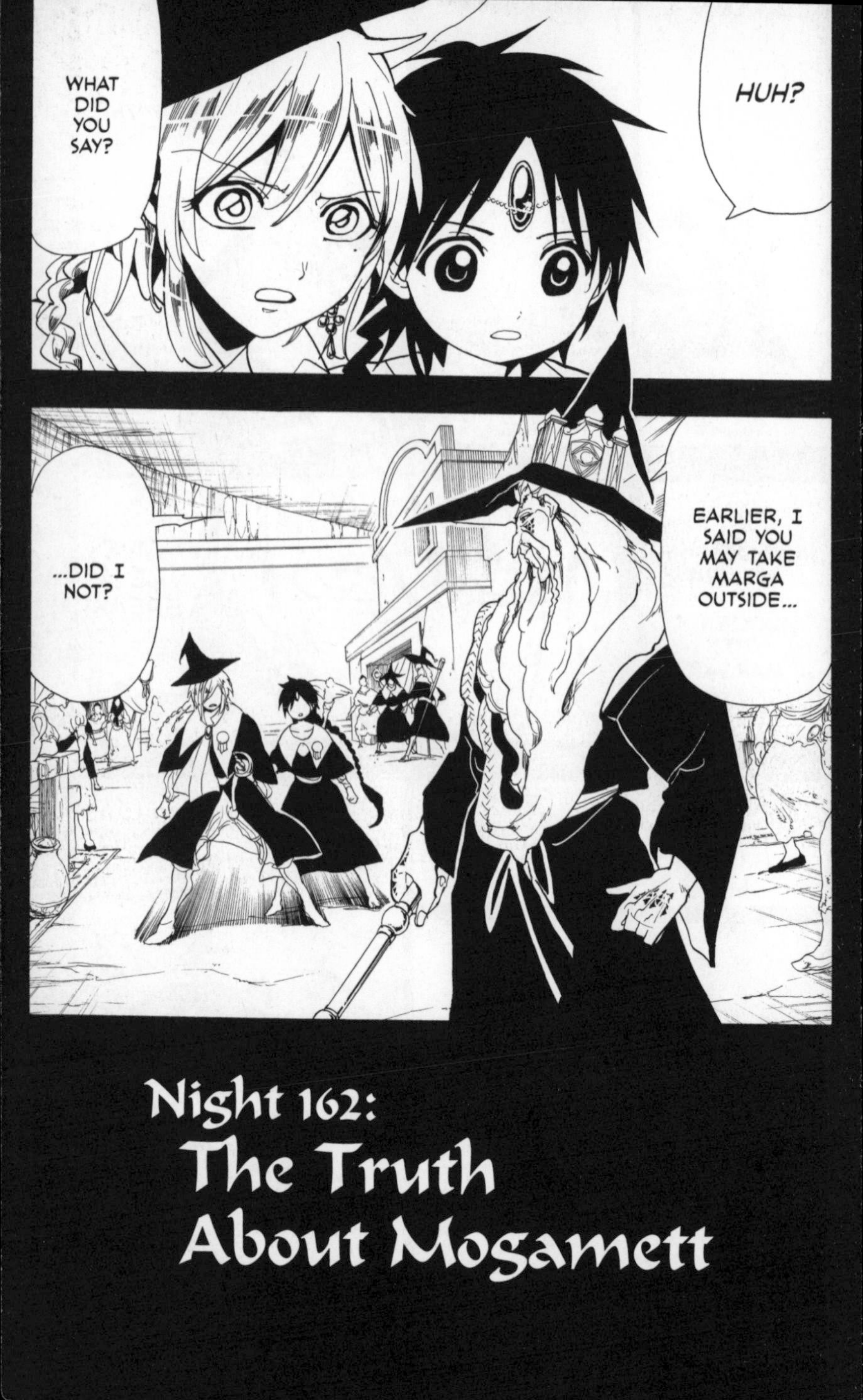
HUH?
WHAT DID YOU SAY?
EARLIER, I SAID YOU MAY TAKE MARGA OUTSIDE...
...DID I NOT?

Night 162: The Truth About Mogamett

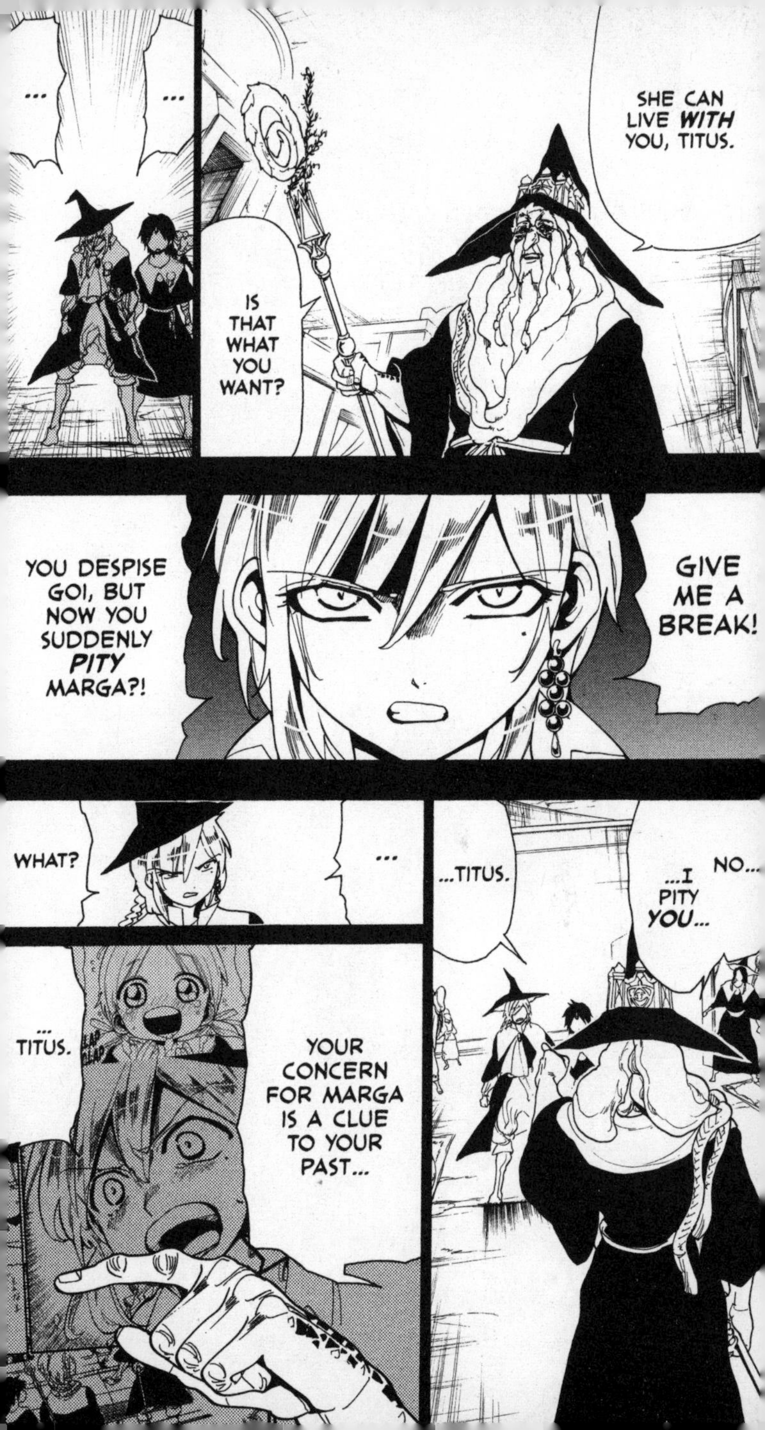
SHE CAN LIVE WITH YOU, TITUS.
IS THAT WHAT YOU WANT?
...
...
GIVE ME A BREAK!
YOU DESPISE GOI, BUT NOW YOU SUDDENLY PITY MARGA?!
NO...
...I PITY YOU...
...TITUS.
...
WHAT?
YOUR CONCERN FOR MARGA IS A CLUE TO YOUR PAST...
... TITUS.

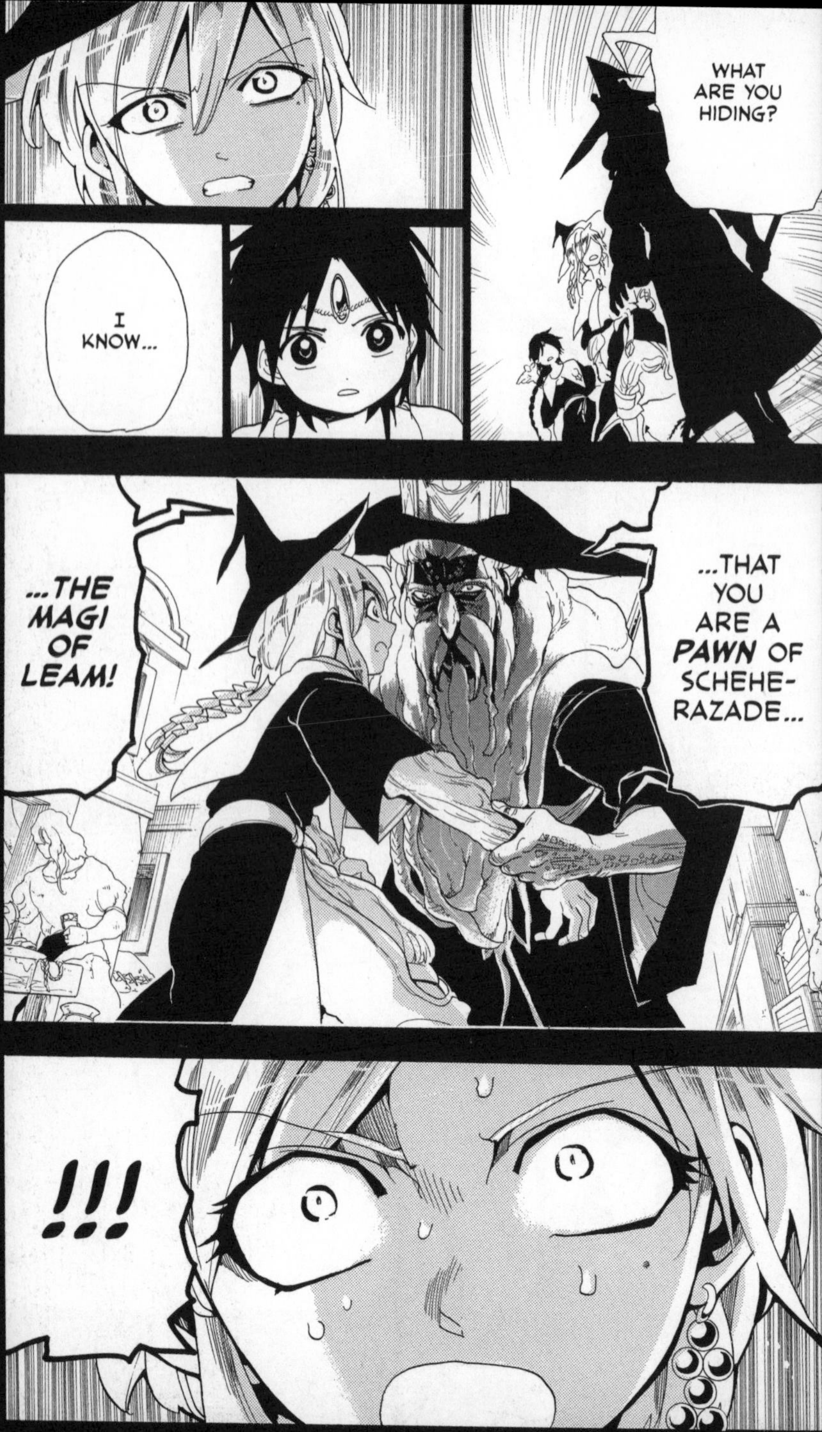
WHAT ARE YOU HIDING?
I KNOW...
...THAT YOU ARE A PAWN OF SCHEHE-RAZADE...
...THE MAGI OF LEAM!
!!!

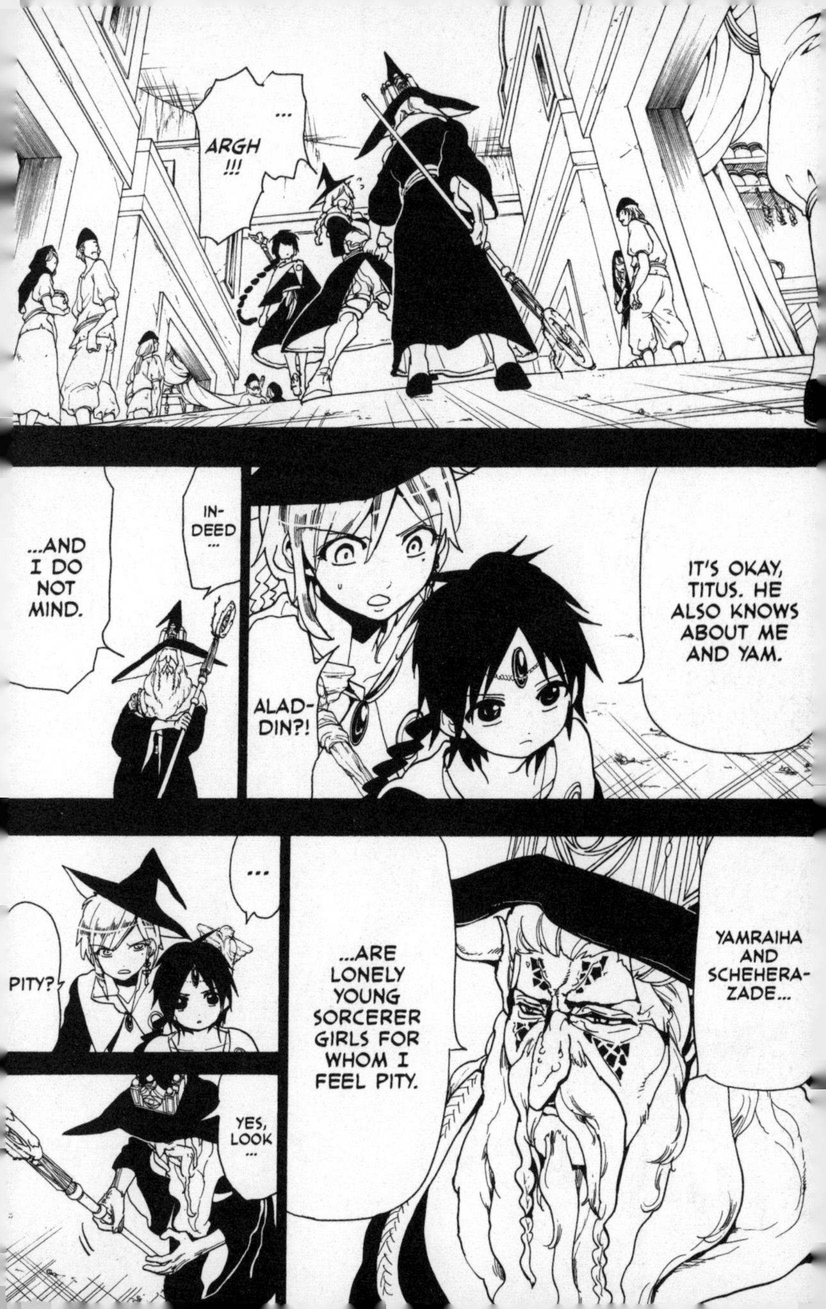
... ARGH !!!
IT'S OKAY, TITUS. HE ALSO KNOWS ABOUT ME AND YAM.
ALAD-DIN?!
IN-DEED ...
...AND I DO NOT MIND.
YAMRAIHA AND SCHEHERA-ZADE...
...ARE LONELY YOUNG SORCERER GIRLS FOR WHOM I FEEL PITY.
...
PITY?
YES, LOOK ...

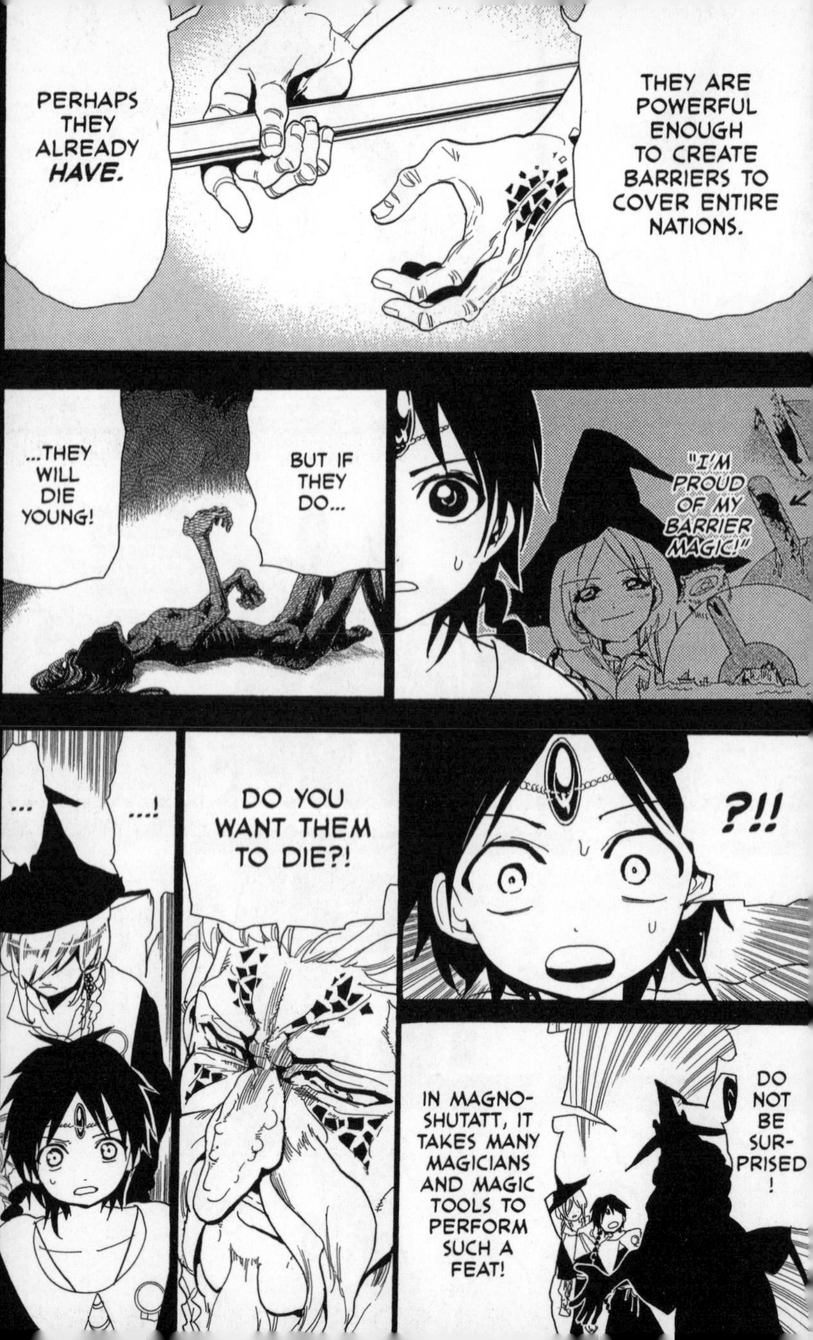
THEY ARE POWERFUL ENOUGH TO CREATE BARRIERS TO COVER ENTIRE NATIONS.
PERHAPS THEY ALREADY *HAVE.*
"I'M PROUD OF MY BARRIER MAGIC!"
BUT IF THEY DO...
...THEY WILL DIE YOUNG!
?!!
DO NOT BE SUR-PRISED!
IN MAGNO-SHUTATT, IT TAKES MANY MAGICIANS AND MAGIC TOOLS TO PERFORM SUCH A FEAT!
DO YOU WANT THEM TO DIE?!
...!
...

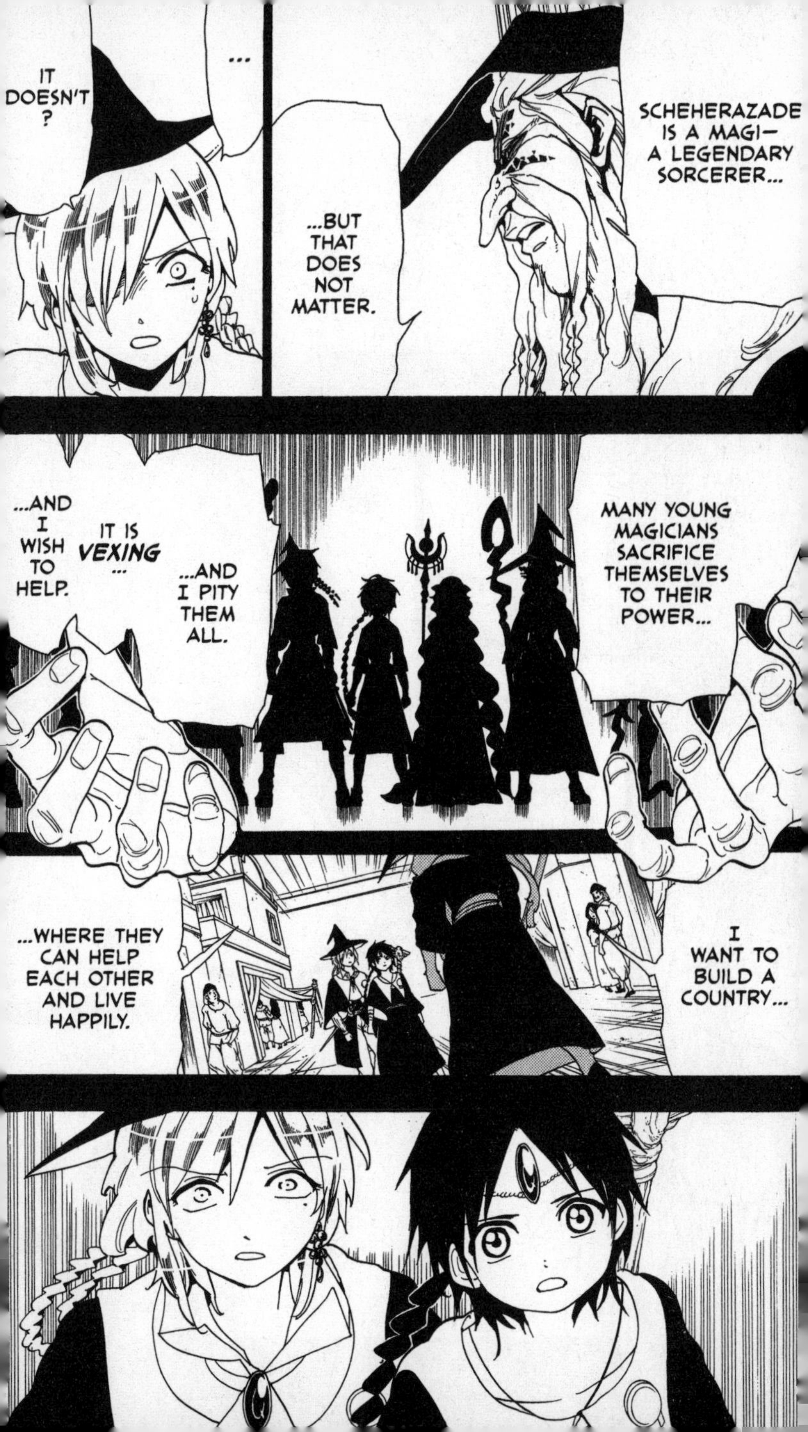
SCHEHERAZADE IS A MAGI— A LEGENDARY SORCERER...
...BUT THAT DOES NOT MATTER.
...
IT DOESN'T ?
MANY YOUNG MAGICIANS SACRIFICE THEMSELVES TO THEIR POWER...
...AND I PITY THEM ALL.
IT IS *VEXING*...
...AND I WISH TO HELP.
I WANT TO BUILD A COUNTRY...
...WHERE THEY CAN HELP EACH OTHER AND LIVE HAPPILY.

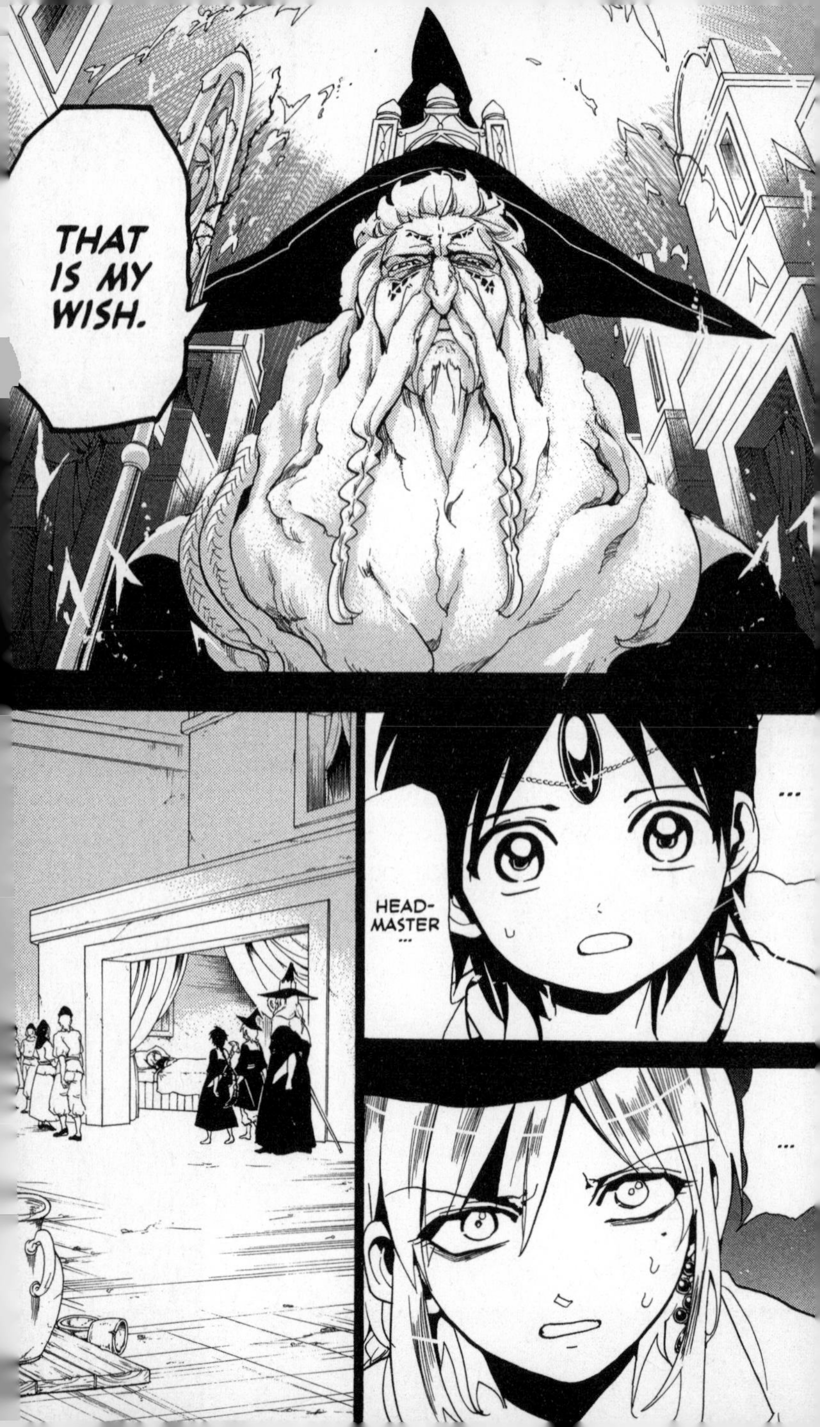
THAT IS MY WISH.
...
HEAD-MASTER ...
...

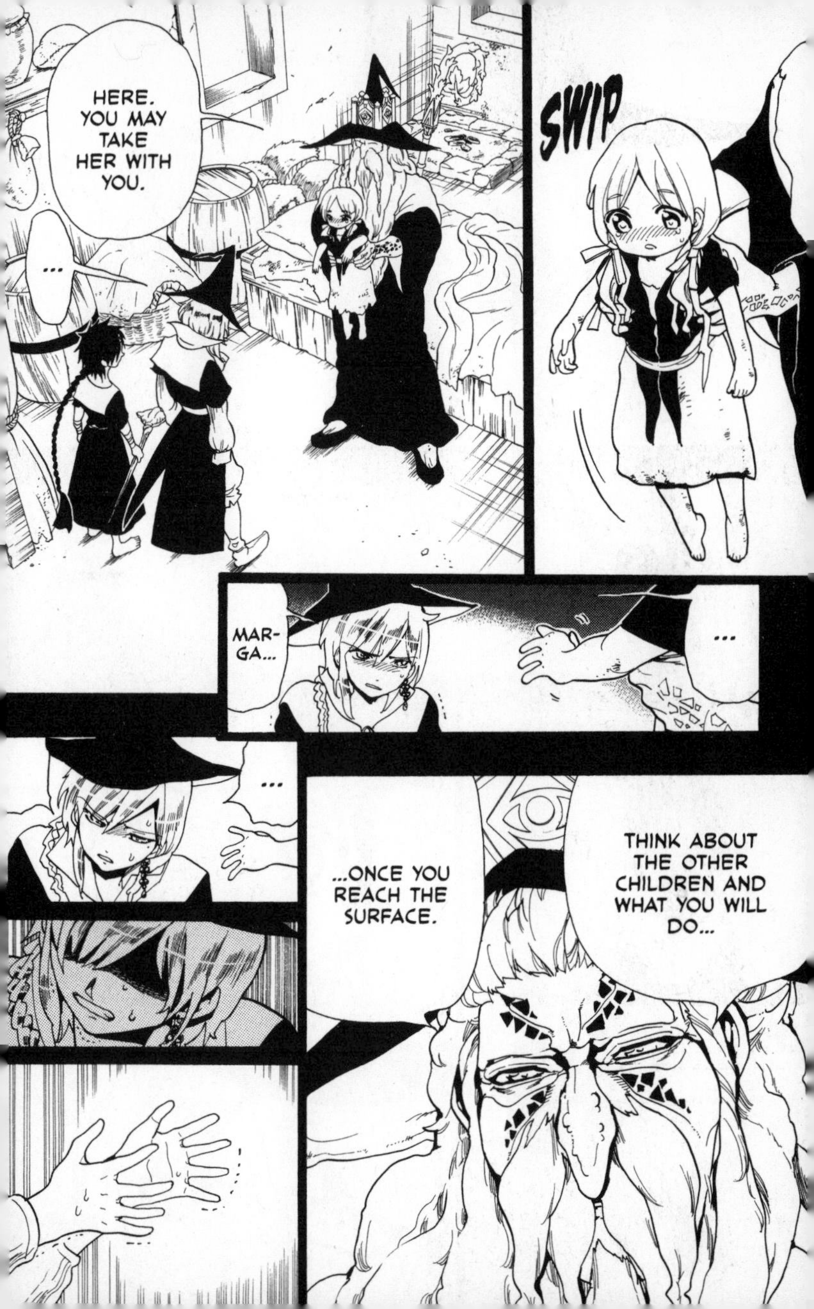
SWIP
HERE. YOU MAY TAKE HER WITH YOU.
...
...
MAR-GA...
THINK ABOUT THE OTHER CHILDREN AND WHAT YOU WILL DO...
...ONCE YOU REACH THE SURFACE.
...

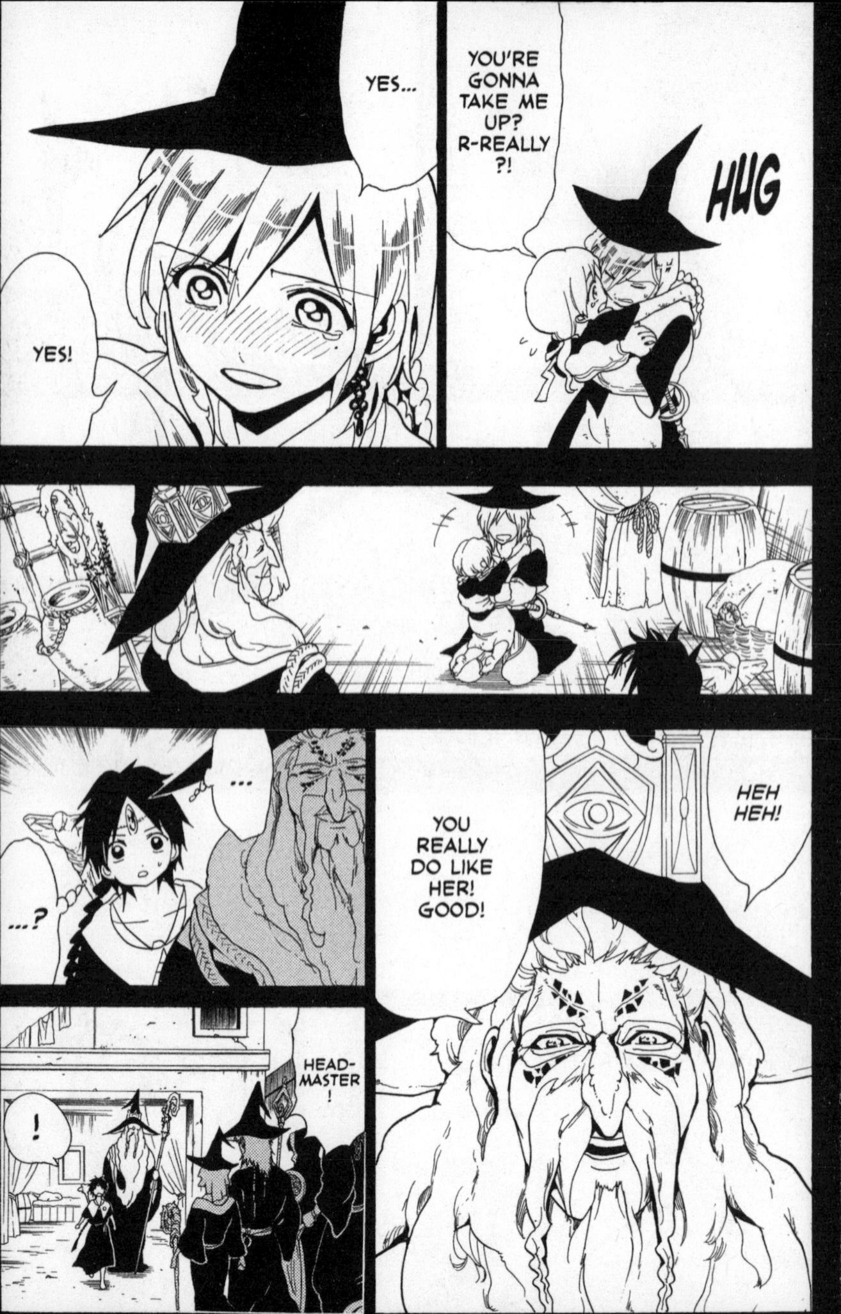
YOU'RE GONNA TAKE ME UP? R-REALLY ?!
HUG
YES...
YES!
HEH HEH!
YOU REALLY DO LIKE HER! GOOD!
...
...?
HEAD-MASTER !
!

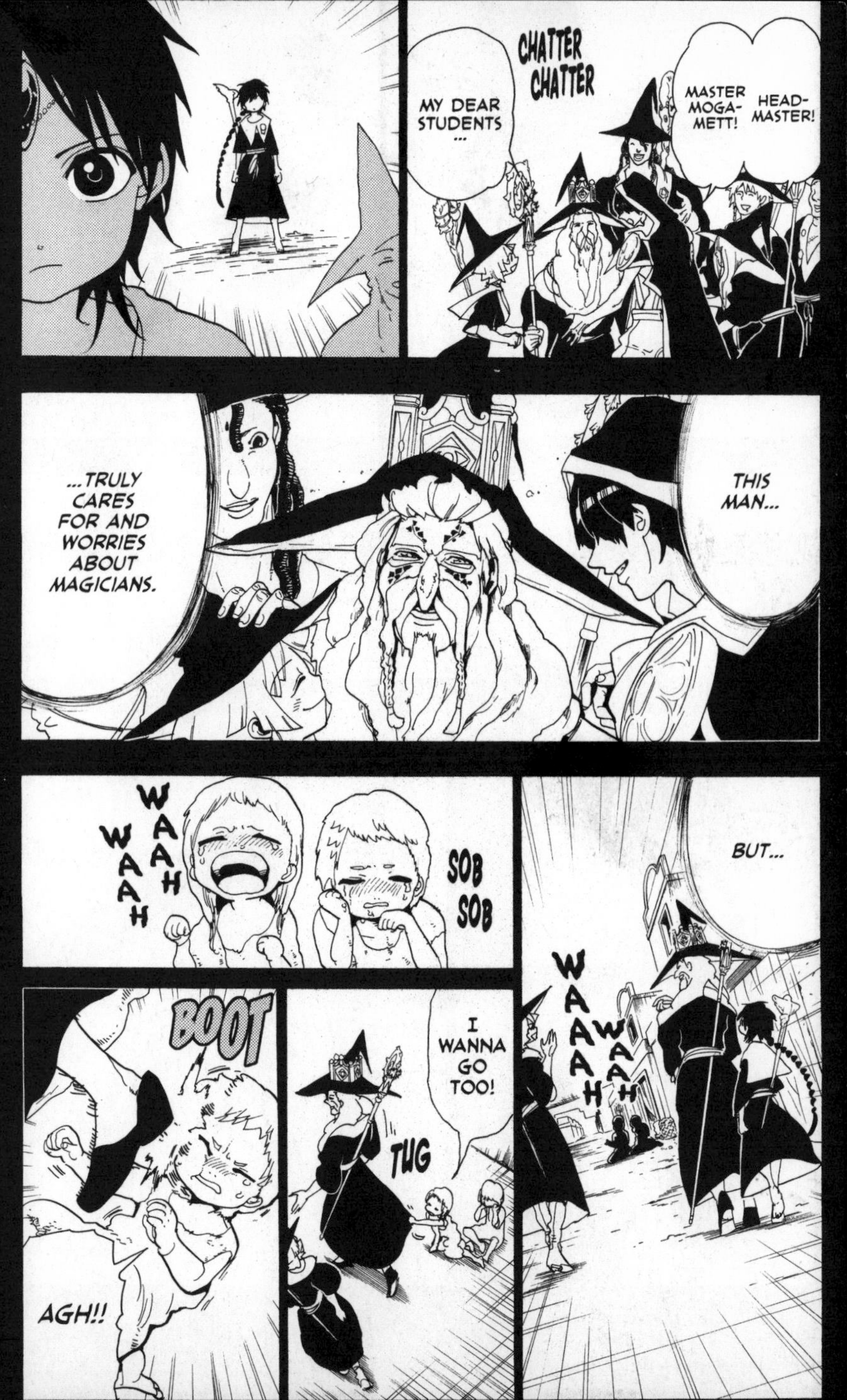
HEAD-MASTER!
MASTER MOGA-METT!
CHATTER CHATTER
MY DEAR STUDENTS ...
THIS MAN...
...TRULY CARES FOR AND WORRIES ABOUT MAGICIANS.
BUT...
WAAH
WAAAAH
SOB SOB
WAAH WAAH
I WANNA GO TOO!
TUG
BOOT
AGH!!

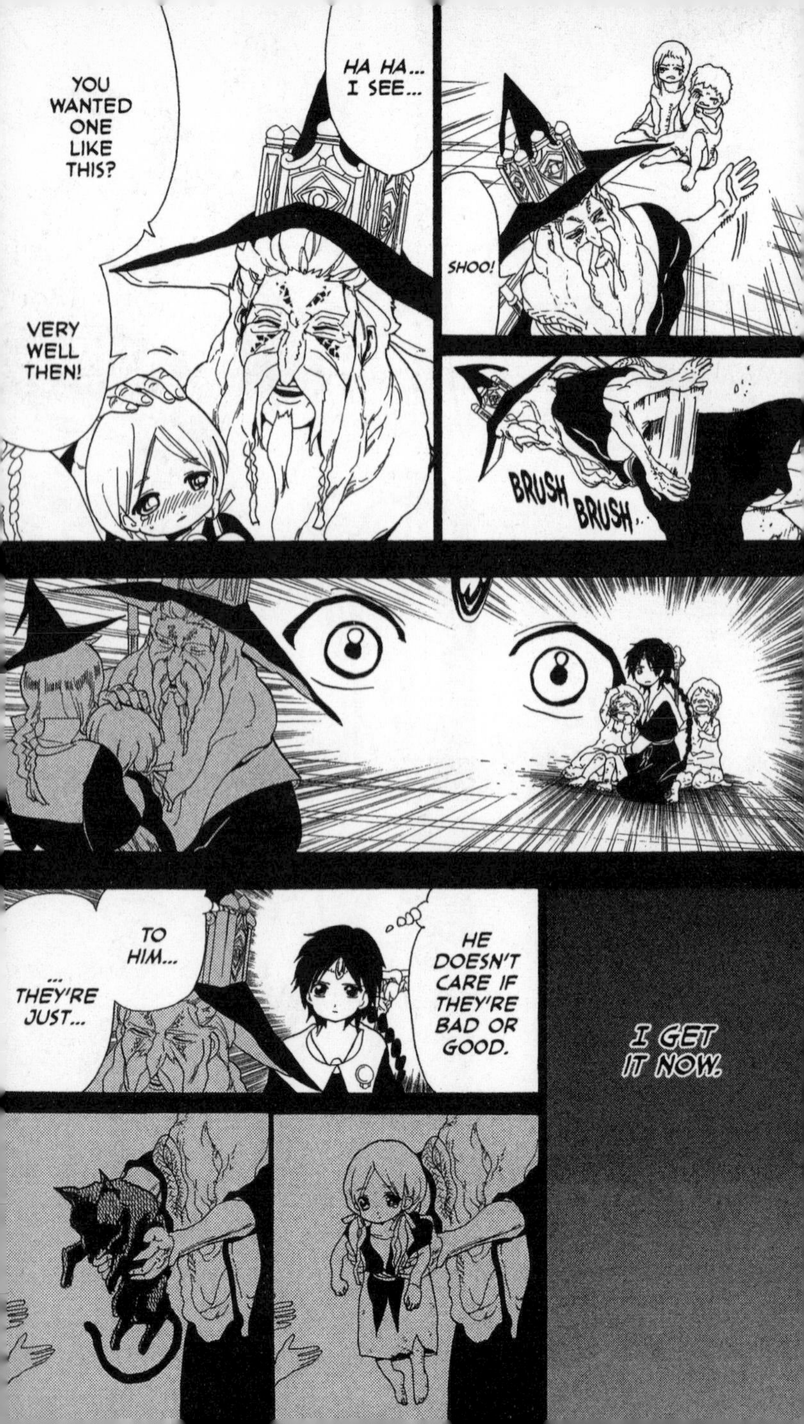
SHOO!
BRUSH BRUSH...
HA HA... I SEE...
YOU WANTED ONE LIKE THIS?
VERY WELL THEN!
I GET IT NOW.
HE DOESN'T CARE IF THEY'RE BAD OR GOOD.
TO HIM...
...THEY'RE JUST...

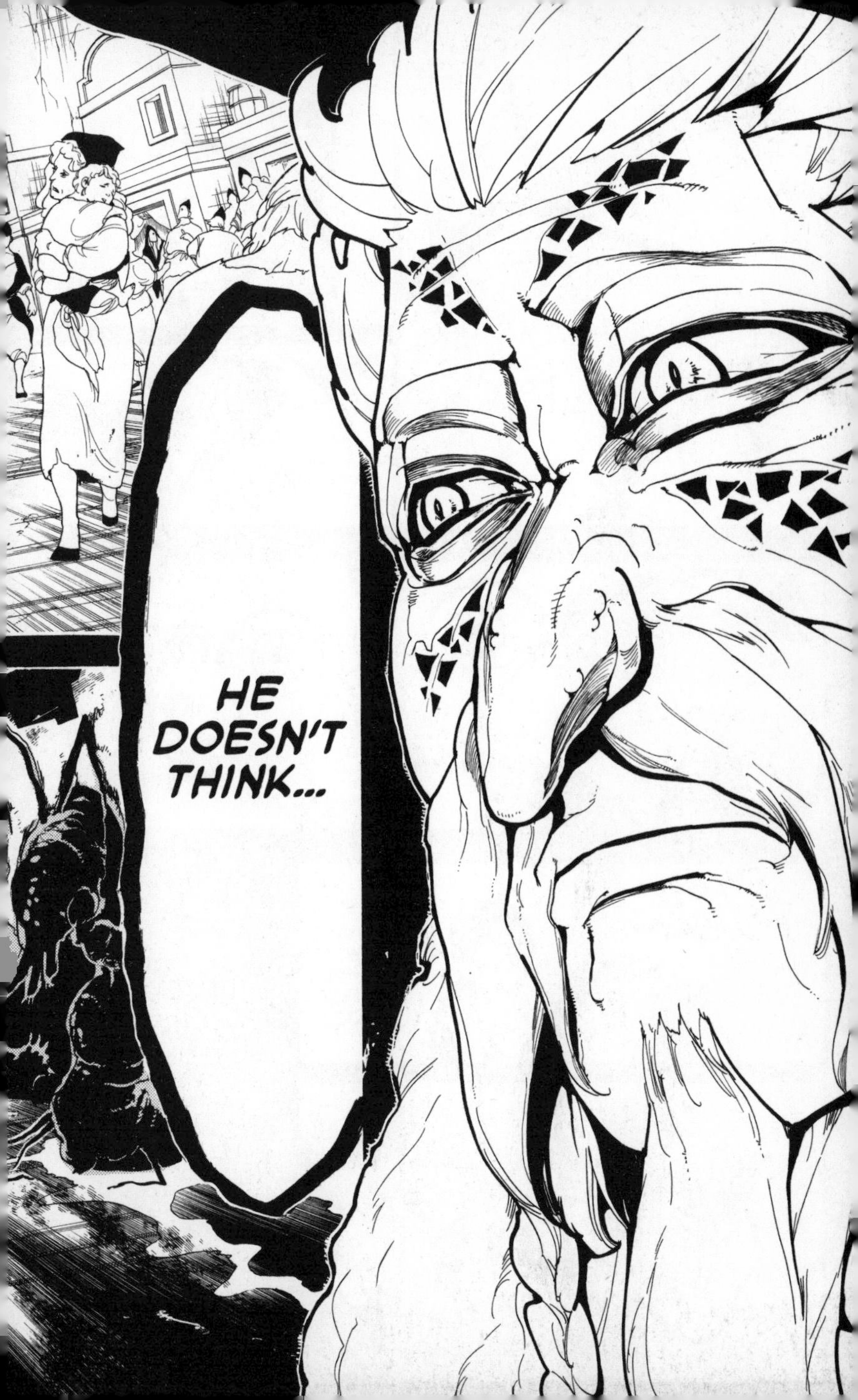
HE DOESN'T THINK...

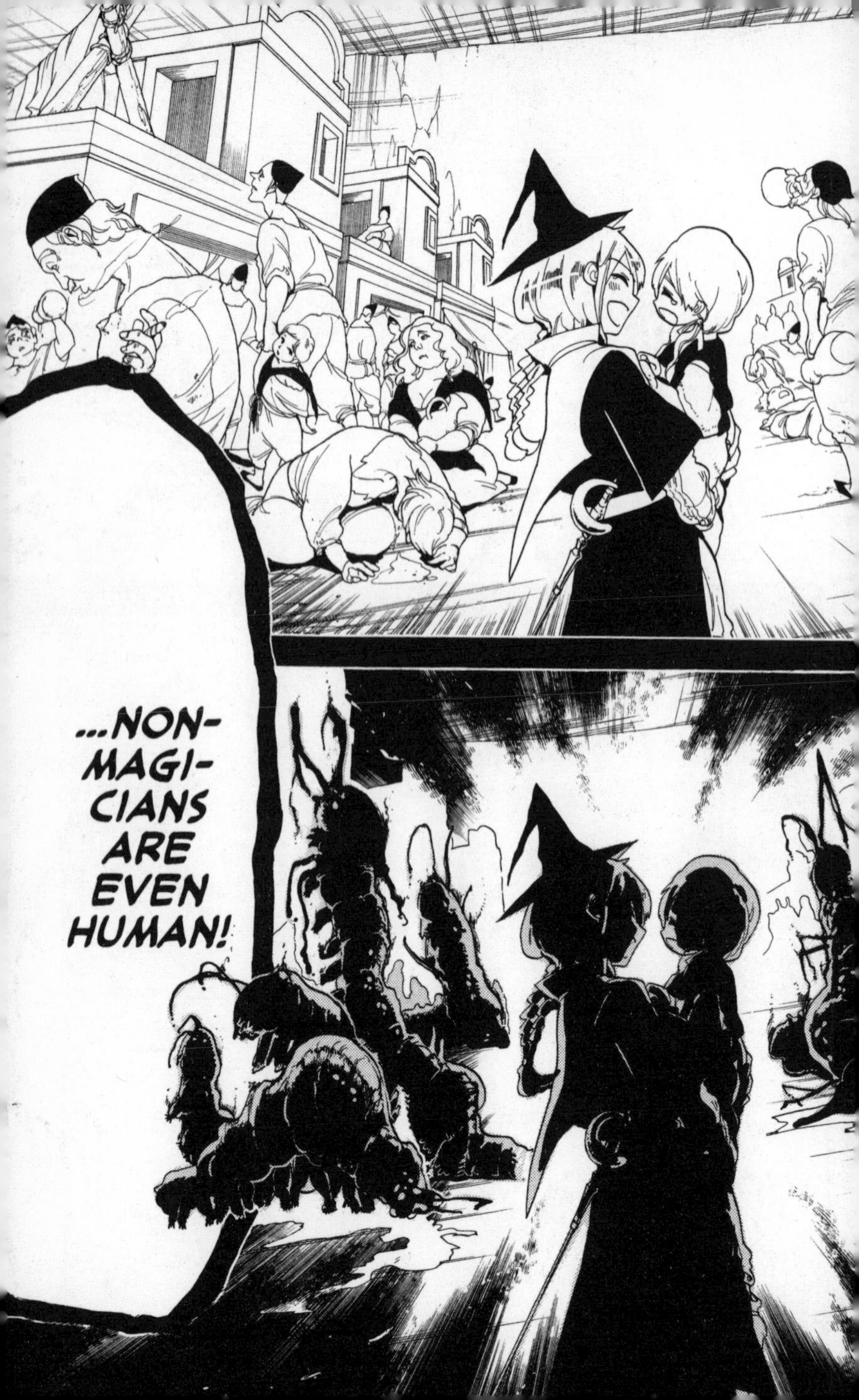
...NON-MAGICIANS ARE EVEN HUMAN!

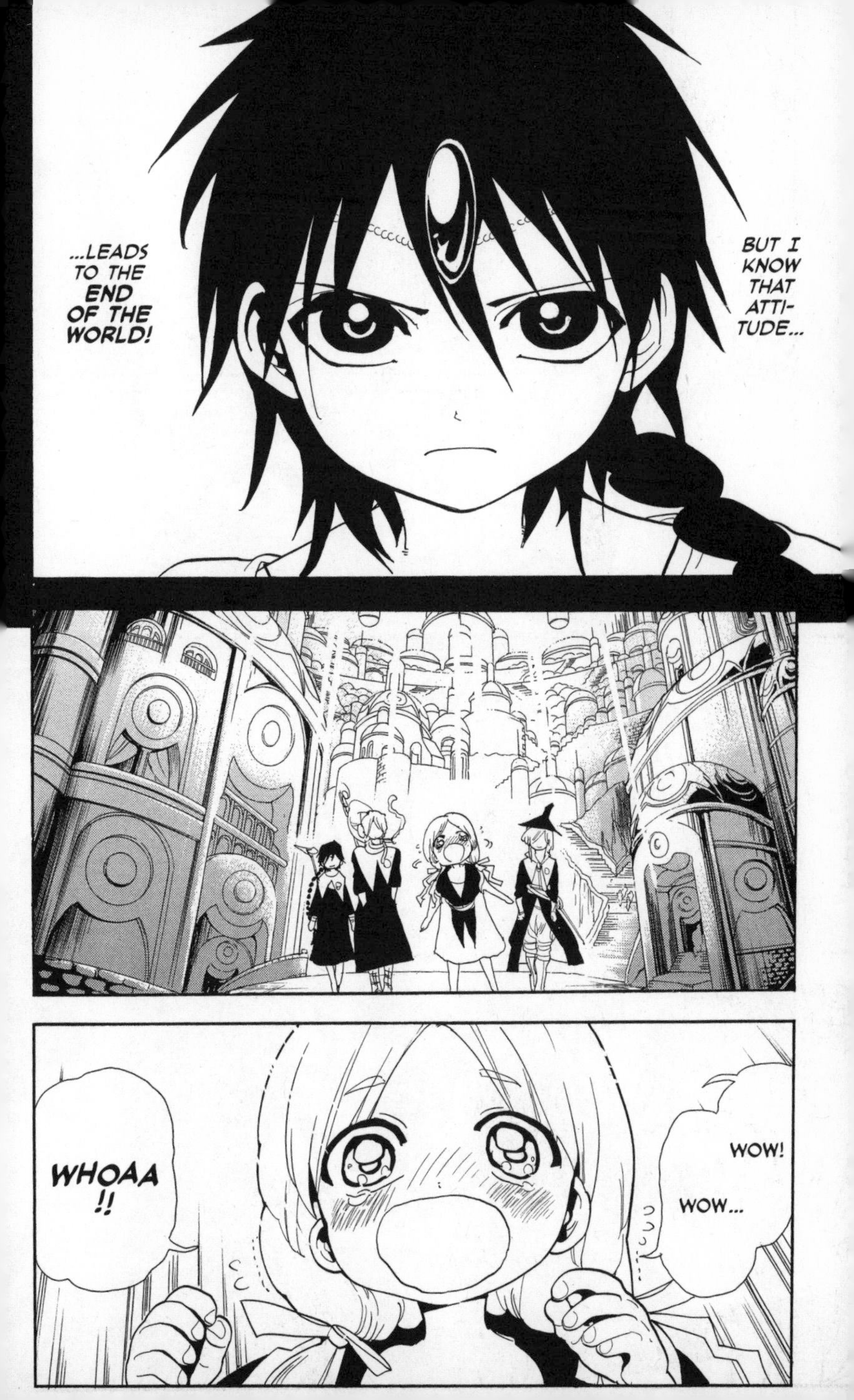
BUT I KNOW THAT ATTI-TUDE...
...LEADS TO THE END OF THE WORLD!
WOW!
WOW...
WHOAA !!

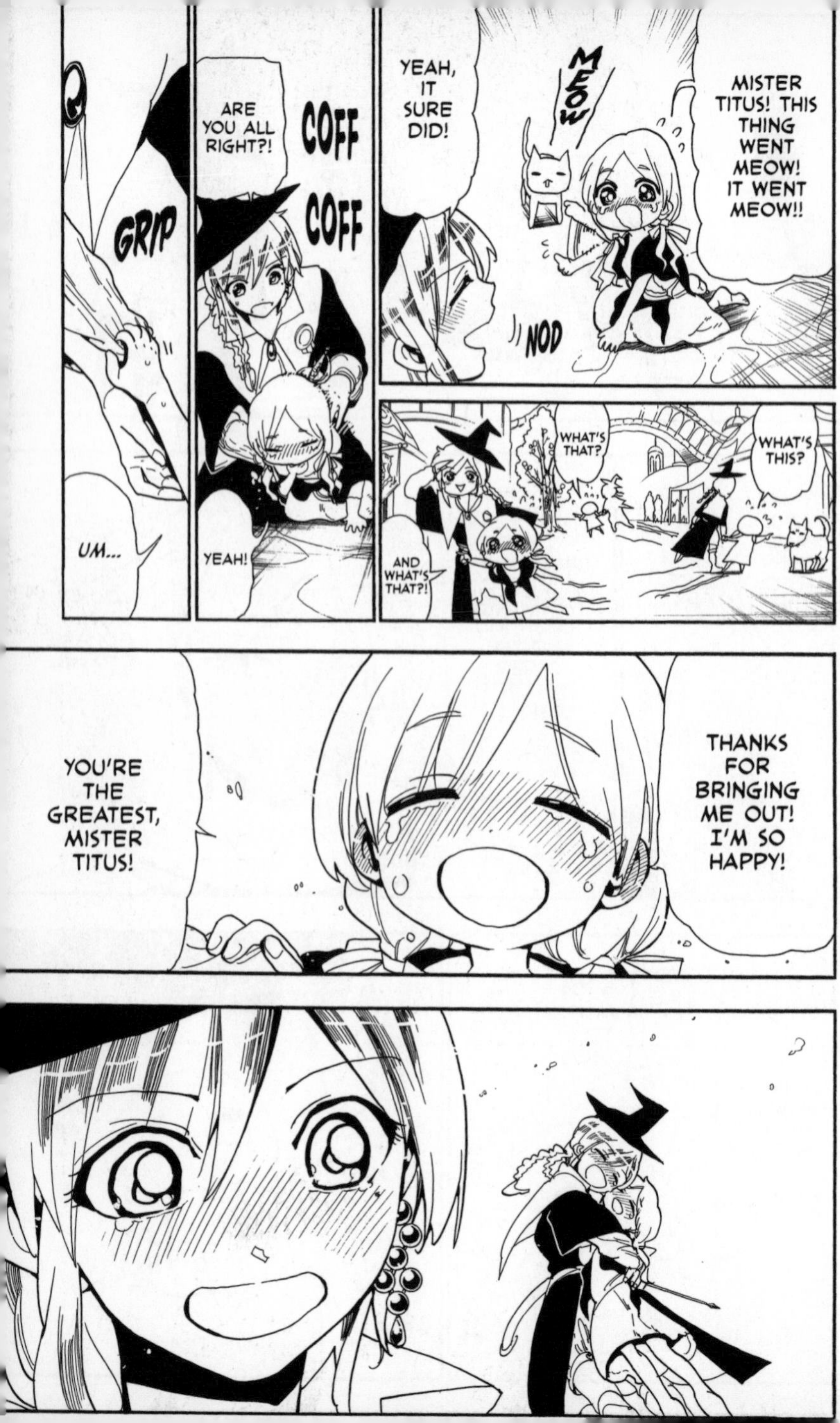
MISTER TITUS! THIS THING WENT MEOW! IT WENT MEOW!!
MEOW
YEAH, IT SURE DID!
NOD
WHAT'S THIS?
WHAT'S THAT?
AND WHAT'S THAT?!
COFF
COFF
ARE YOU ALL RIGHT?!
YEAH!
GRIP
UM...
THANKS FOR BRINGING ME OUT! I'M SO HAPPY!
YOU'RE THE GREATEST, MISTER TITUS!

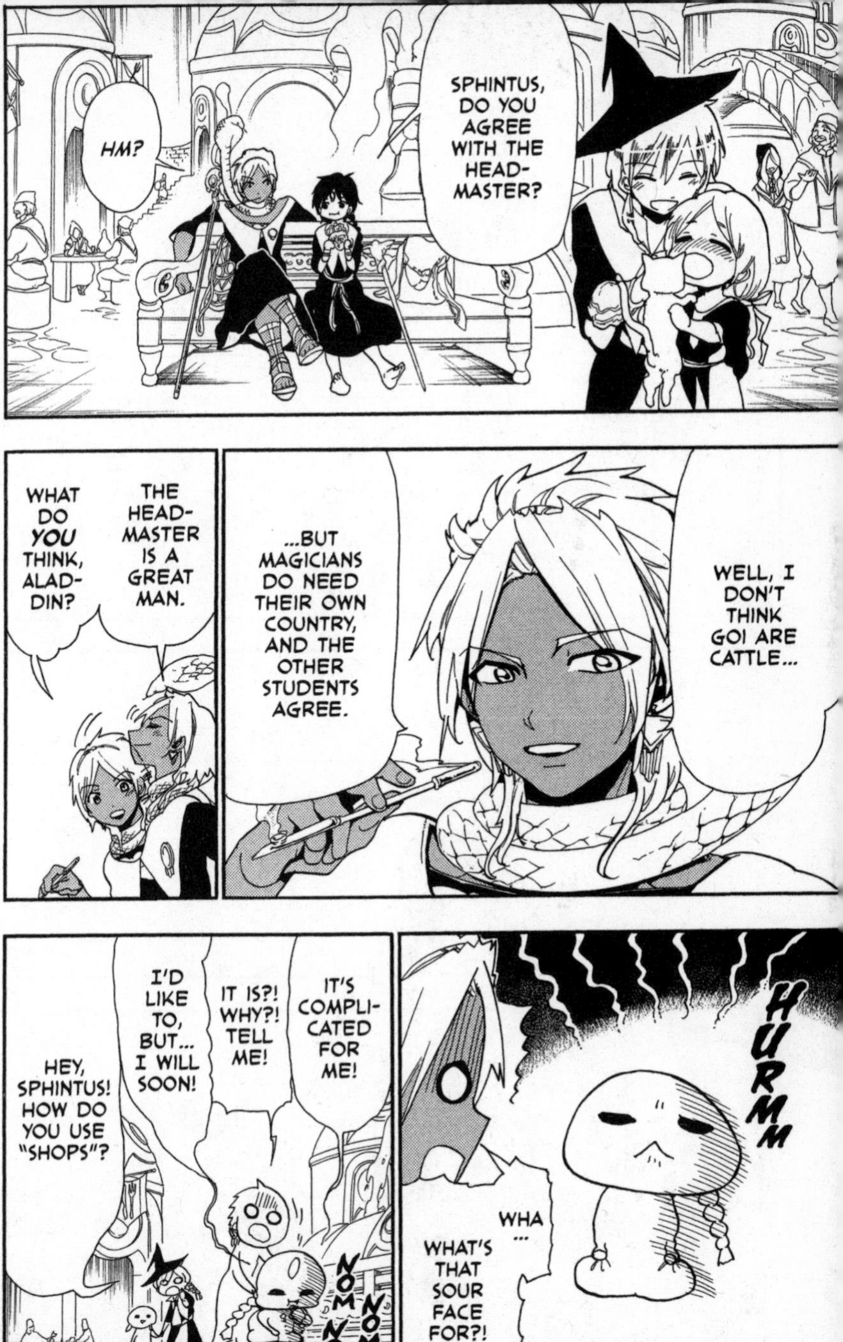
SPHINTUS, DO YOU AGREE WITH THE HEADMASTER?
HM?
WELL, I DON'T THINK GOI ARE CATTLE...
...BUT MAGICIANS DO NEED THEIR OWN COUNTRY, AND THE OTHER STUDENTS AGREE.
THE HEADMASTER IS A GREAT MAN.
WHAT DO *YOU* THINK, ALADDIN?
HURMM
WHA...
WHAT'S THAT SOUR FACE FOR?!
IT'S COMPLICATED FOR ME!
IT IS?! WHY?! TELL ME!
I'D LIKE TO, BUT... I WILL SOON!
HEY, SPHINTUS! HOW DO YOU USE "SHOPS"?
NOM NOM
NOM NOM

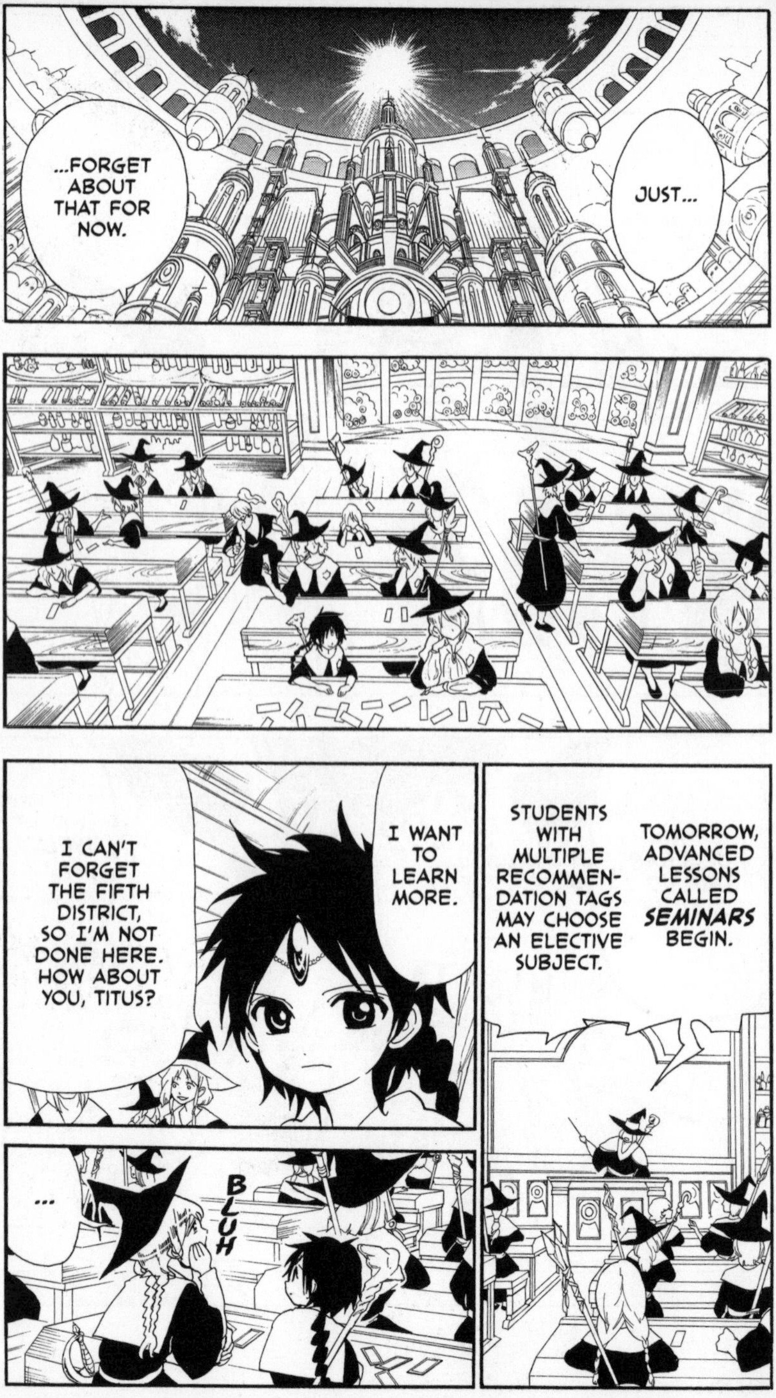
JUST...
...FORGET ABOUT THAT FOR NOW.
TOMORROW, ADVANCED LESSONS CALLED *SEMINARS* BEGIN.
STUDENTS WITH MULTIPLE RECOMMEN-DATION TAGS MAY CHOOSE AN ELECTIVE SUBJECT.
I WANT TO LEARN MORE.
I CAN'T FORGET THE FIFTH DISTRICT, SO I'M NOT DONE HERE. HOW ABOUT YOU, TITUS?
BLUH
...

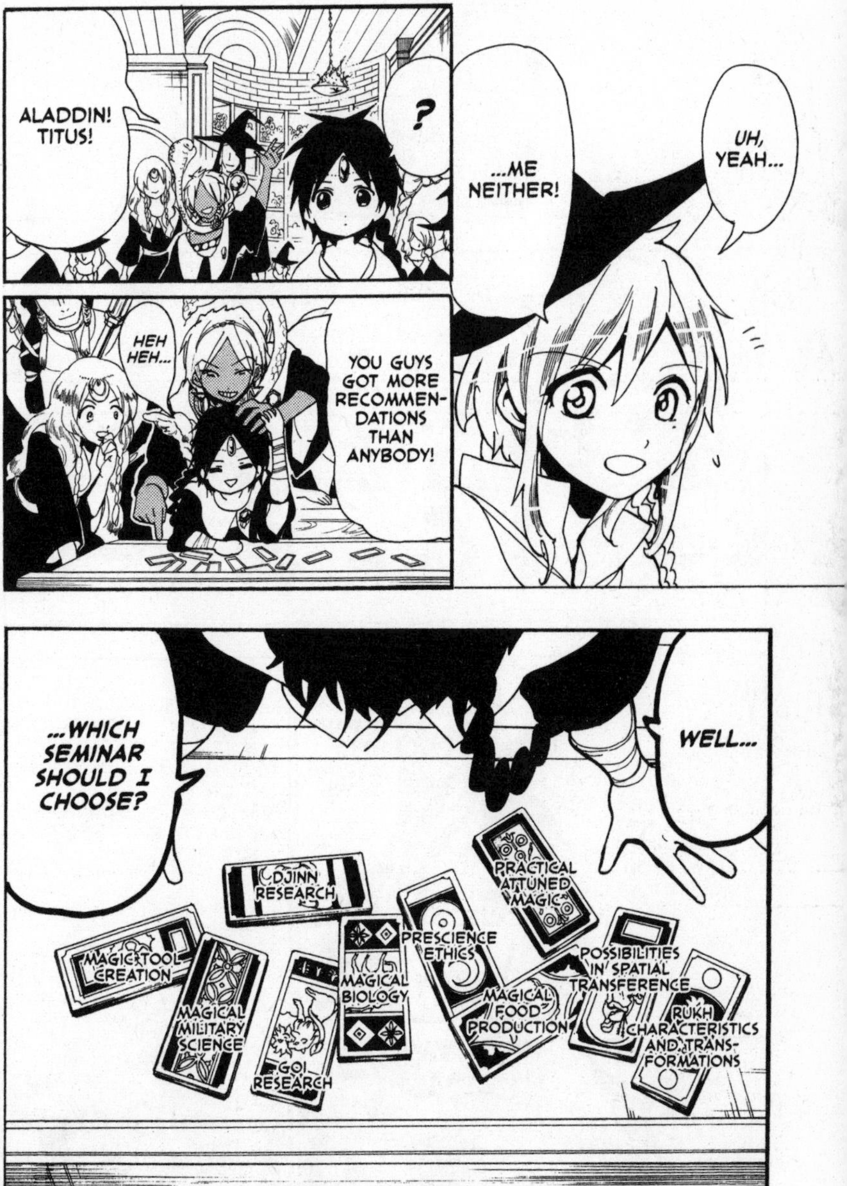
UH, YEAH...
...ME NEITHER!
ALADDIN! TITUS!
?
YOU GUYS GOT MORE RECOMMEN-DATIONS THAN ANYBODY!
HEH HEH...
WELL...
...WHICH SEMINAR SHOULD I CHOOSE?
PRACTICAL ATTUNED MAGIC
DJINN RESEARCH
POSSIBILITIES IN SPATIAL TRANSFERENCE
PRESCIENCE ETHICS
RUKH CHARACTERISTICS AND TRANS-FORMATIONS
MAGICAL FOOD PRODUCTION
MAGICAL BIOLOGY
GOI RESEARCH
MAGICAL MILITARY SCIENCE
MAGIC TOOL CREATION

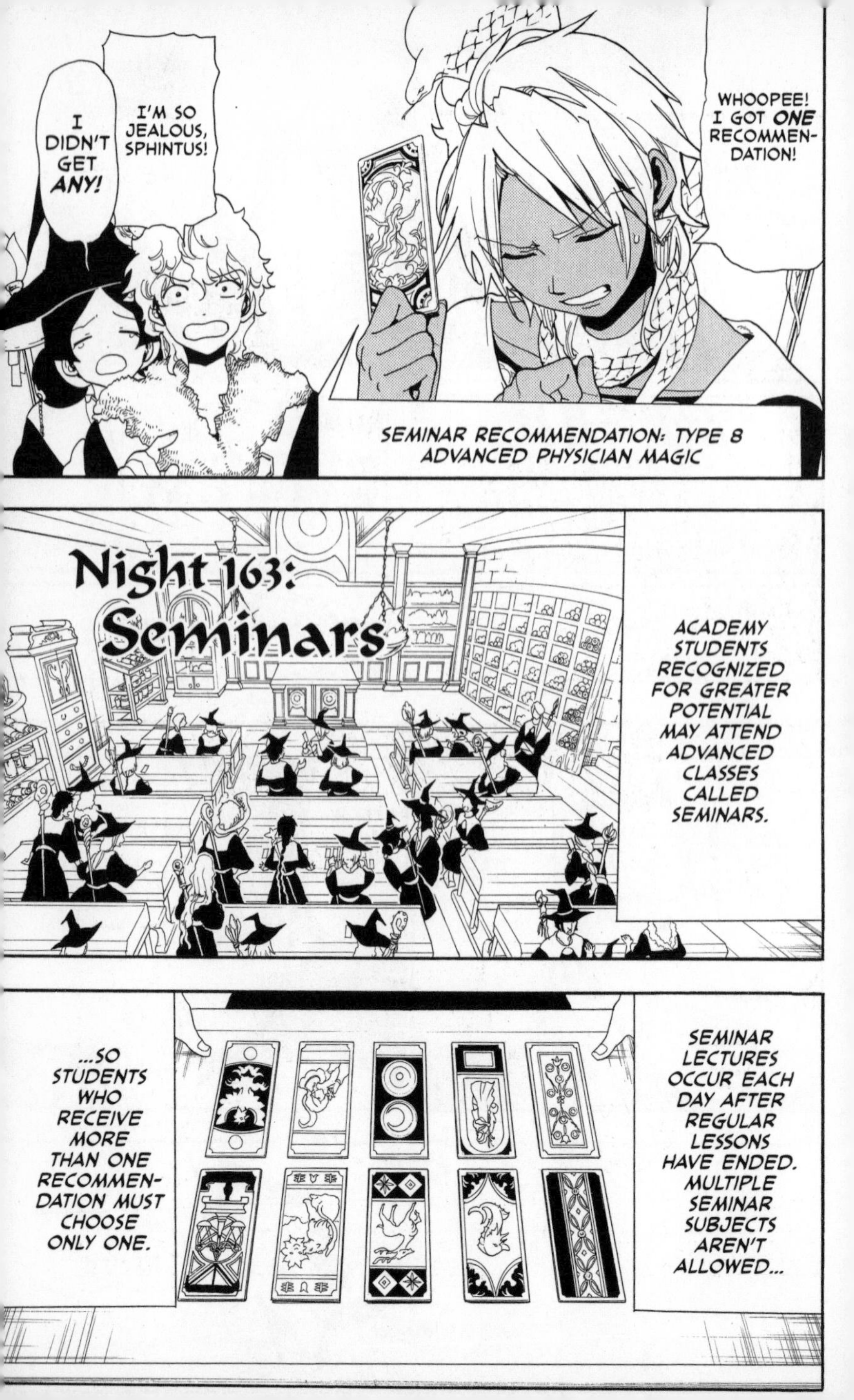
WHOOPEE! I GOT ONE RECOMMENDATION!
SEMINAR RECOMMENDATION: TYPE 8 ADVANCED PHYSICIAN MAGIC
I'M SO JEALOUS, SPHINTUS!
I DIDN'T GET ANY!
ACADEMY STUDENTS RECOGNIZED FOR GREATER POTENTIAL MAY ATTEND ADVANCED CLASSES CALLED SEMINARS.
Night 163: Seminars
SEMINAR LECTURES OCCUR EACH DAY AFTER REGULAR LESSONS HAVE ENDED. MULTIPLE SEMINAR SUBJECTS AREN'T ALLOWED...
...SO STUDENTS WHO RECEIVE MORE THAN ONE RECOMMENDATION MUST CHOOSE ONLY ONE.

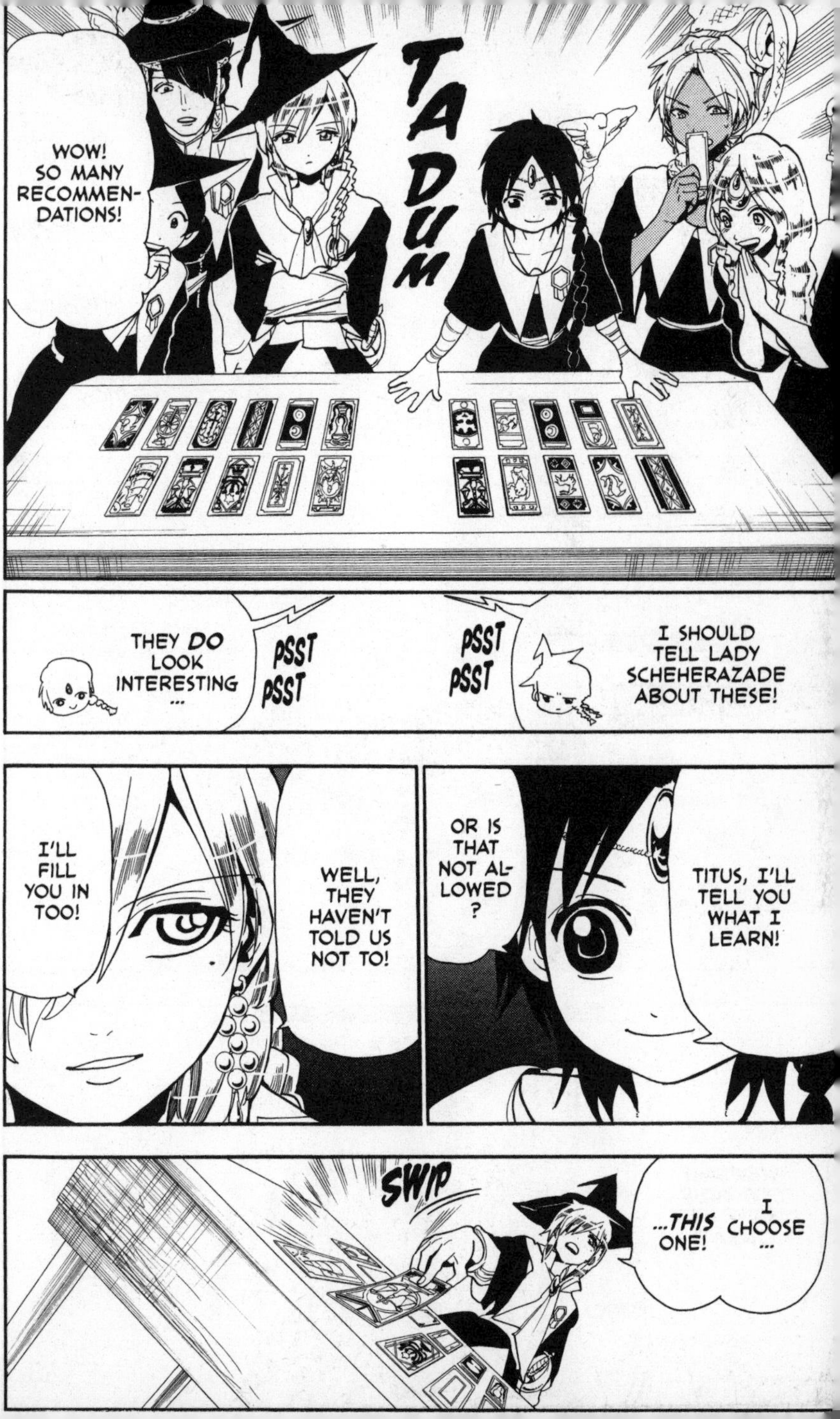
TADUM
WOW! SO MANY RECOMMEN-DATIONS!
I SHOULD TELL LADY SCHEHERAZADE ABOUT THESE!
PSST PSST
PSST PSST
THEY DO LOOK INTERESTING...
TITUS, I'LL TELL YOU WHAT I LEARN!
OR IS THAT NOT AL-LOWED?
WELL, THEY HAVEN'T TOLD US NOT TO!
I'LL FILL YOU IN TOO!
I CHOOSE...
...THIS ONE!
SWIP

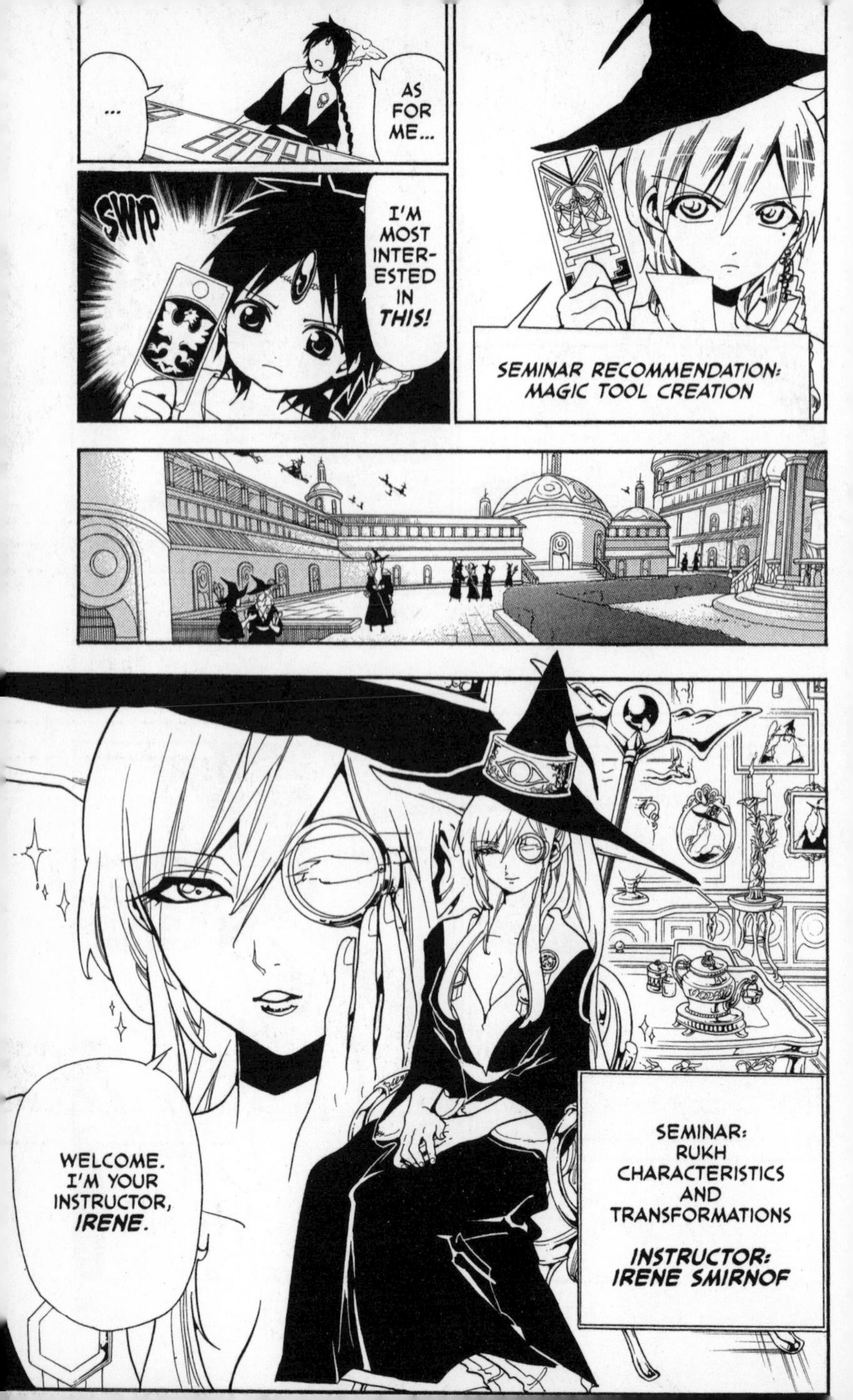
SEMINAR RECOMMENDATION: MAGIC TOOL CREATION
AS FOR ME...
...
I'M MOST INTERESTED IN THIS!
SWIP
SEMINAR: RUKH CHARACTERISTICS AND TRANSFORMATIONS
INSTRUCTOR: IRENE SMIRNOF
WELCOME. I'M YOUR INSTRUCTOR, IRENE.

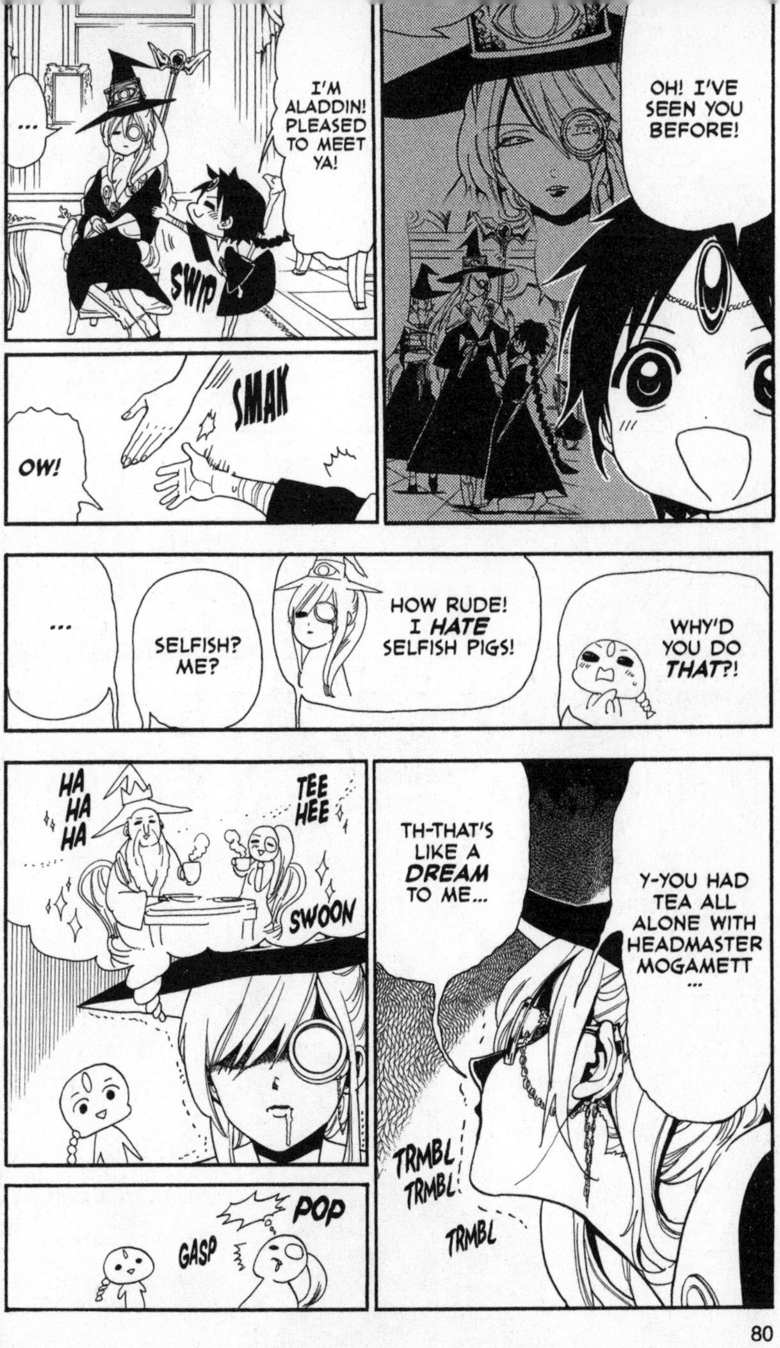
OH! I'VE SEEN YOU BEFORE!
I'M ALADDIN! PLEASED TO MEET YA!
...
SWIP
SMAK
OW!
WHY'D YOU DO THAT?!
HOW RUDE! I HATE SELFISH PIGS!
SELFISH? ME?
...
Y-YOU HAD TEA ALL ALONE WITH HEADMASTER MOGAMETT ...
TH-THAT'S LIKE A DREAM TO ME...
TRMBL TRMBL
TRMBL
TEE HEE
HA HA HA
SWOON
POP
GASP

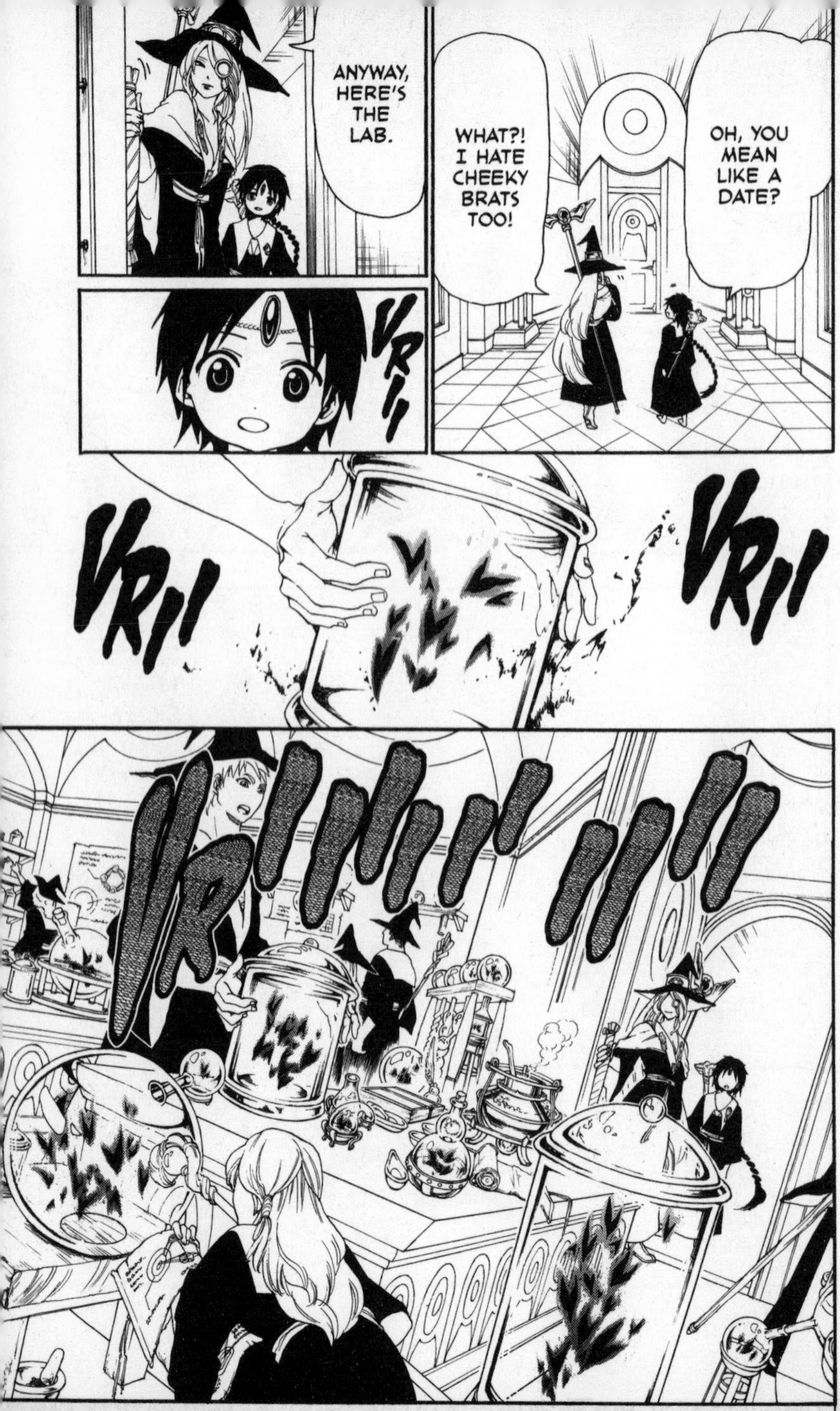
OH, YOU MEAN LIKE A DATE?
WHAT?! I HATE CHEEKY BRATS TOO!
ANYWAY, HERE'S THE LAB.
VRII
VRII
VRII
VRIIIIII IIII

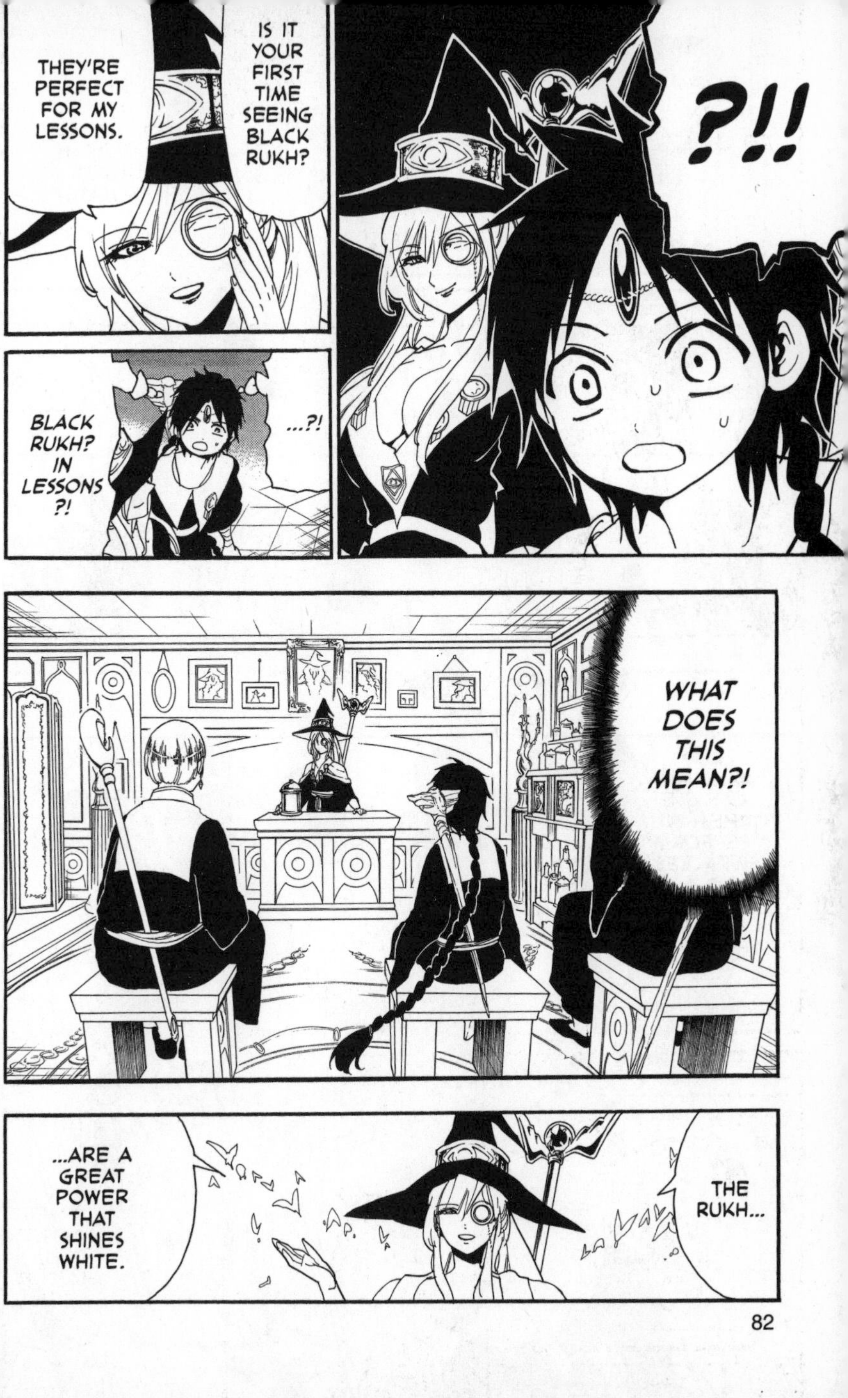
?!!
IS IT YOUR FIRST TIME SEEING BLACK RUKH?
THEY'RE PERFECT FOR MY LESSONS.
...?!
BLACK RUKH? IN LESSONS?!
WHAT DOES THIS MEAN?!
THE RUKH...
...ARE A GREAT POWER THAT SHINES WHITE.

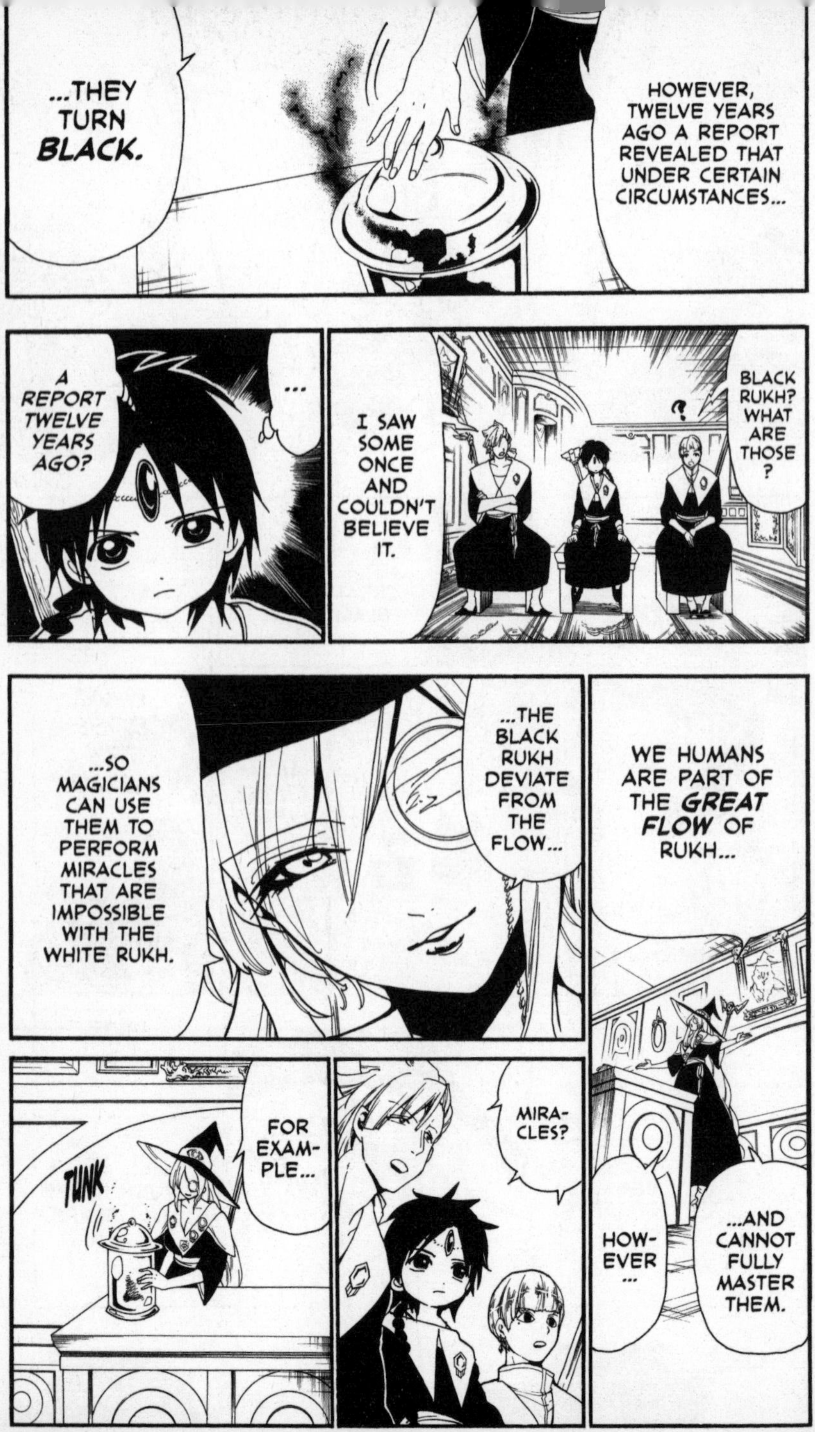
HOWEVER, TWELVE YEARS AGO A REPORT REVEALED THAT UNDER CERTAIN CIRCUMSTANCES...
...THEY TURN *BLACK.*
BLACK RUKH? WHAT ARE THOSE?
?
I SAW SOME ONCE AND COULDN'T BELIEVE IT.
...
A REPORT TWELVE YEARS AGO?
WE HUMANS ARE PART OF THE *GREAT FLOW* OF RUKH...
...AND CANNOT FULLY MASTER THEM.
HOW-EVER...
...THE BLACK RUKH DEVIATE FROM THE FLOW...
...SO MAGICIANS CAN USE THEM TO PERFORM MIRACLES THAT ARE IMPOSSIBLE WITH THE WHITE RUKH.
MIRA-CLES?
FOR EXAM-PLE...
TUNK

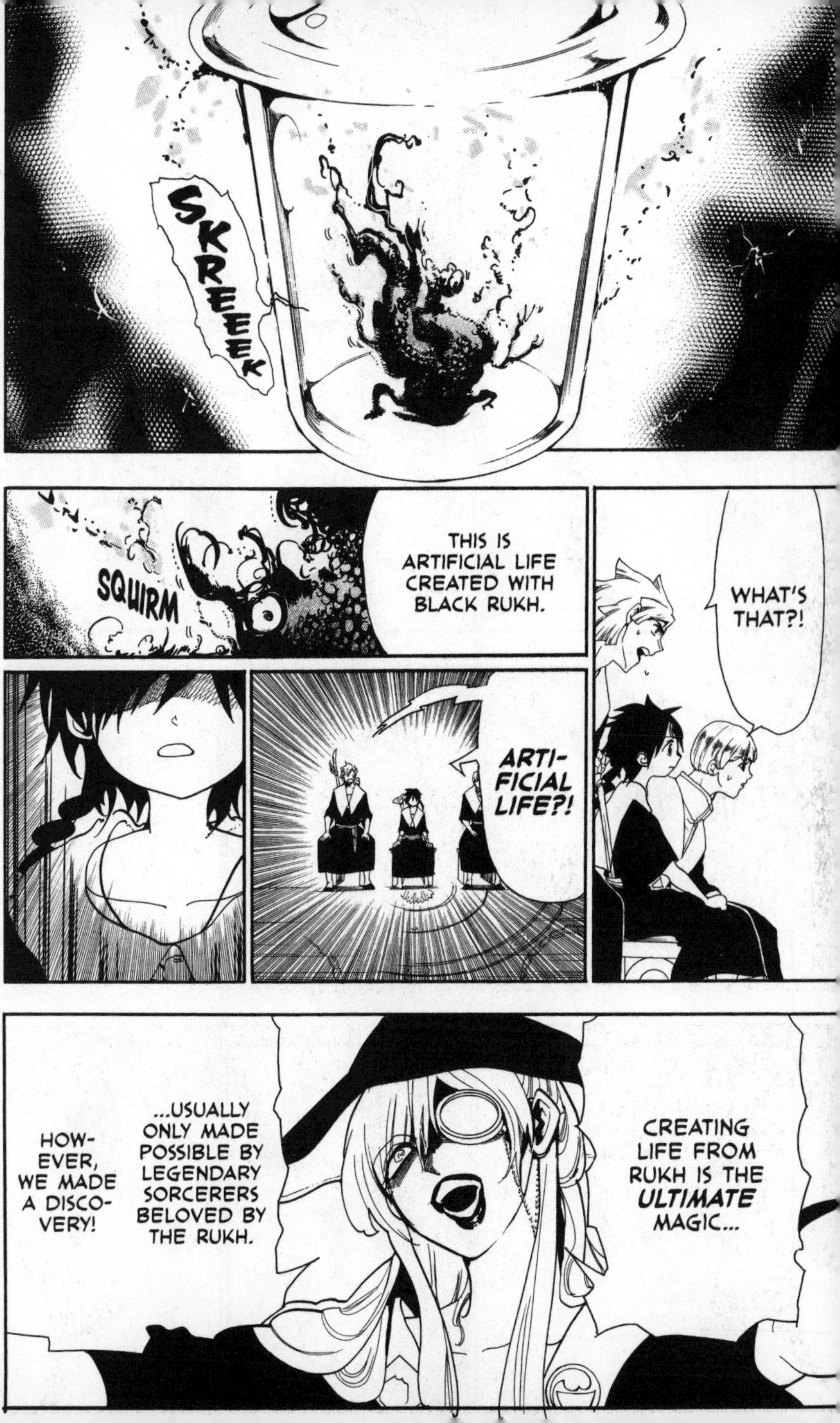
SKREEEEK
WHAT'S THAT?!
THIS IS ARTIFICIAL LIFE CREATED WITH BLACK RUKH.
SQUIRM
ARTI-FICIAL LIFE?!
CREATING LIFE FROM RUKH IS THE ULTIMATE MAGIC...
...USUALLY ONLY MADE POSSIBLE BY LEGENDARY SORCERERS BELOVED BY THE RUKH.
HOW-EVER, WE MADE A DISCO-VERY!

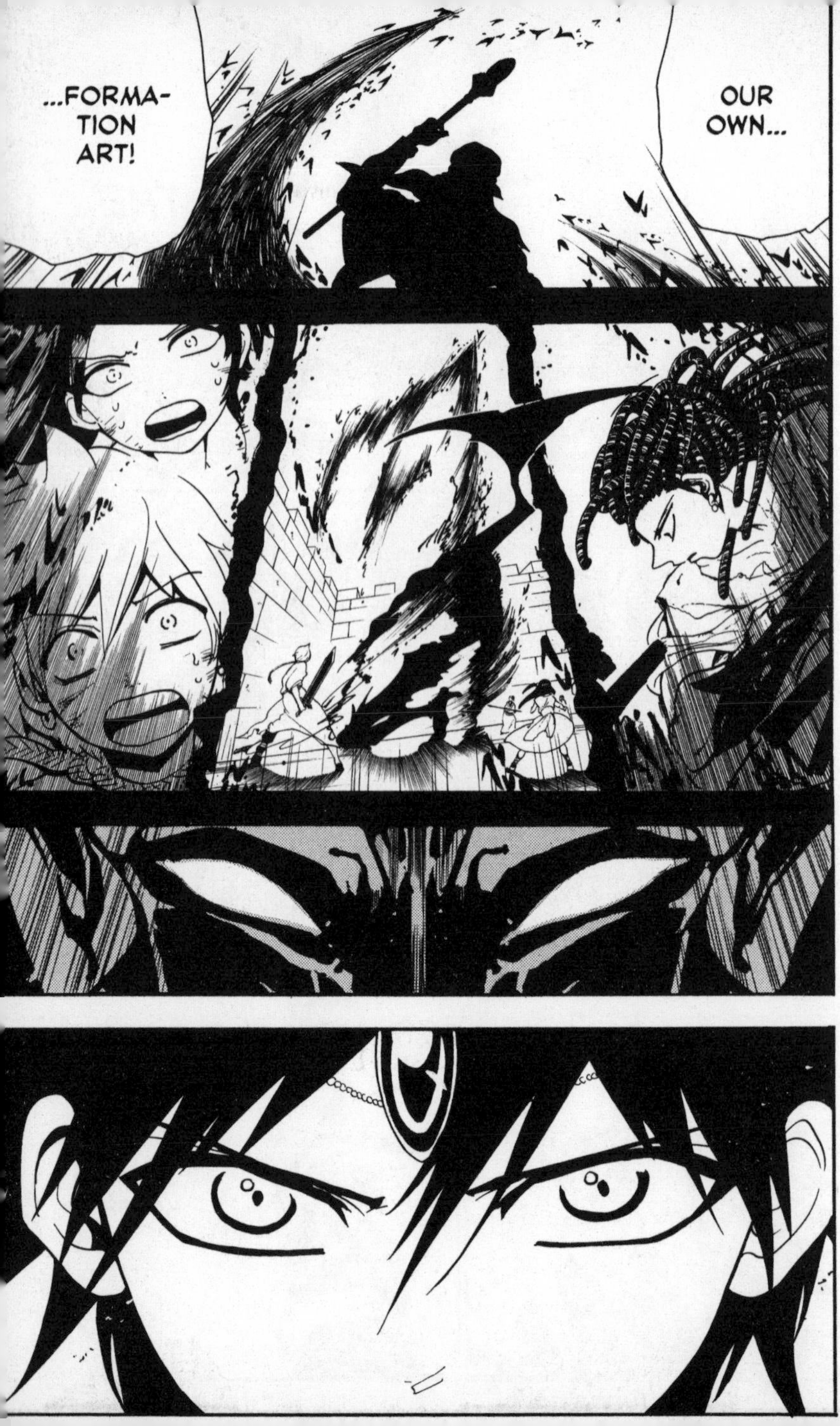
OUR OWN...
...FORMA-TION ART!

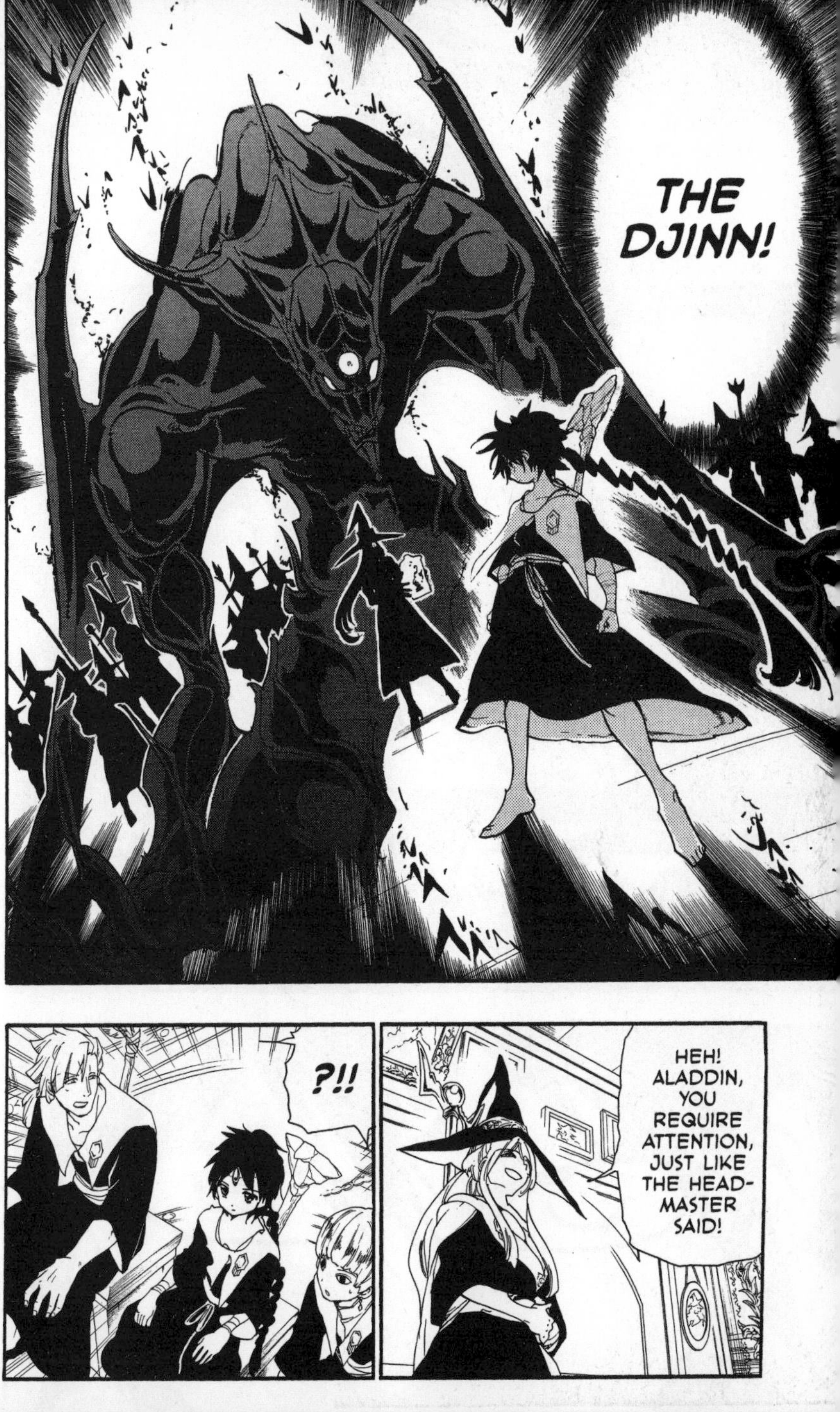
THE DJINN!
HEH! ALADDIN, YOU REQUIRE ATTENTION, JUST LIKE THE HEAD-MASTER SAID!
?!!

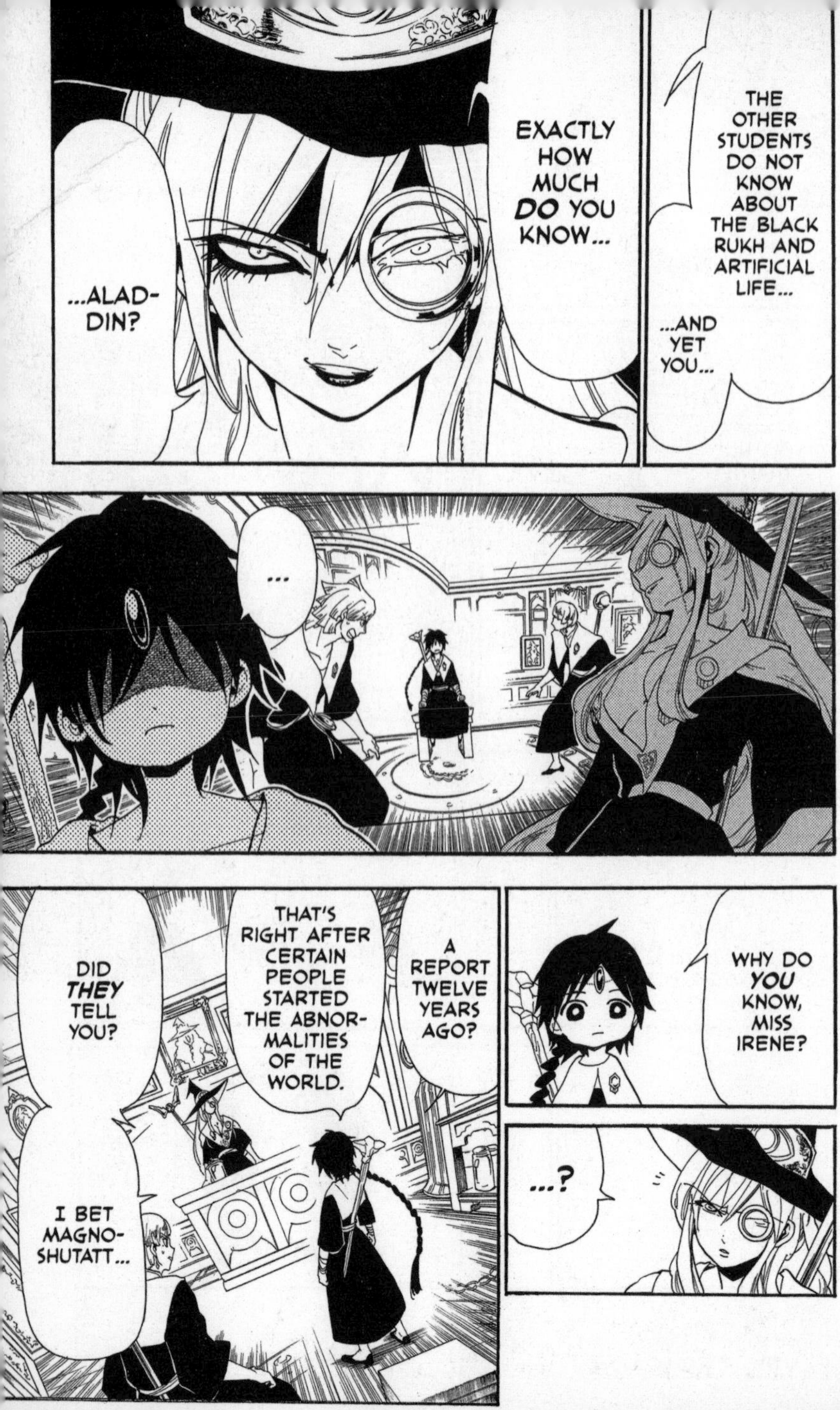
THE OTHER STUDENTS DO NOT KNOW ABOUT THE BLACK RUKH AND ARTIFICIAL LIFE...
...AND YET YOU...
EXACTLY HOW MUCH *DO* YOU KNOW...
...ALAD-DIN?
...
WHY DO *YOU* KNOW, MISS IRENE?
...?
A REPORT TWELVE YEARS AGO?
THAT'S RIGHT AFTER CERTAIN PEOPLE STARTED THE ABNOR-MALITIES OF THE WORLD.
DID *THEY* TELL YOU?
I BET MAGNO-SHUTATT...

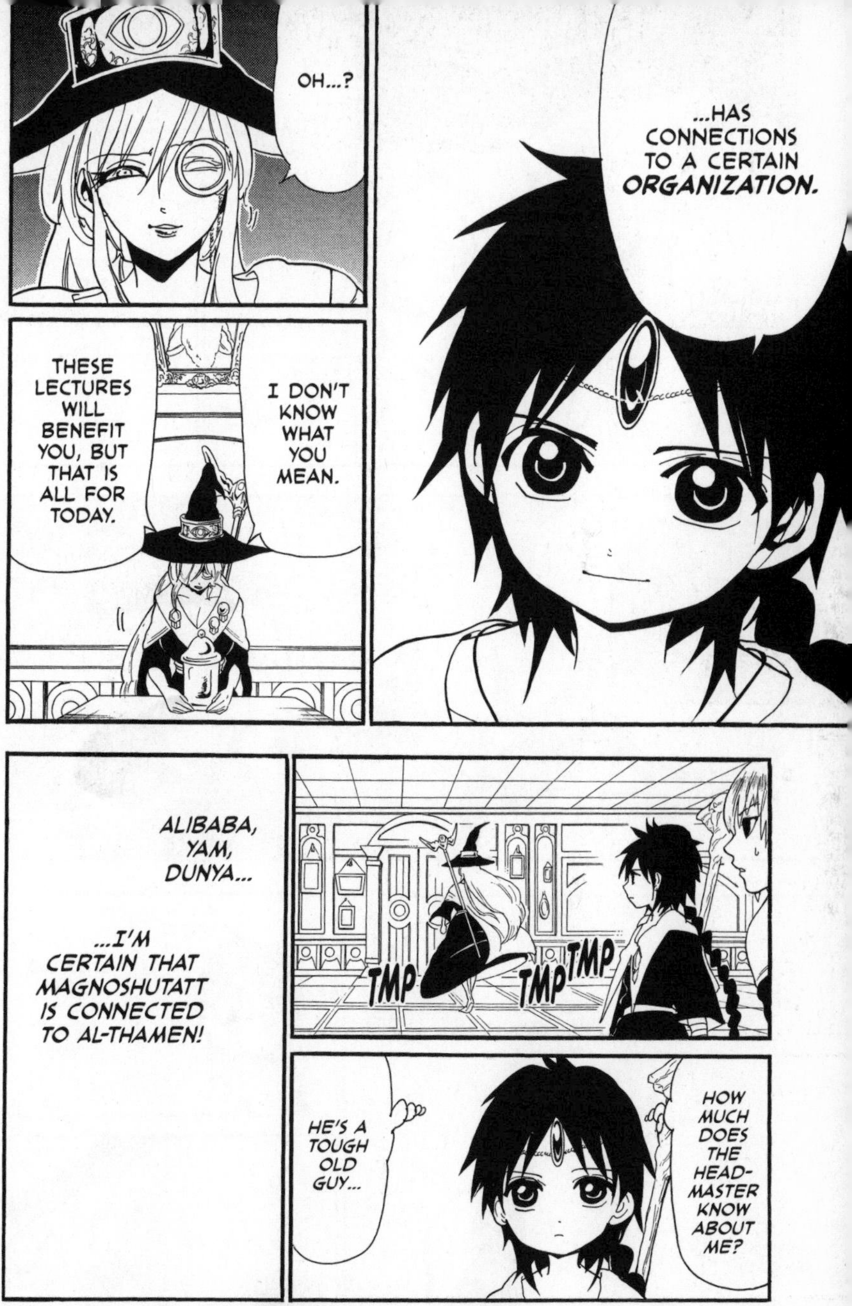
...HAS CONNECTIONS TO A CERTAIN ORGANIZATION.
OH...?
I DON'T KNOW WHAT YOU MEAN.
THESE LECTURES WILL BENEFIT YOU, BUT THAT IS ALL FOR TODAY.
TMP
TMP TMP
HOW MUCH DOES THE HEAD-MASTER KNOW ABOUT ME?
HE'S A TOUGH OLD GUY...
ALIBABA, YAM, DUNYA...
...I'M CERTAIN THAT MAGNOSHUTATT IS CONNECTED TO AL-THAMEN!

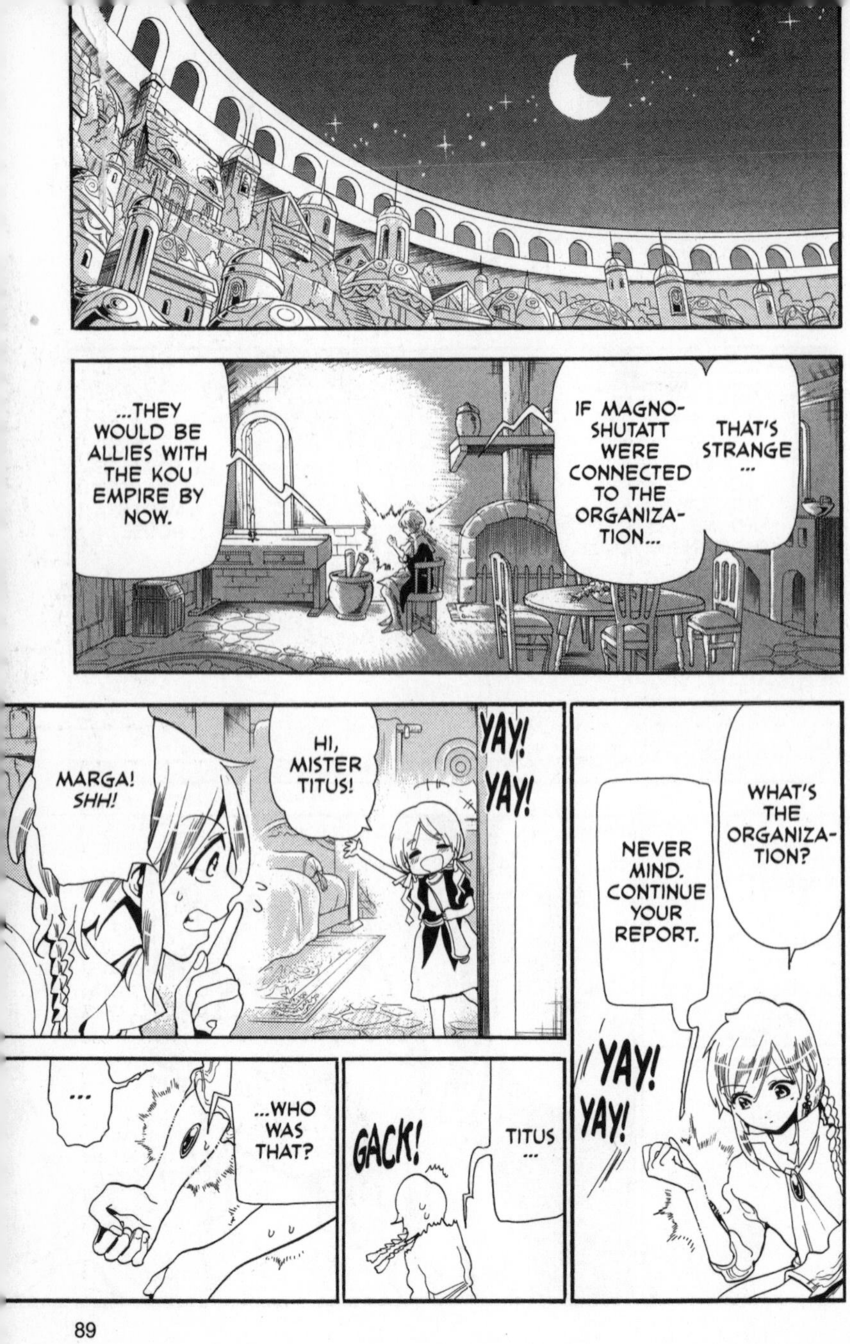
THAT'S STRANGE...
IF MAGNOSHUTATT WERE CONNECTED TO THE ORGANIZATION...
...THEY WOULD BE ALLIES WITH THE KOU EMPIRE BY NOW.
WHAT'S THE ORGANIZATION?
NEVER MIND. CONTINUE YOUR REPORT.
YAY! YAY!
YAY! YAY!
HI, MISTER TITUS!
MARGA! SHH!
TITUS...
GACK!
...WHO WAS THAT?
...

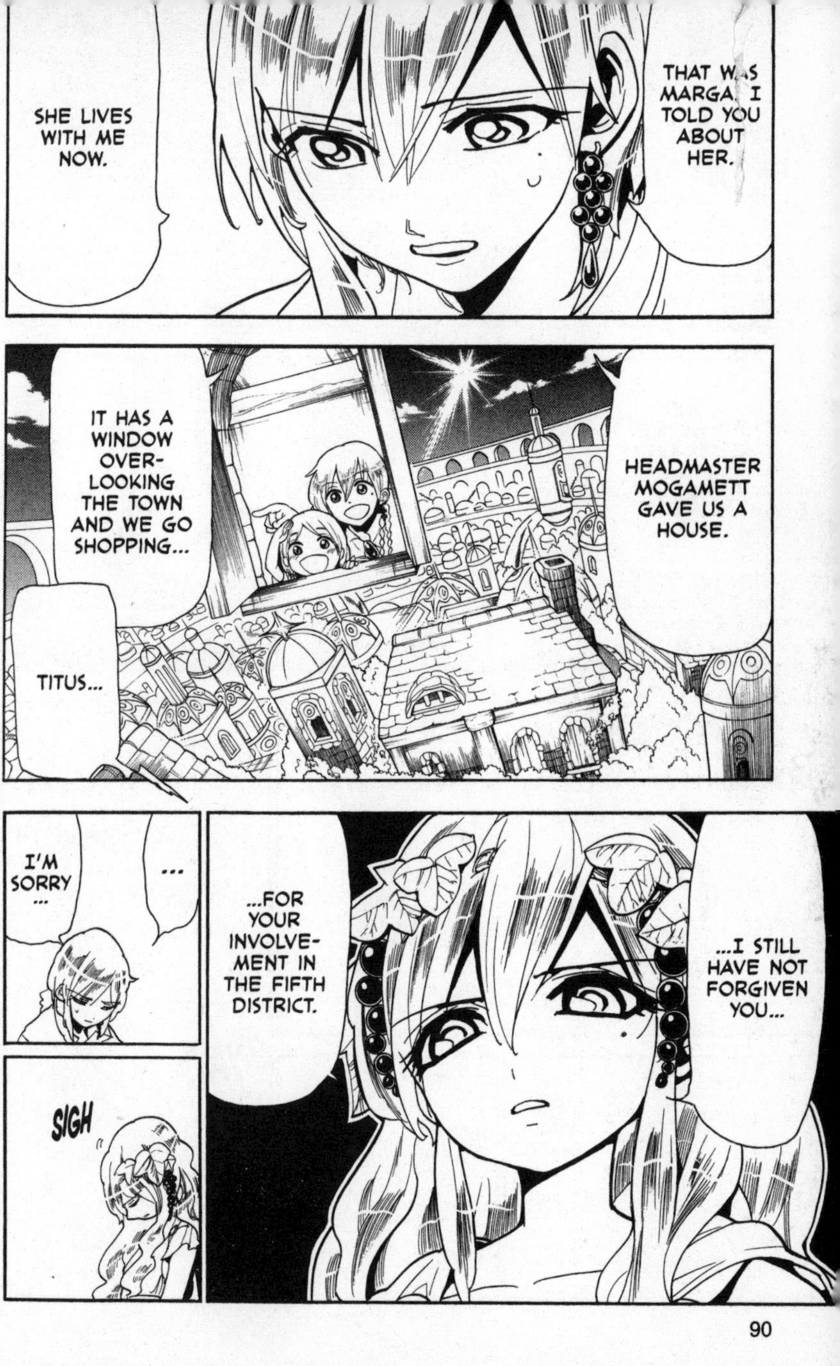
THAT WAS MARGA. I TOLD YOU ABOUT HER.
SHE LIVES WITH ME NOW.
HEADMASTER MOGAMETT GAVE US A HOUSE.
IT HAS A WINDOW OVER-LOOKING THE TOWN AND WE GO SHOPPING...
TITUS...
...I STILL HAVE NOT FORGIVEN YOU...
...FOR YOUR INVOLVEMENT IN THE FIFTH DISTRICT.
...
I'M SORRY ...
SIGH

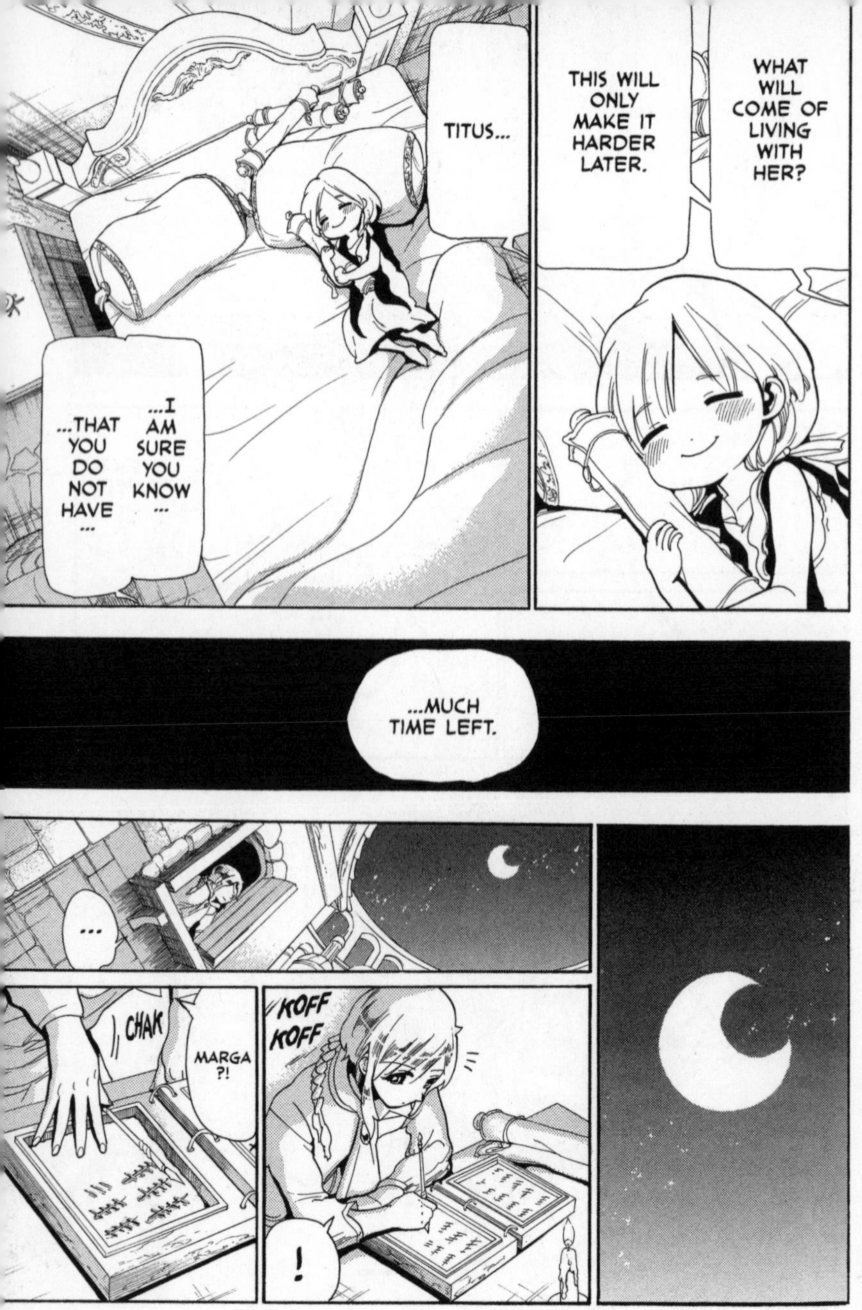
WHAT WILL COME OF LIVING WITH HER?
THIS WILL ONLY MAKE IT HARDER LATER.
TITUS...
...I AM SURE YOU KNOW...
...THAT YOU DO NOT HAVE...
...MUCH TIME LEFT.
...
KOFF KOFF
!
MARGA?!
CHAK

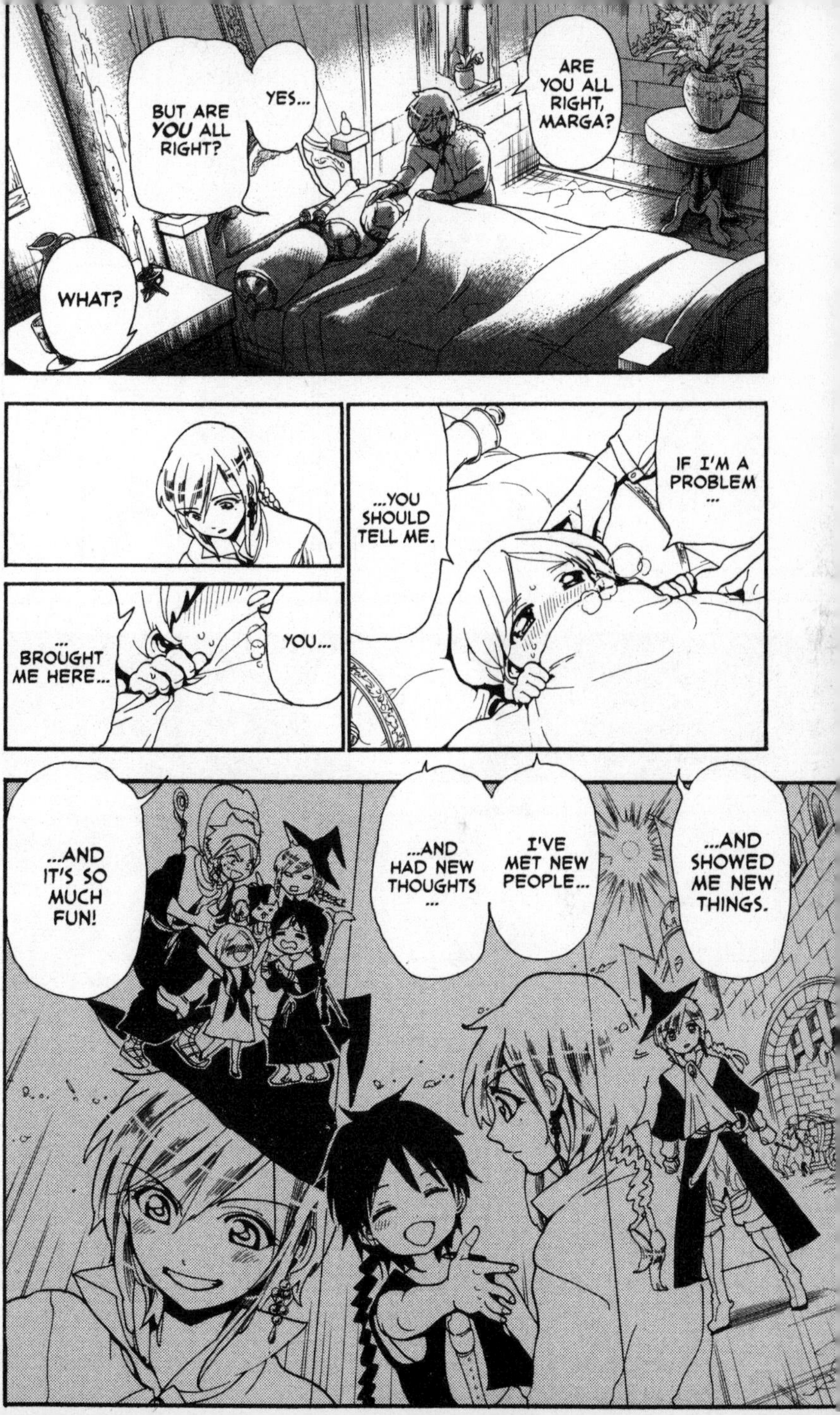
ARE YOU ALL RIGHT, MARGA?
YES...
BUT ARE *YOU* ALL RIGHT?
WHAT?
IF I'M A PROBLEM ...
...YOU SHOULD TELL ME.
YOU...
... BROUGHT ME HERE...
...AND SHOWED ME NEW THINGS.
I'VE MET NEW PEOPLE...
...AND HAD NEW THOUGHTS ...
...AND IT'S SO MUCH FUN!

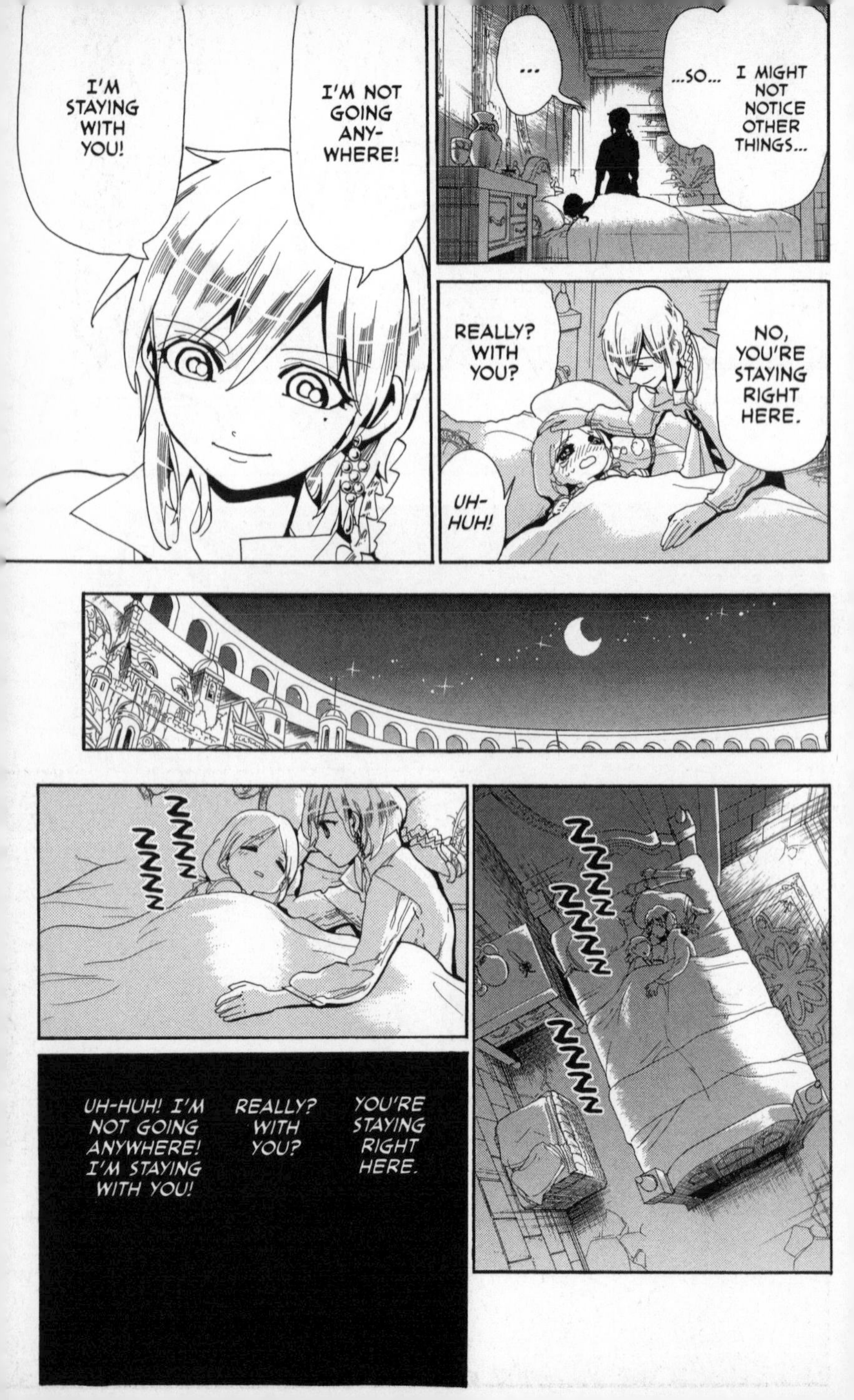
...SO... I MIGHT NOT NOTICE OTHER THINGS...
...
NO, YOU'RE STAYING RIGHT HERE.
REALLY? WITH YOU?
UH-HUH!
I'M NOT GOING ANYWHERE!
I'M STAYING WITH YOU!
ZZZZZZ
ZZZZ
ZZZZ
ZZZZ
YOU'RE STAYING RIGHT HERE.
REALLY? WITH YOU?
UH-HUH! I'M NOT GOING ANYWHERE! I'M STAYING WITH YOU!

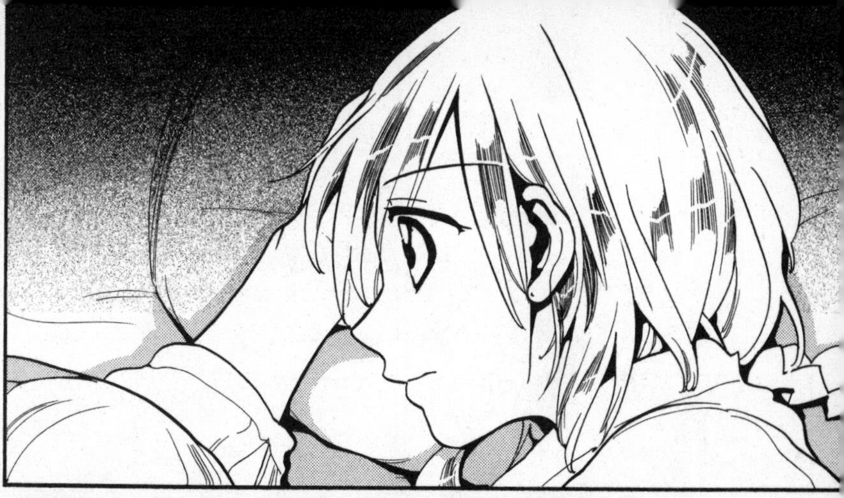
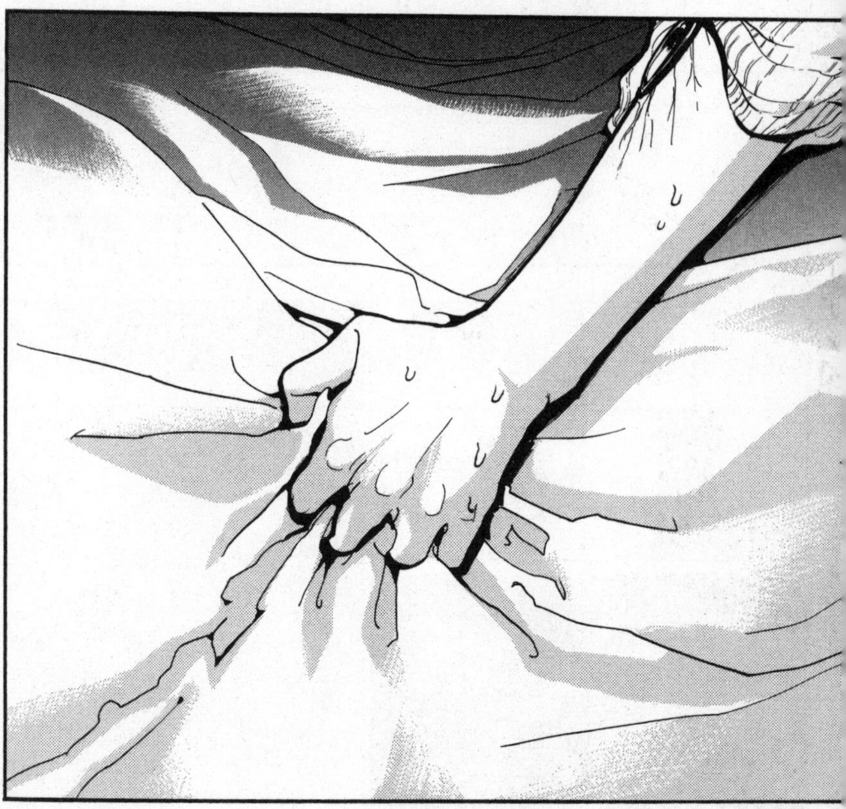

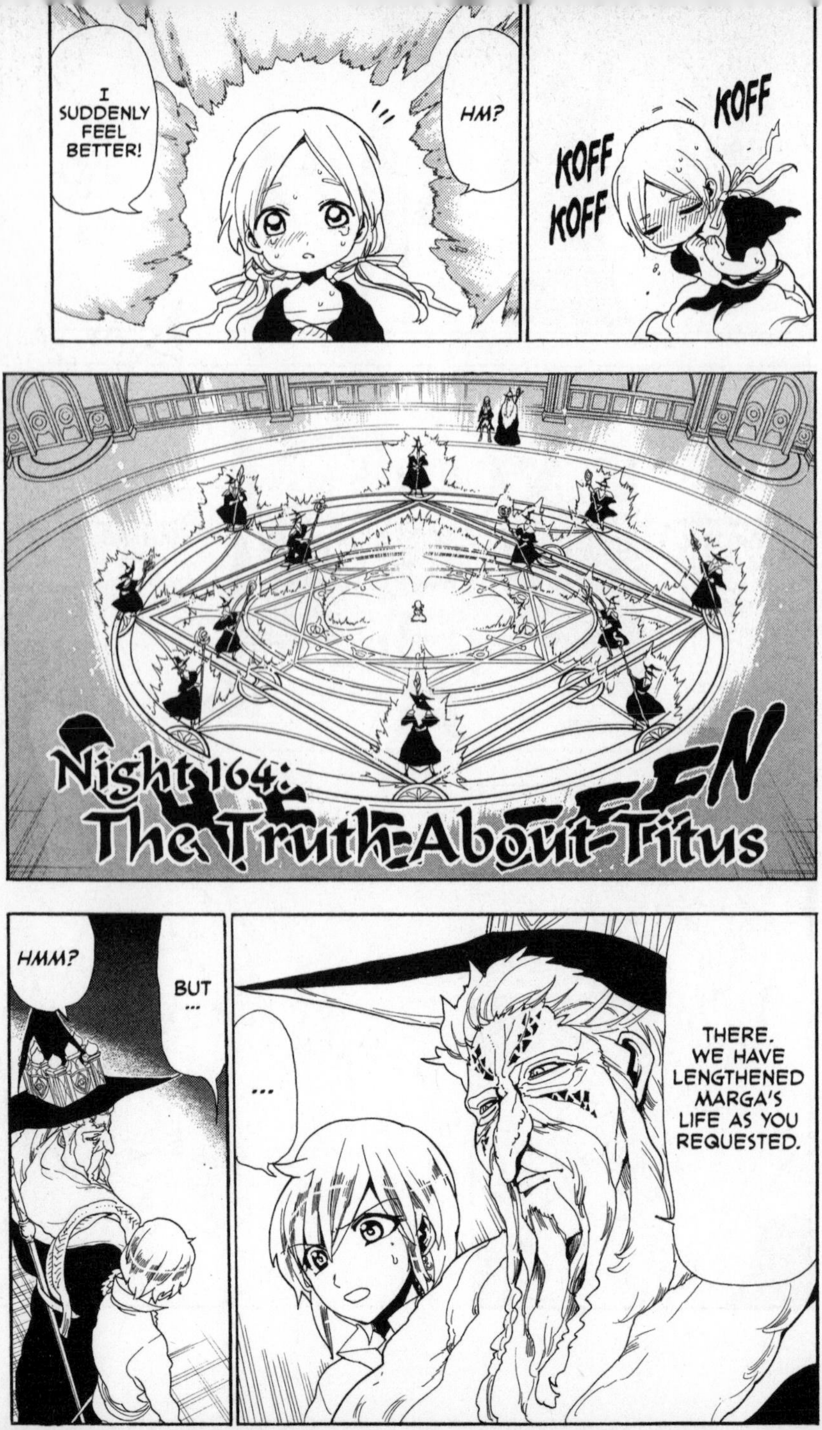
KOFF
KOFF KOFF
HM?
I SUDDENLY FEEL BETTER!
Night 164:
The Truth About Titus
THERE. WE HAVE LENGTHENED MARGA'S LIFE AS YOU REQUESTED.
...
BUT ...
HMM?

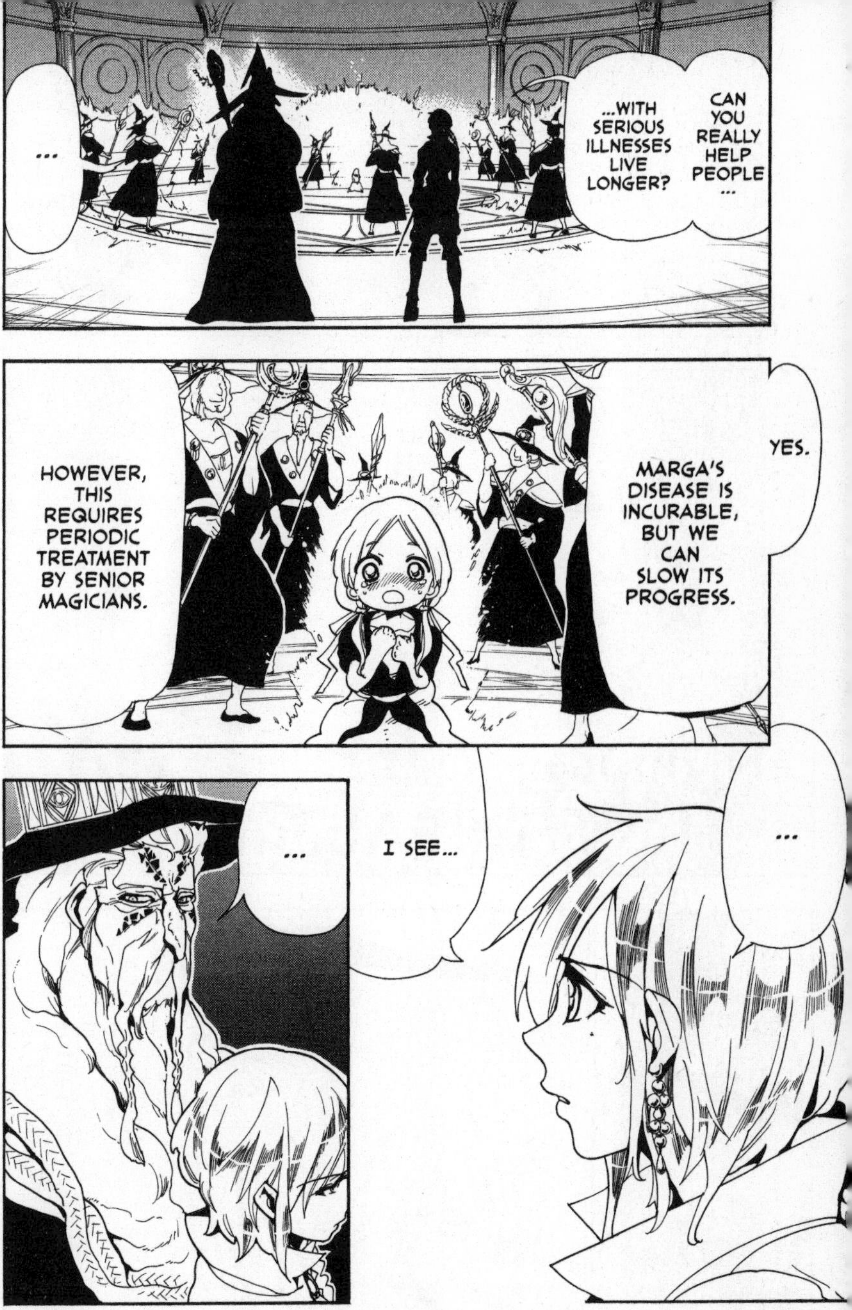
CAN YOU REALLY HELP PEOPLE ...
...WITH SERIOUS ILLNESSES LIVE LONGER?
...
YES.
MARGA'S DISEASE IS INCURABLE, BUT WE CAN SLOW ITS PROGRESS.
HOWEVER, THIS REQUIRES PERIODIC TREATMENT BY SENIOR MAGICIANS.
...
I SEE...
...

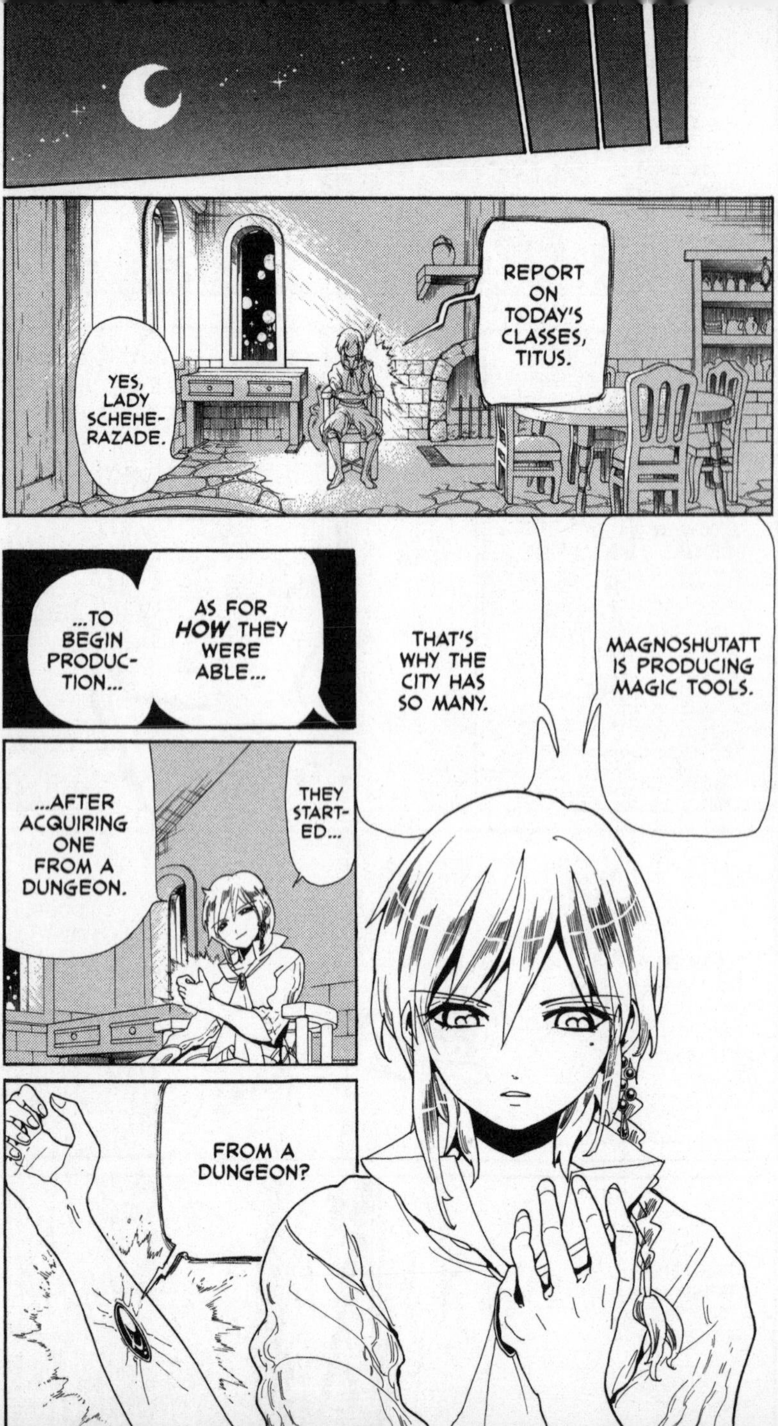
REPORT ON TODAY'S CLASSES, TITUS.
YES, LADY SCHEHERAZADE.
MAGNOSHUTATT IS PRODUCING MAGIC TOOLS.
THAT'S WHY THE CITY HAS SO MANY.
AS FOR *HOW* THEY WERE ABLE...
...TO BEGIN PRODUCTION...
THEY STARTED...
...AFTER ACQUIRING ONE FROM A DUNGEON.
FROM A DUNGEON?

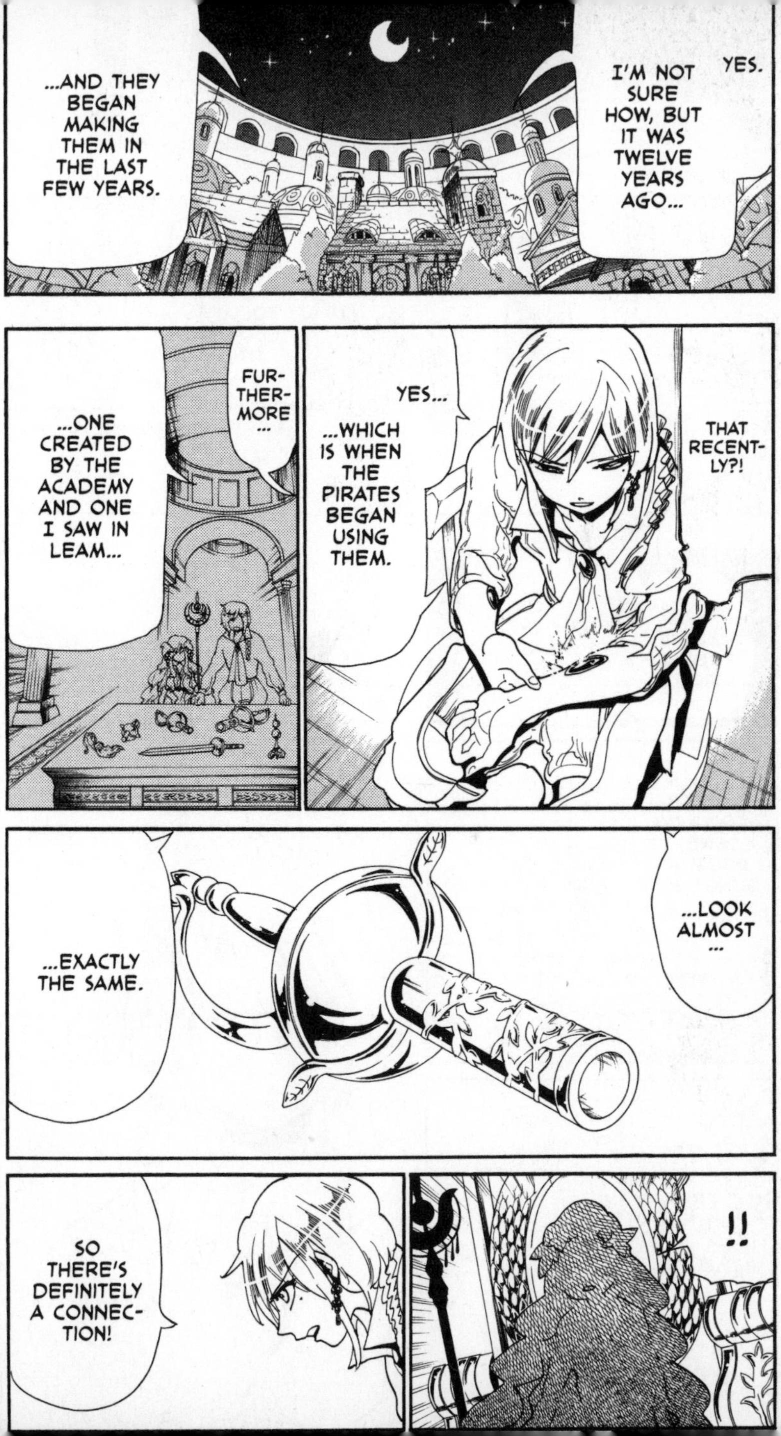
YES.
I'M NOT SURE HOW, BUT IT WAS TWELVE YEARS AGO...
...AND THEY BEGAN MAKING THEM IN THE LAST FEW YEARS.
THAT RECENTLY?!
YES...
...WHICH IS WHEN THE PIRATES BEGAN USING THEM.
FURTHERMORE...
...ONE CREATED BY THE ACADEMY AND ONE I SAW IN LEAM...
...LOOK ALMOST...
...EXACTLY THE SAME.
!!
SO THERE'S DEFINITELY A CONNECTION!

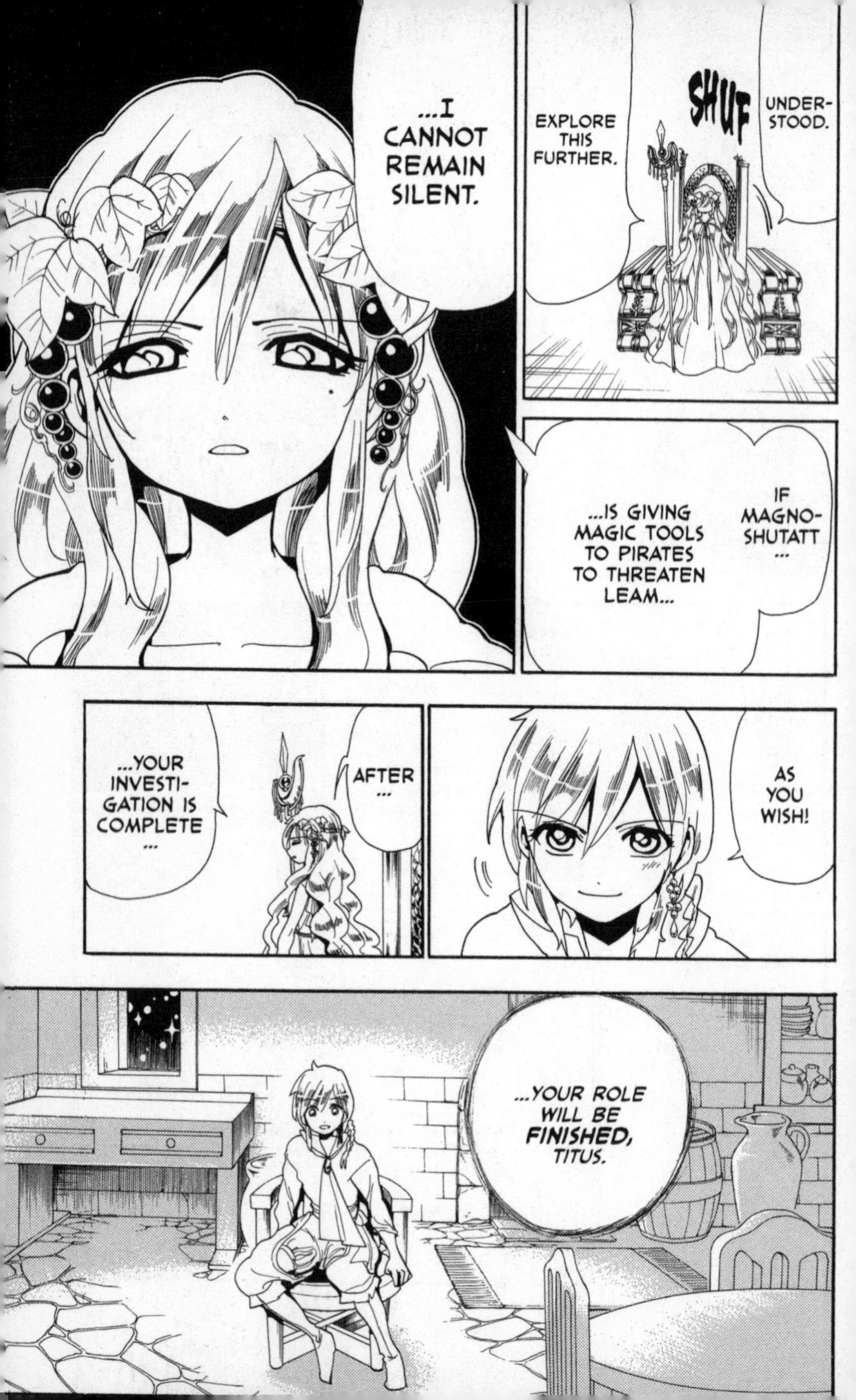
UNDER-STOOD.
SHUF
EXPLORE THIS FURTHER.
IF MAGNO-SHUTATT...
...IS GIVING MAGIC TOOLS TO PIRATES TO THREATEN LEAM...
...I CANNOT REMAIN SILENT.
AS YOU WISH!
AFTER...
...YOUR INVESTI-GATION IS COMPLETE...
...YOUR ROLE WILL BE FINISHED, TITUS.

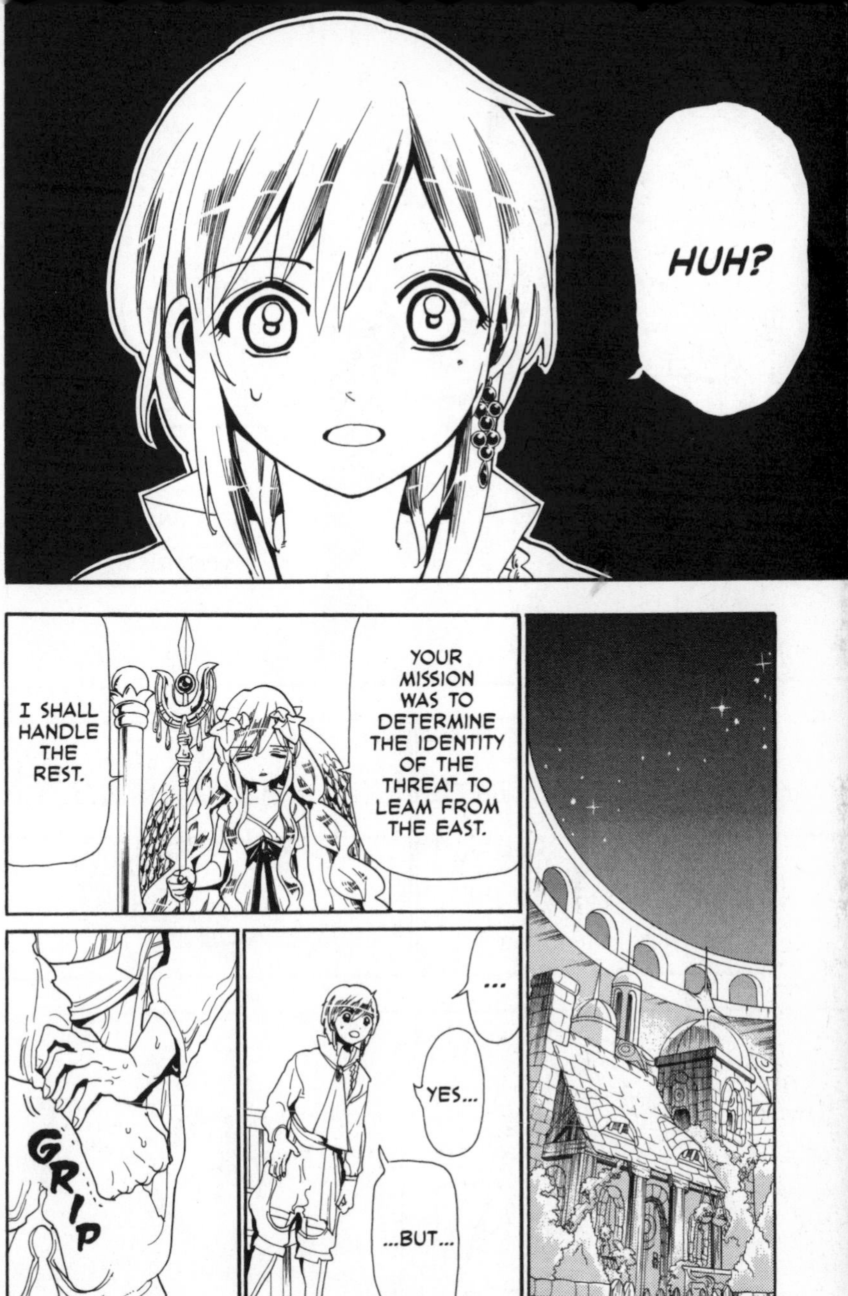
HUH?
YOUR MISSION WAS TO DETERMINE THE IDENTITY OF THE THREAT TO LEAM FROM THE EAST.
I SHALL HANDLE THE REST.
...
YES...
...BUT...
GRIP

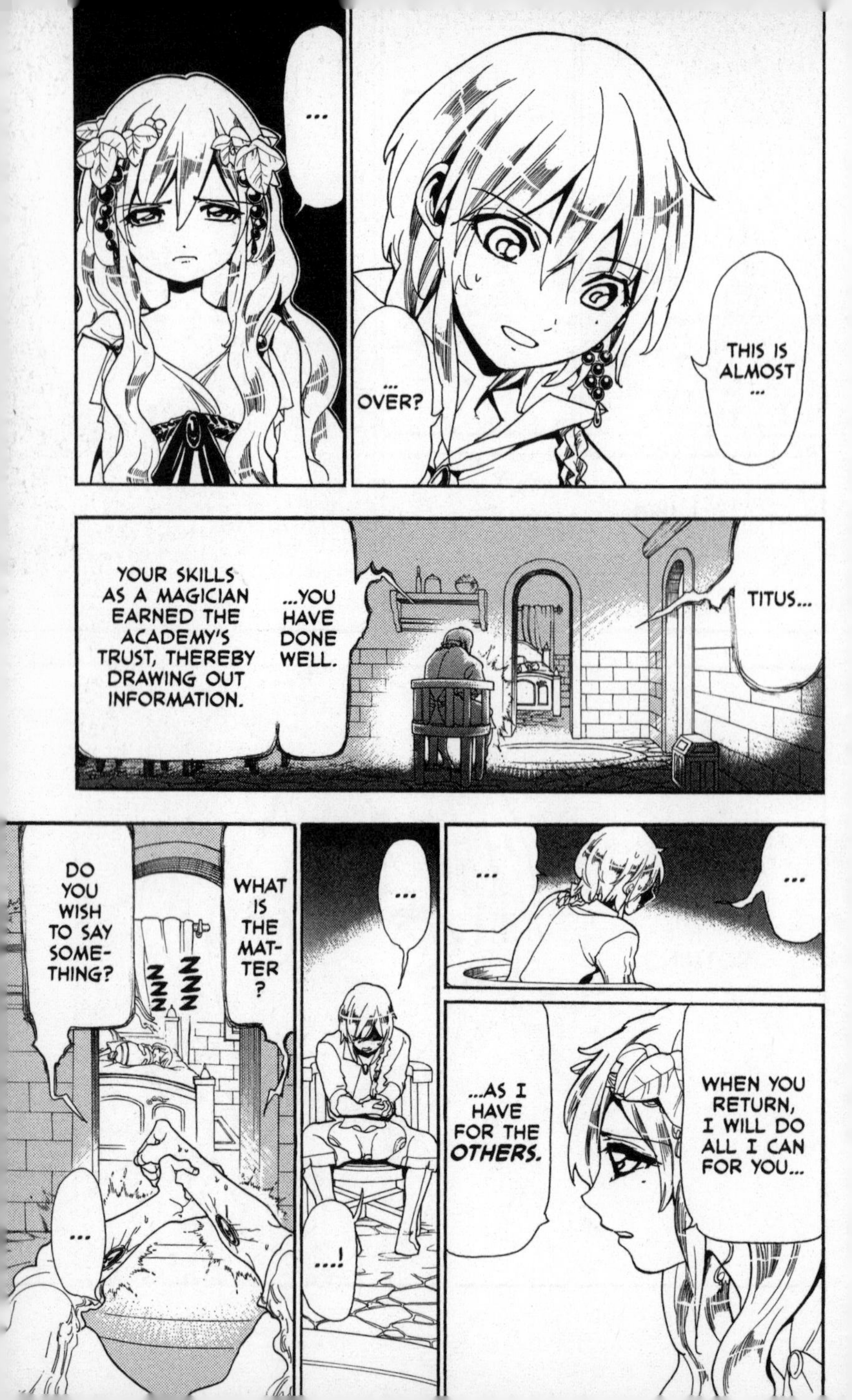
THIS IS ALMOST ...
... OVER?
...
TITUS...
...YOU HAVE DONE WELL.
YOUR SKILLS AS A MAGICIAN EARNED THE ACADEMY'S TRUST, THEREBY DRAWING OUT INFORMATION.
...
...
WHEN YOU RETURN, I WILL DO ALL I CAN FOR YOU...
...AS I HAVE FOR THE *OTHERS.*
...
...!
WHAT IS THE MAT-TER?
DO YOU WISH TO SAY SOME-THING?
ZZZ ZZZ
...

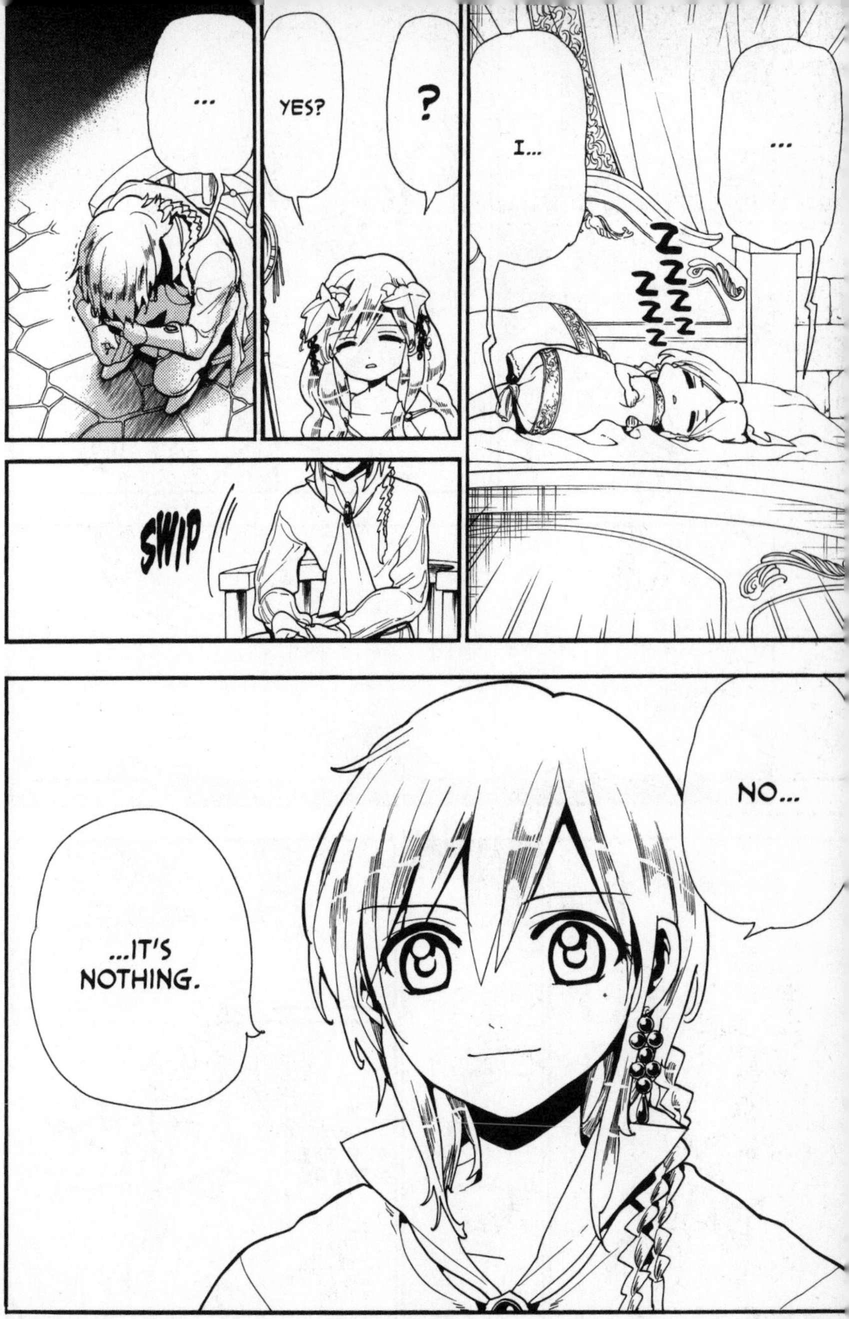
...
I...
Z Z Z Z Z Z Z Z
?
YES?
...
SWIP
NO...
...IT'S NOTHING.

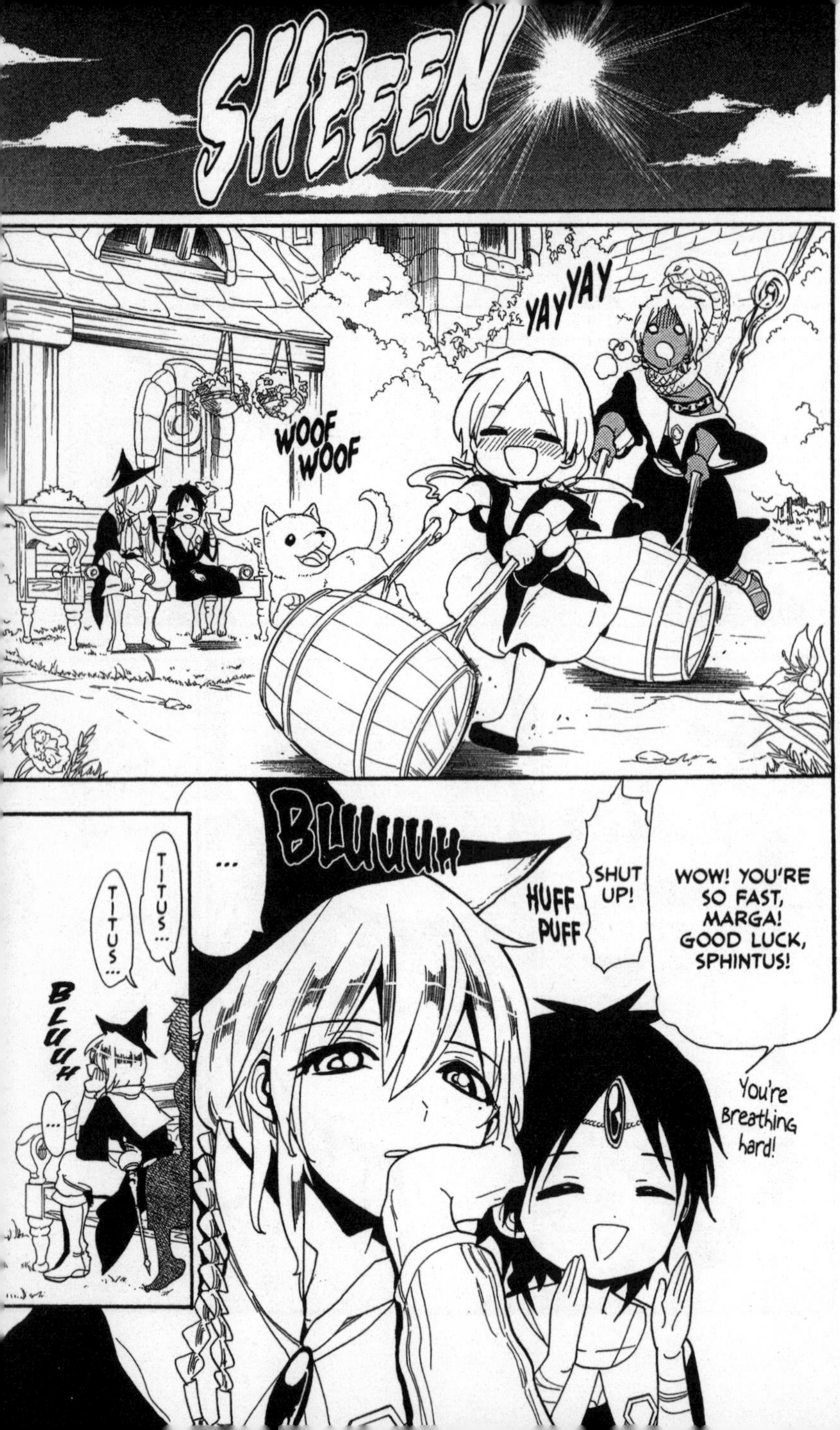
SHEEEN
YAY YAY
WOOF WOOF
WOW! YOU'RE SO FAST, MARGA! GOOD LUCK, SPHINTUS!
You're Breathing hard!
SHUT UP!
HUFF PUFF
BLUUUH
...
TITUS...
TITUS...
BLUUH
...

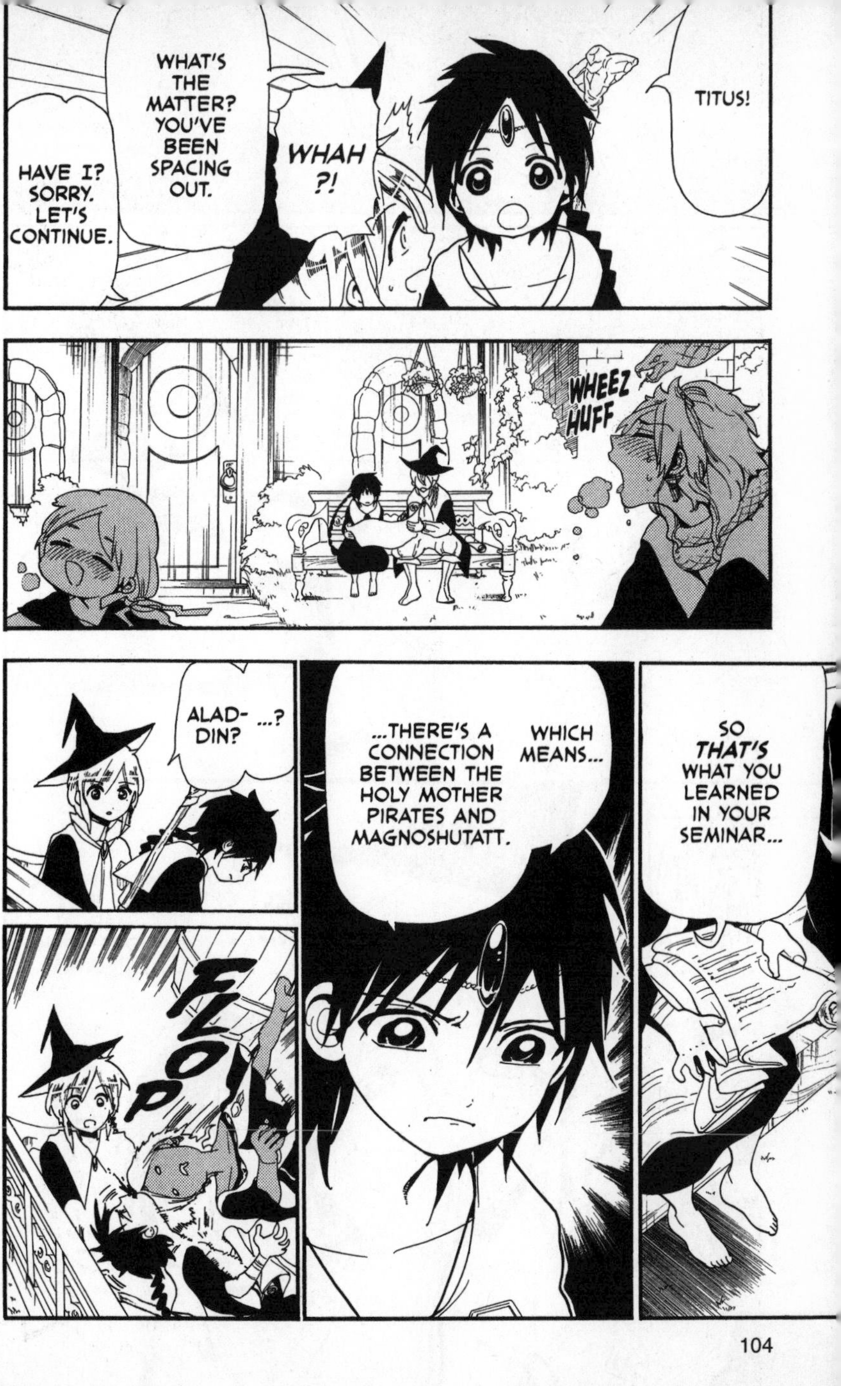
TITUS!
WHAH ?!
WHAT'S THE MATTER? YOU'VE BEEN SPACING OUT.
HAVE I? SORRY. LET'S CONTINUE.
WHEEZ HUFF
SO THAT'S WHAT YOU LEARNED IN YOUR SEMINAR...
WHICH MEANS...
...THERE'S A CONNECTION BETWEEN THE HOLY MOTHER PIRATES AND MAGNOSHUTATT.
...?
ALAD- DIN?
FLOP

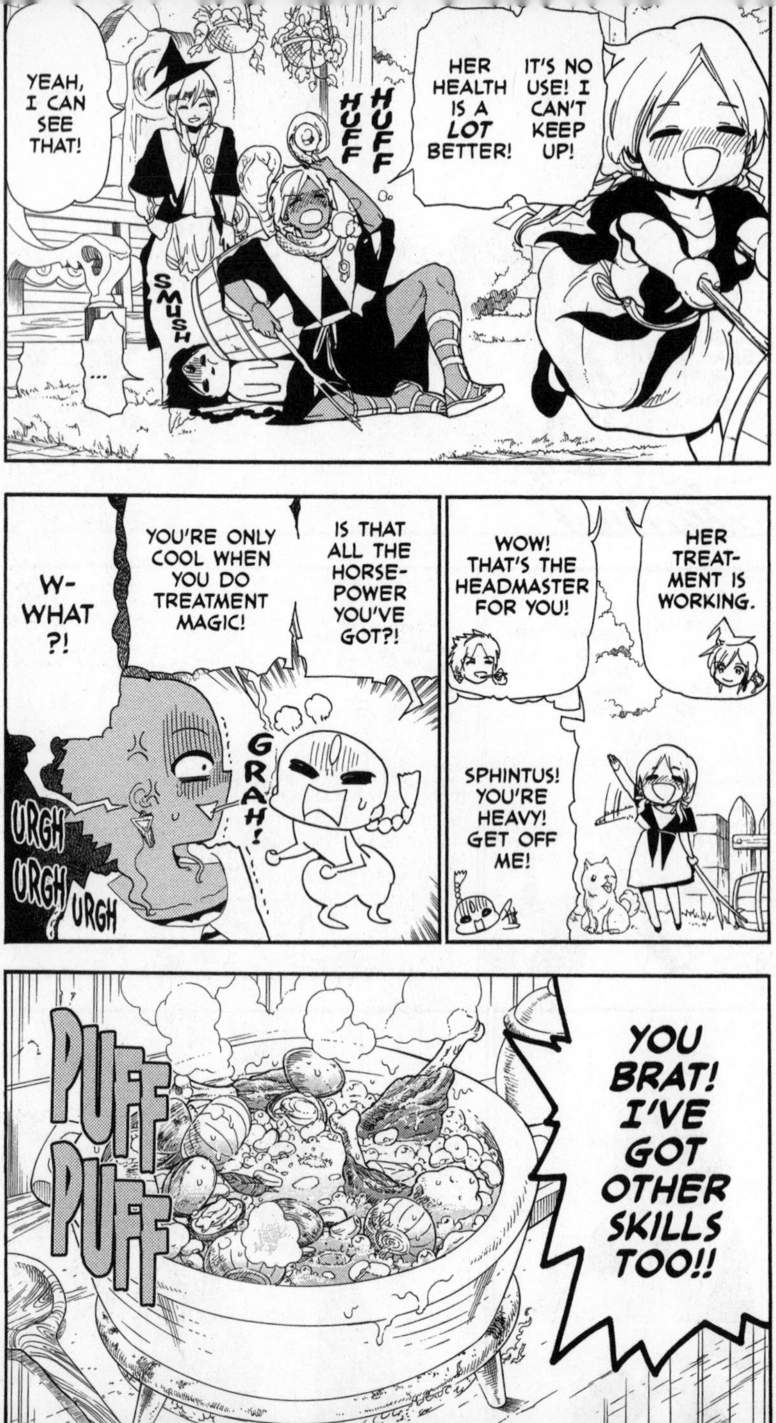
IT'S NO USE! I CAN'T KEEP UP!
HER HEALTH IS A *LOT* BETTER!
HUFF HUFF
YEAH, I CAN SEE THAT!
SMUSH
...
HER TREAT-MENT IS WORKING.
WOW! THAT'S THE HEADMASTER FOR YOU!
SPHINTUS! YOU'RE HEAVY! GET OFF ME!
IS THAT ALL THE HORSE-POWER YOU'VE GOT?!
YOU'RE ONLY COOL WHEN YOU DO TREATMENT MAGIC!
W-WHAT?!
GRAH!
URGH URGH URGH
YOU BRAT! I'VE GOT OTHER SKILLS TOO!!
PUFF PUFF

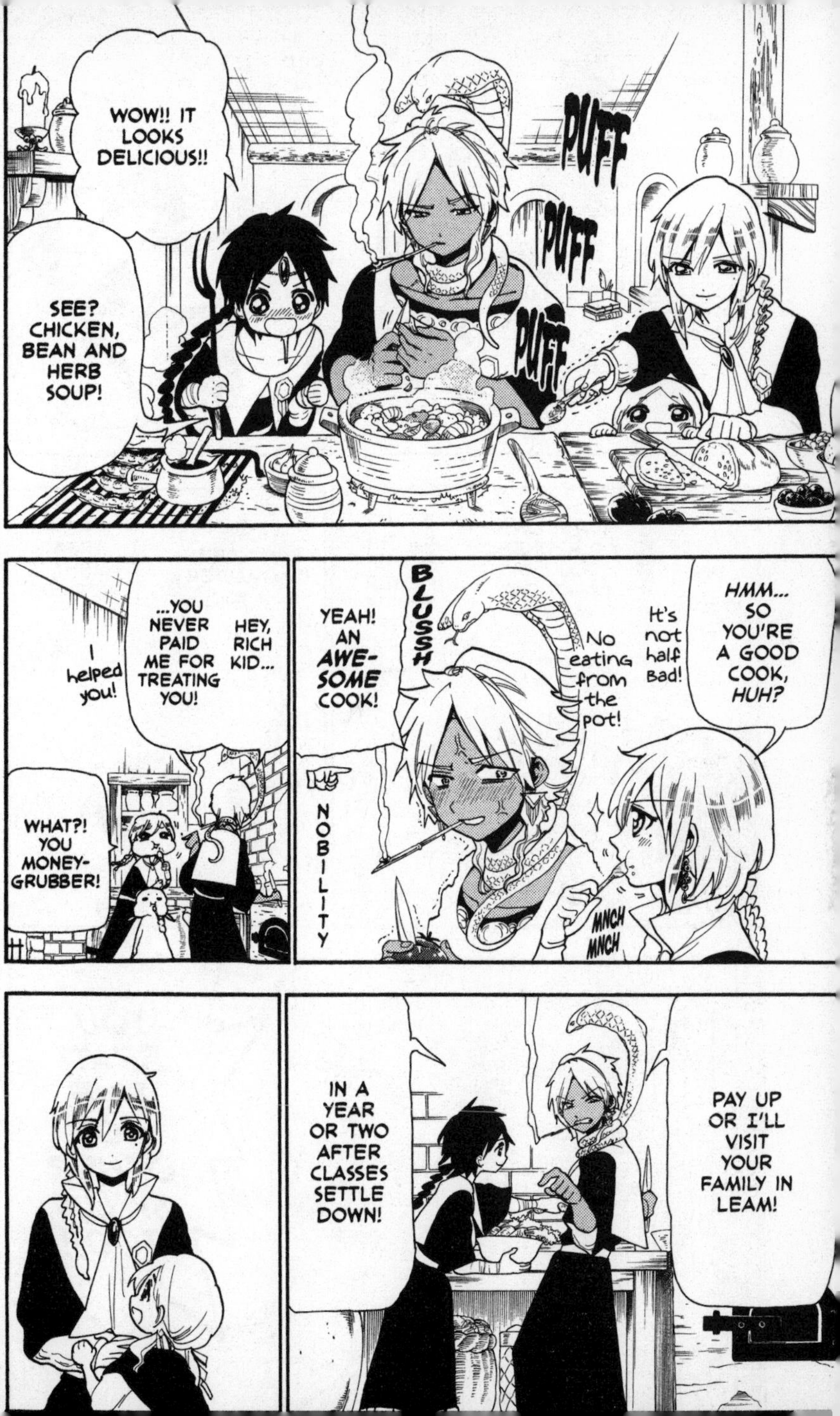
PUFF PUFF PUFF
WOW!! IT LOOKS DELICIOUS!!
SEE? CHICKEN, BEAN AND HERB SOUP!
HMM... SO YOU'RE A GOOD COOK, HUH?
It's not half Bad!
No eating from the pot!
BLUSSH
YEAH! AN AWESOME COOK!
NOBILITY
MNCH MNCH
HEY, RICH KID...
...YOU NEVER PAID ME FOR TREATING YOU!
I helped you!
WHAT?! YOU MONEY-GRUBBER!
PAY UP OR I'LL VISIT YOUR FAMILY IN LEAM!
IN A YEAR OR TWO AFTER CLASSES SETTLE DOWN!

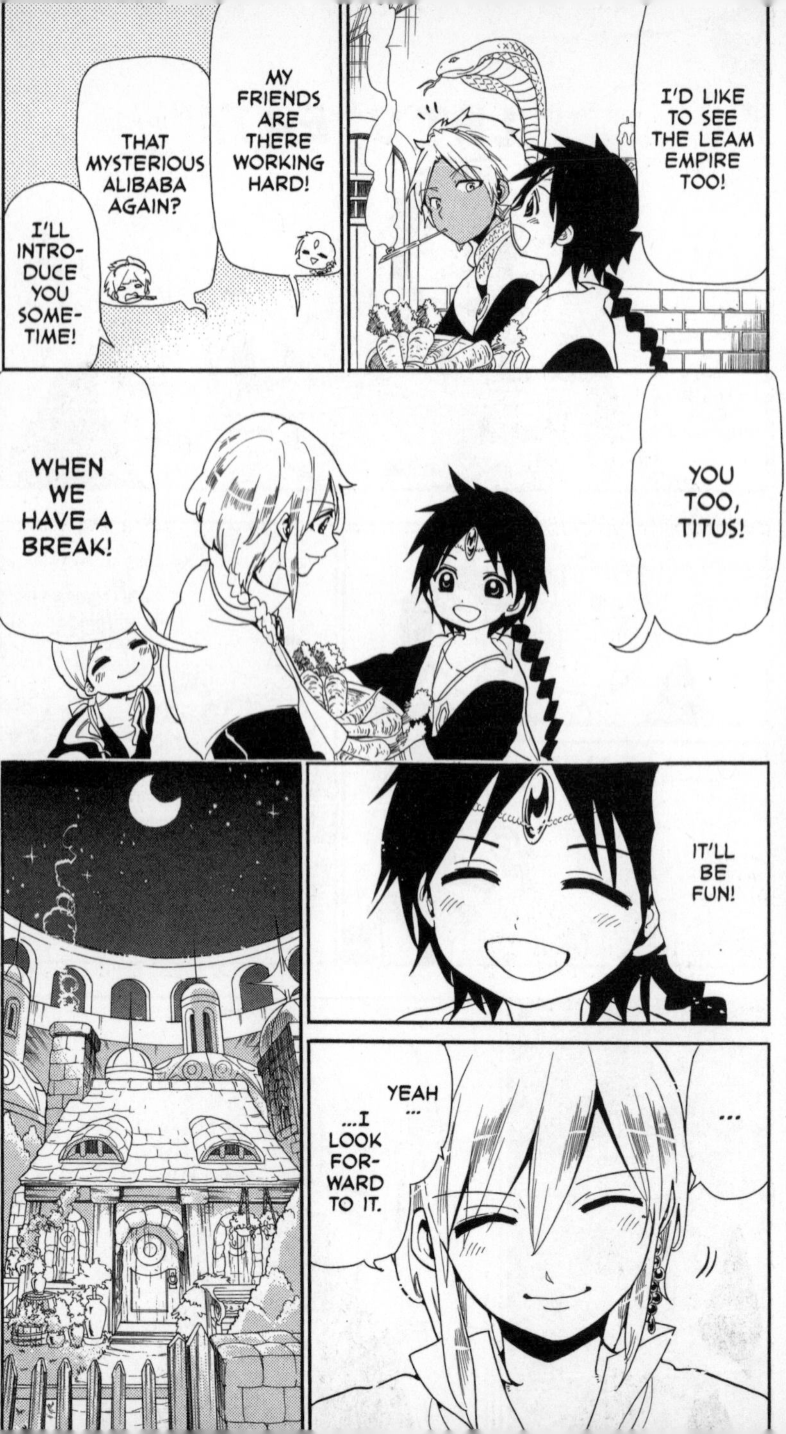
I'D LIKE TO SEE THE LEAM EMPIRE TOO!
MY FRIENDS ARE THERE WORKING HARD!
THAT MYSTERIOUS ALIBABA AGAIN?
I'LL INTRODUCE YOU SOMETIME!
YOU TOO, TITUS!
WHEN WE HAVE A BREAK!
IT'LL BE FUN!
...
YEAH ...
...I LOOK FORWARD TO IT.

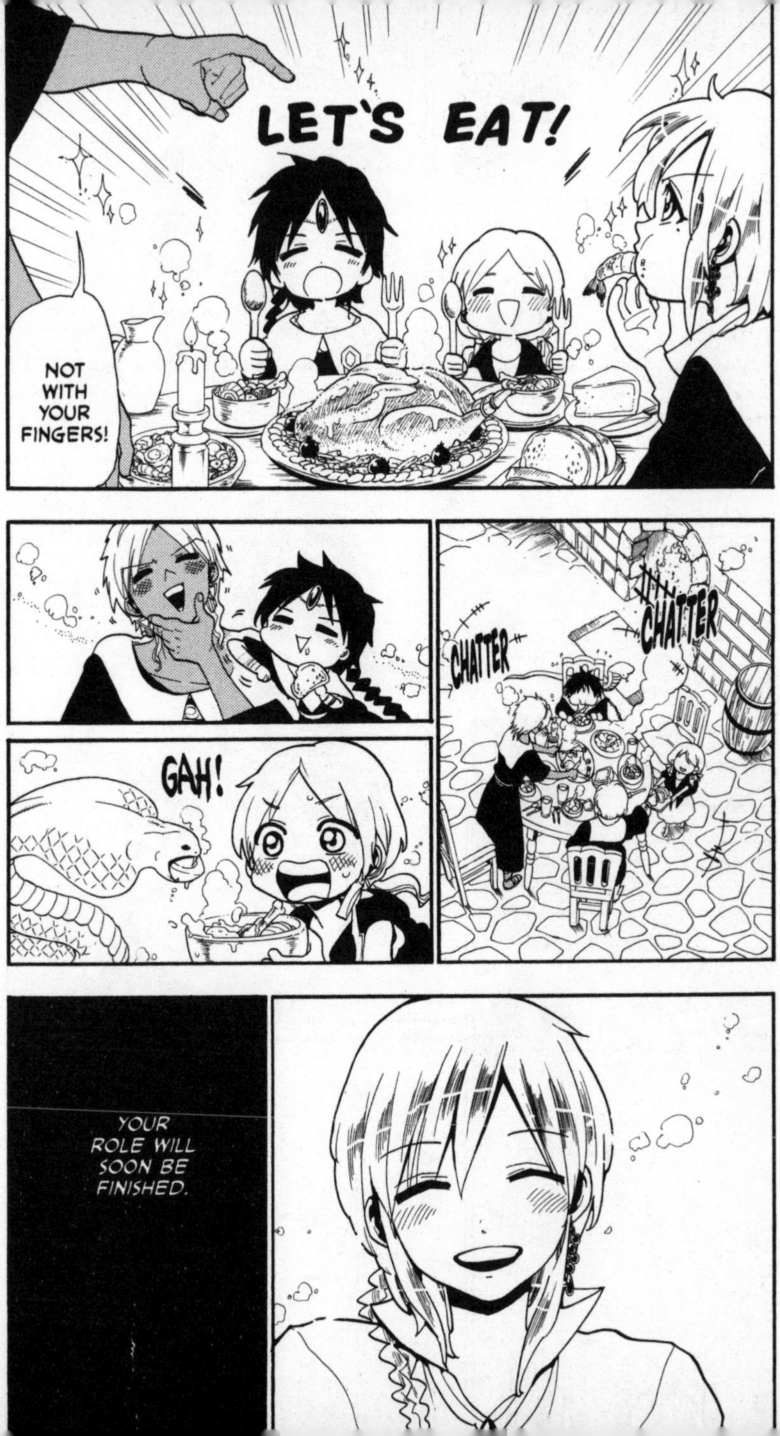
LET'S EAT!
NOT WITH YOUR FINGERS!
CHATTER
CHATTER
GAH!
YOUR ROLE WILL SOON BE FINISHED.

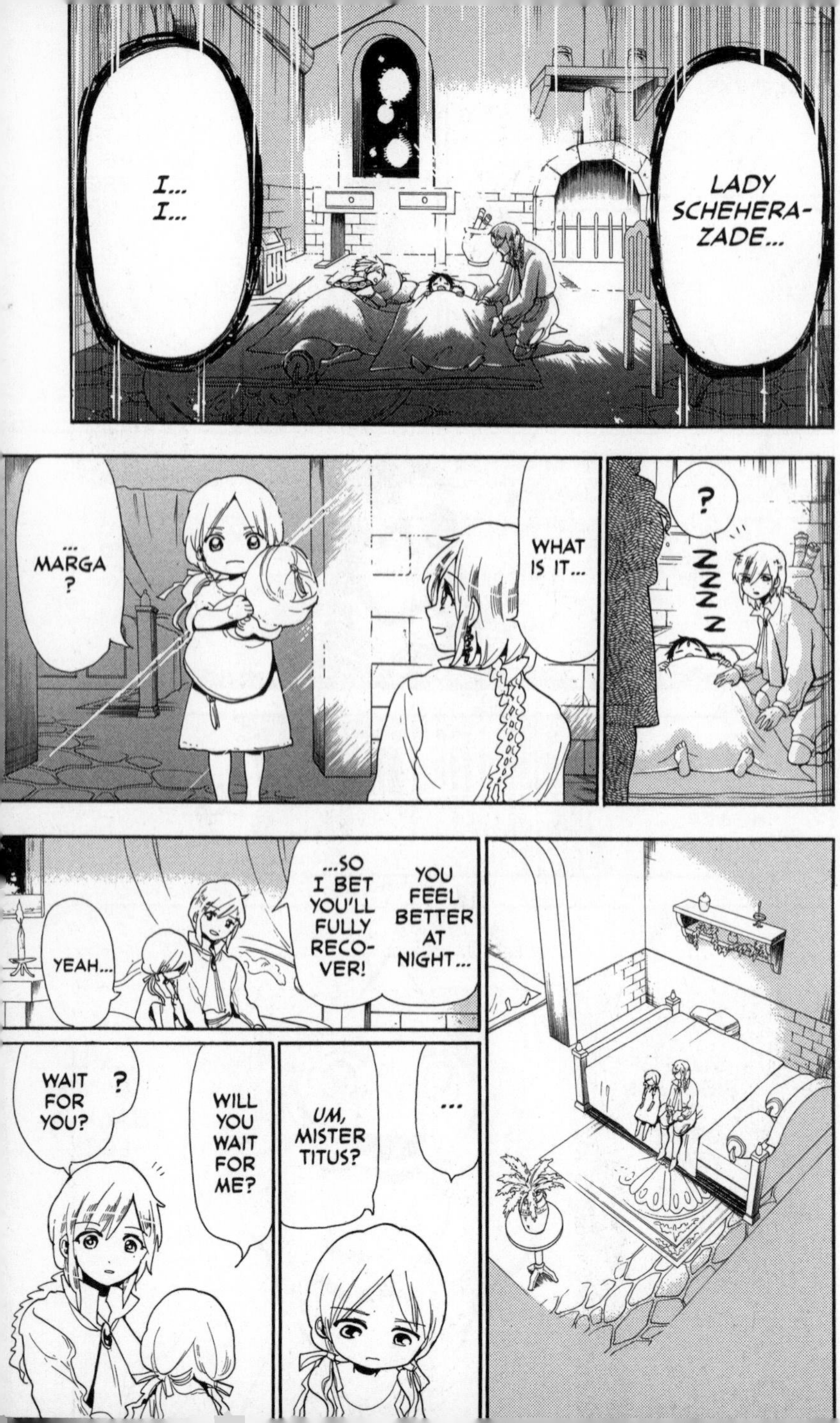
LADY SCHEHERA-ZADE...
I... I...
?
ZZZZ
WHAT IS IT...
...MARGA?
YOU FEEL BETTER AT NIGHT...
...SO I BET YOU'LL FULLY RECO-VER!
YEAH...
...
UM, MISTER TITUS?
WILL YOU WAIT FOR ME?
WAIT FOR YOU?

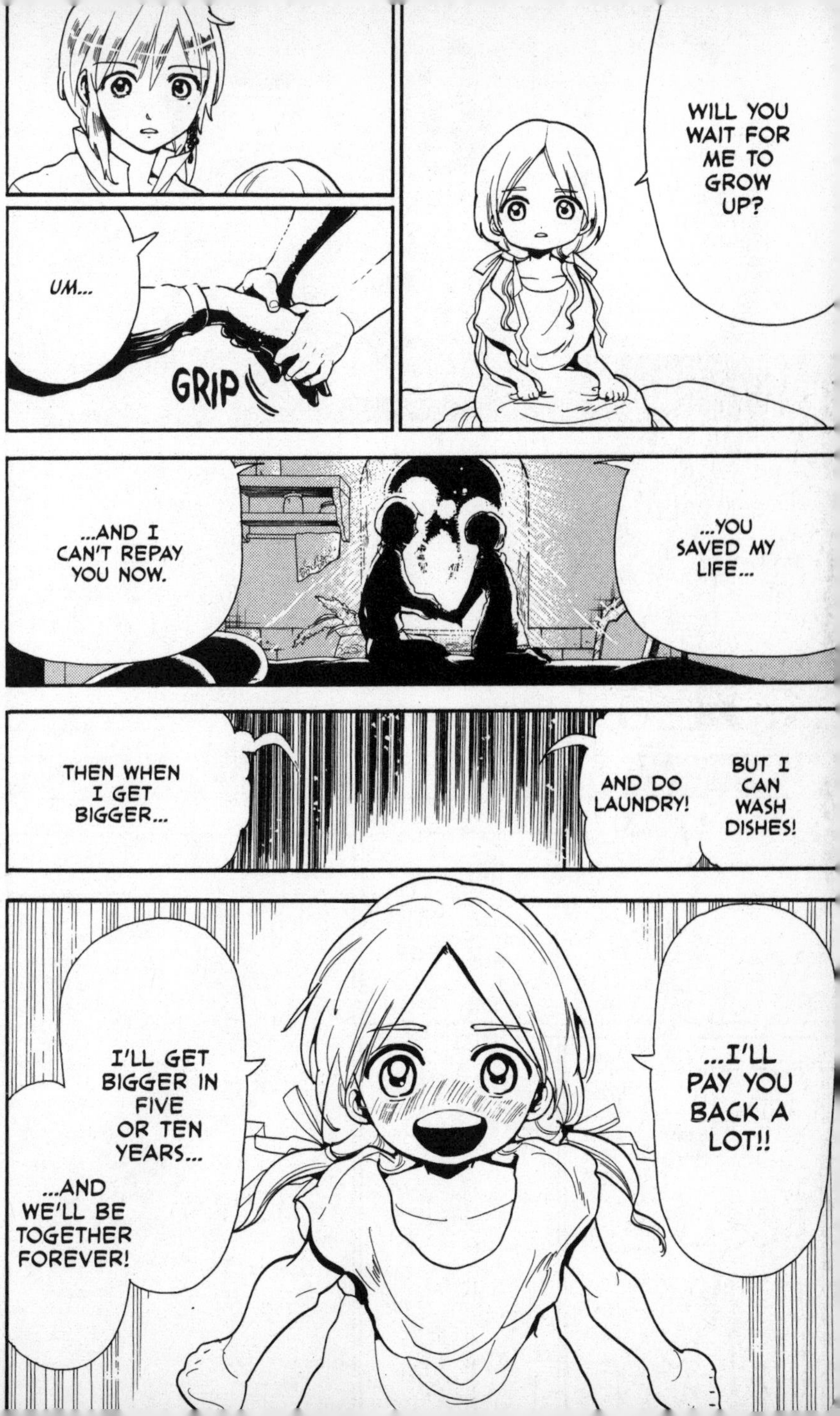
WILL YOU WAIT FOR ME TO GROW UP?
UM...
GRIP
...YOU SAVED MY LIFE...
...AND I CAN'T REPAY YOU NOW.
BUT I CAN WASH DISHES!
AND DO LAUNDRY!
THEN WHEN I GET BIGGER...
...I'LL PAY YOU BACK A LOT!!
I'LL GET BIGGER IN FIVE OR TEN YEARS...
...AND WE'LL BE TOGETHER FOREVER!

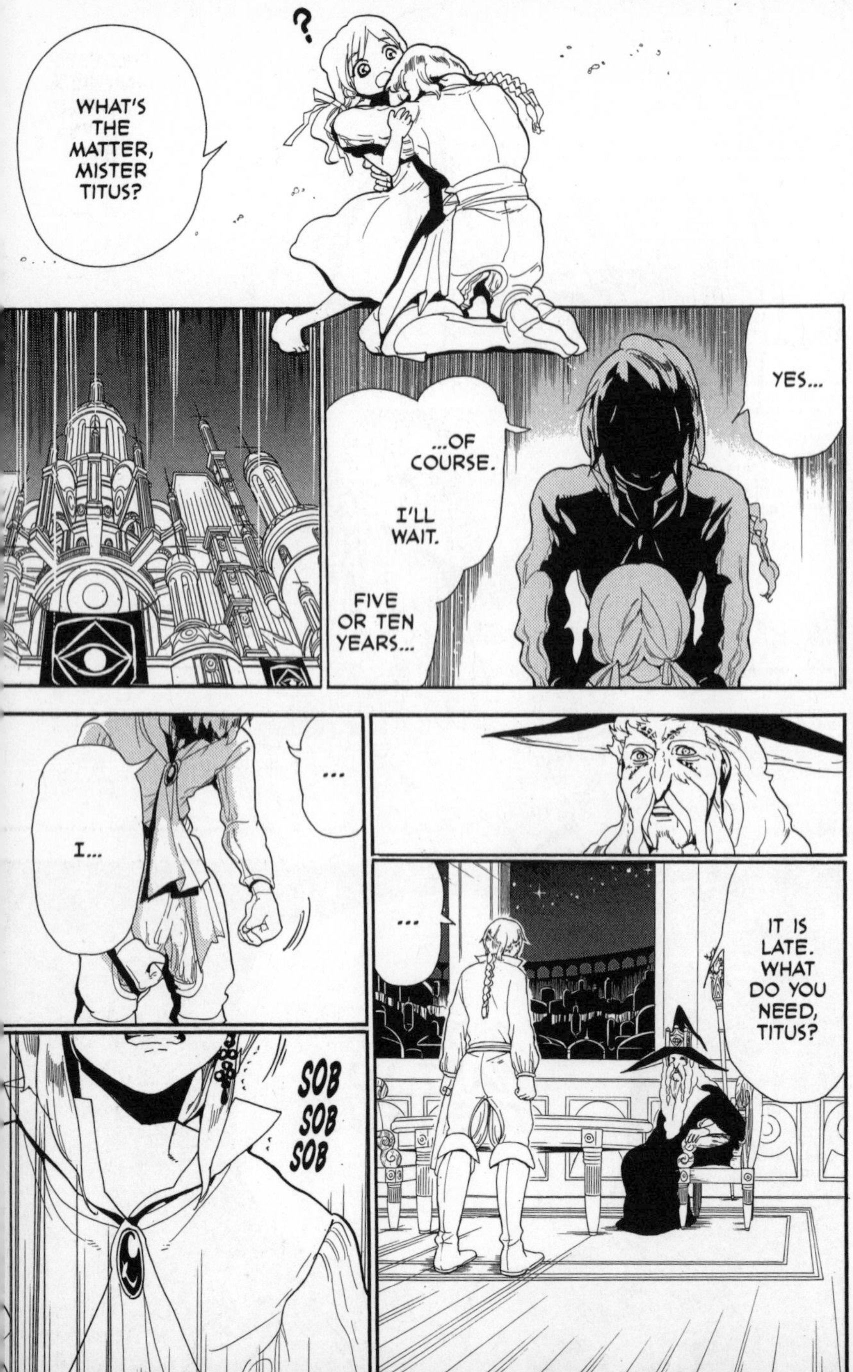
?
WHAT'S THE MATTER, MISTER TITUS?
YES...
...OF COURSE.
I'LL WAIT.
FIVE OR TEN YEARS...
IT IS LATE. WHAT DO YOU NEED, TITUS?
...
...
I...
SOB SOB SOB

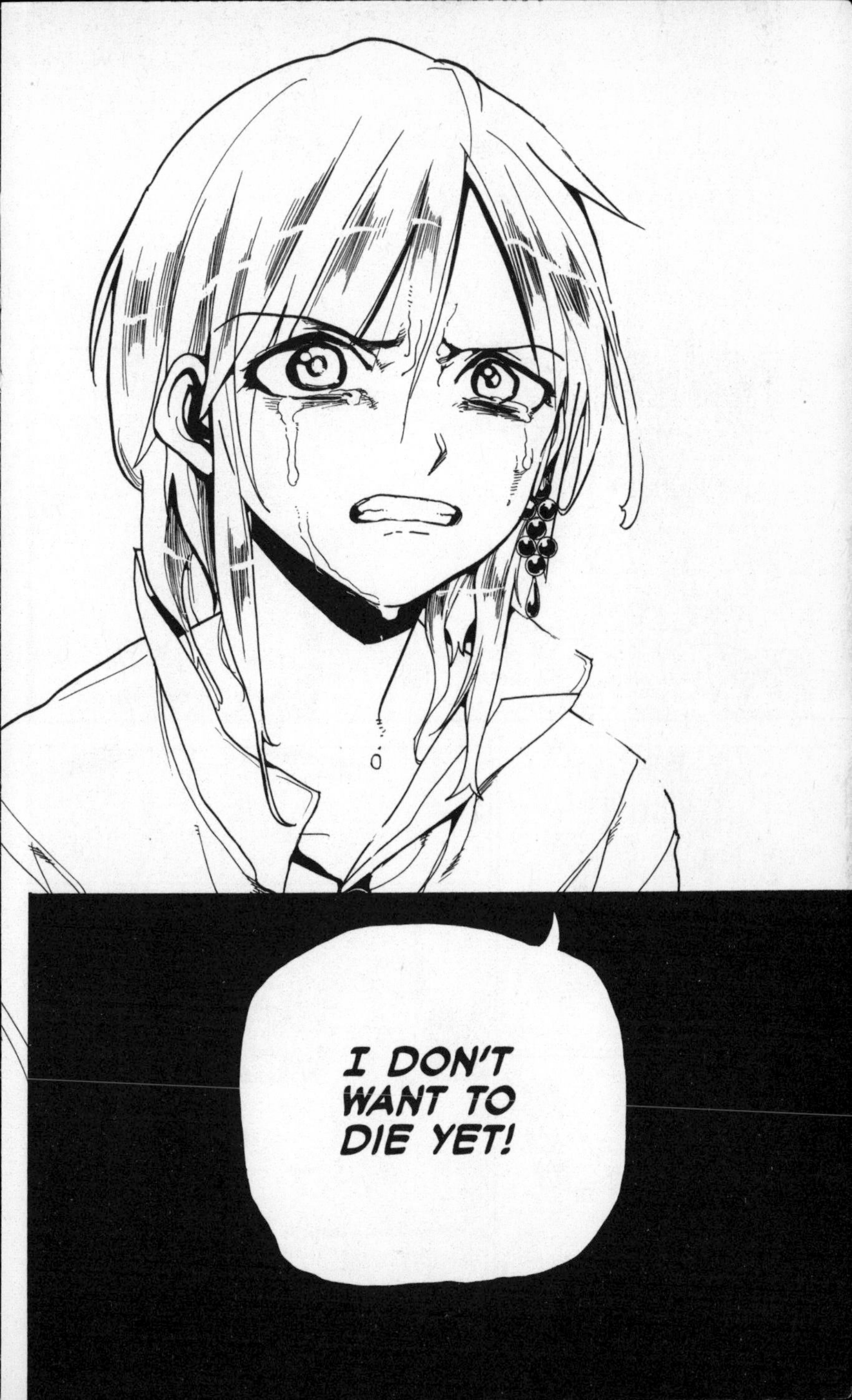
I DON'T WANT TO DIE YET!

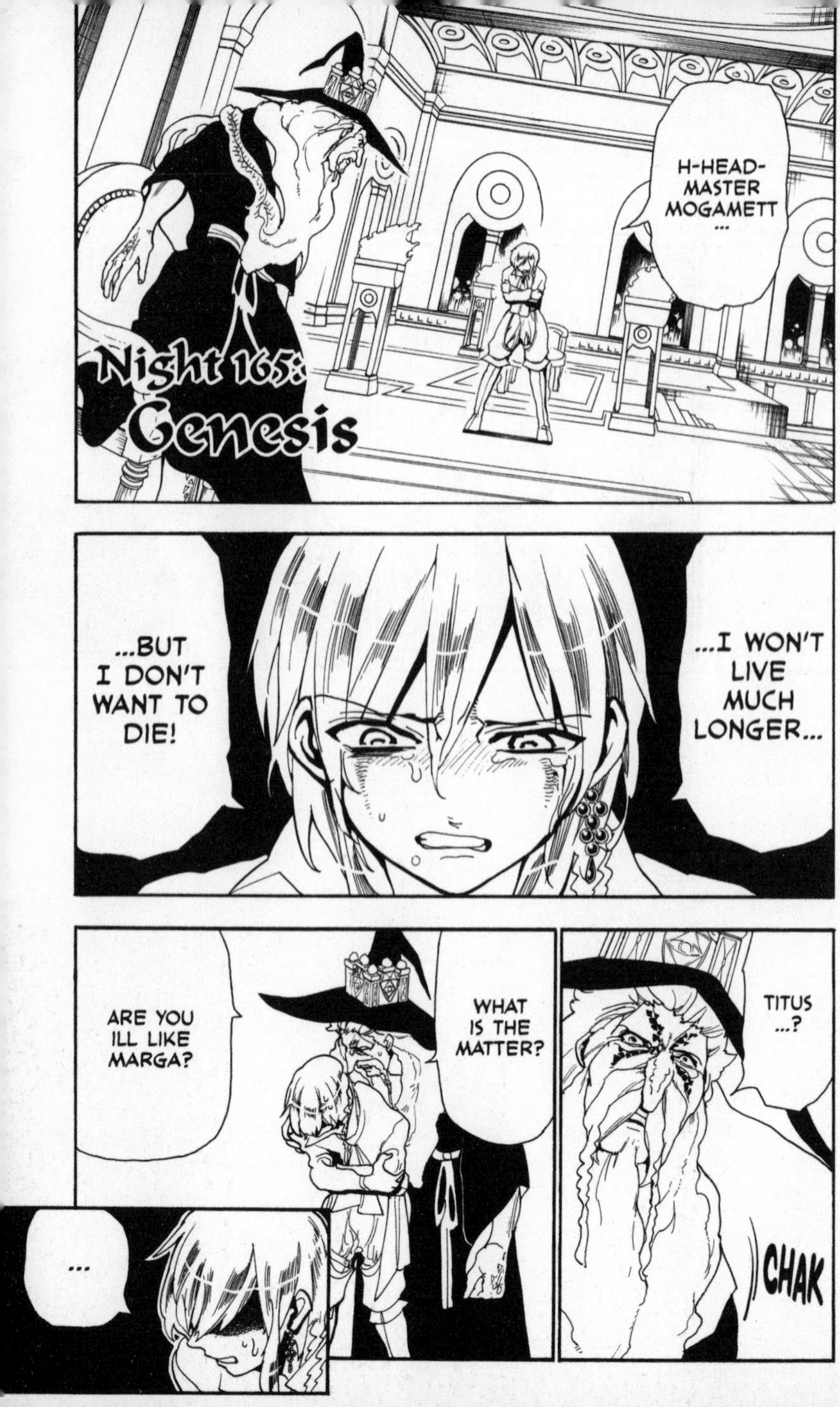
H-HEAD-MASTER MOGAMETT ...
Night 165: Genesis
...I WON'T LIVE MUCH LONGER...
...BUT I DON'T WANT TO DIE!
TITUS ...?
CHAK
WHAT IS THE MATTER?
ARE YOU ILL LIKE MARGA?
...

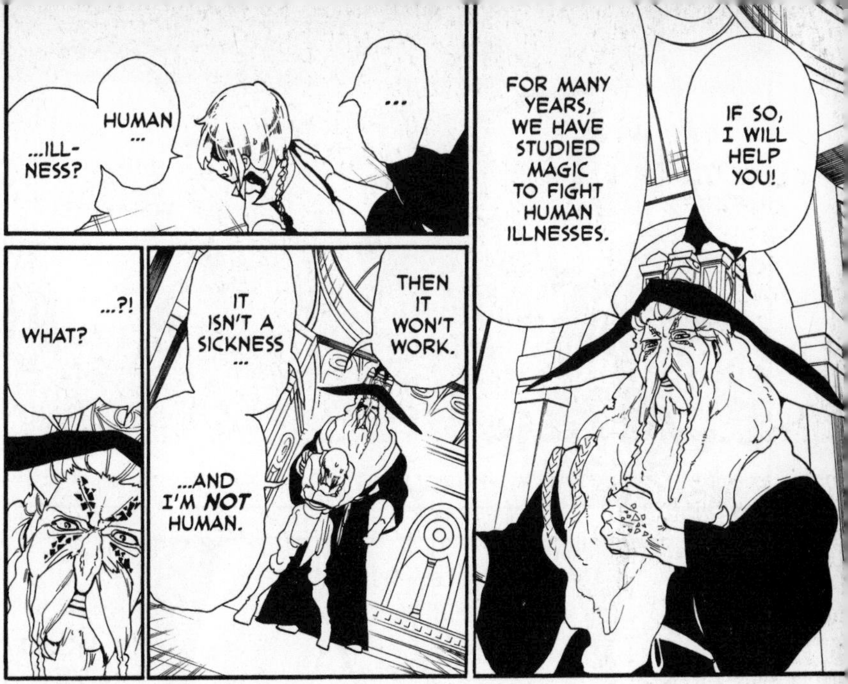
IF SO, I WILL HELP YOU!
FOR MANY YEARS, WE HAVE STUDIED MAGIC TO FIGHT HUMAN ILLNESSES.
...
HUMAN ...
...ILL-NESS?
THEN IT WON'T WORK.
IT ISN'T A SICKNESS ...
...AND I'M ***NOT*** HUMAN.
...?!
WHAT?

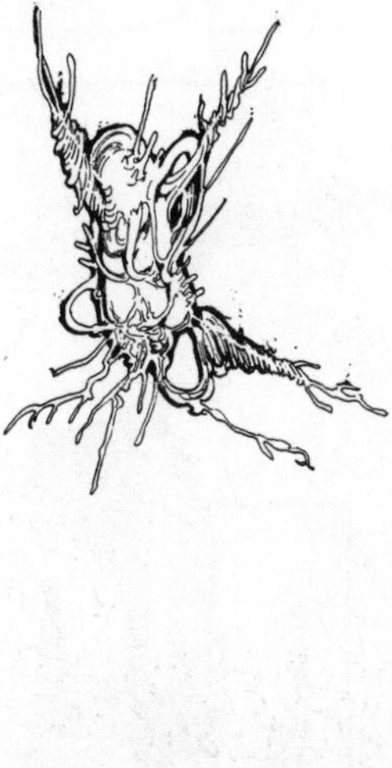

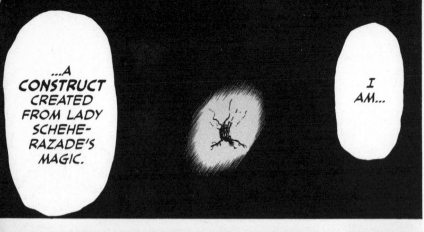

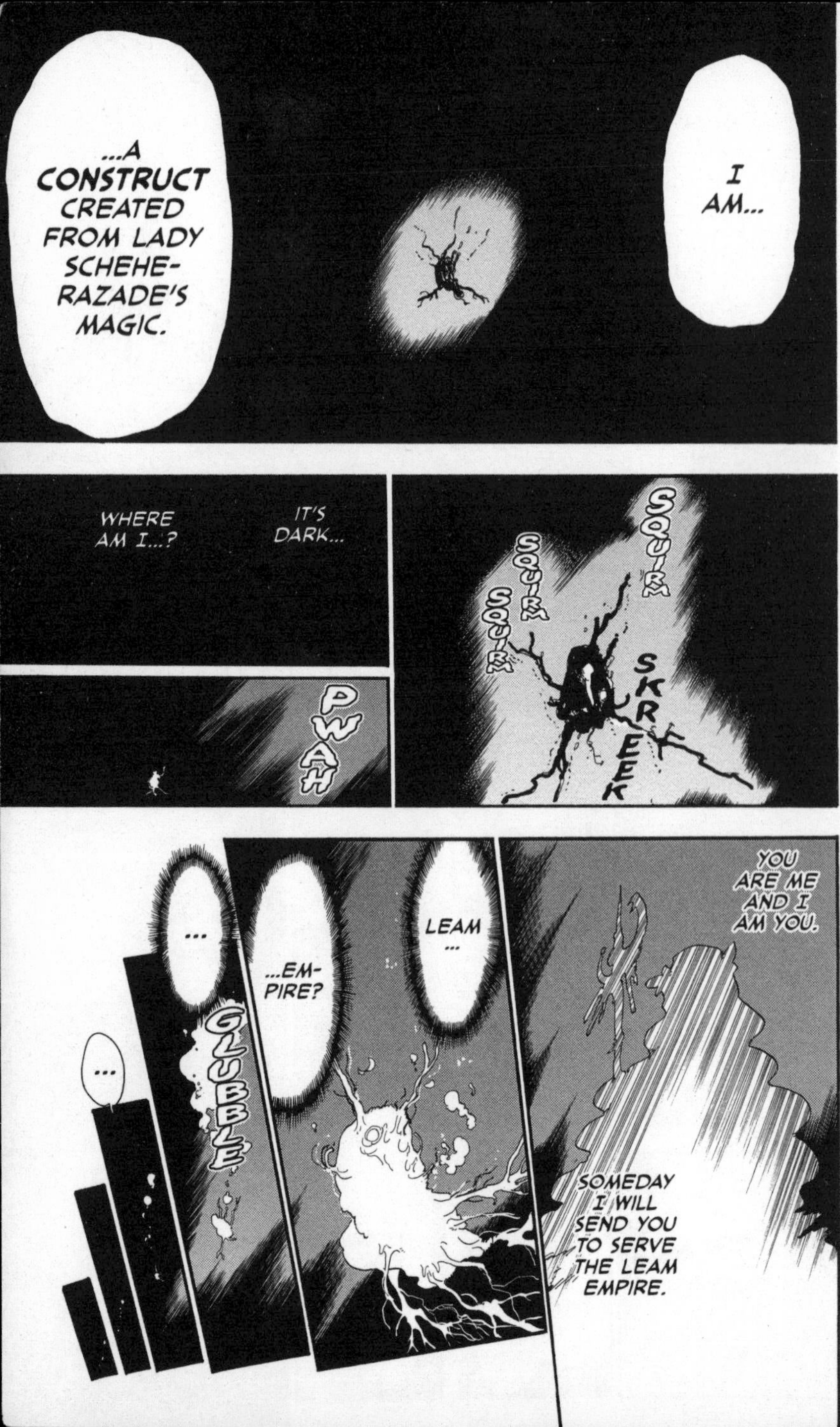

...A **CONSTRUCT** CREATED FROM LADY SCHEHE-RAZADE'S MAGIC.

I AM...

WHERE AM I...?

IT'S DARK...

SQUIRM SQUIRM SQUIRM SKREEK

PWAH

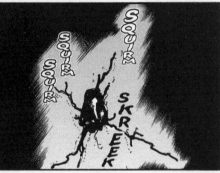

YOU ARE ME AND I AM YOU.

LEAM ...

...EM-PIRE?

...

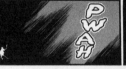

GLUBBLE

...

SOMEDAY I WILL SEND YOU TO SERVE THE LEAM EMPIRE.

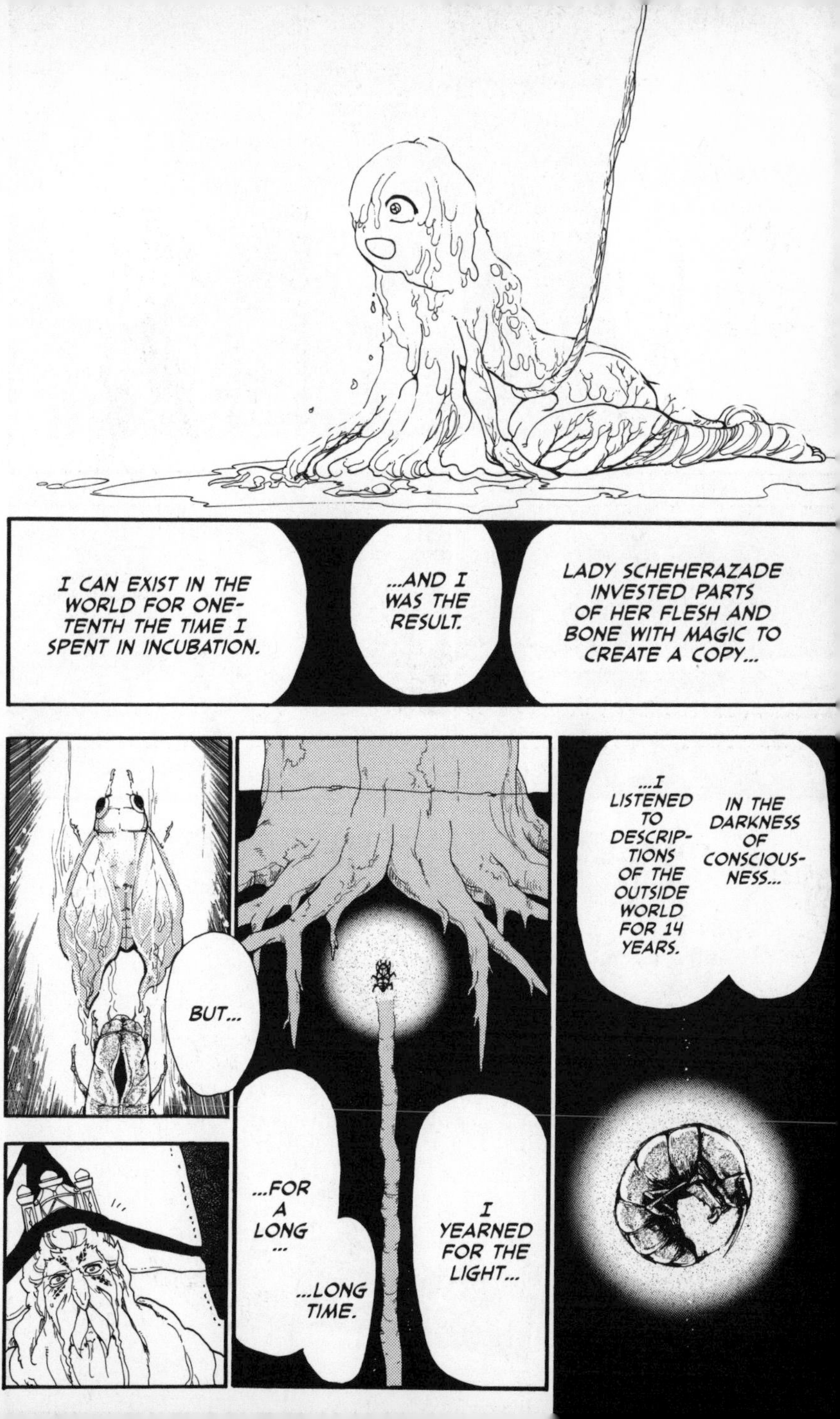
LADY SCHEHERAZADE INVESTED PARTS OF HER FLESH AND BONE WITH MAGIC TO CREATE A COPY...
...AND I WAS THE RESULT.
I CAN EXIST IN THE WORLD FOR ONE-TENTH THE TIME I SPENT IN INCUBATION.
IN THE DARKNESS OF CONSCIOUSNESS...
...I LISTENED TO DESCRIPTIONS OF THE OUTSIDE WORLD FOR 14 YEARS.
I YEARNED FOR THE LIGHT...
...FOR A LONG ...
...LONG TIME.
BUT...

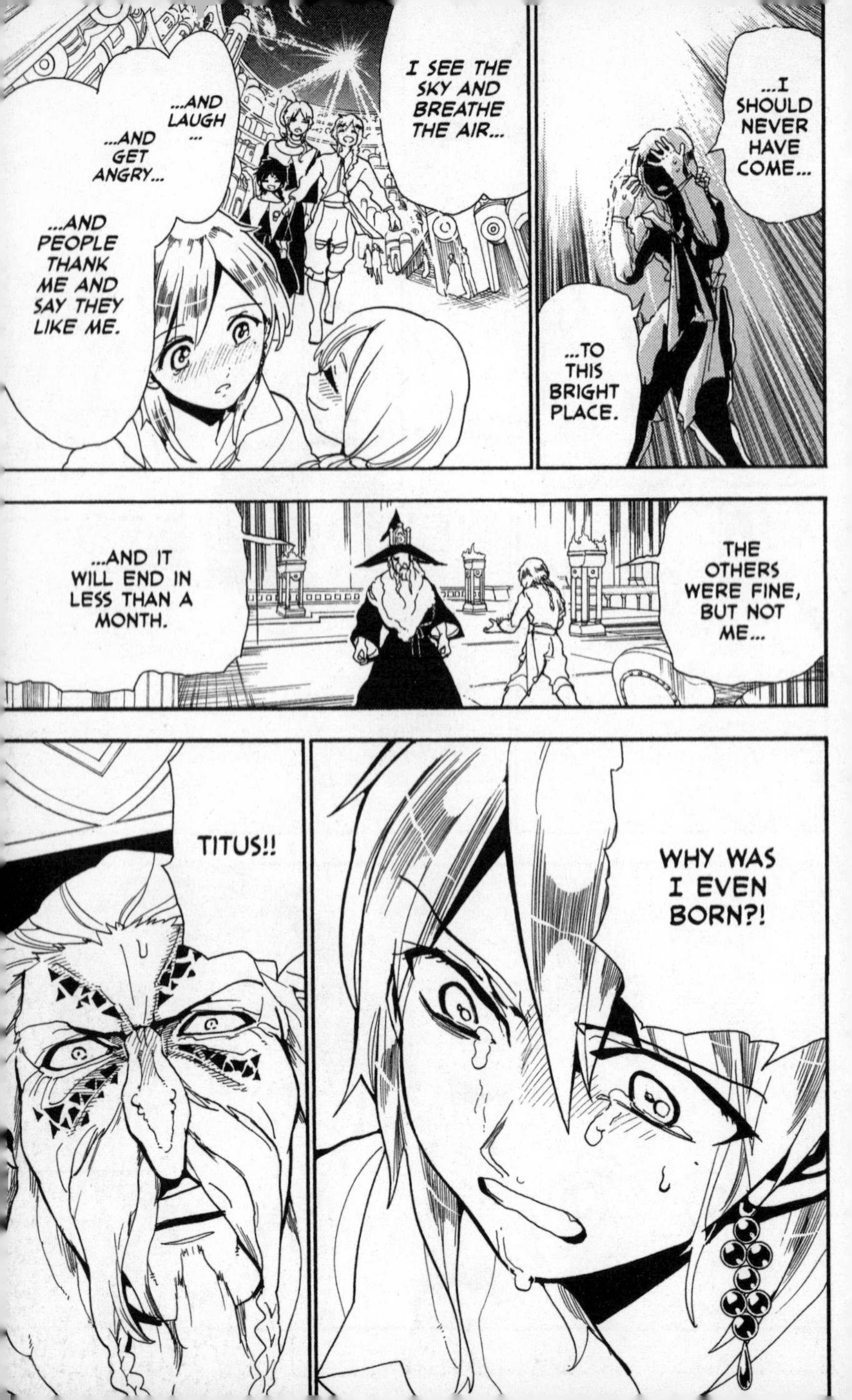
...I SHOULD NEVER HAVE COME...
...TO THIS BRIGHT PLACE.
I SEE THE SKY AND BREATHE THE AIR...
...AND LAUGH...
...AND GET ANGRY...
...AND PEOPLE THANK ME AND SAY THEY LIKE ME.
THE OTHERS WERE FINE, BUT NOT ME...
...AND IT WILL END IN LESS THAN A MONTH.
WHY WAS I EVEN BORN?!
TITUS!!

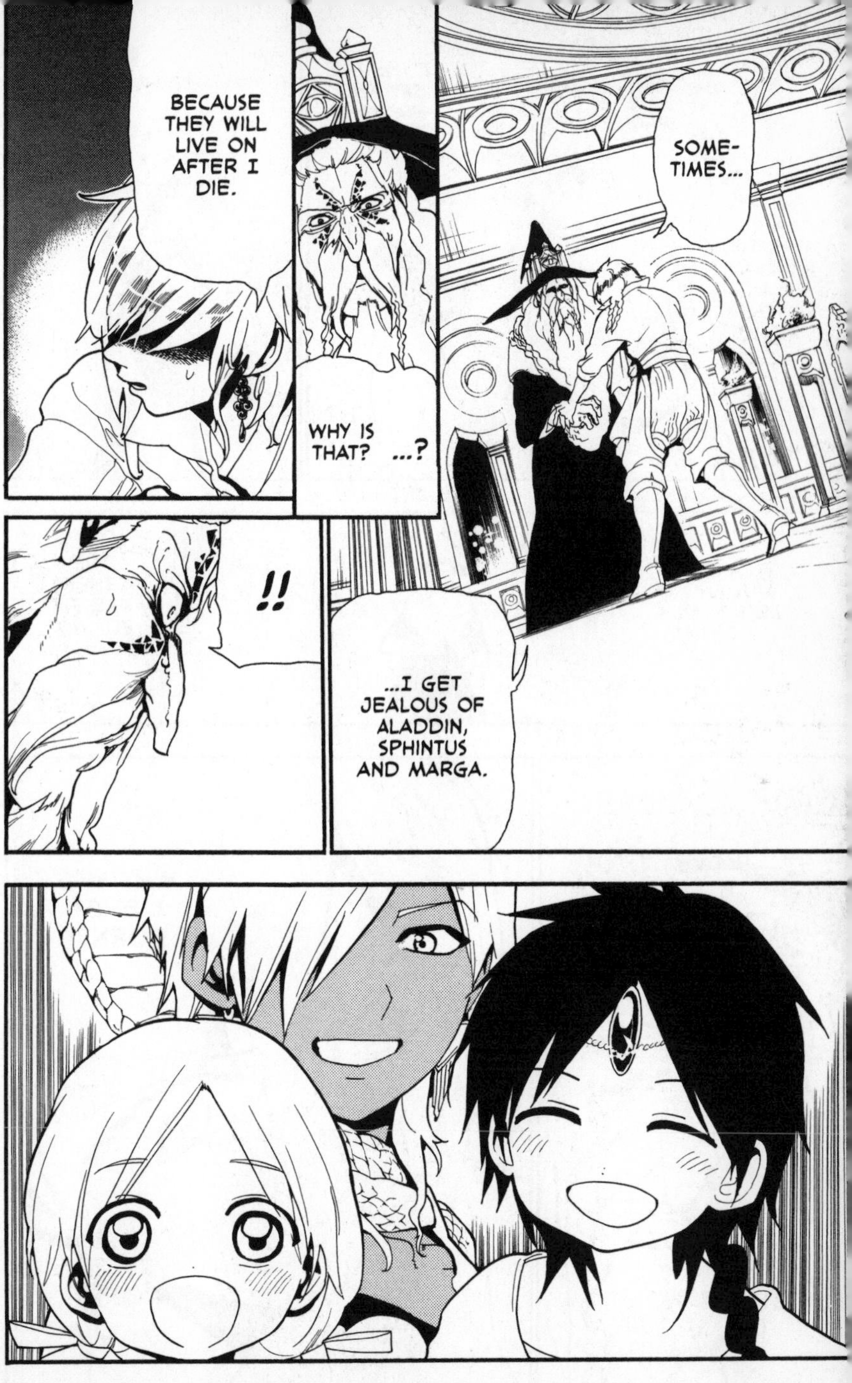
SOME-TIMES...
...I GET JEALOUS OF ALADDIN, SPHINTUS AND MARGA.
...?
WHY IS THAT?
BECAUSE THEY WILL LIVE ON AFTER I DIE.
!!

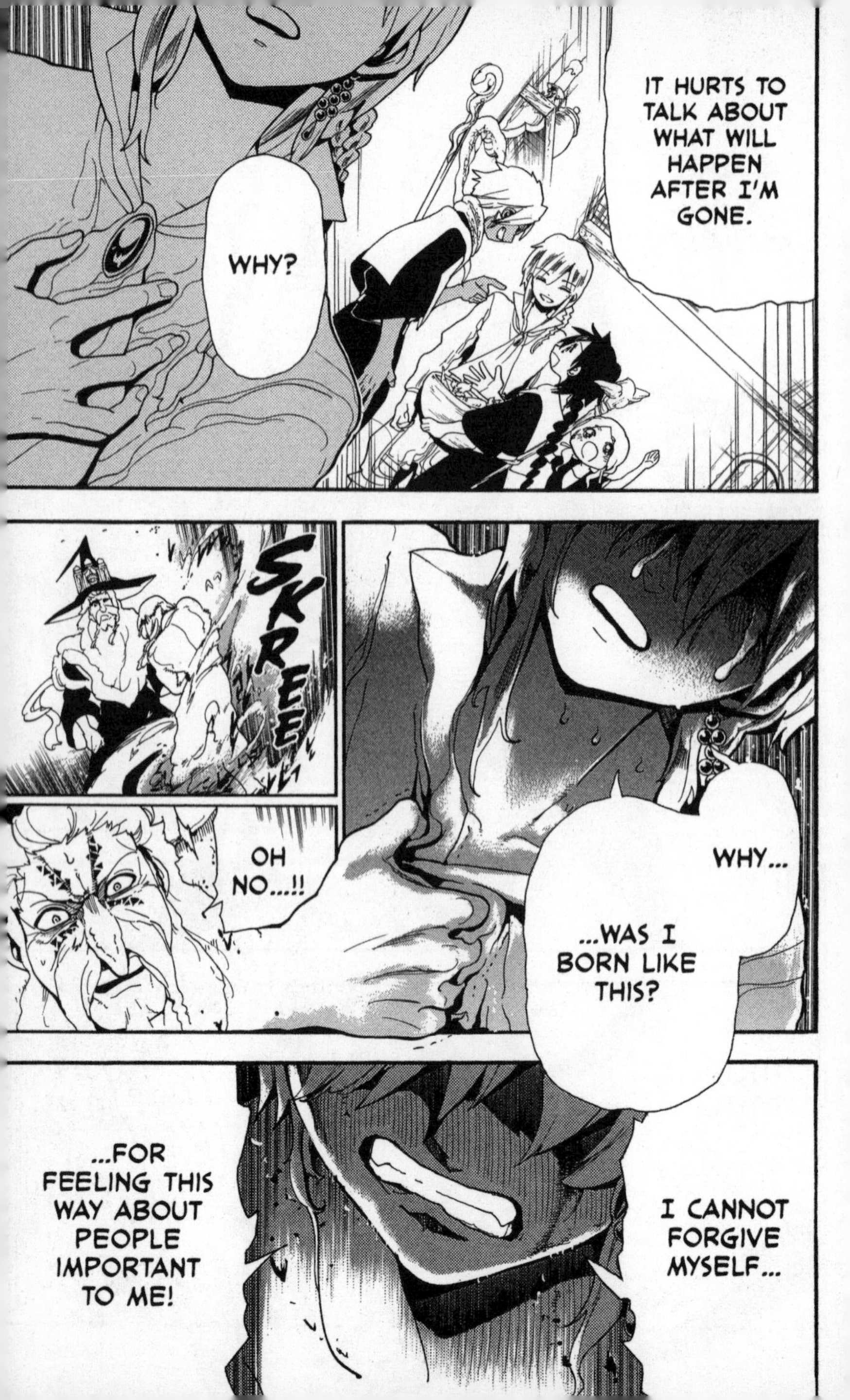
IT HURTS TO TALK ABOUT WHAT WILL HAPPEN AFTER I'M GONE.
WHY?
WHY...
...WAS I BORN LIKE THIS?
SKREE
OH NO...!!
I CANNOT FORGIVE MYSELF...
...FOR FEELING THIS WAY ABOUT PEOPLE IMPORTANT TO ME!

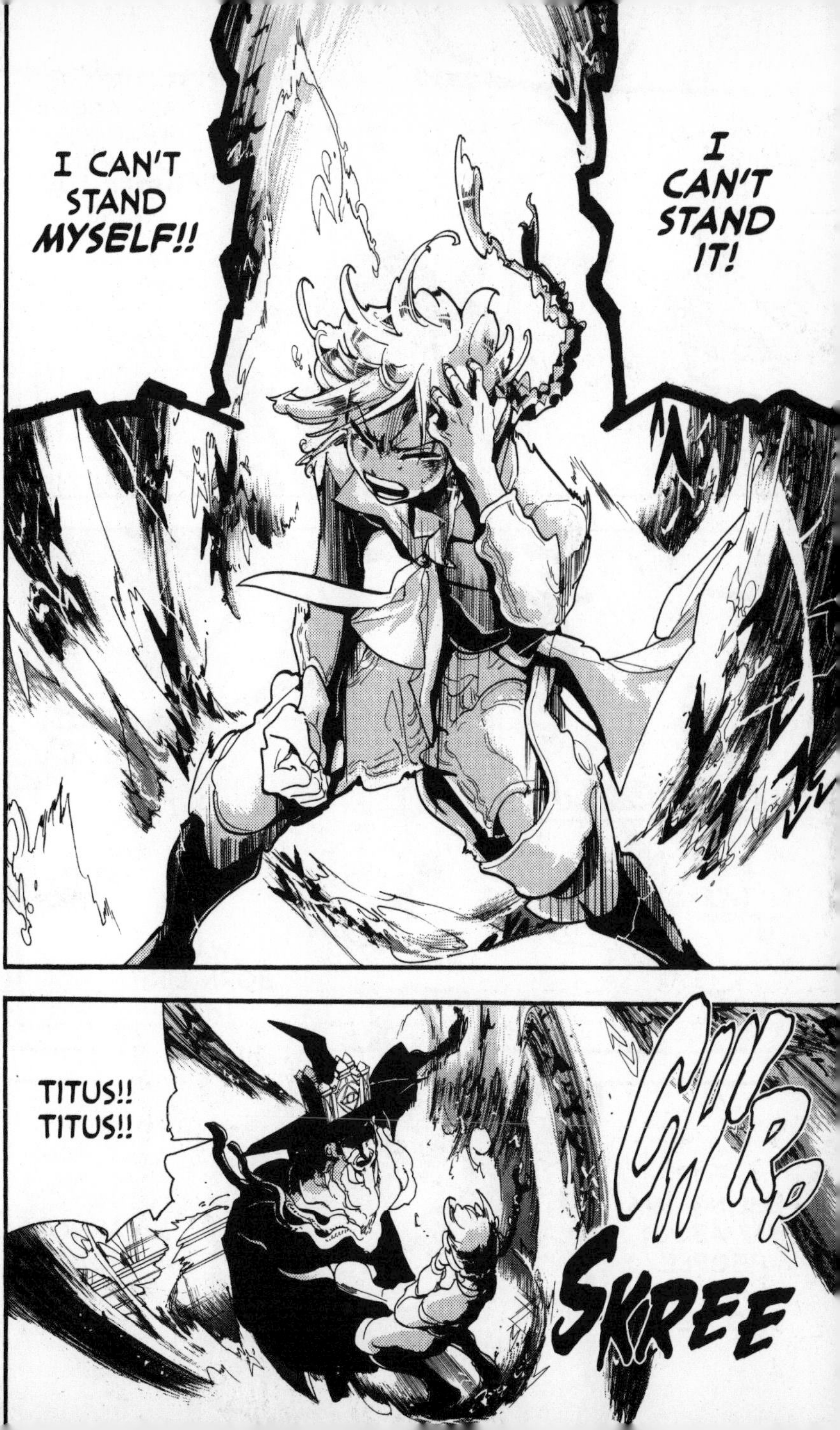
I CAN'T STAND IT!
I CAN'T STAND MYSELF!!
CHIRP
SKREE
TITUS!! TITUS!!

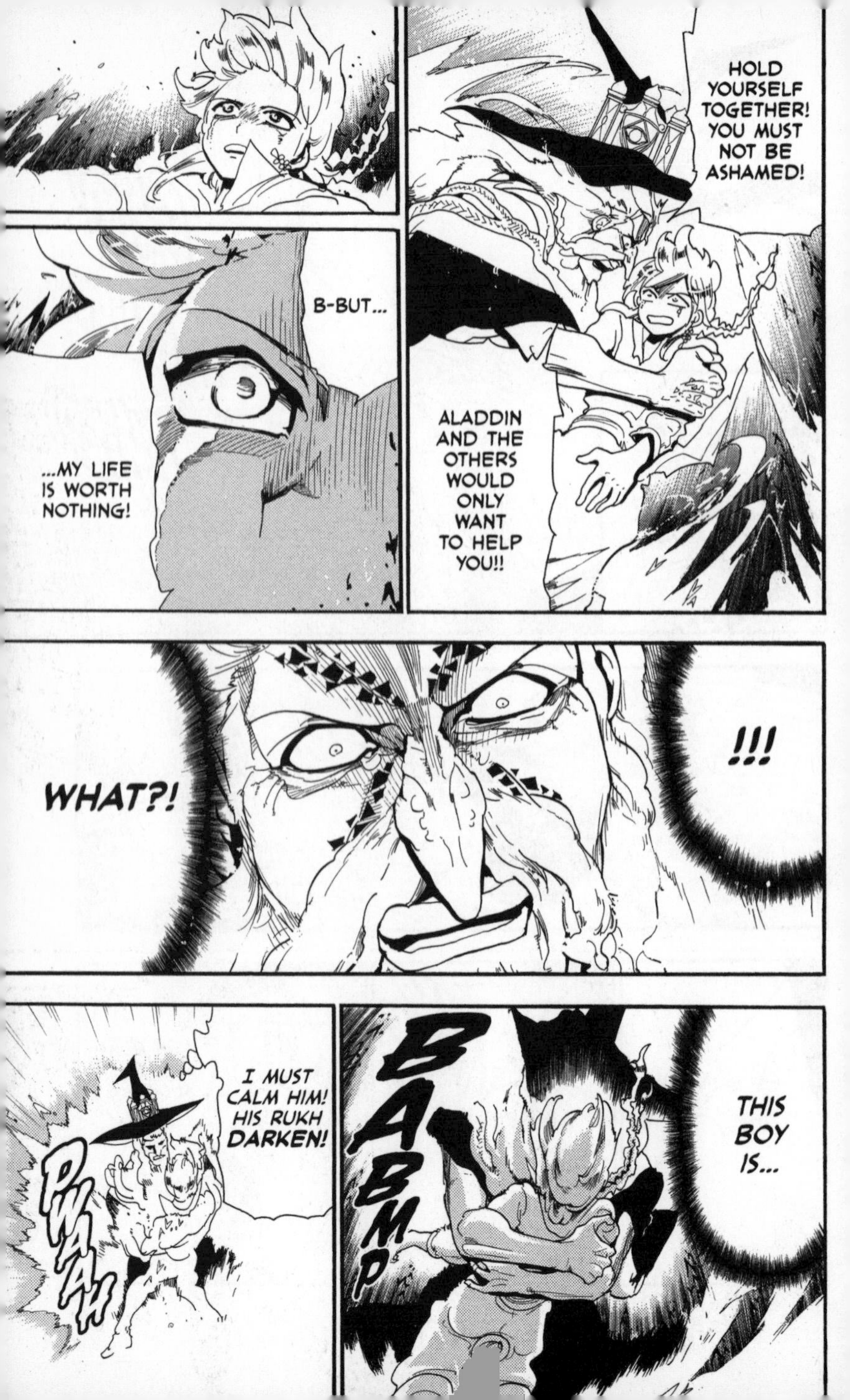
HOLD YOURSELF TOGETHER! YOU MUST NOT BE ASHAMED!
ALADDIN AND THE OTHERS WOULD ONLY WANT TO HELP YOU!!
B-BUT...
...MY LIFE IS WORTH NOTHING!
!!!
WHAT?!
THIS BOY IS...
BABMP
I MUST CALM HIM! HIS RUKH DARKEN!
PWAAH

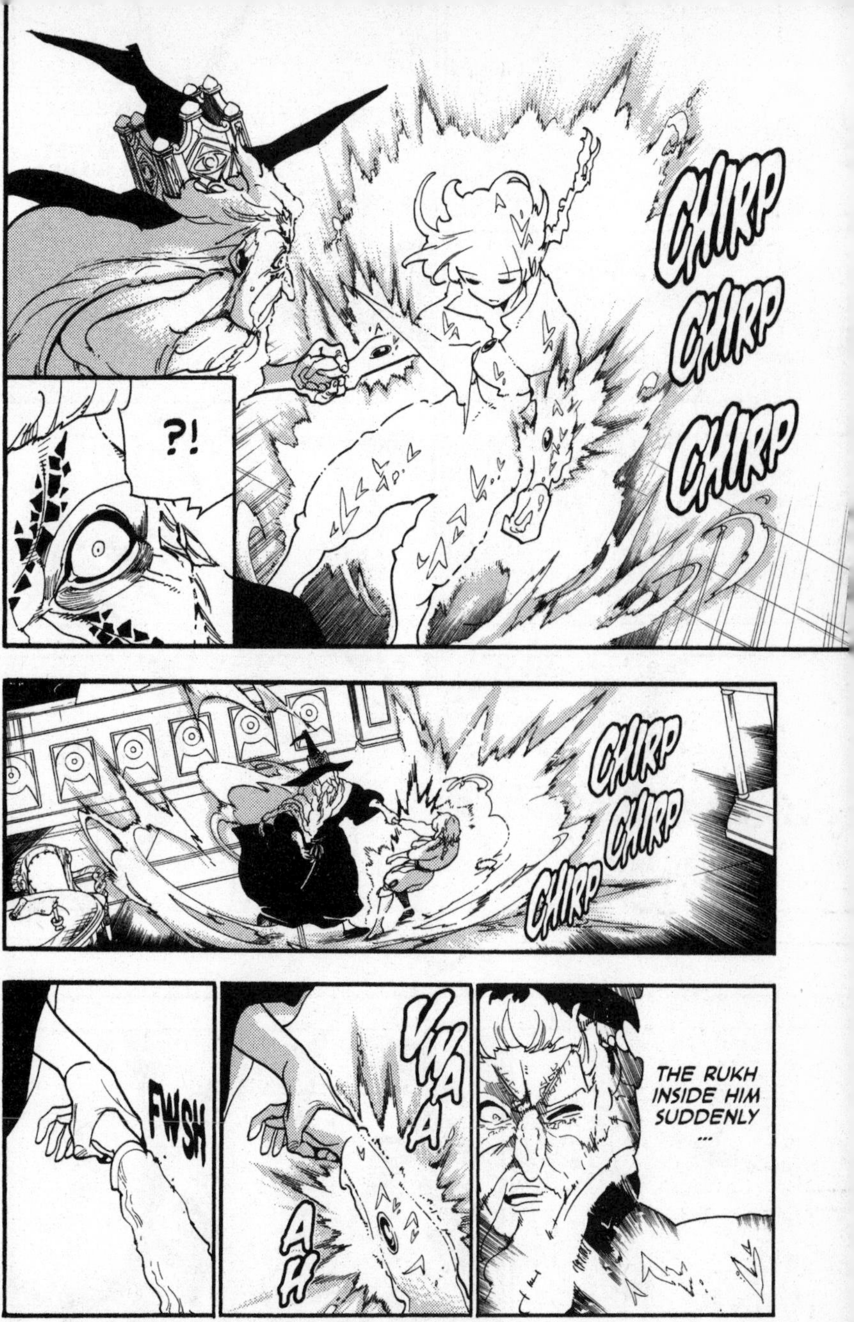
CHIRP
CHIRP
CHIRP
?!
CHIRP
CHIRP
CHIRP
THE RUKH INSIDE HIM SUDDENLY ...
VWAAAH
FWSH

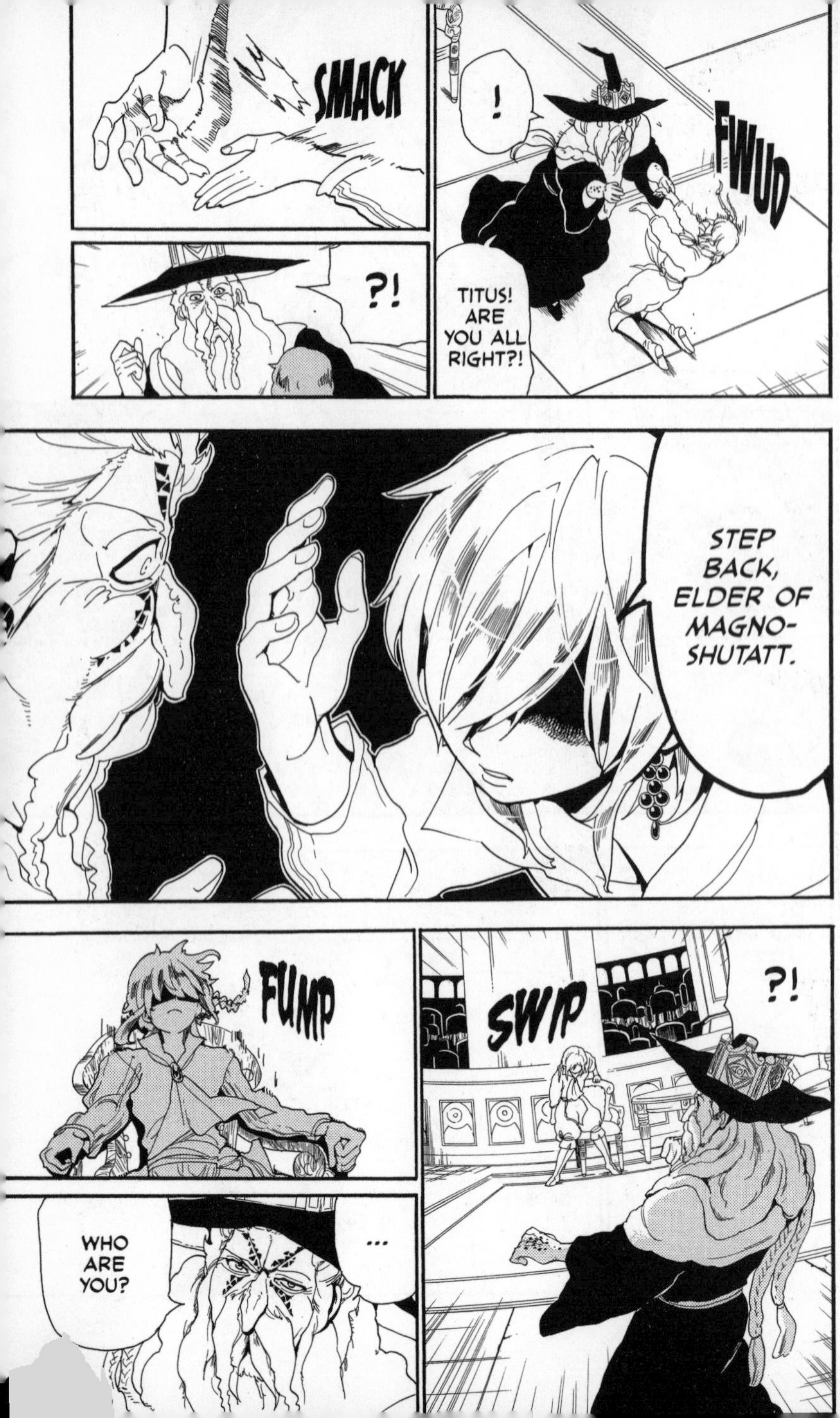
!
FWUD
TITUS! ARE YOU ALL RIGHT?!
SMACK
?!
STEP BACK, ELDER OF MAGNO-SHUTATT.
?!
SWIP
FUMP
...
WHO ARE YOU?

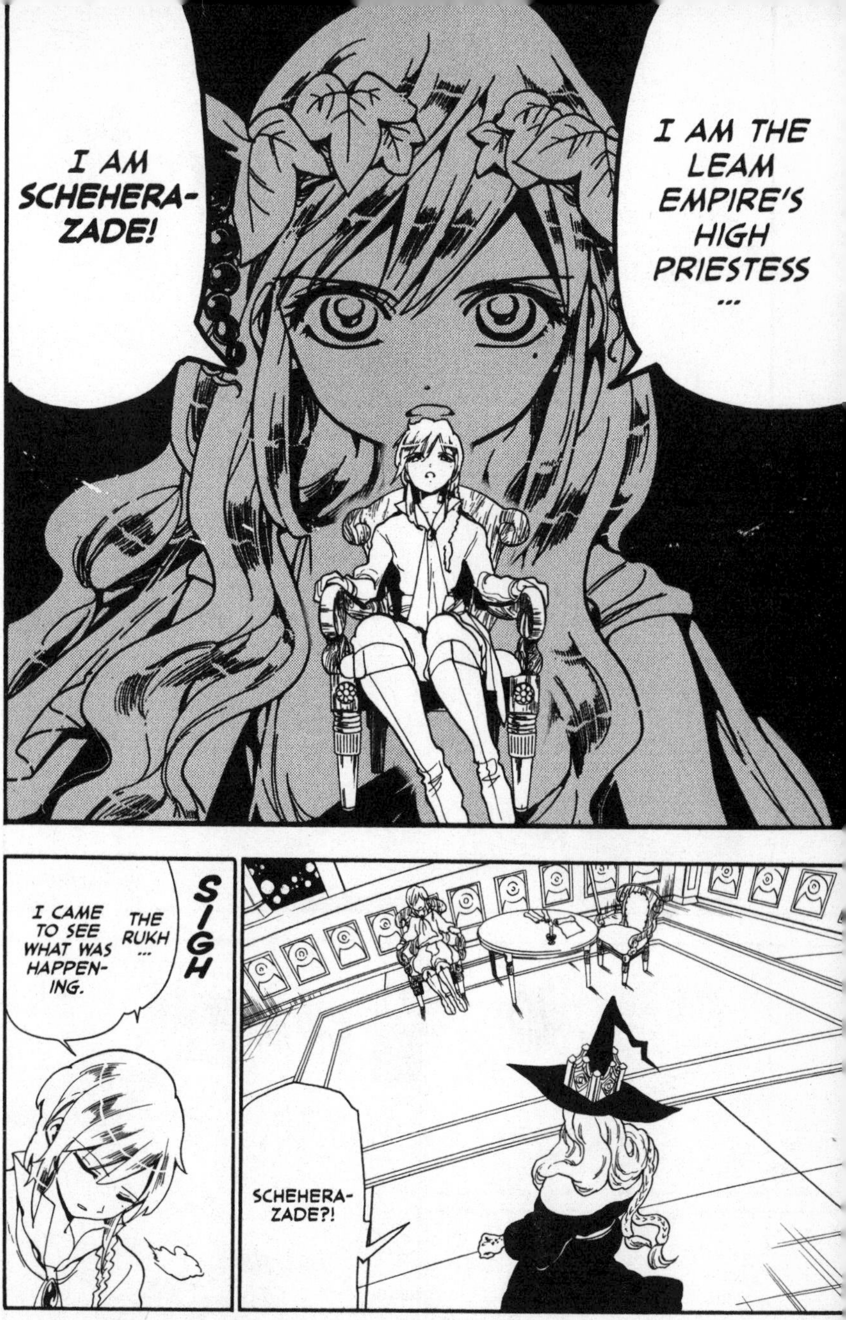
I AM THE LEAM EMPIRE'S HIGH PRIESTESS ...
I AM SCHEHERAZADE!
SCHEHERAZADE?!
SIGH
THE RUKH ...
I CAME TO SEE WHAT WAS HAPPENING.

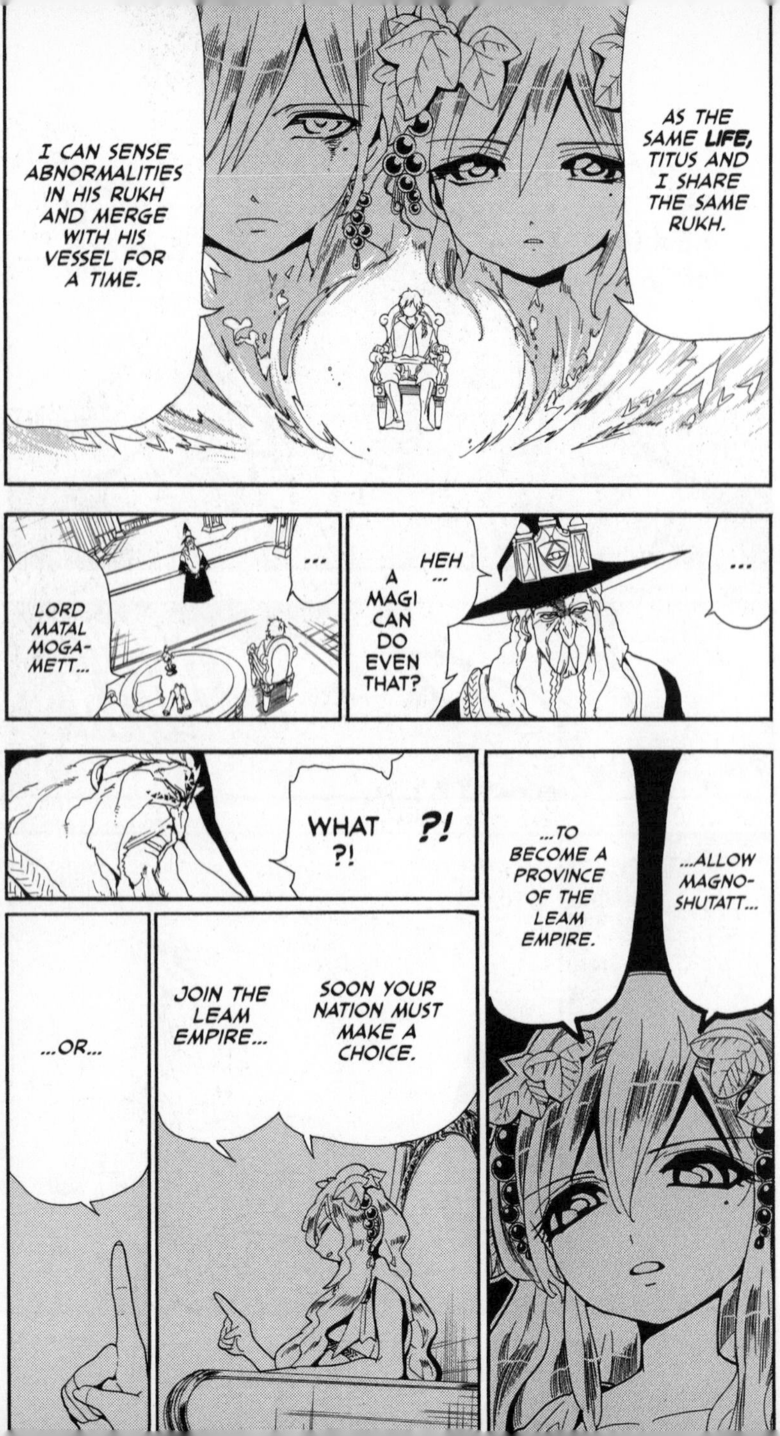

AS THE SAME **LIFE,** TITUS AND I SHARE THE SAME RUKH.
I CAN SENSE ABNORMALITIES IN HIS RUKH AND MERGE WITH HIS VESSEL FOR A TIME.
...
HEH ...
A MAGI CAN DO EVEN THAT?
...
LORD MATAL MOGAMETT...
...ALLOW MAGNO-SHUTATT...
...TO BECOME A PROVINCE OF THE LEAM EMPIRE.
WHAT ?!
?!
SOON YOUR NATION MUST MAKE A CHOICE.
JOIN THE LEAM EMPIRE...
...OR...

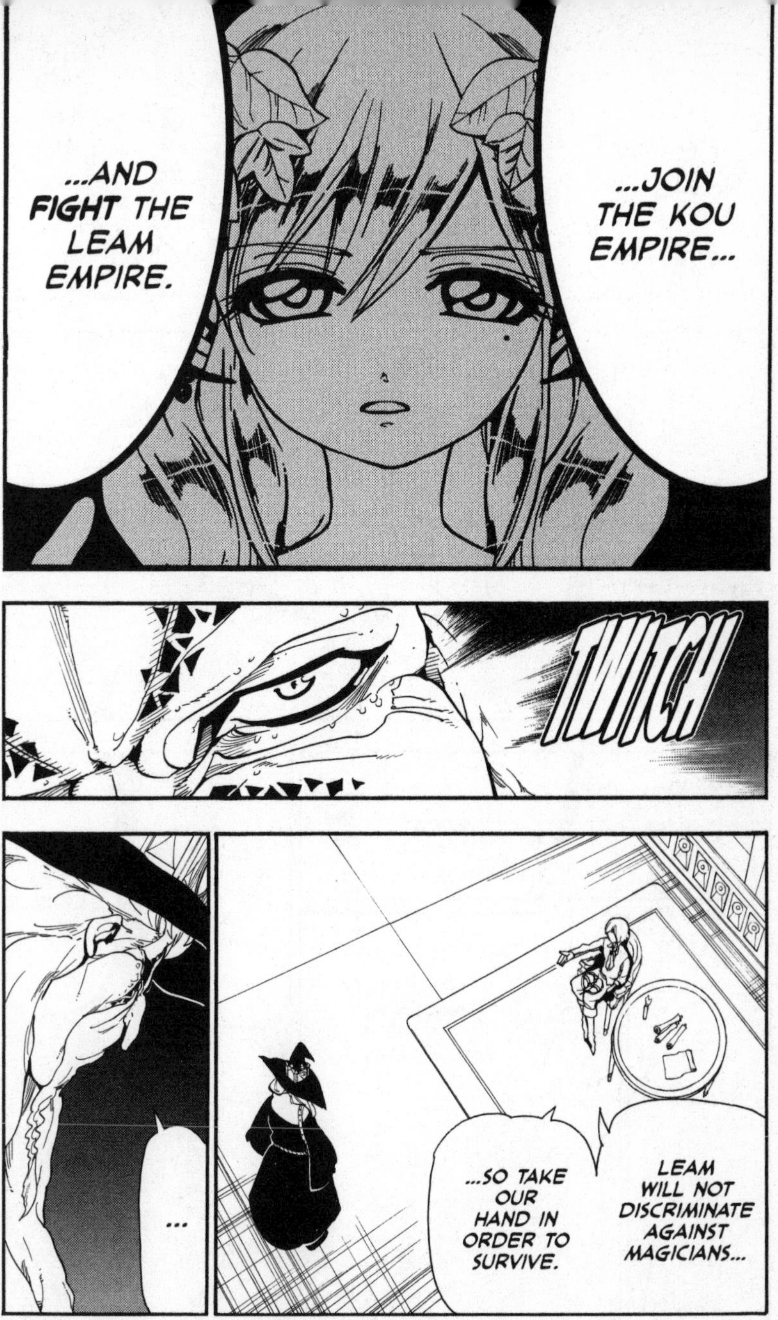
...JOIN THE KOU EMPIRE...
...AND FIGHT THE LEAM EMPIRE.
TWITCH
LEAM WILL NOT DISCRIMINATE AGAINST MAGICIANS...
...SO TAKE OUR HAND IN ORDER TO SURVIVE.
...

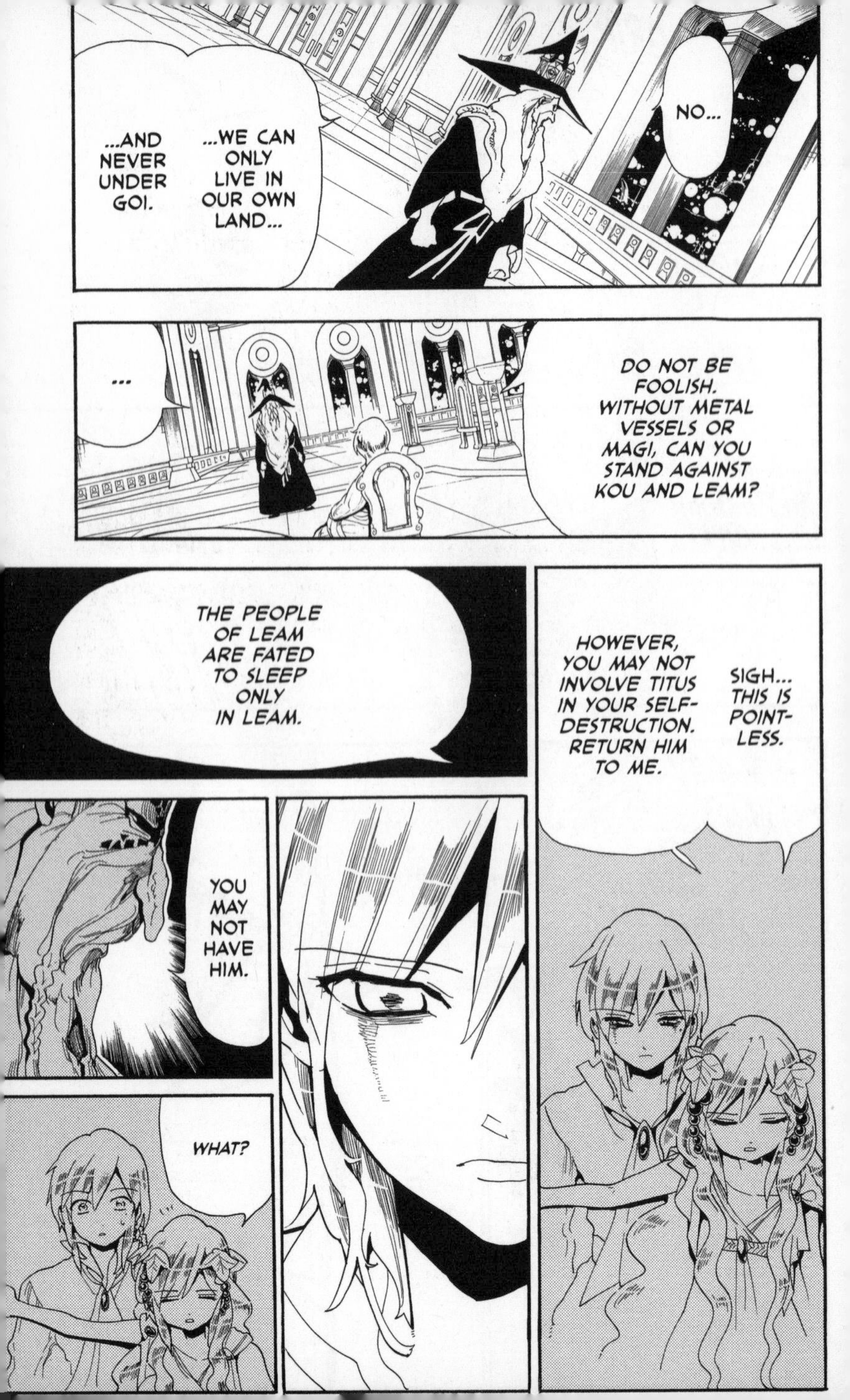
NO...
...WE CAN ONLY LIVE IN OUR OWN LAND...
...AND NEVER UNDER GOI.
DO NOT BE FOOLISH. WITHOUT METAL VESSELS OR MAGI, CAN YOU STAND AGAINST KOU AND LEAM?
...
SIGH... THIS IS POINTLESS.
HOWEVER, YOU MAY NOT INVOLVE TITUS IN YOUR SELF-DESTRUCTION. RETURN HIM TO ME.
THE PEOPLE OF LEAM ARE FATED TO SLEEP ONLY IN LEAM.
YOU MAY NOT HAVE HIM.
WHAT?

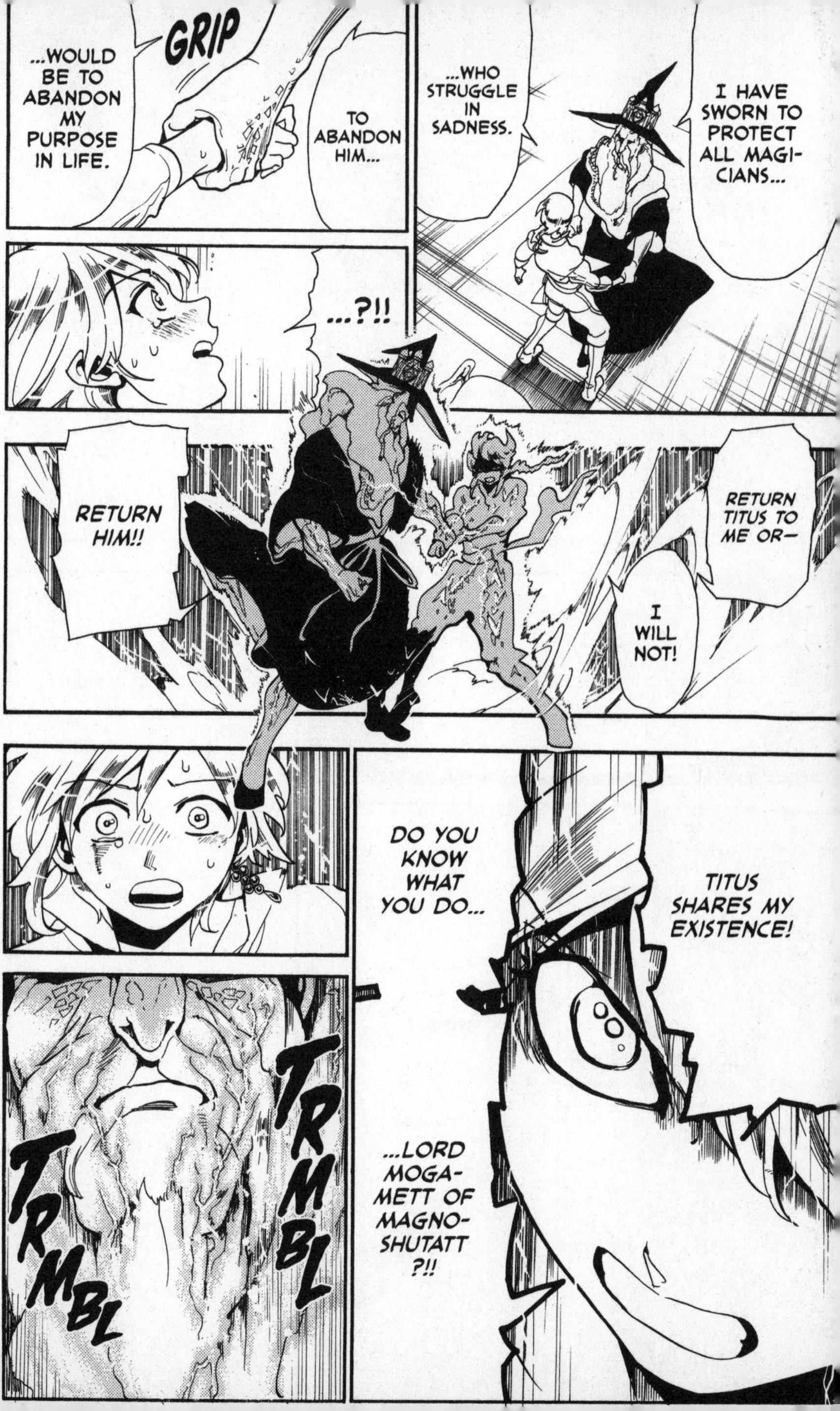
I HAVE SWORN TO PROTECT ALL MAGICIANS...
...WHO STRUGGLE IN SADNESS.
GRIP
TO ABANDON HIM...
...WOULD BE TO ABANDON MY PURPOSE IN LIFE.
...?!!
RETURN TITUS TO ME OR—
I WILL NOT!
RETURN HIM!!
TITUS SHARES MY EXISTENCE!
DO YOU KNOW WHAT YOU DO...
...LORD MOGAMETT OF MAGNOSHUTATT ?!!
TRMBL
TRMBL

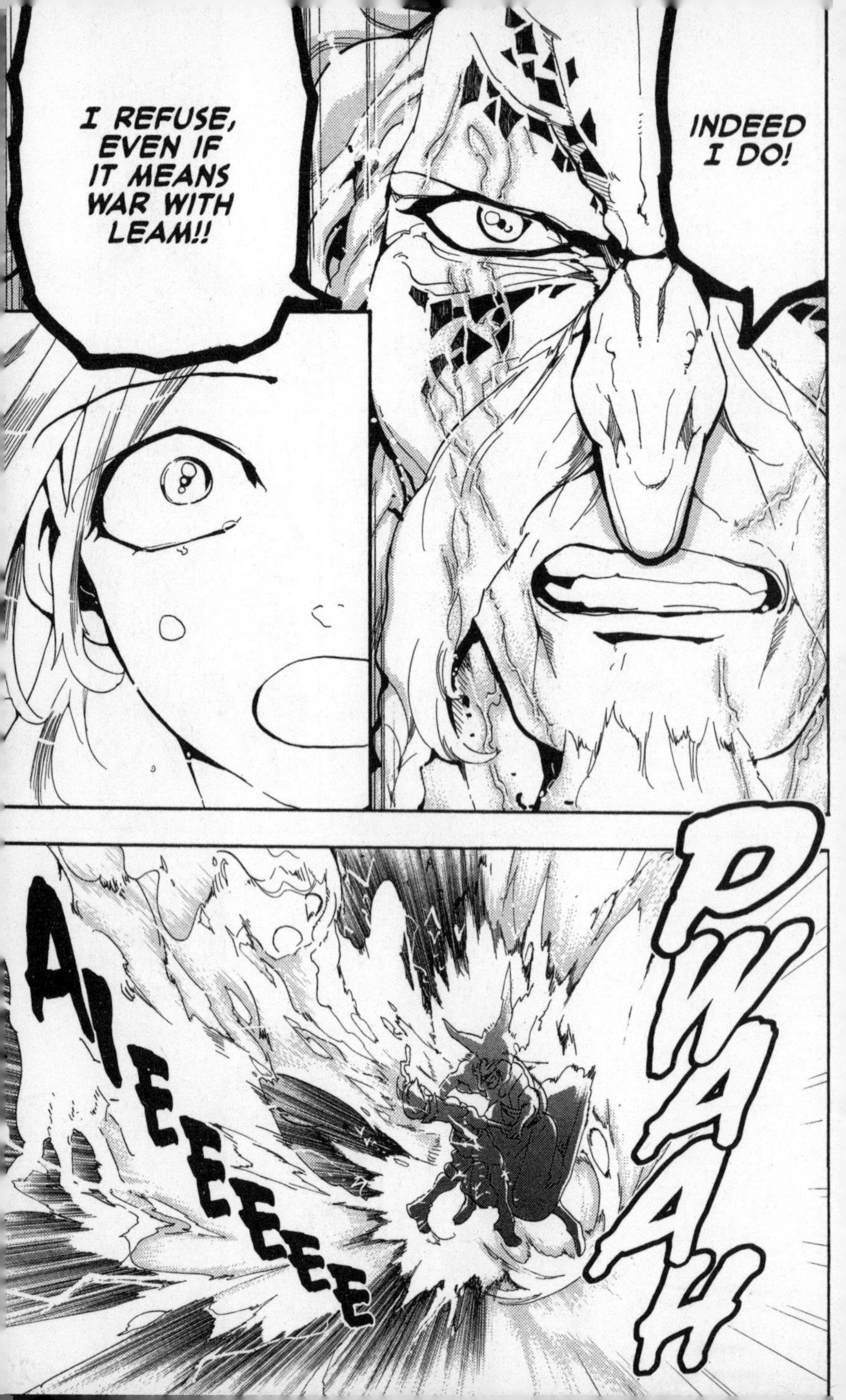
INDEED I DO!
I REFUSE, EVEN IF IT MEANS WAR WITH LEAM!!
PWAAH
AIEEEEEEE

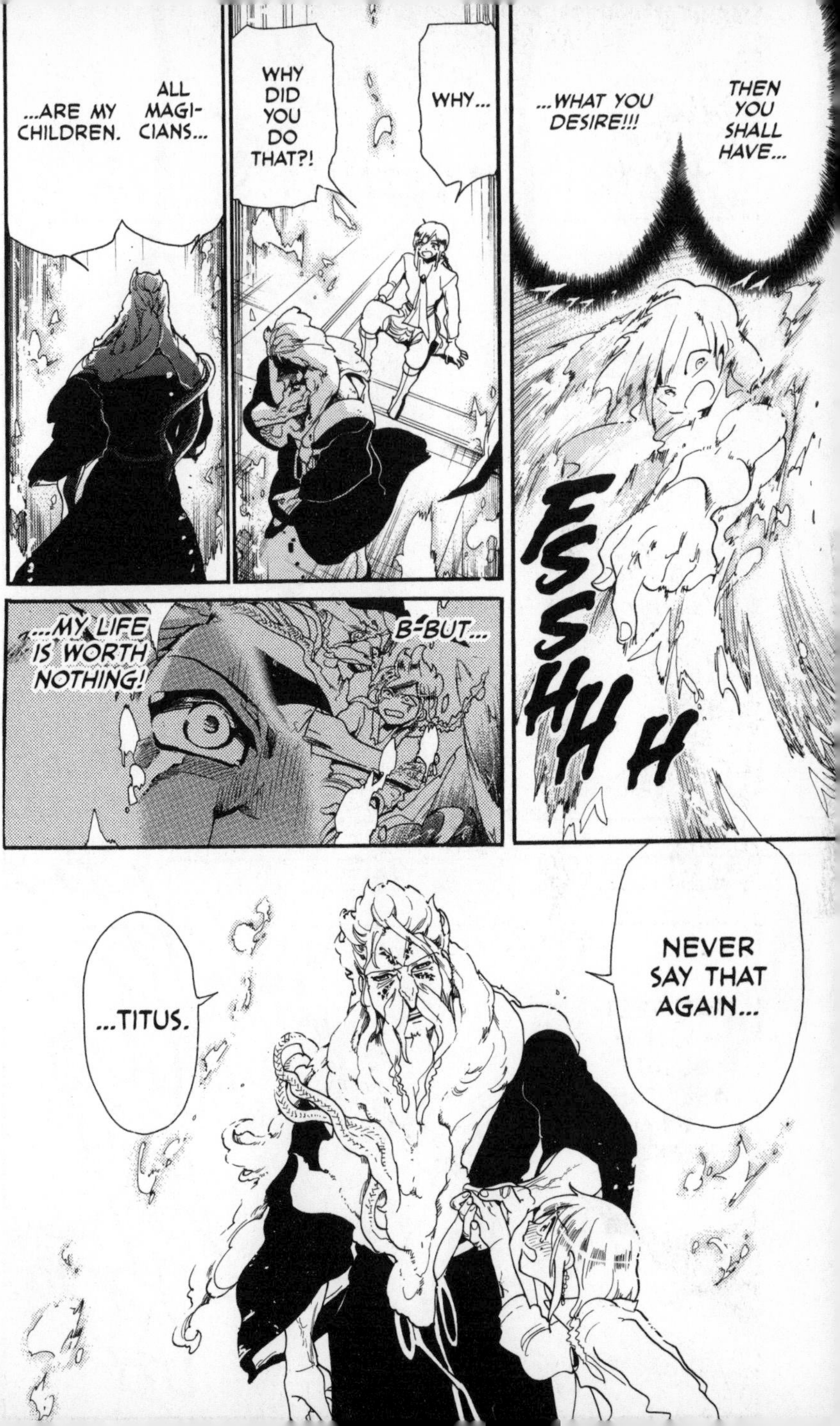
THEN YOU SHALL HAVE...
...WHAT YOU DESIRE!!!
FSSHHHH
WHY...
WHY DID YOU DO THAT?!
ALL MAGICIANS...
...ARE MY CHILDREN.
B-BUT...
...MY LIFE IS WORTH NOTHING!
NEVER SAY THAT AGAIN...
...TITUS.

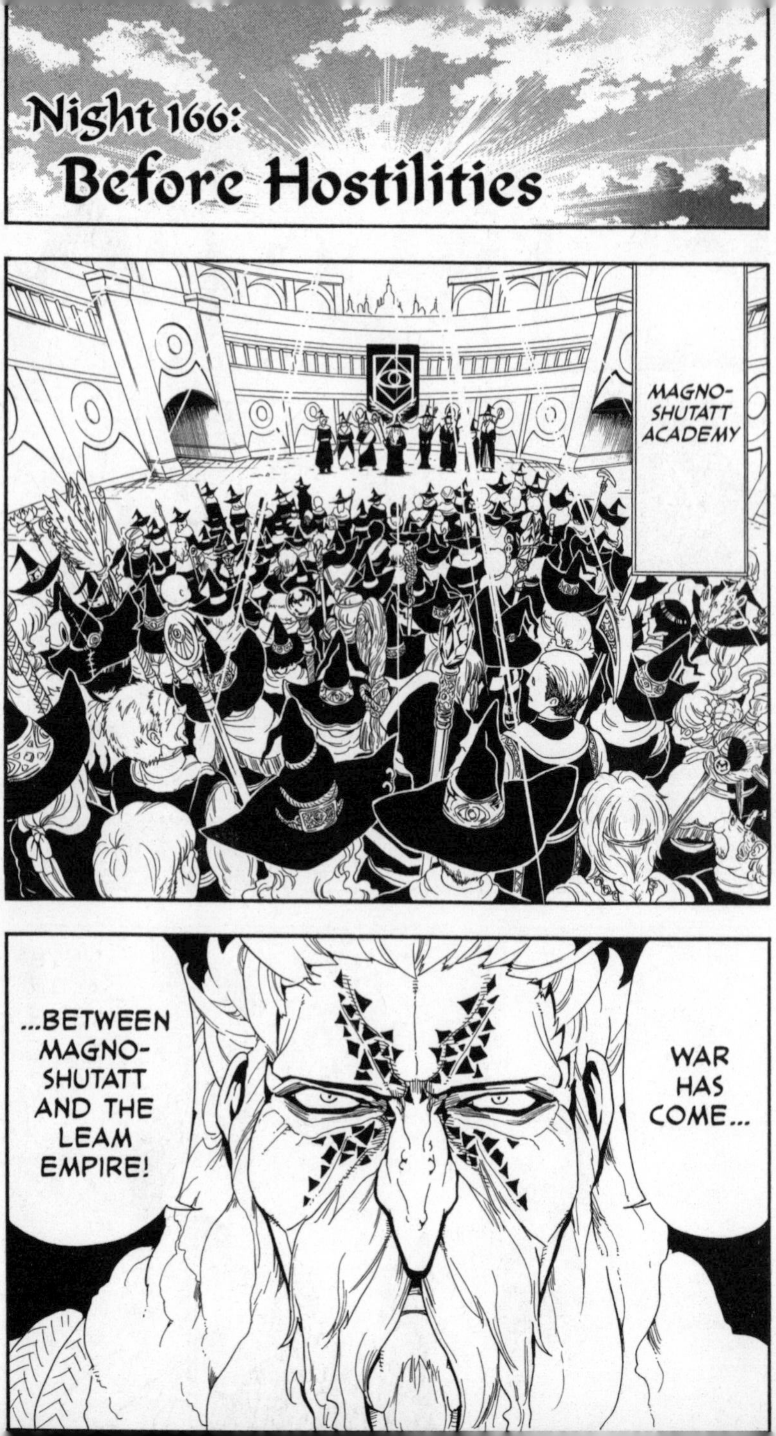
Night 166:
Before Hostilities
MAGNO-SHUTATT ACADEMY
WAR HAS COME...
...BETWEEN MAGNO-SHUTATT AND THE LEAM EMPIRE!

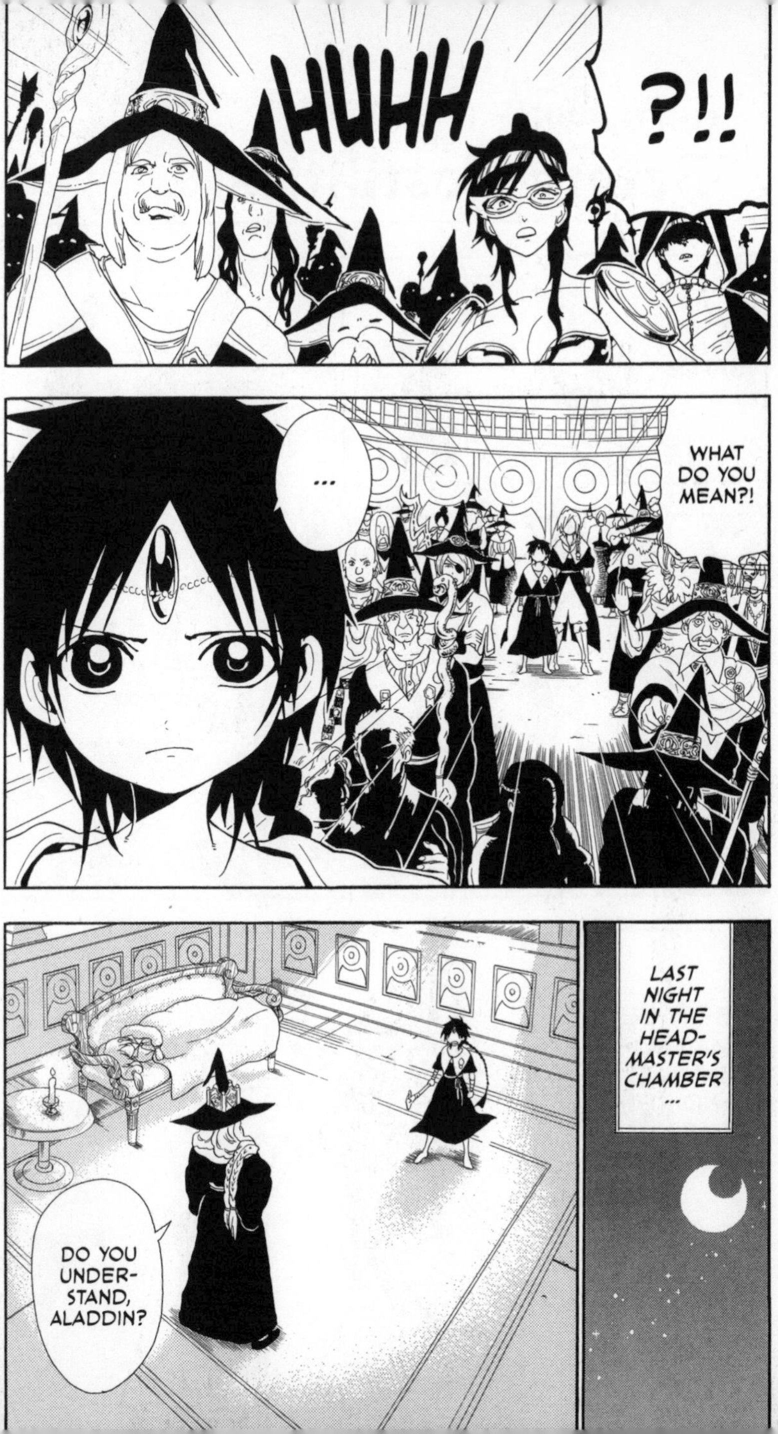
HUHH
?!!
WHAT DO YOU MEAN?!
...
LAST NIGHT IN THE HEAD-MASTER'S CHAMBER...
DO YOU UNDER-STAND, ALADDIN?

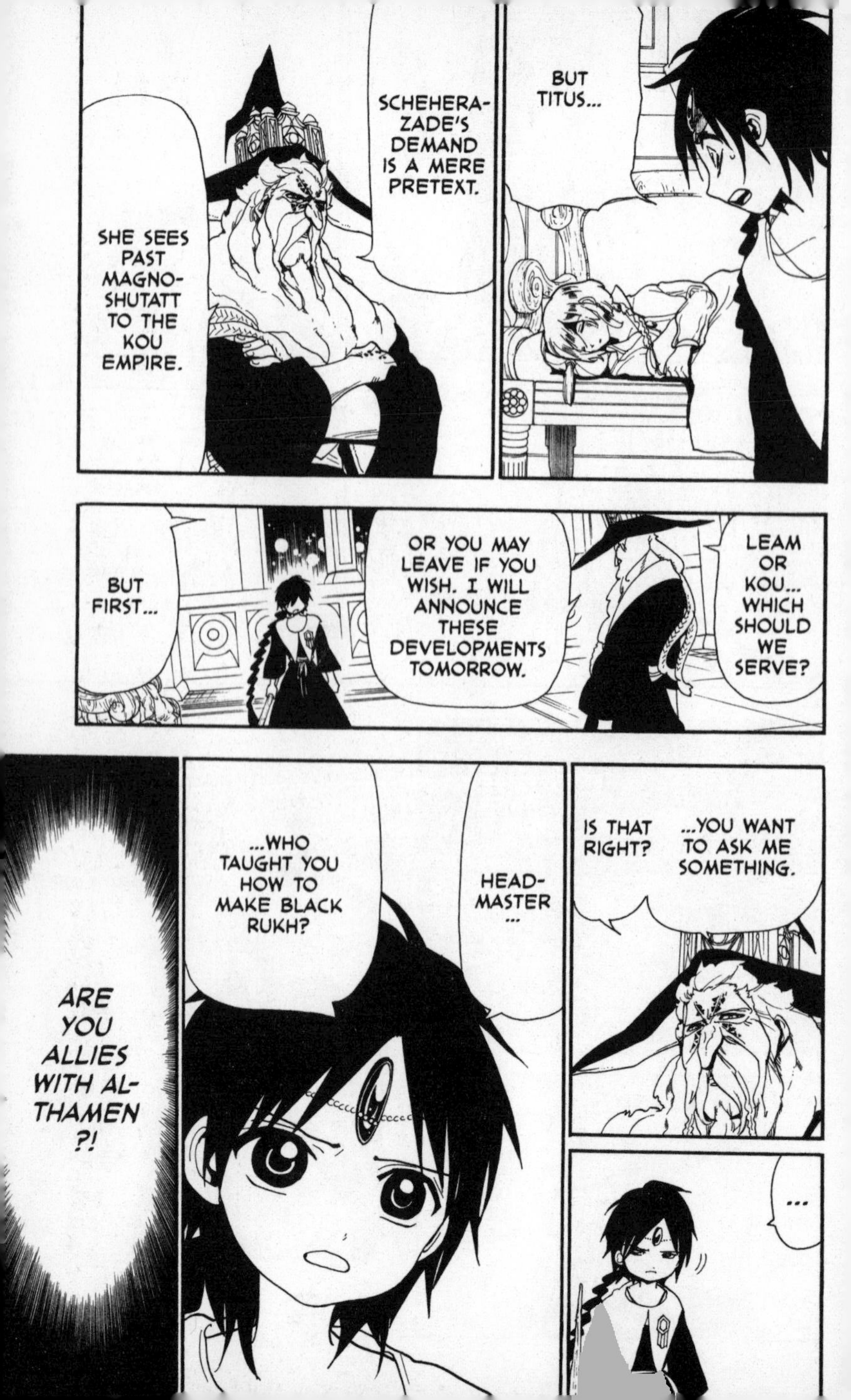
BUT TITUS...
SCHEHERAZADE'S DEMAND IS A MERE PRETEXT.
SHE SEES PAST MAGNOSHUTATT TO THE KOU EMPIRE.
LEAM OR KOU... WHICH SHOULD WE SERVE?
OR YOU MAY LEAVE IF YOU WISH. I WILL ANNOUNCE THESE DEVELOPMENTS TOMORROW.
BUT FIRST...
...YOU WANT TO ASK ME SOMETHING.
IS THAT RIGHT?
...
HEADMASTER...
...WHO TAUGHT YOU HOW TO MAKE BLACK RUKH?
ARE YOU ALLIES WITH AL-THAMEN?!

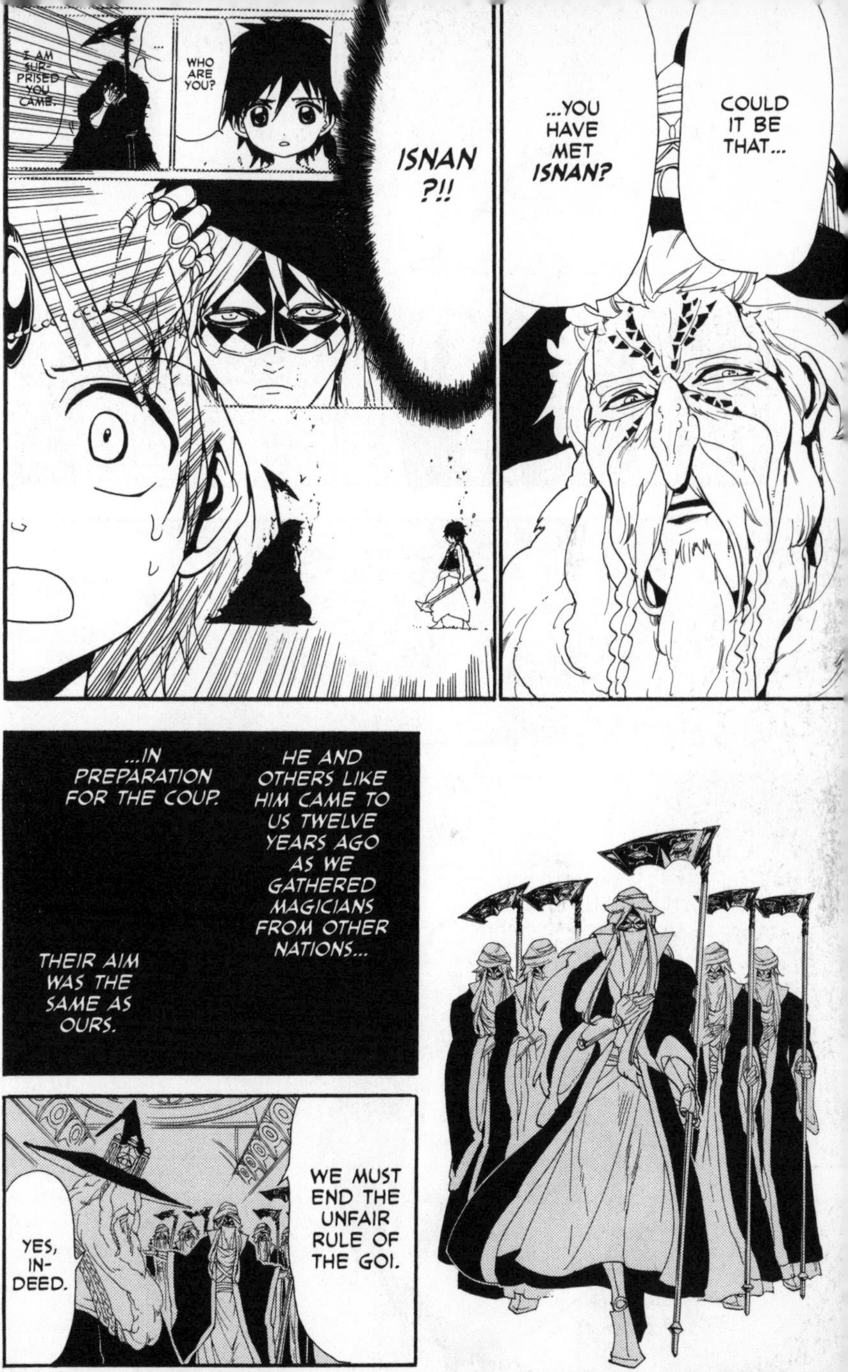
COULD IT BE THAT...
...YOU HAVE MET ISNAN?
ISNAN ?!!
WHO ARE YOU?
...
I AM SUR-PRISED YOU CAME.
HE AND OTHERS LIKE HIM CAME TO US TWELVE YEARS AGO AS WE GATHERED MAGICIANS FROM OTHER NATIONS...
...IN PREPARATION FOR THE COUP.
THEIR AIM WAS THE SAME AS OURS.
WE MUST END THE UNFAIR RULE OF THE GOI.
YES, IN-DEED.

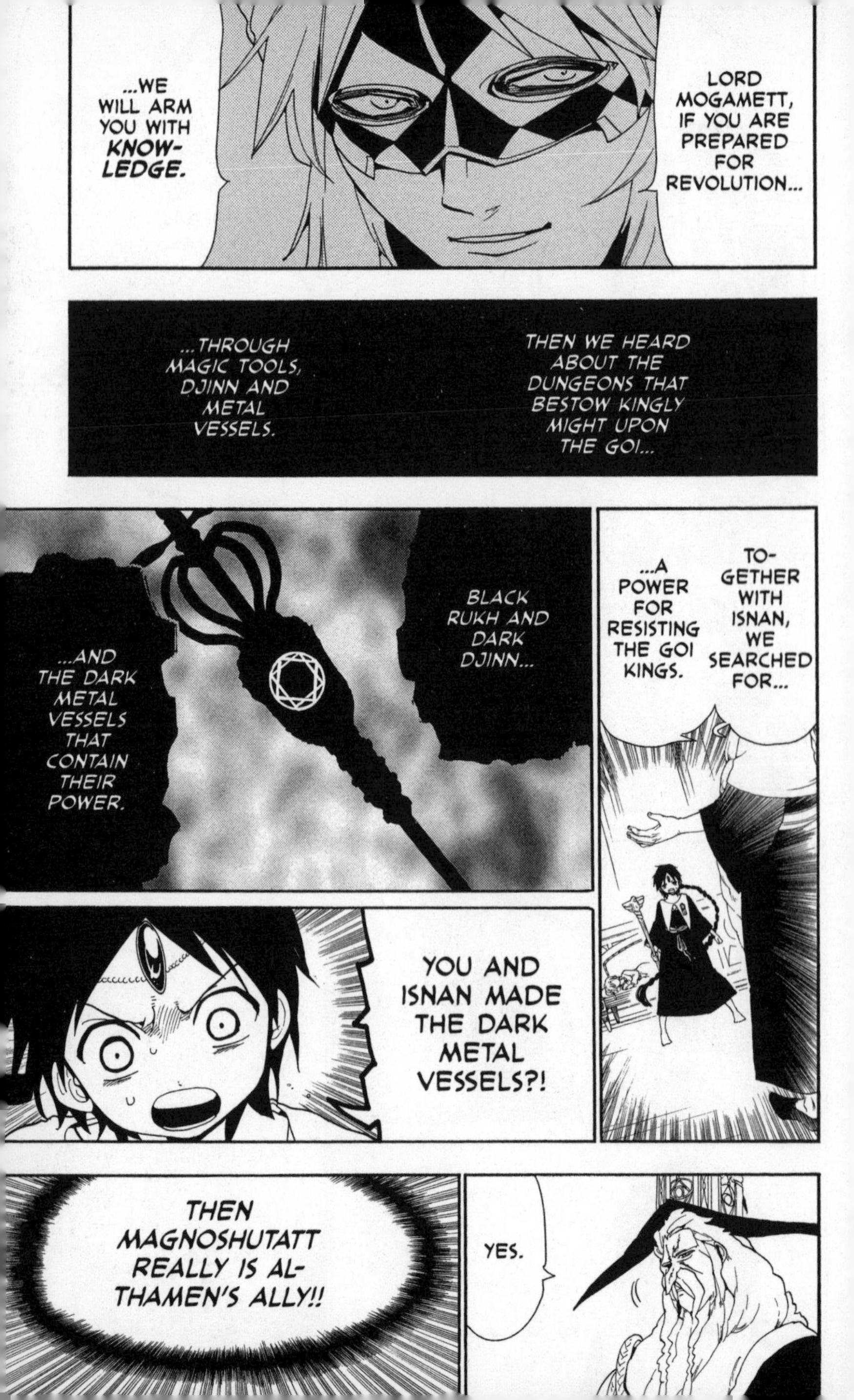

LORD MOGAMETT, IF YOU ARE PREPARED FOR REVOLUTION...
...WE WILL ARM YOU WITH KNOWLEDGE.
THEN WE HEARD ABOUT THE DUNGEONS THAT BESTOW KINGLY MIGHT UPON THE GOI...
...THROUGH MAGIC TOOLS, DJINN AND METAL VESSELS.
TOGETHER WITH ISNAN, WE SEARCHED FOR...
...A POWER FOR RESISTING THE GOI KINGS.
BLACK RUKH AND DARK DJINN...
...AND THE DARK METAL VESSELS THAT CONTAIN THEIR POWER.
YOU AND ISNAN MADE THE DARK METAL VESSELS?!
YES.
THEN MAGNOSHUTATT REALLY IS AL-THAMEN'S ALLY!!

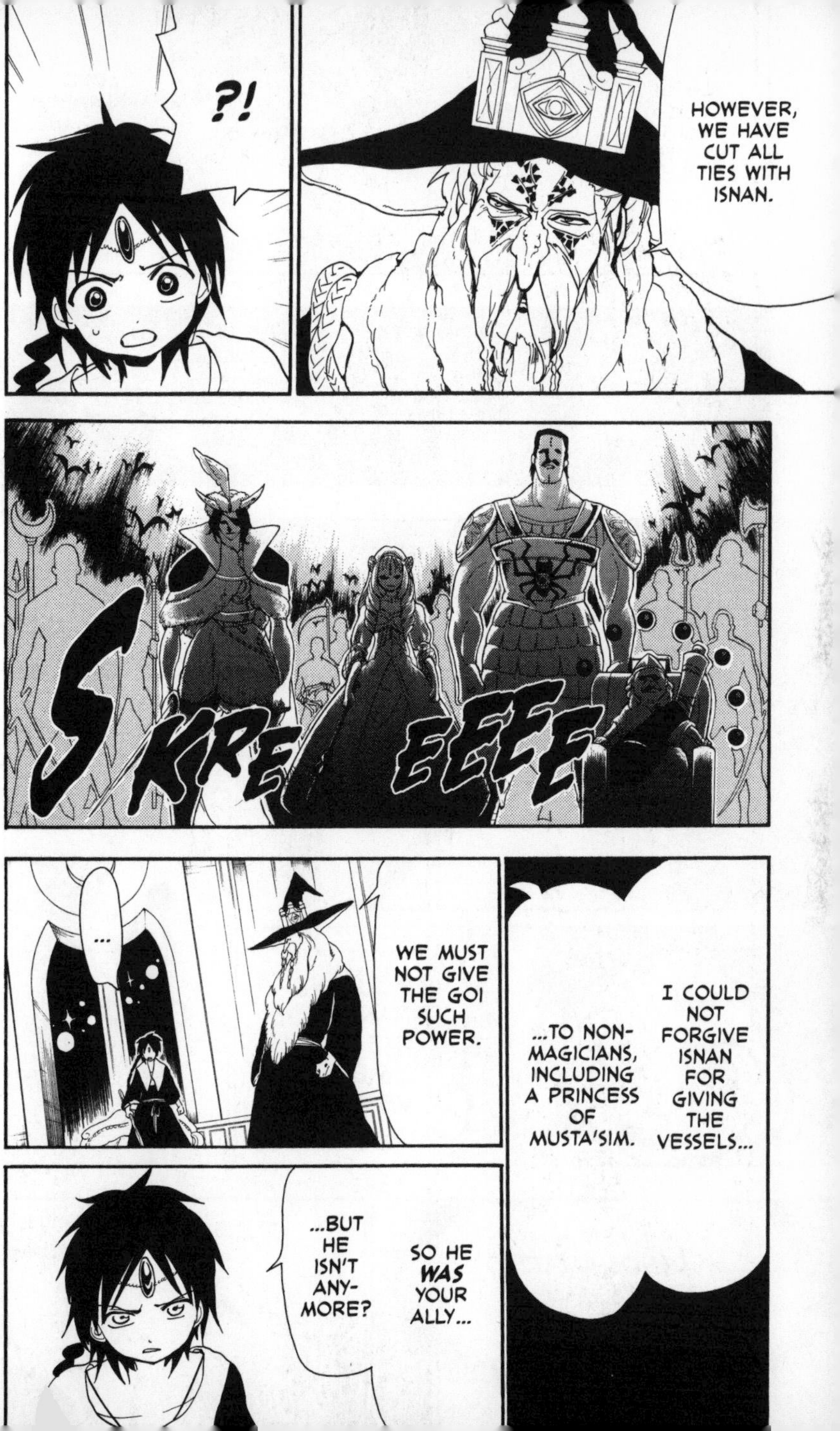
HOWEVER, WE HAVE CUT ALL TIES WITH ISNAN.
?!
SKREEEEEE
I COULD NOT FORGIVE ISNAN FOR GIVING THE VESSELS...
...TO NON-MAGICIANS, INCLUDING A PRINCESS OF MUSTA'SIM.
WE MUST NOT GIVE THE GOI SUCH POWER.
...
SO HE WAS YOUR ALLY...
...BUT HE ISN'T ANYMORE?

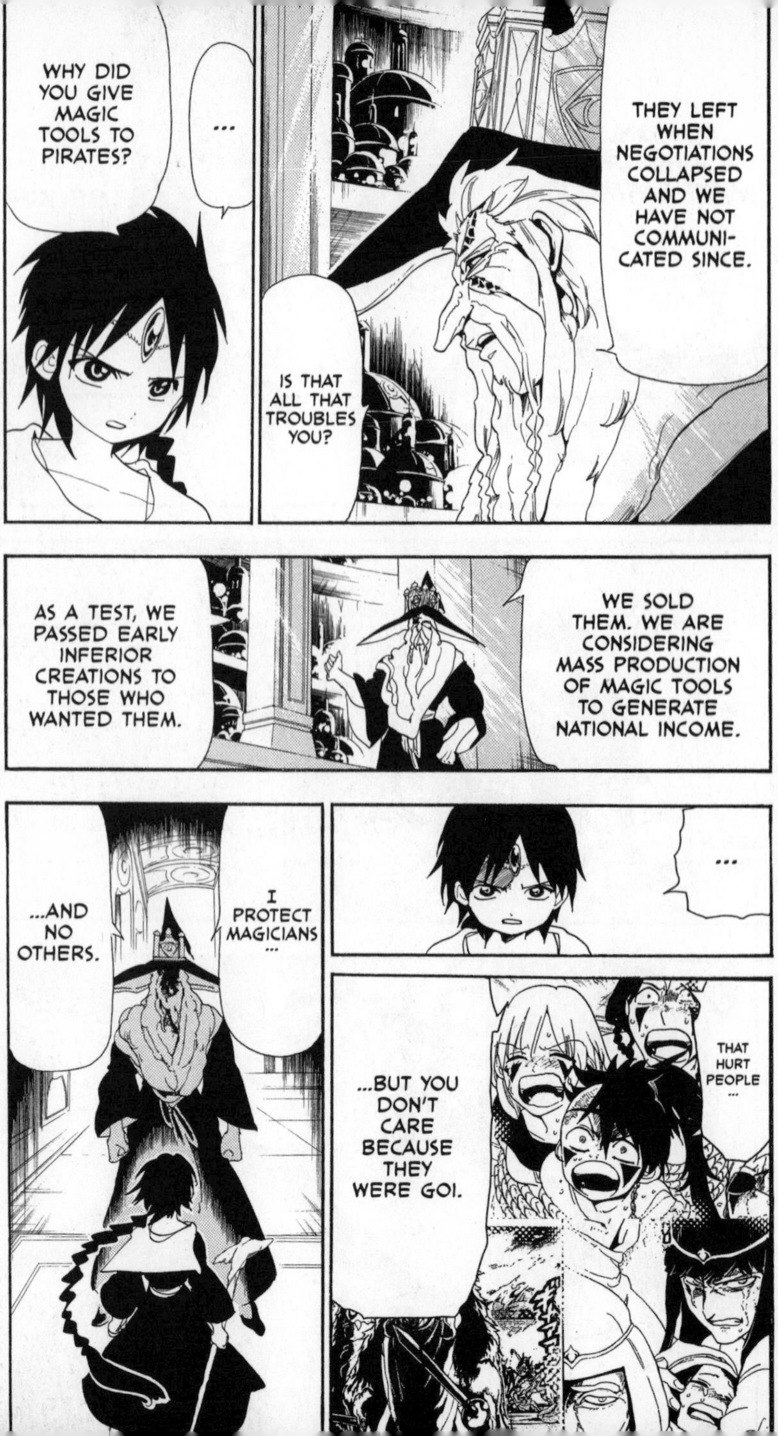
THEY LEFT WHEN NEGOTIATIONS COLLAPSED AND WE HAVE NOT COMMUNICATED SINCE.
IS THAT ALL THAT TROUBLES YOU?
...
WHY DID YOU GIVE MAGIC TOOLS TO PIRATES?
WE SOLD THEM. WE ARE CONSIDERING MASS PRODUCTION OF MAGIC TOOLS TO GENERATE NATIONAL INCOME.
AS A TEST, WE PASSED EARLY INFERIOR CREATIONS TO THOSE WHO WANTED THEM.
...
THAT HURT PEOPLE ...
...BUT YOU DON'T CARE BECAUSE THEY WERE GOI.
I PROTECT MAGICIANS ...
...AND NO OTHERS.

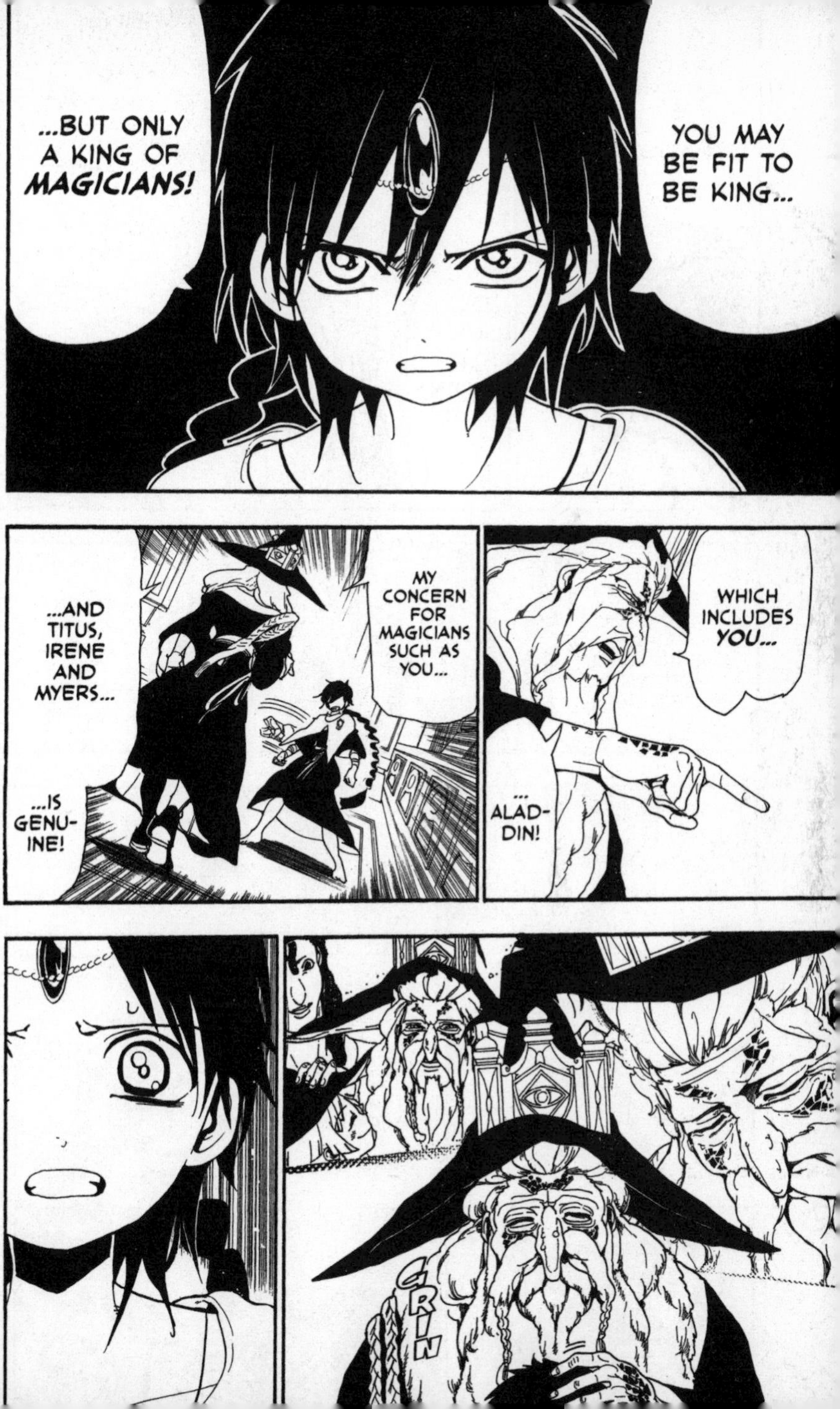
YOU MAY BE FIT TO BE KING...
...BUT ONLY A KING OF MAGICIANS!
WHICH INCLUDES YOU...
...ALAD-DIN!
MY CONCERN FOR MAGICIANS SUCH AS YOU...
...AND TITUS, IRENE AND MYERS...
...IS GENU-INE!
GRIN

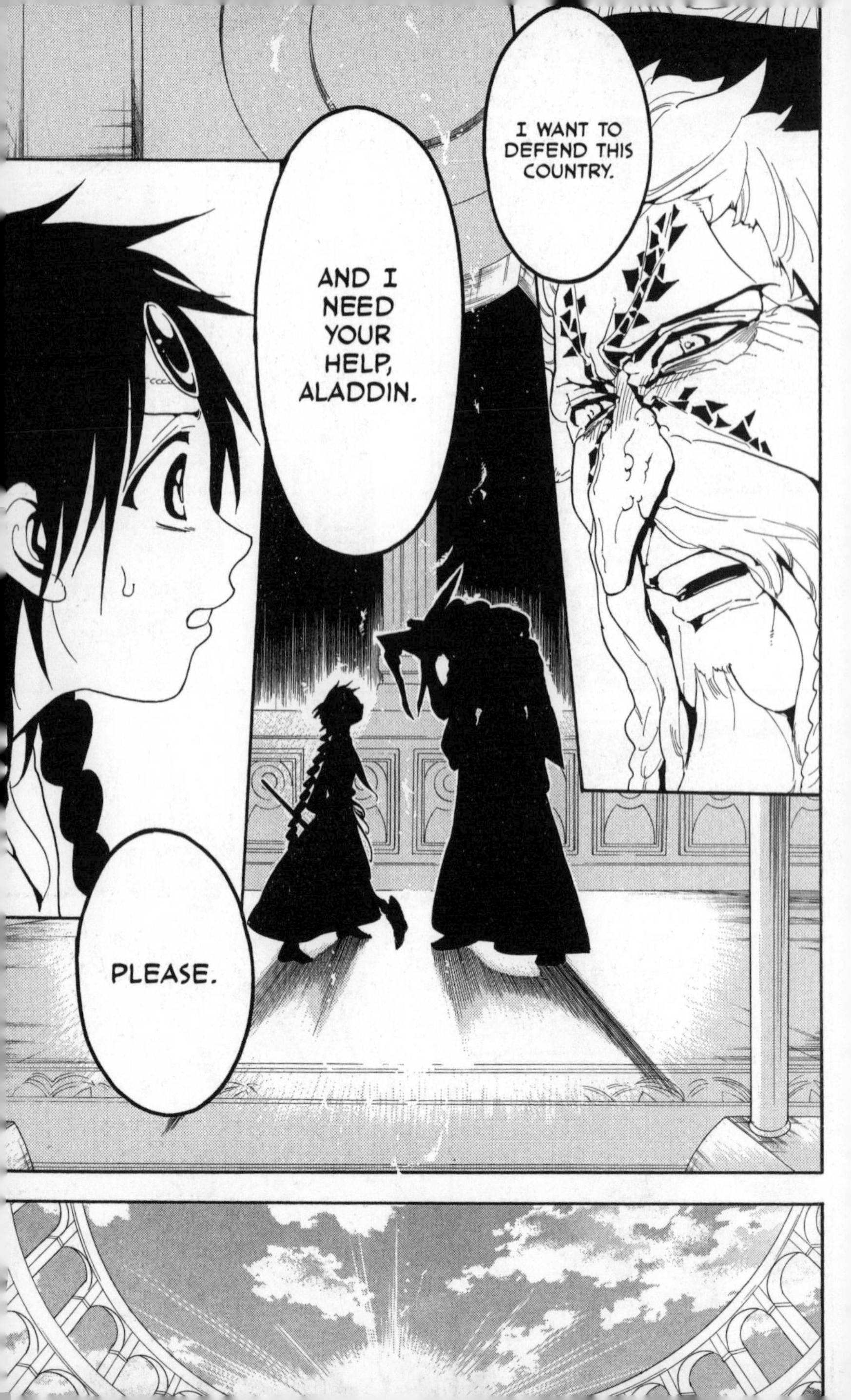
I WANT TO DEFEND THIS COUNTRY.
AND I NEED YOUR HELP, ALADDIN.
PLEASE.

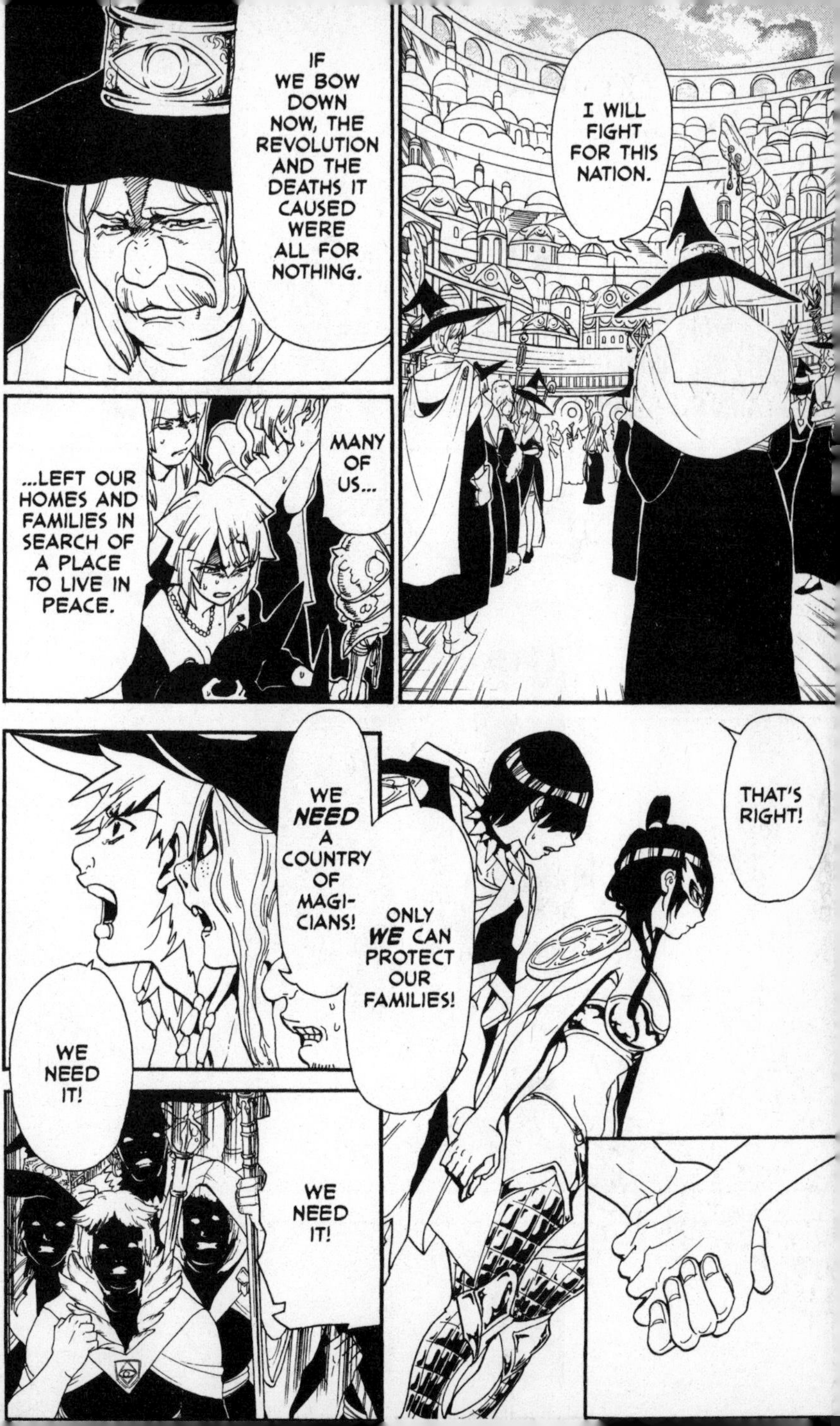

I WILL FIGHT FOR THIS NATION.
IF WE BOW DOWN NOW, THE REVOLUTION AND THE DEATHS IT CAUSED WERE ALL FOR NOTHING.
MANY OF US...
...LEFT OUR HOMES AND FAMILIES IN SEARCH OF A PLACE TO LIVE IN PEACE.
THAT'S RIGHT!
ONLY *WE* CAN PROTECT OUR FAMILIES!
WE *NEED* A COUNTRY OF MAGICIANS!
WE NEED IT!
WE NEED IT!

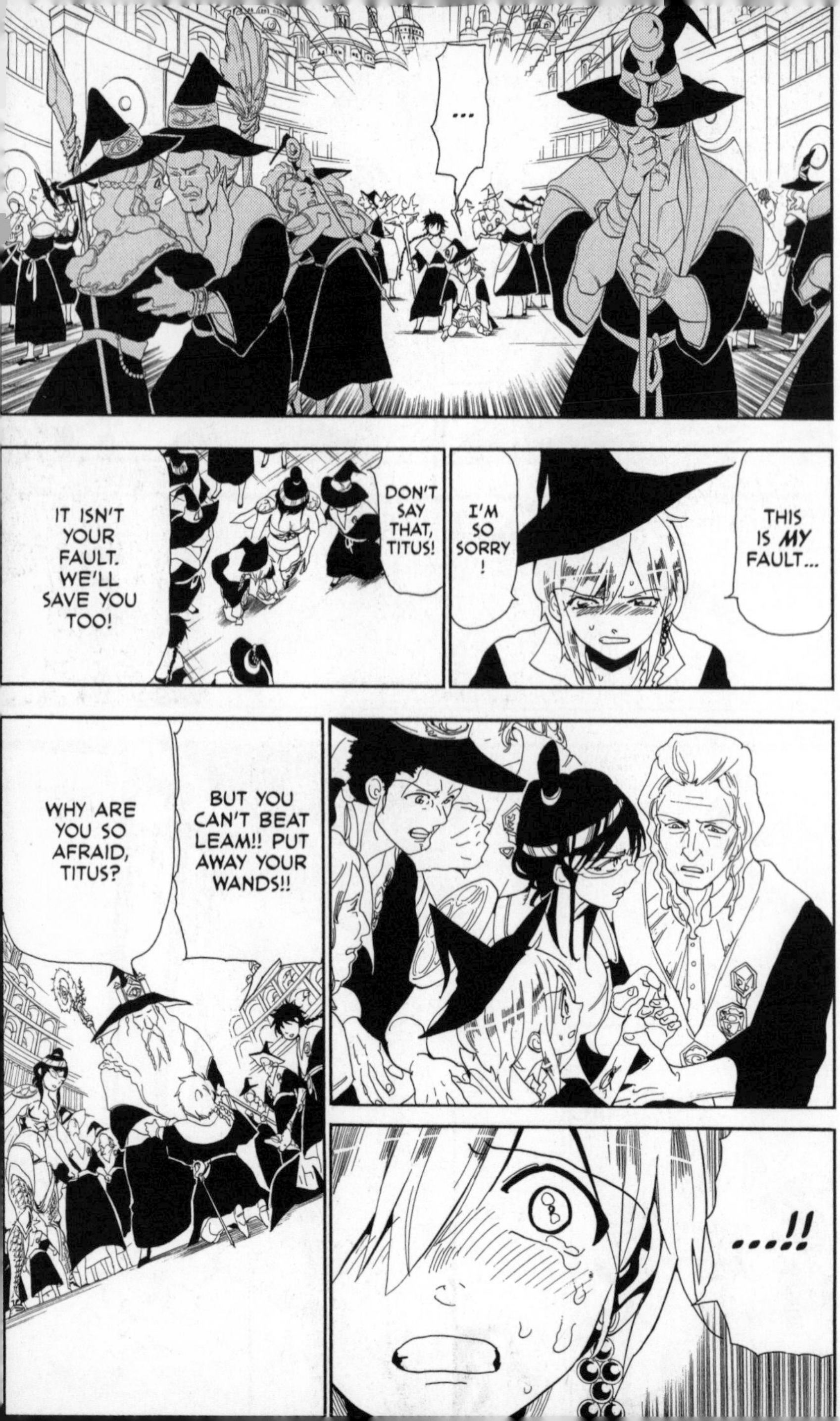
...
THIS IS MY FAULT...
I'M SO SORRY!
DON'T SAY THAT, TITUS!
IT ISN'T YOUR FAULT. WE'LL SAVE YOU TOO!
...!!
BUT YOU CAN'T BEAT LEAM!! PUT AWAY YOUR WANDS!!
WHY ARE YOU SO AFRAID, TITUS?

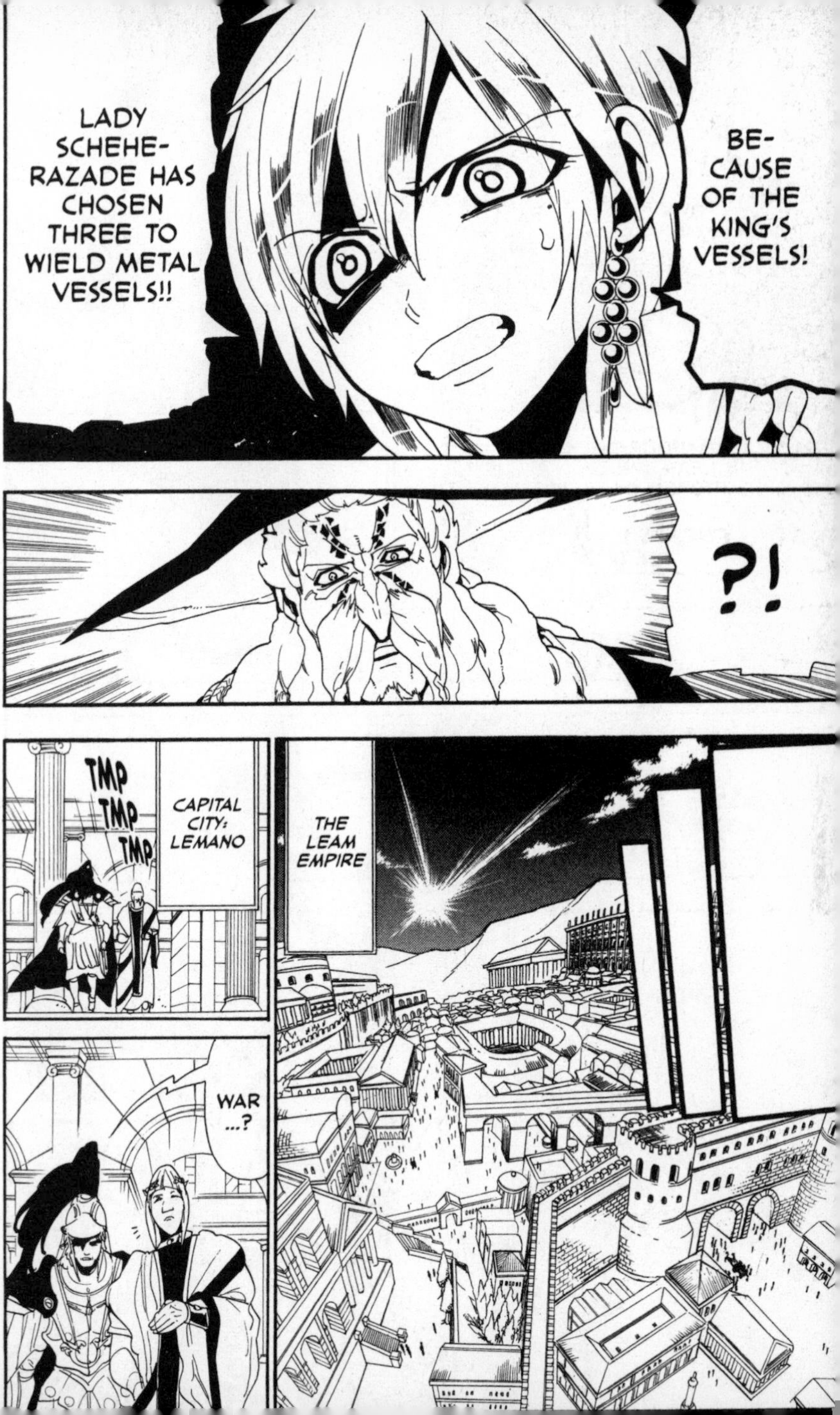
BE-CAUSE OF THE KING'S VESSELS!
LADY SCHEHE-RAZADE HAS CHOSEN THREE TO WIELD METAL VESSELS!!
?!
THE LEAM EMPIRE
CAPITAL CITY: LEMANO
TMP TMP TMP
WAR ...?

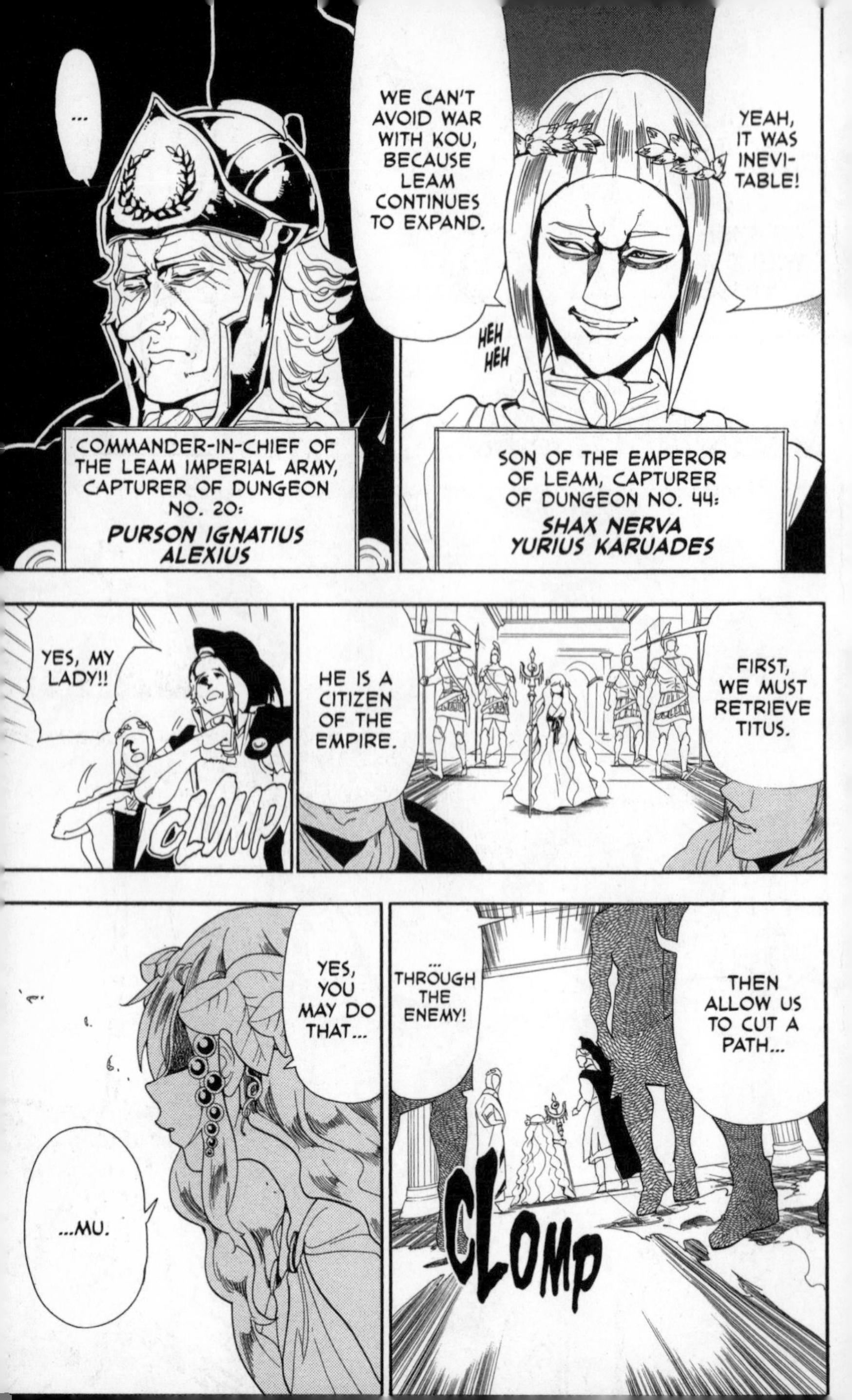
YEAH, IT WAS INEVITABLE!
WE CAN'T AVOID WAR WITH KOU, BECAUSE LEAM CONTINUES TO EXPAND.
HEH HEH
SON OF THE EMPEROR OF LEAM, CAPTURER OF DUNGEON NO. 44: SHAX NERVA YURIUS KARUADES
...
COMMANDER-IN-CHIEF OF THE LEAM IMPERIAL ARMY, CAPTURER OF DUNGEON NO. 20: PURSON IGNATIUS ALEXIUS
FIRST, WE MUST RETRIEVE TITUS.
HE IS A CITIZEN OF THE EMPIRE.
YES, MY LADY!!
CLOMP
THEN ALLOW US TO CUT A PATH...
...THROUGH THE ENEMY!
CLOMP
YES, YOU MAY DO THAT...
...MU.

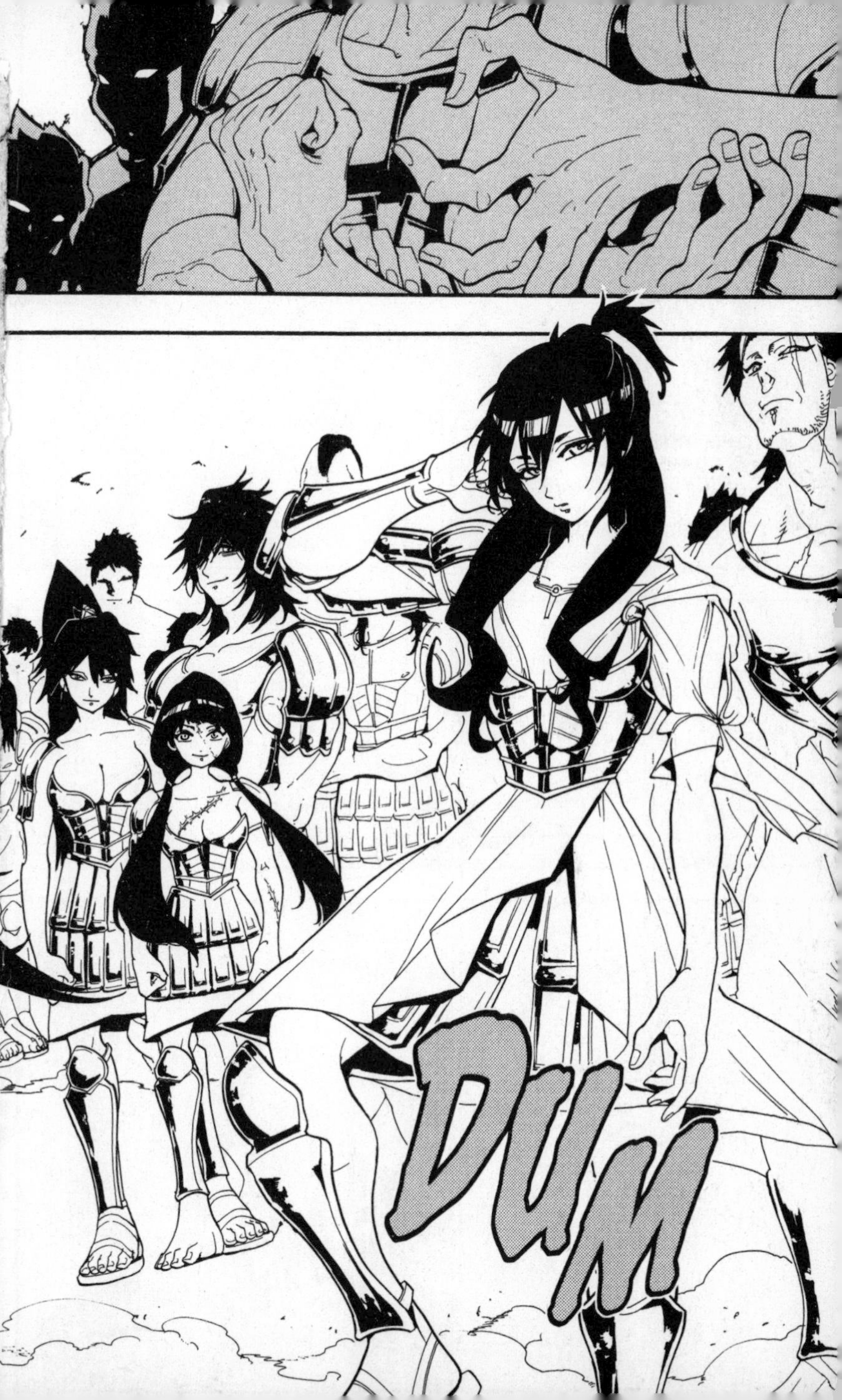
DUM

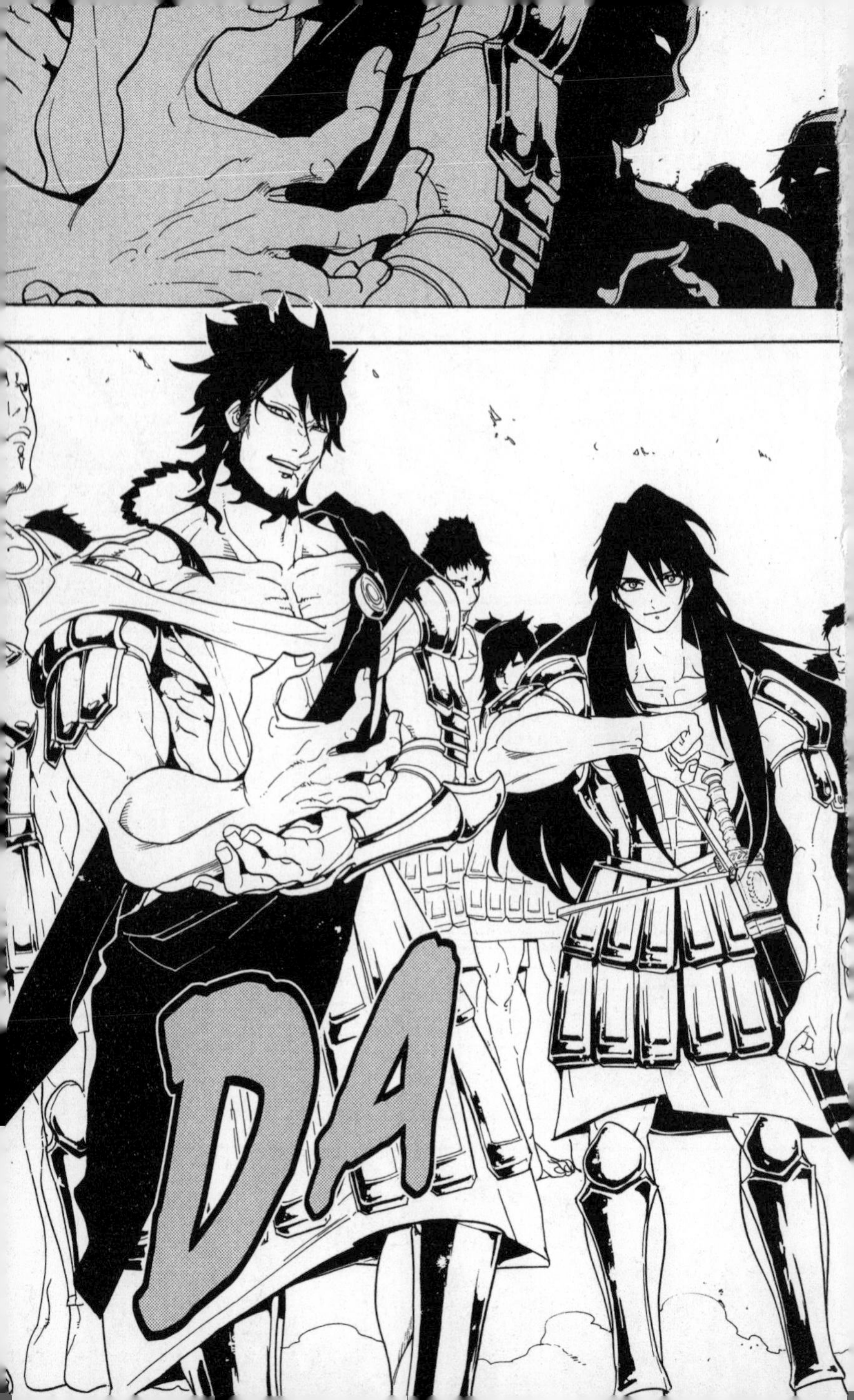
DA

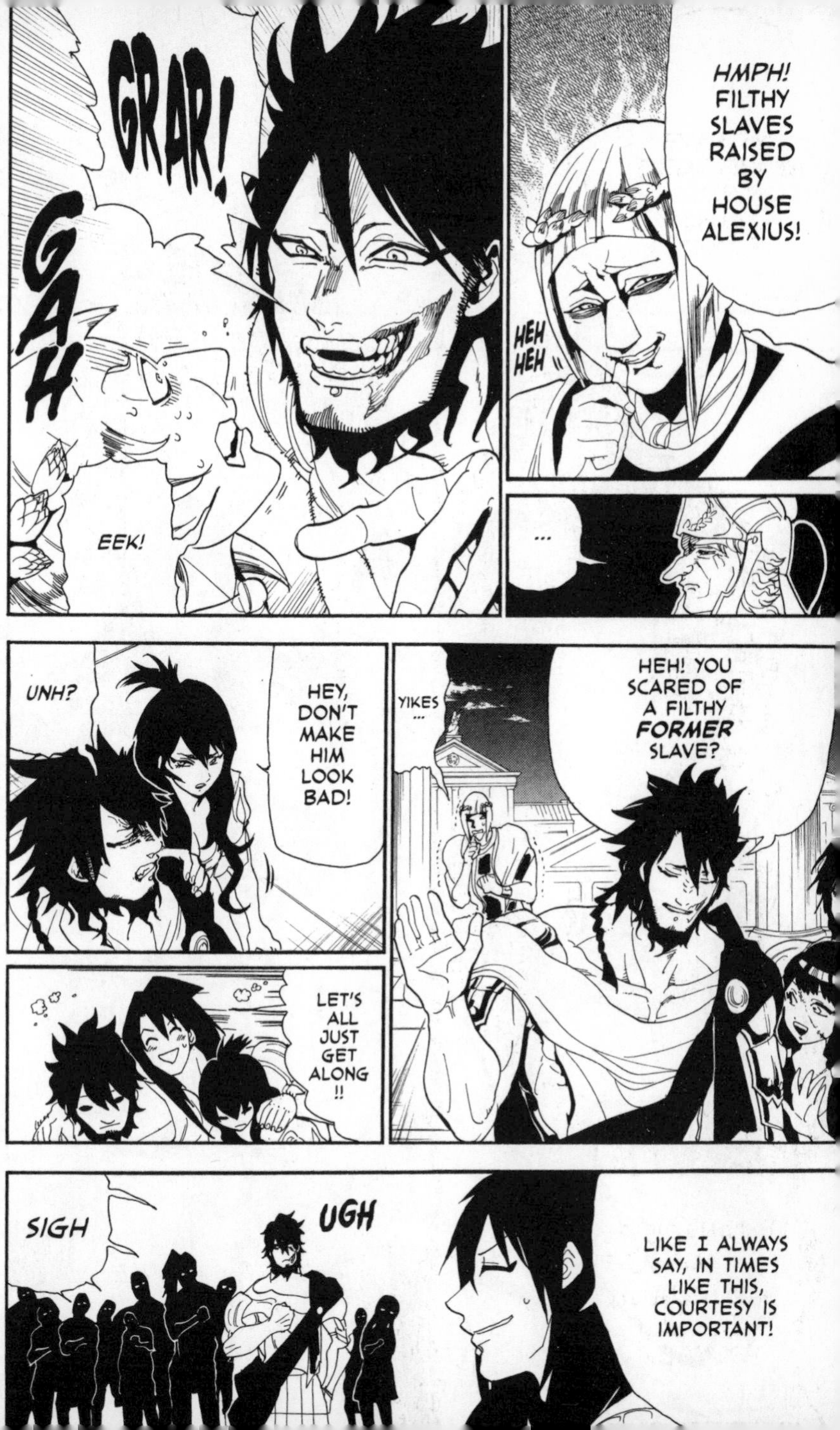
HMPH! FILTHY SLAVES RAISED BY HOUSE ALEXIUS!
HEH HEH
...
GRAR!
GAH
EEK!
HEH! YOU SCARED OF A FILTHY *FORMER* SLAVE?
YIKES ...
HEY, DON'T MAKE HIM LOOK BAD!
UNH?
LET'S ALL JUST GET ALONG !!
LIKE I ALWAYS SAY, IN TIMES LIKE THIS, COURTESY IS IMPORTANT!
UGH
SIGH

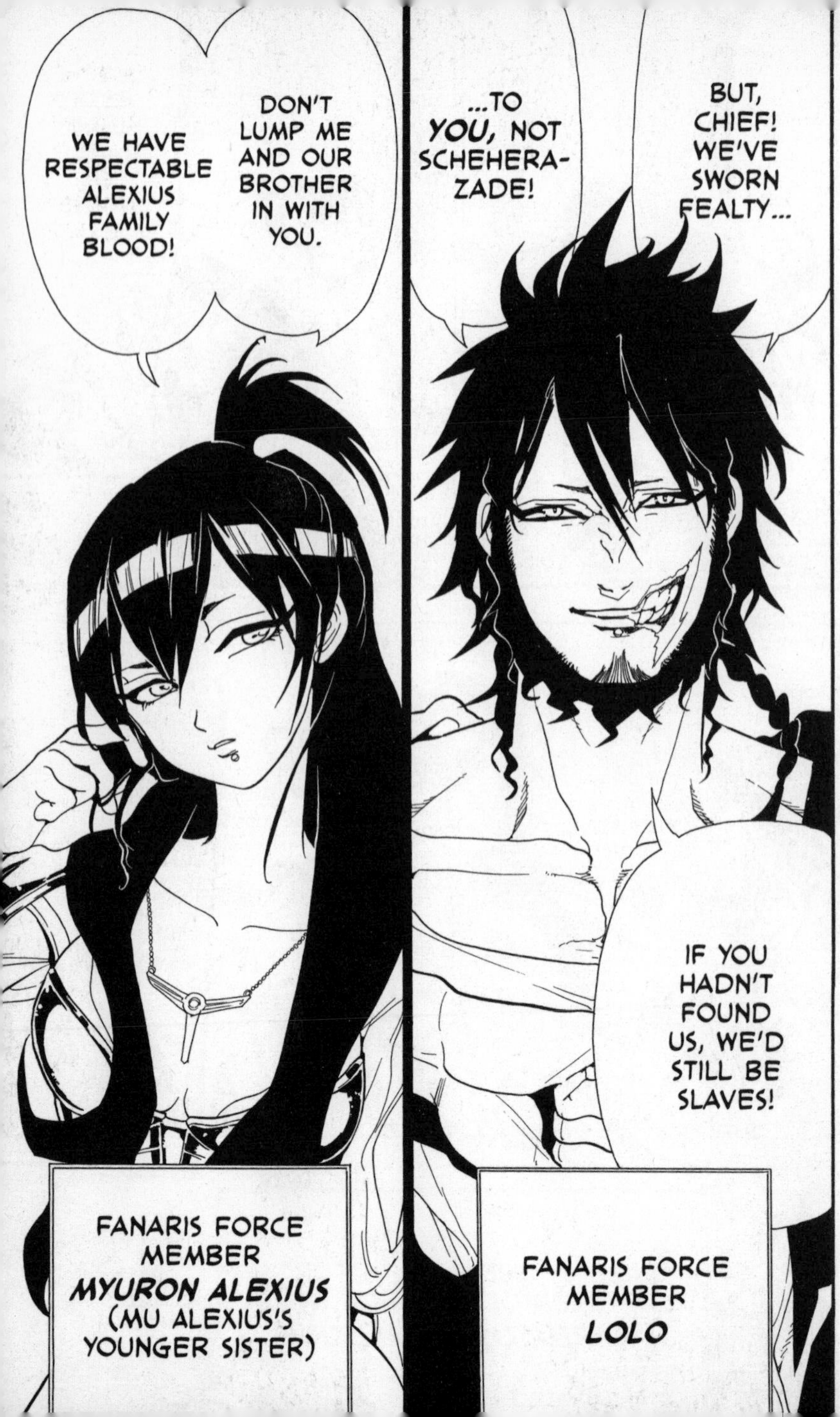
BUT, CHIEF! WE'VE SWORN FEALTY...
...TO YOU, NOT SCHEHERA-ZADE!
IF YOU HADN'T FOUND US, WE'D STILL BE SLAVES!
FANARIS FORCE MEMBER LOLO
DON'T LUMP ME AND OUR BROTHER IN WITH YOU.
WE HAVE RESPECTABLE ALEXIUS FAMILY BLOOD!
FANARIS FORCE MEMBER MYURON ALEXIUS (MU ALEXIUS'S YOUNGER SISTER)

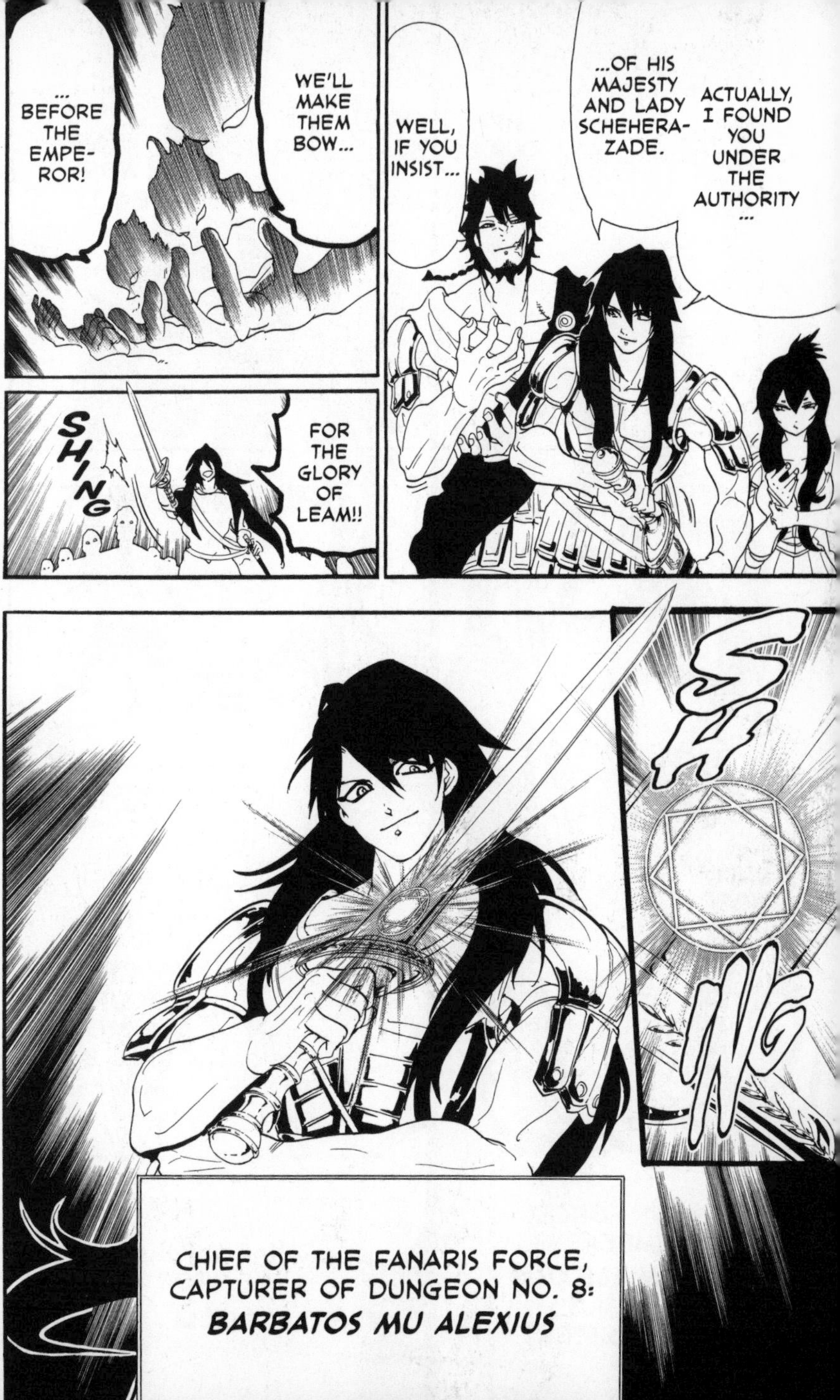

ACTUALLY, I FOUND YOU UNDER THE AUTHORITY...
...OF HIS MAJESTY AND LADY SCHEHERAZADE.
WELL, IF YOU INSIST...
WE'LL MAKE THEM BOW...
...BEFORE THE EMPEROR!
FOR THE GLORY OF LEAM!!
SHING
SHAING
CHIEF OF THE FANARIS FORCE,
CAPTURER OF DUNGEON NO. 8:
BARBATOS MU ALEXIUS

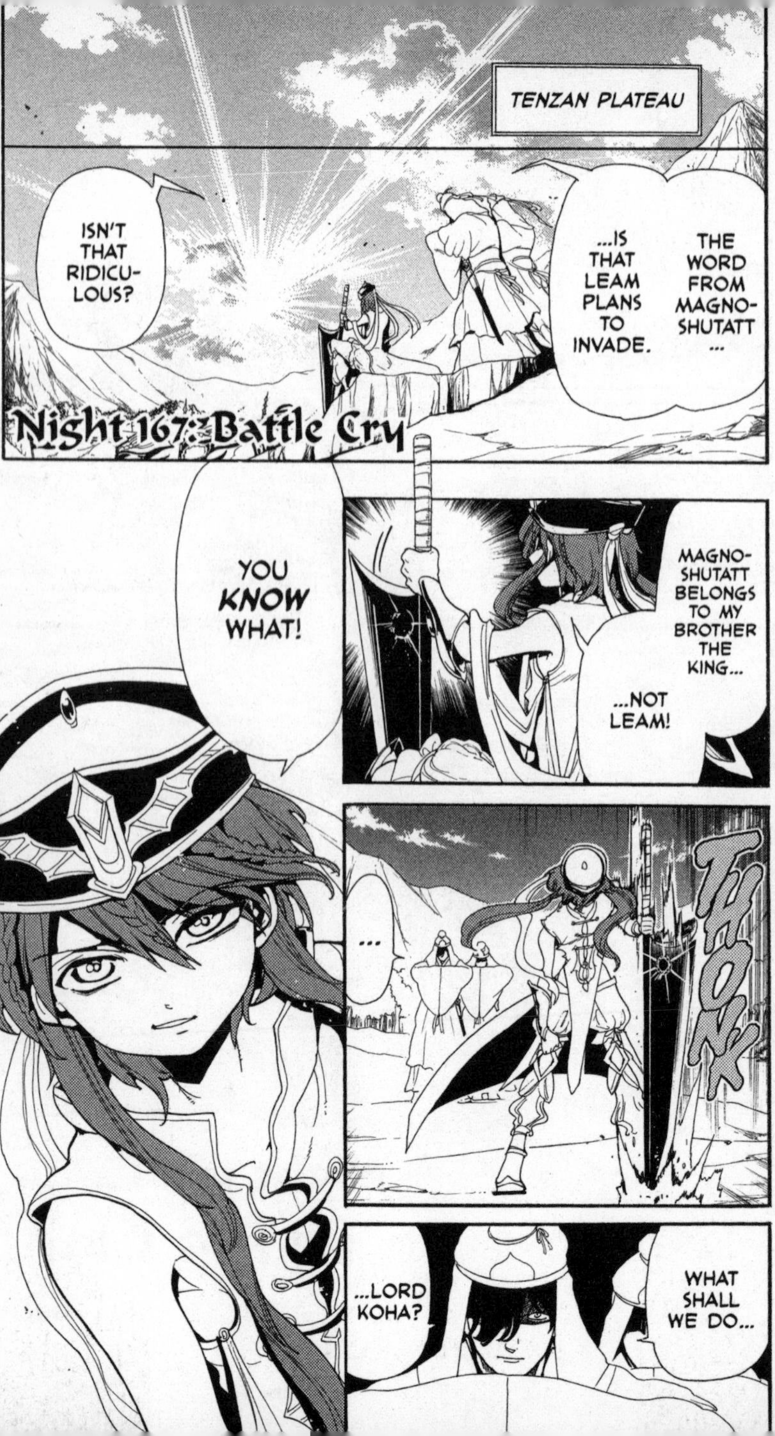
TENZAN PLATEAU
THE WORD FROM MAGNO-SHUTATT ...
...IS THAT LEAM PLANS TO INVADE.
ISN'T THAT RIDICULOUS?
Night 167: Battle Cry
MAGNO-SHUTATT BELONGS TO MY BROTHER THE KING...
...NOT LEAM!
THONK
...
WHAT SHALL WE DO...
...LORD KOHA?
YOU KNOW WHAT!

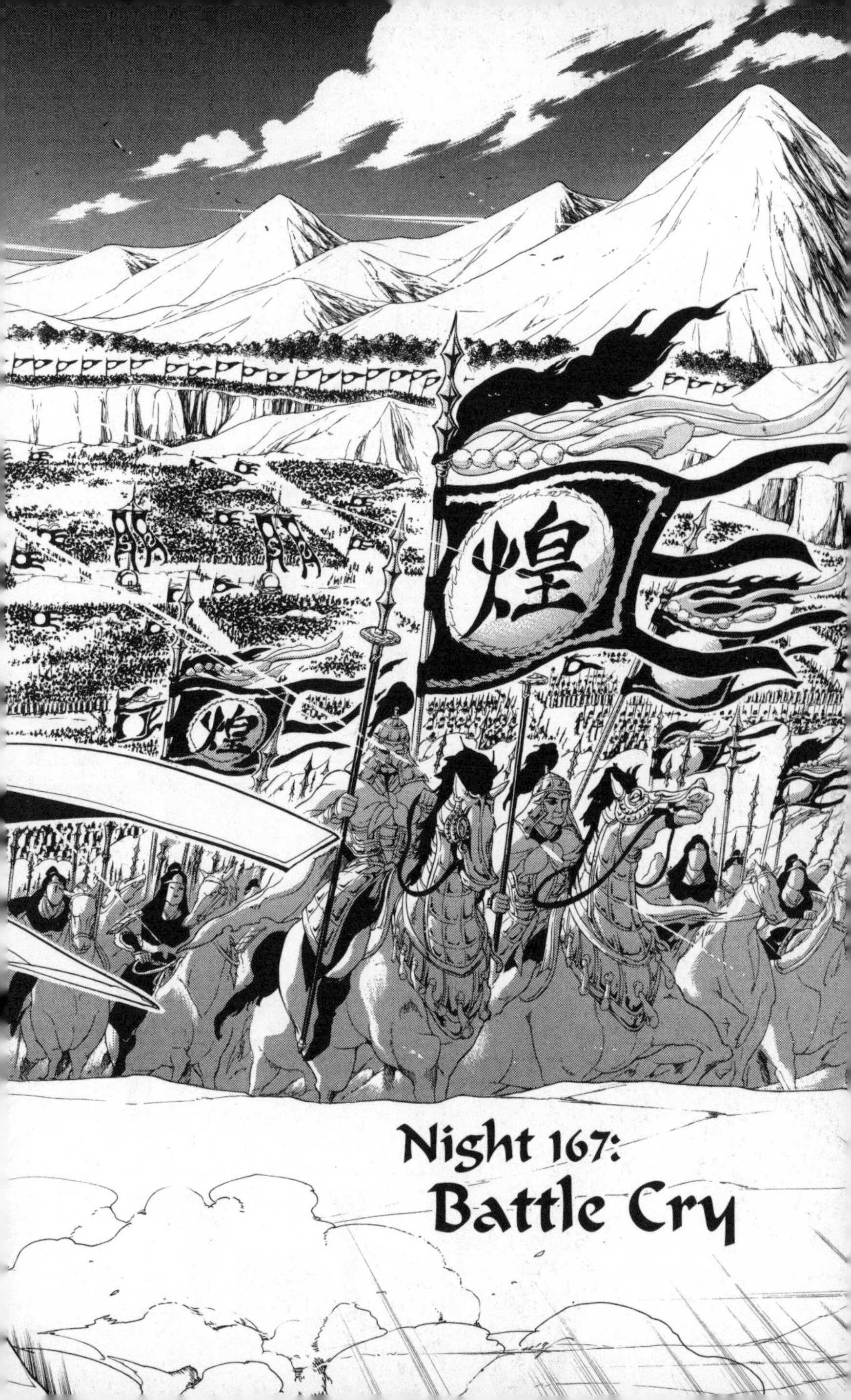
煌
煌
Night 167:
Battle Cry

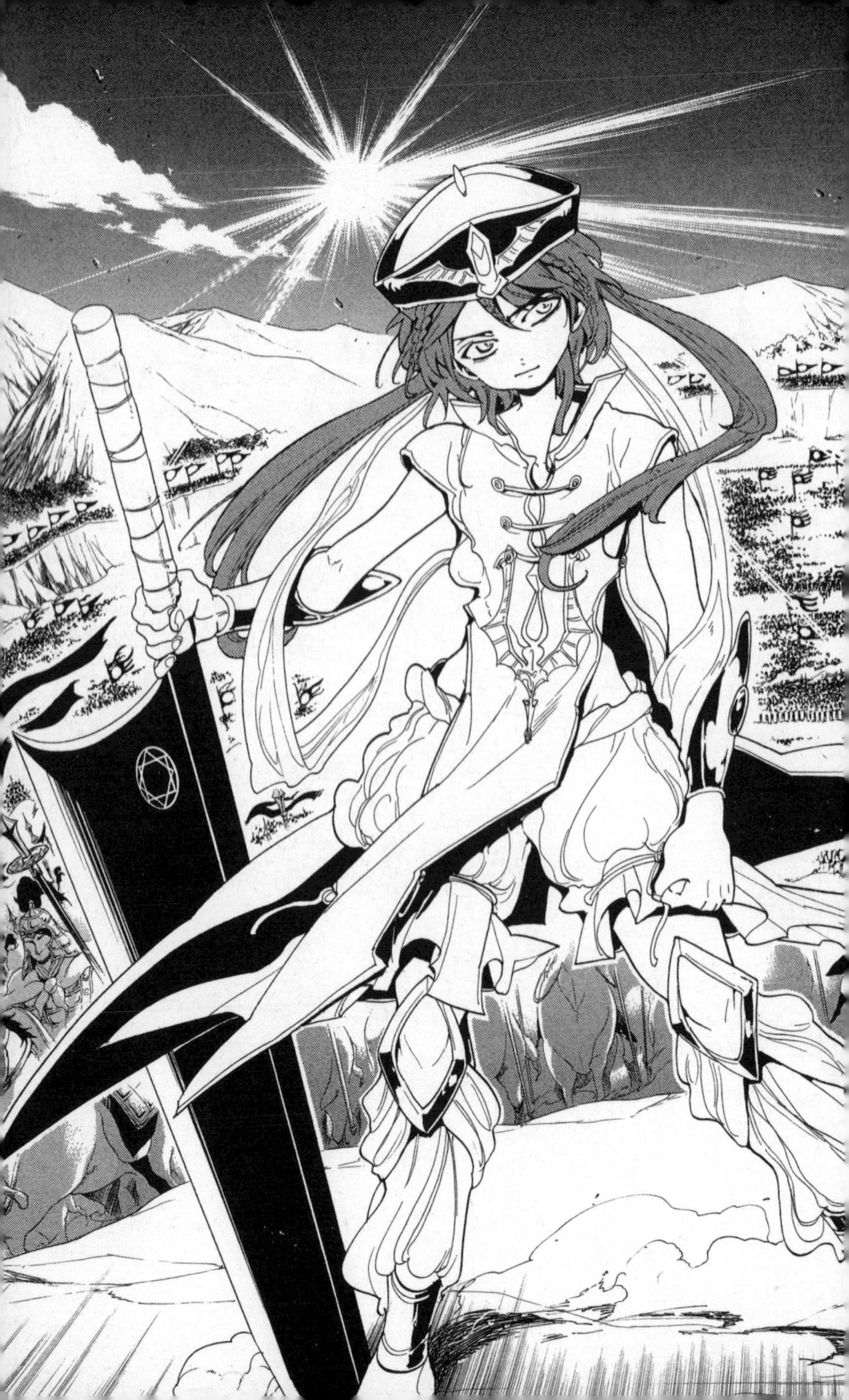

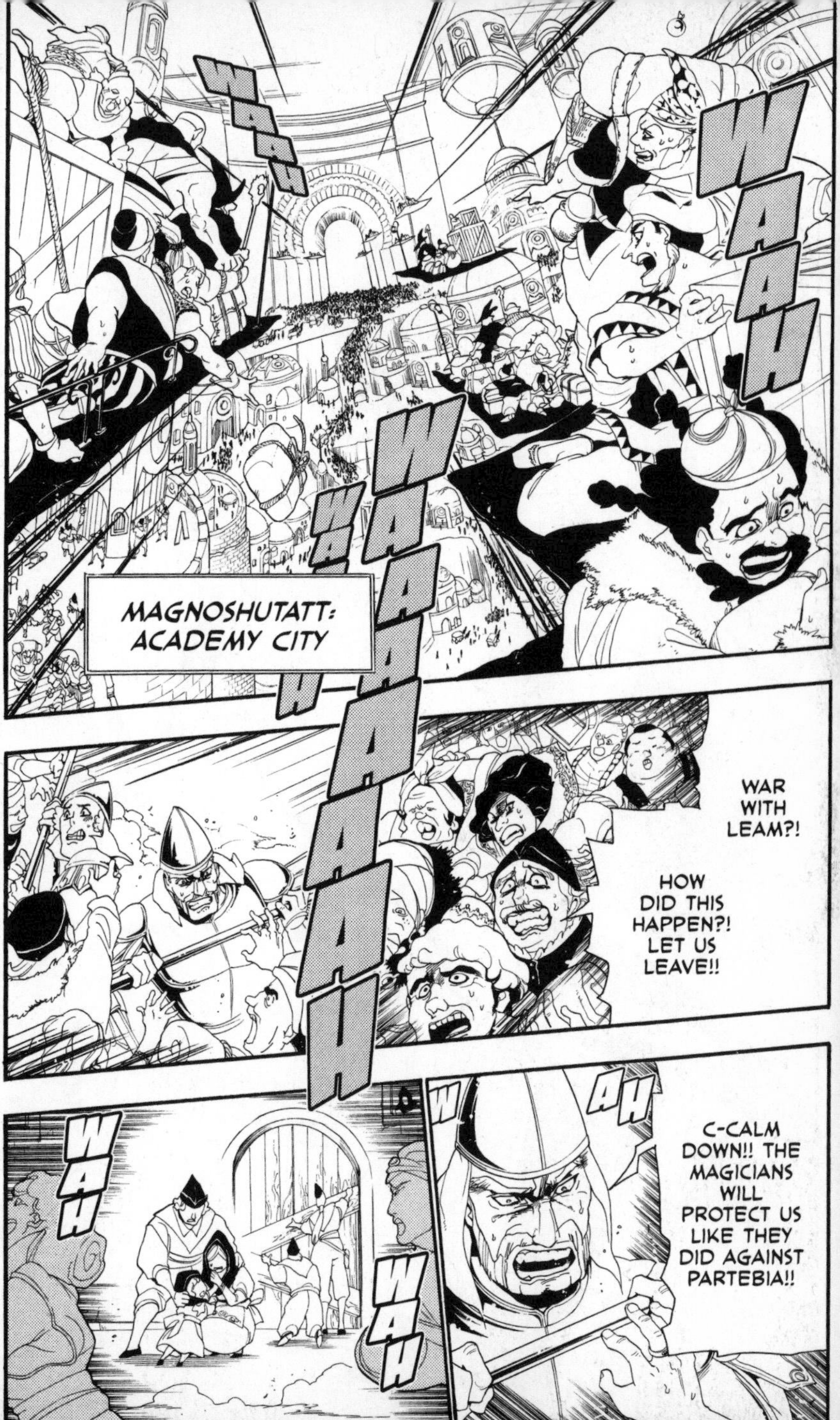
WAAAH
WAAAH
MAGNOSHUTATT: ACADEMY CITY
WAAAAAAAAH
WAAAH
WAR WITH LEAM?!
HOW DID THIS HAPPEN?! LET US LEAVE!!
C-CALM DOWN!! THE MAGICIANS WILL PROTECT US LIKE THEY DID AGAINST PARTEBIA!!
WAH
WAH
WAH

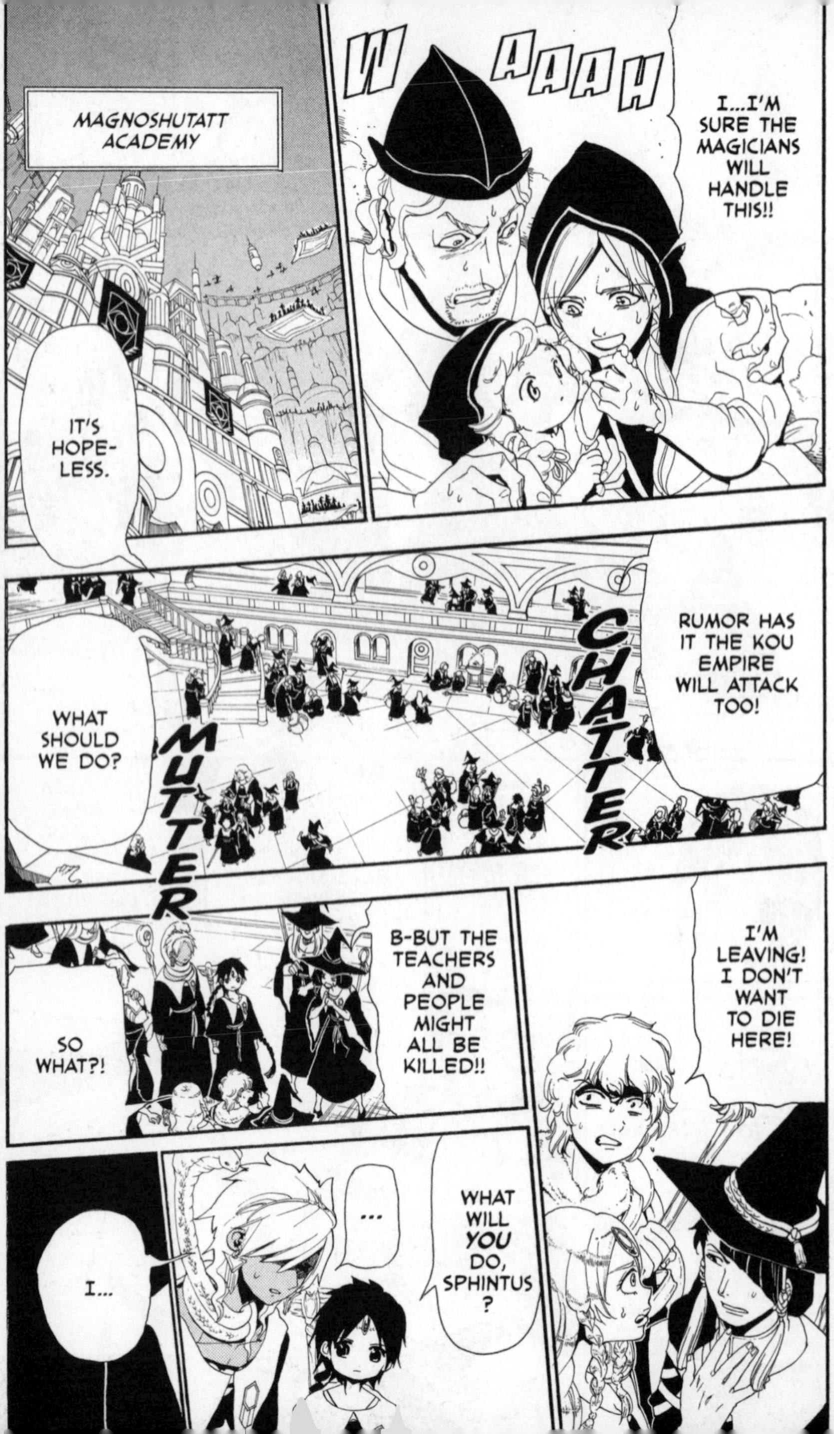
WAAAH
I...I'M SURE THE MAGICIANS WILL HANDLE THIS!!
MAGNOSHUTATT ACADEMY
IT'S HOPE-LESS.
RUMOR HAS IT THE KOU EMPIRE WILL ATTACK TOO!
CHATTER
MUTTER
WHAT SHOULD WE DO?
I'M LEAVING! I DON'T WANT TO DIE HERE!
B-BUT THE TEACHERS AND PEOPLE MIGHT ALL BE KILLED!!
SO WHAT?!
WHAT WILL *YOU* DO, SPHINTUS?
...
I...

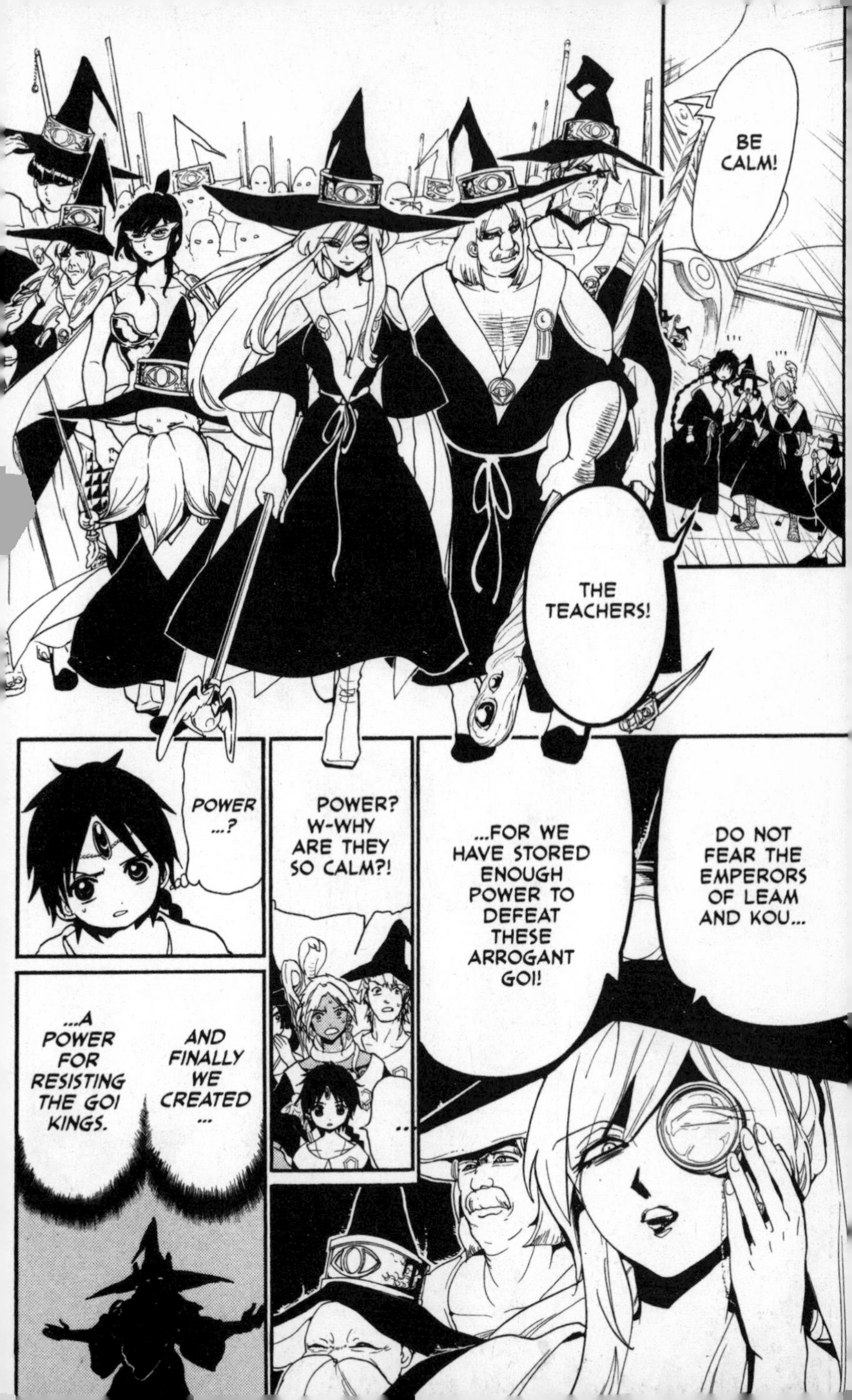
BE CALM!
THE TEACHERS!
DO NOT FEAR THE EMPERORS OF LEAM AND KOU...
...FOR WE HAVE STORED ENOUGH POWER TO DEFEAT THESE ARROGANT GOI!
POWER? W-WHY ARE THEY SO CALM?!
..
POWER ...?
AND FINALLY WE CREATED ...
...A POWER FOR RESISTING THE GOI KINGS.

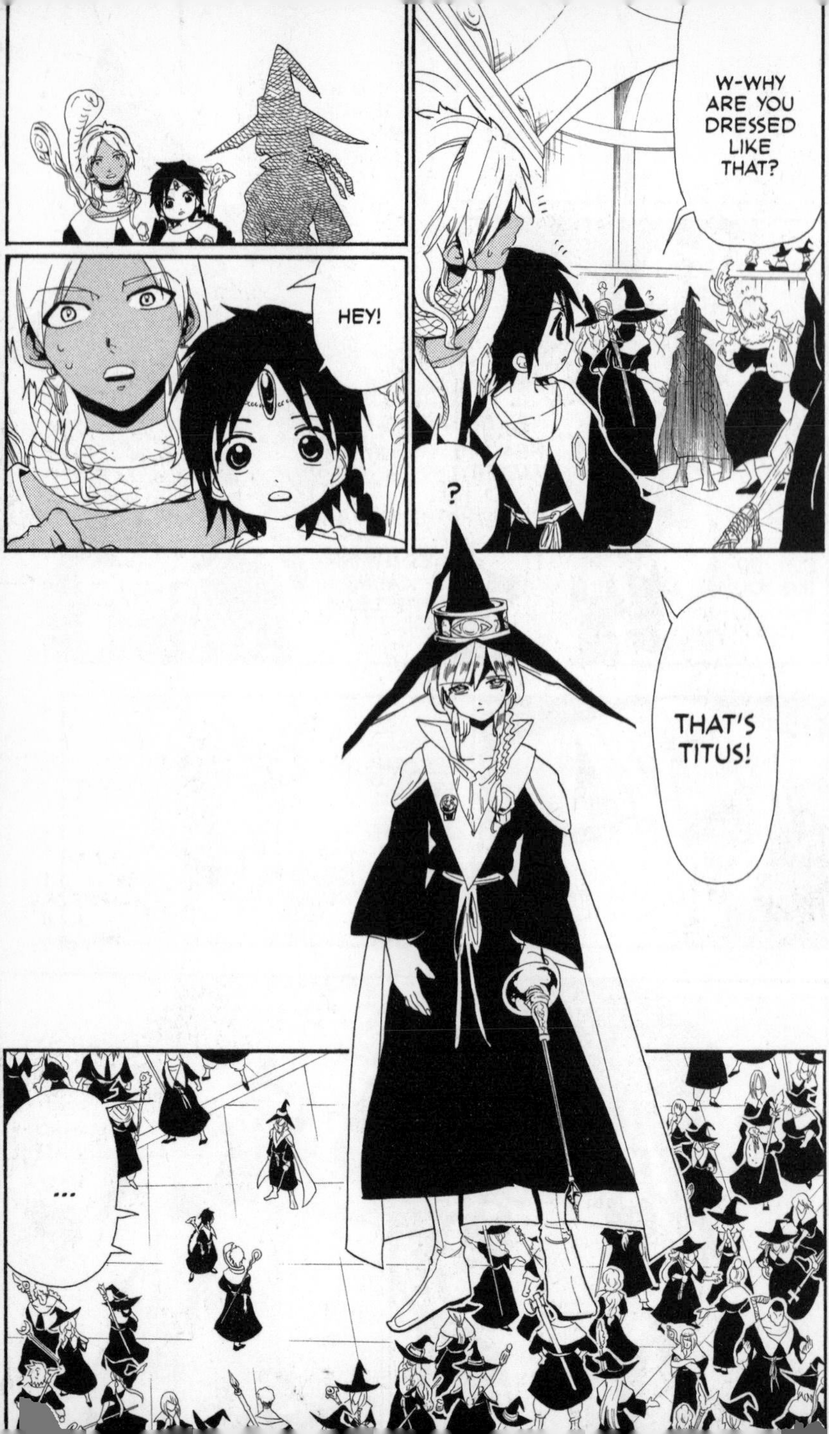
W-WHY ARE YOU DRESSED LIKE THAT?
?
HEY!
THAT'S TITUS!
...

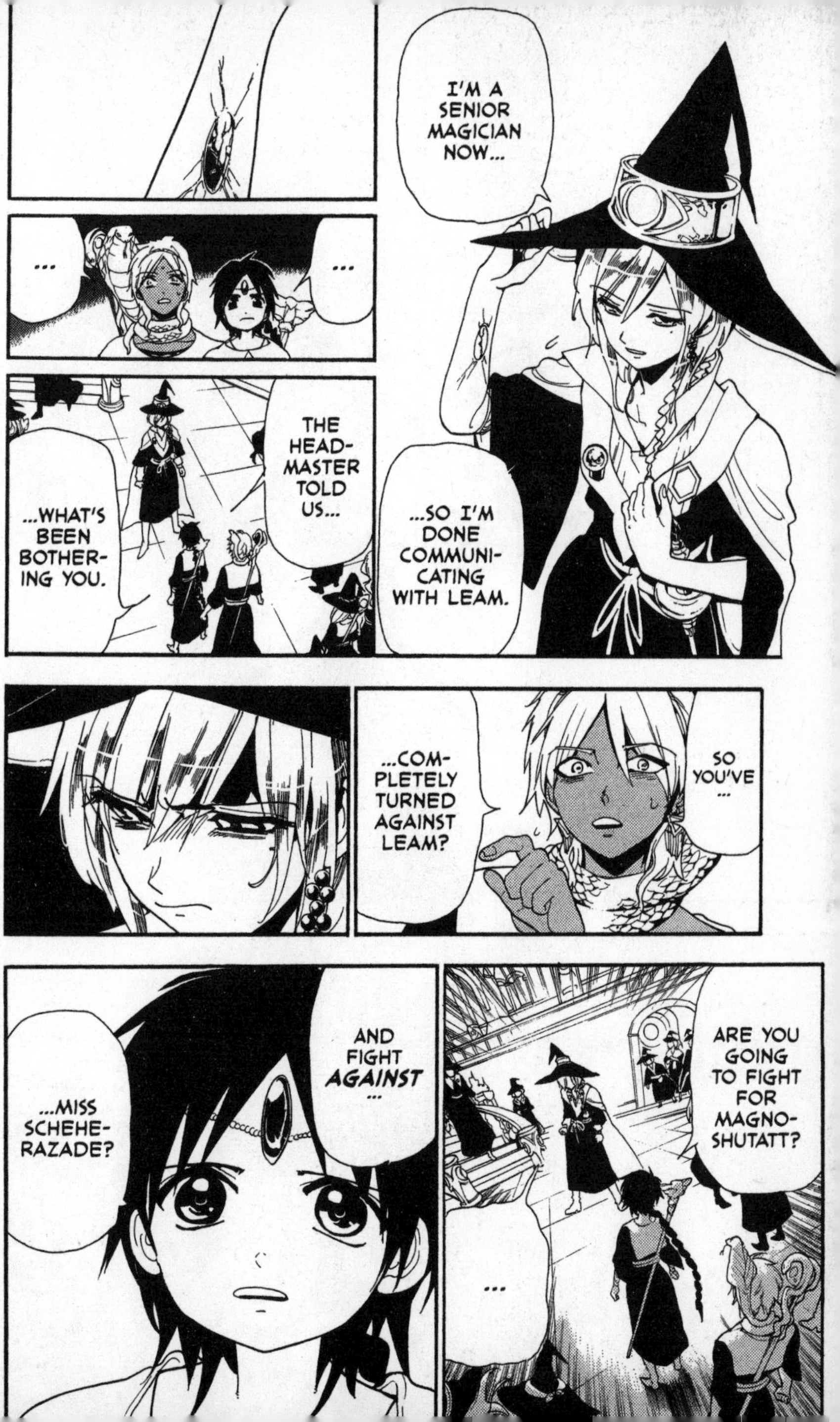
I'M A SENIOR MAGICIAN NOW...
...SO I'M DONE COMMUNICATING WITH LEAM.
...
...
THE HEADMASTER TOLD US...
...WHAT'S BEEN BOTHERING YOU.
SO YOU'VE...
...COMPLETELY TURNED AGAINST LEAM?
ARE YOU GOING TO FIGHT FOR MAGNOSHUTATT?
...
AND FIGHT *AGAINST*...
...MISS SCHEHERAZADE?

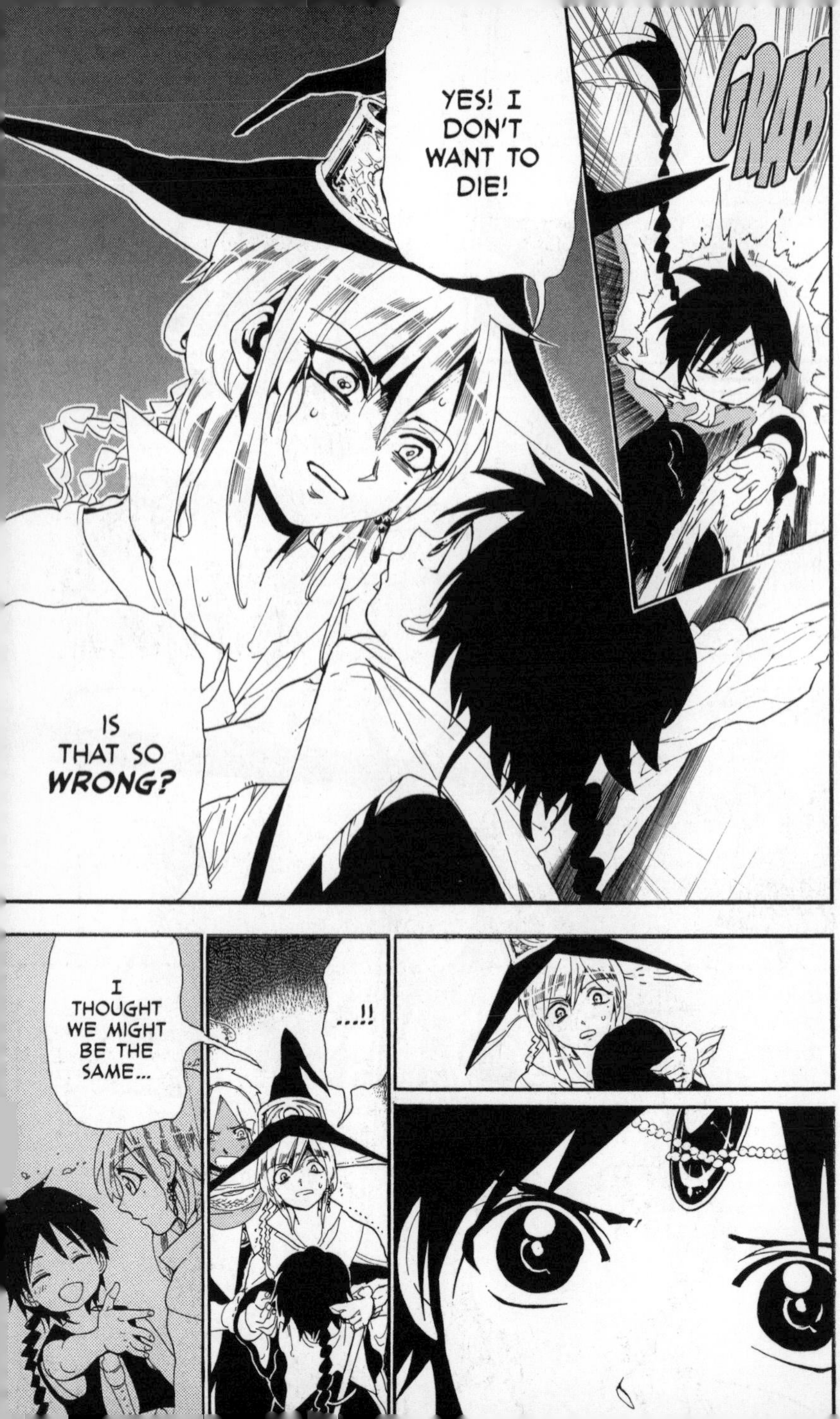
GRAB
YES! I DON'T WANT TO DIE!
IS THAT SO *WRONG?*
...!!
I THOUGHT WE MIGHT BE THE SAME...

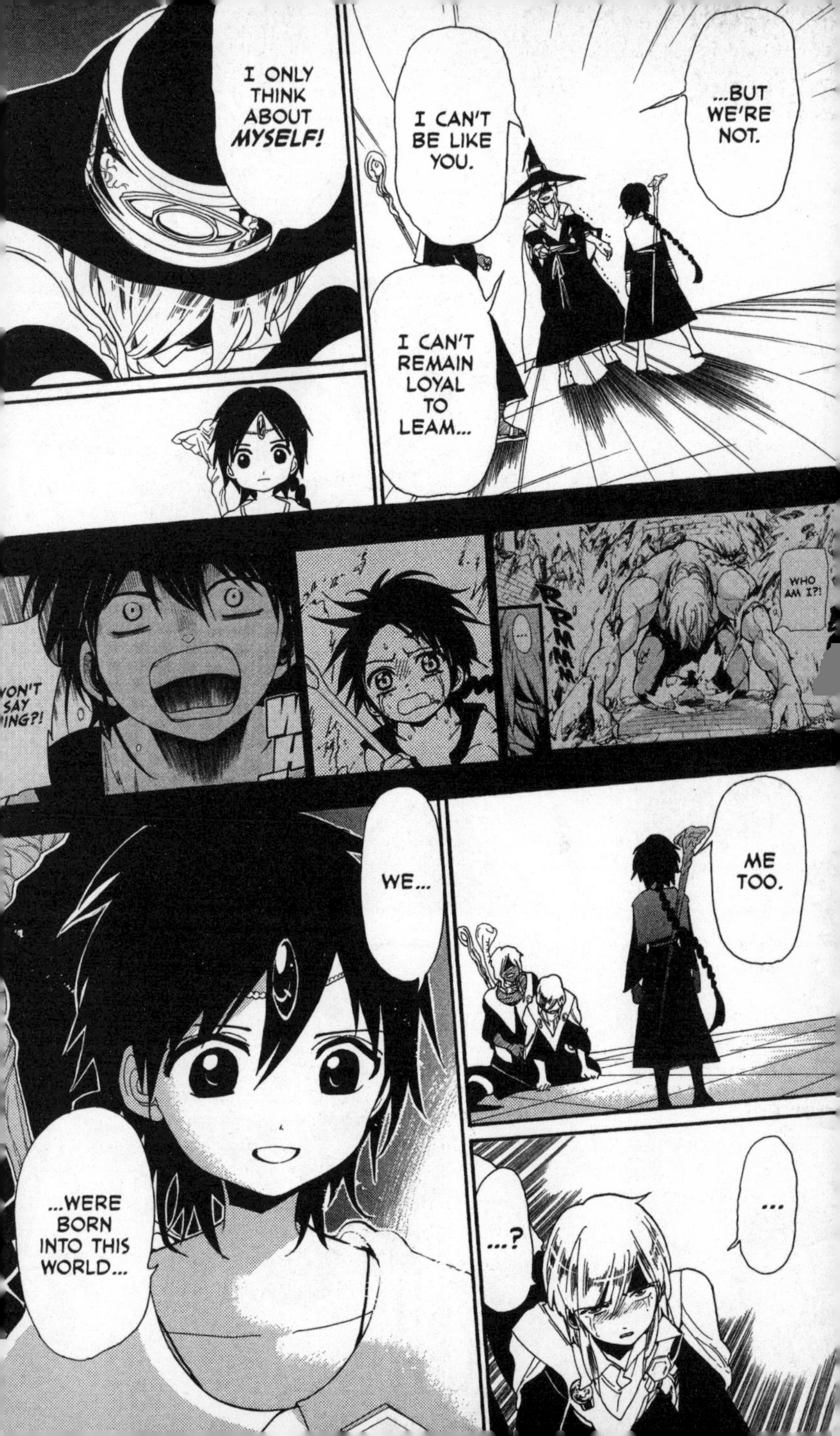
...BUT WE'RE NOT.
I CAN'T BE LIKE YOU.
I CAN'T REMAIN LOYAL TO LEAM...
I ONLY THINK ABOUT *MYSELF!*
WHO AM I?!
RRRMMM
...
ME TOO.
...
...?
WE...
...WERE BORN INTO THIS WORLD...

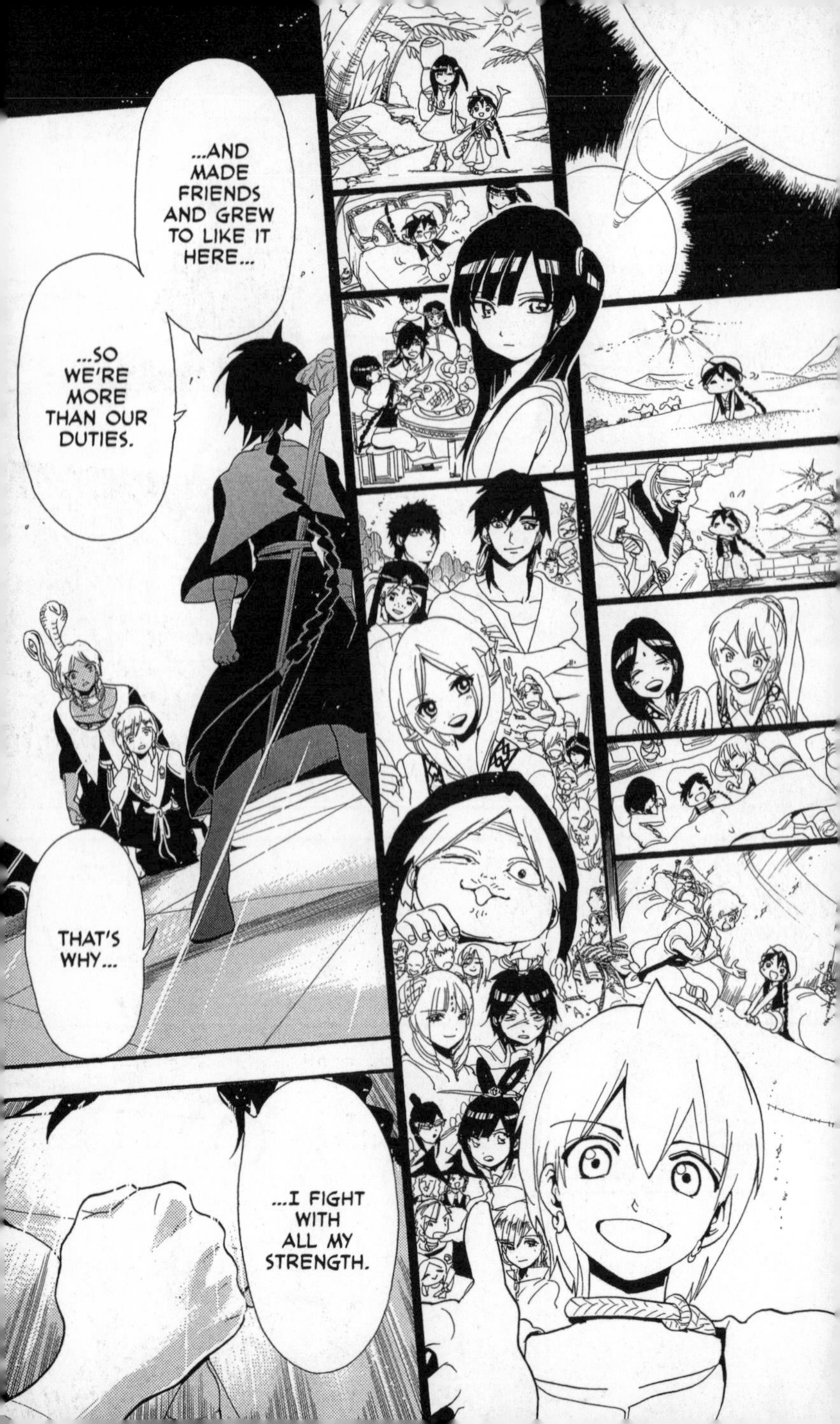
...AND MADE FRIENDS AND GREW TO LIKE IT HERE...
...SO WE'RE MORE THAN OUR DUTIES.
THAT'S WHY...
...I FIGHT WITH ALL MY STRENGTH.

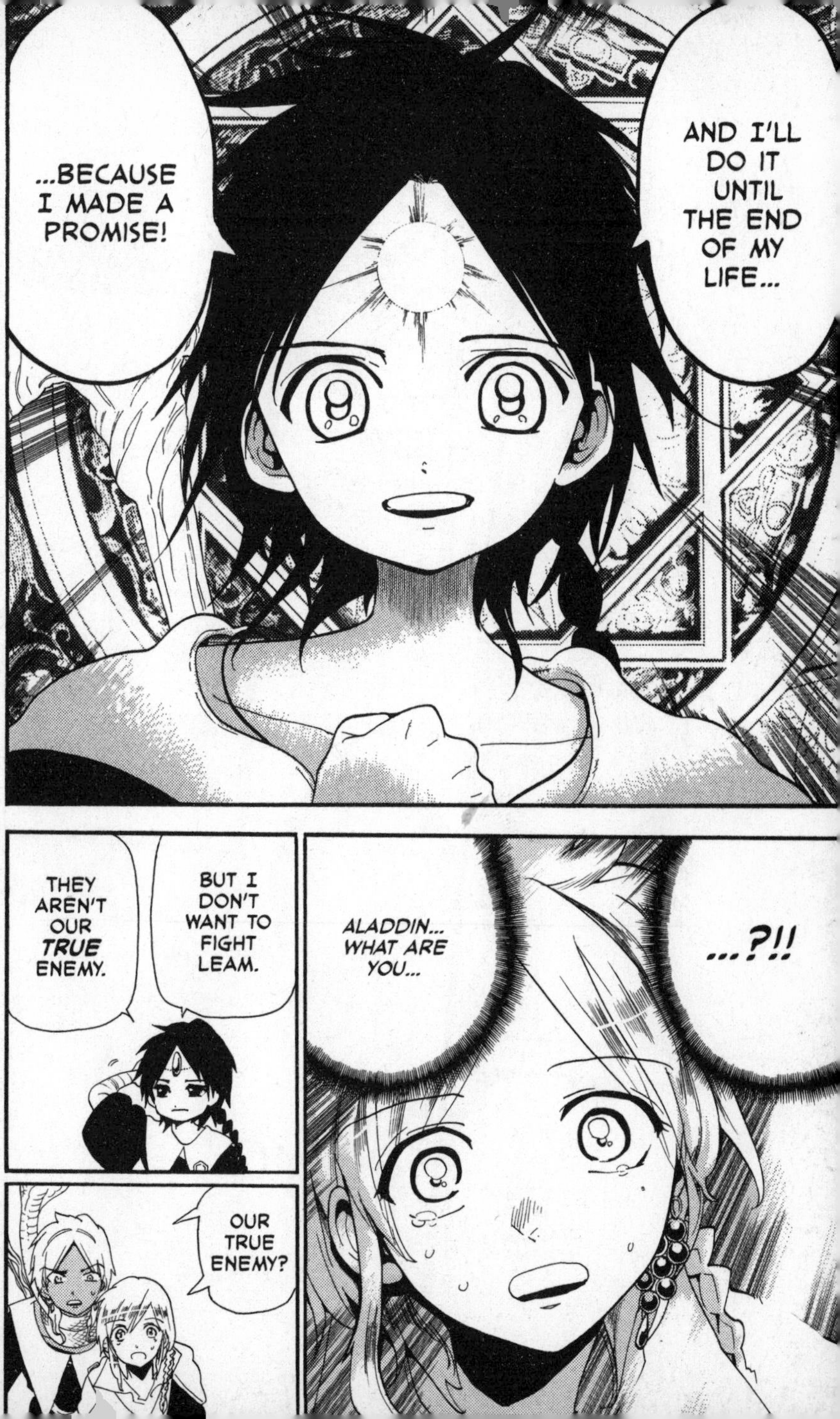
AND I'LL DO IT UNTIL THE END OF MY LIFE...
...BECAUSE I MADE A PROMISE!
...?!!
ALADDIN... WHAT ARE YOU...
BUT I DON'T WANT TO FIGHT LEAM.
THEY AREN'T OUR *TRUE* ENEMY.
OUR TRUE ENEMY?

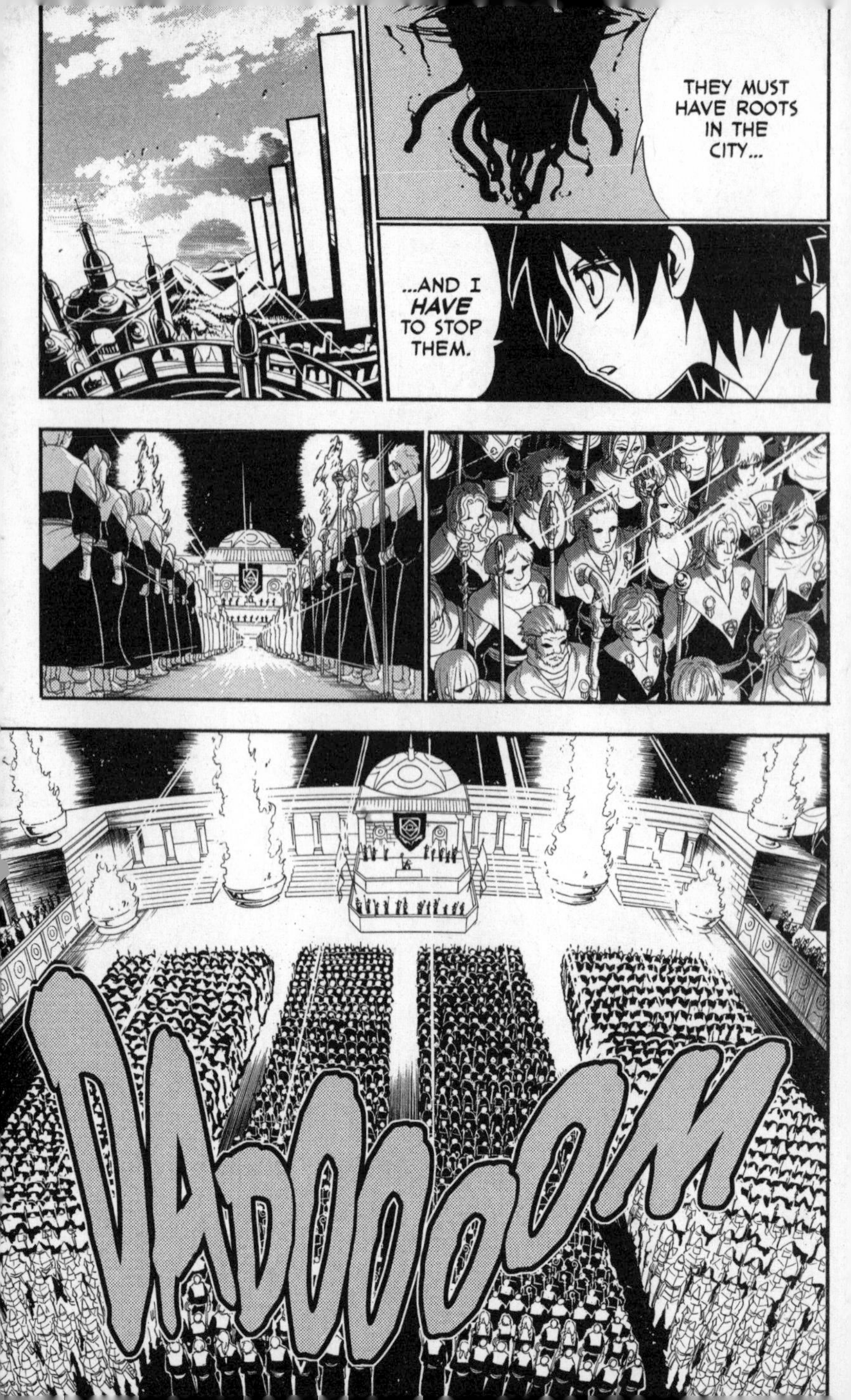
THEY MUST HAVE ROOTS IN THE CITY...
...AND I *HAVE* TO STOP THEM.
DADOOOOM

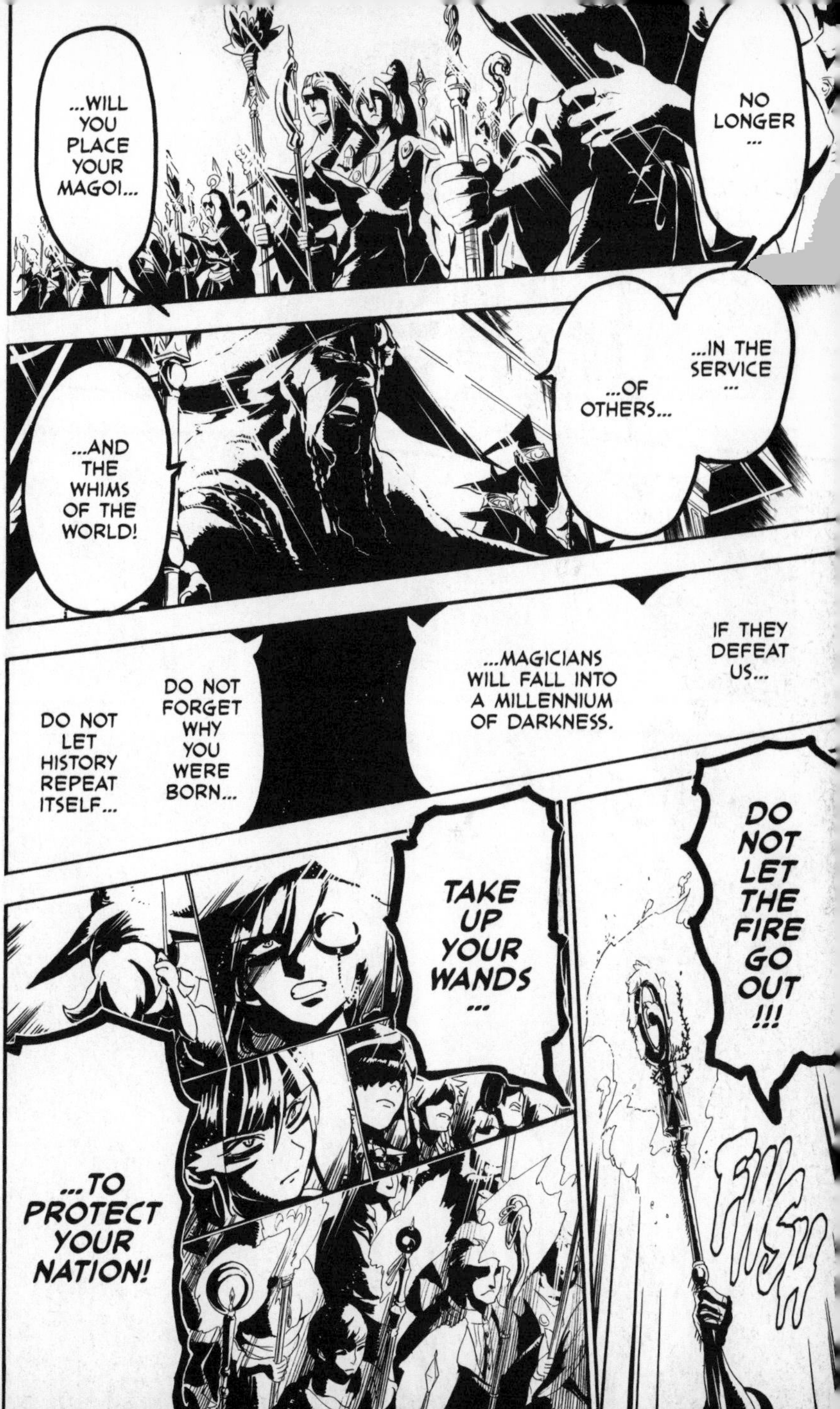
NO LONGER ...
...WILL YOU PLACE YOUR MAGOI...
...IN THE SERVICE ...
...OF OTHERS...
...AND THE WHIMS OF THE WORLD!
IF THEY DEFEAT US...
...MAGICIANS WILL FALL INTO A MILLENNIUM OF DARKNESS.
DO NOT FORGET WHY YOU WERE BORN...
DO NOT LET HISTORY REPEAT ITSELF...
DO NOT LET THE FIRE GO OUT!!!
FWSH
TAKE UP YOUR WANDS ...
...TO PROTECT YOUR NATION!

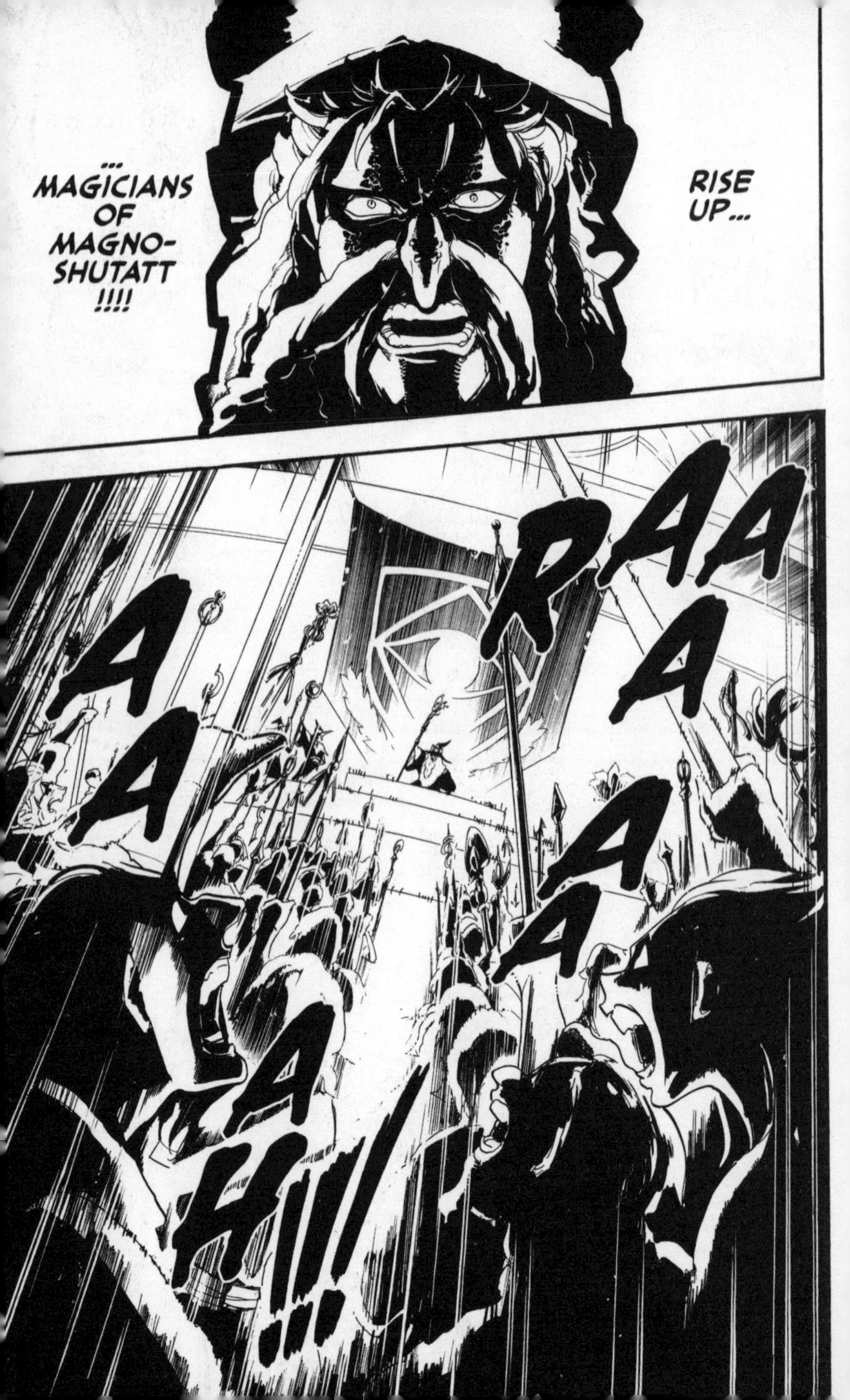
RISE UP...
...MAGICIANS OF MAGNO-SHUTATT!!!!
RAAAAAAAAAH!!!

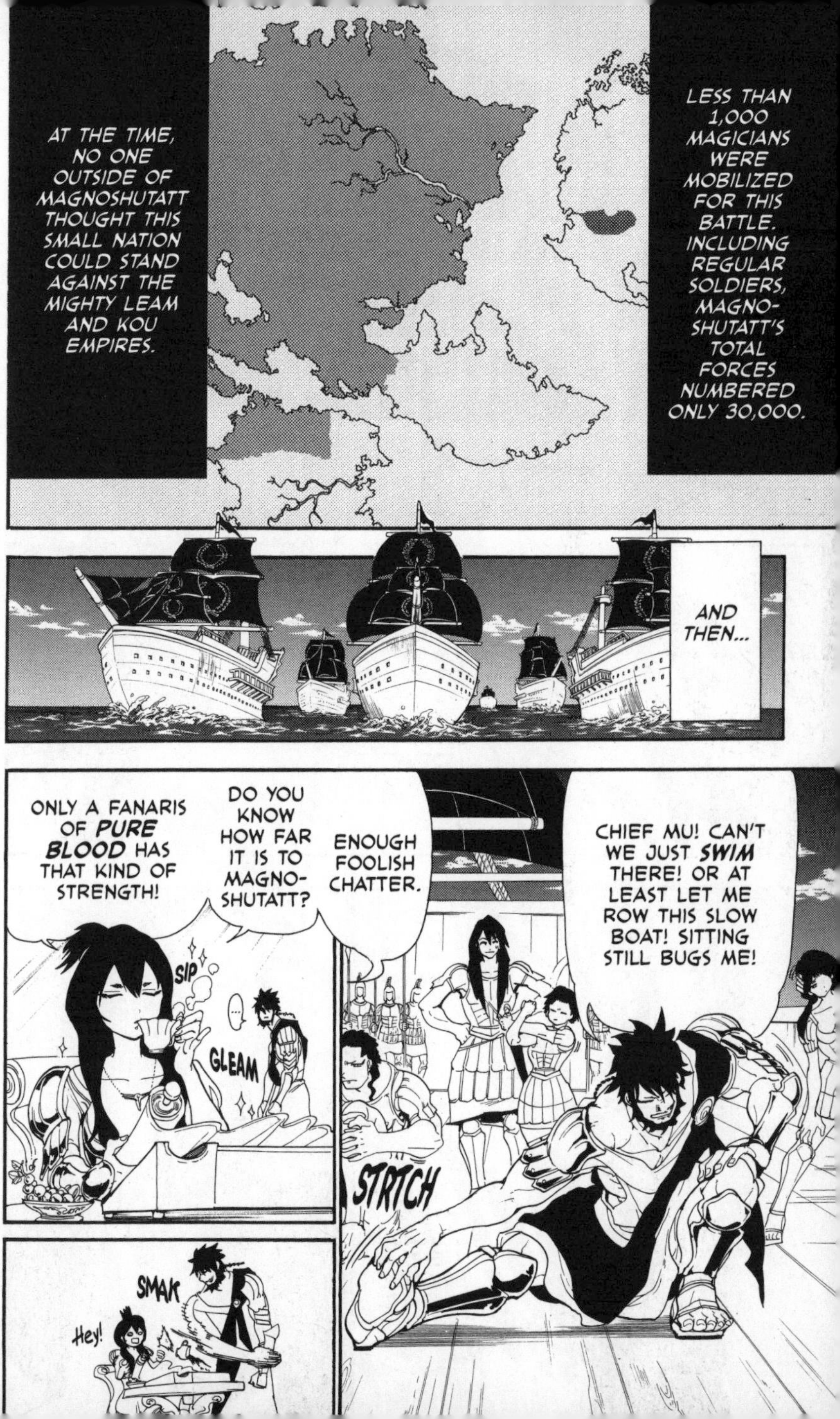
LESS THAN 1,000 MAGICIANS WERE MOBILIZED FOR THIS BATTLE. INCLUDING REGULAR SOLDIERS, MAGNO-SHUTATT'S TOTAL FORCES NUMBERED ONLY 30,000.
AT THE TIME, NO ONE OUTSIDE OF MAGNOSHUTATT THOUGHT THIS SMALL NATION COULD STAND AGAINST THE MIGHTY LEAM AND KOU EMPIRES.
AND THEN...
CHIEF MU! CAN'T WE JUST SWIM THERE! OR AT LEAST LET ME ROW THIS SLOW BOAT! SITTING STILL BUGS ME!
STRTCH
ENOUGH FOOLISH CHATTER.
DO YOU KNOW HOW FAR IT IS TO MAGNO-SHUTATT?
ONLY A FANARIS OF PURE BLOOD HAS THAT KIND OF STRENGTH!
SIP
...
GLEAM
SMAK
Hey!

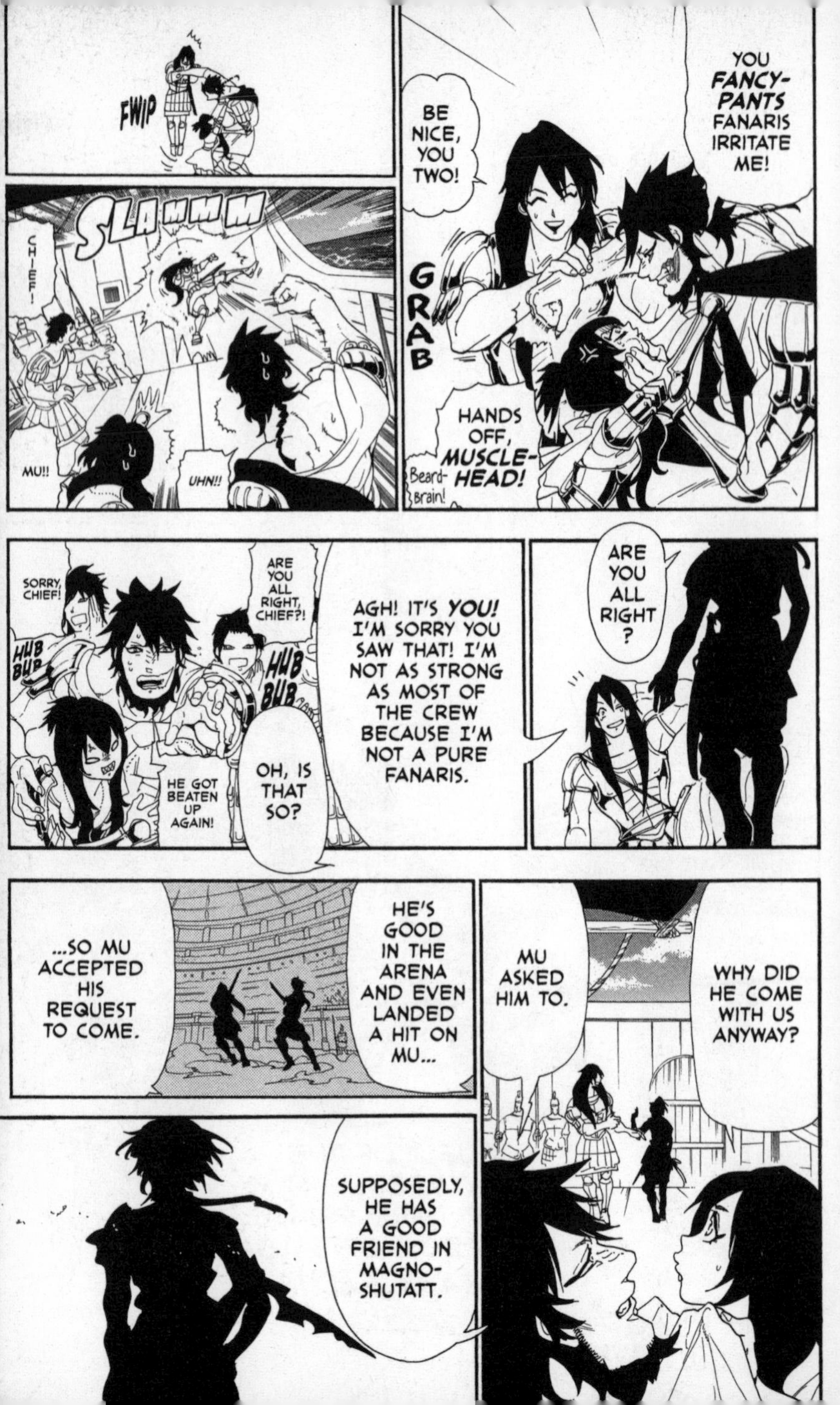
YOU FANCY-PANTS FANARIS IRRITATE ME!
BE NICE, YOU TWO!
GRAB
HANDS OFF, MUSCLE-HEAD!
Beard-Brain!
FWIP
SLAMMM
CHIEF!
UHN!!
MU!!
ARE YOU ALL RIGHT?
AGH! IT'S YOU! I'M SORRY YOU SAW THAT! I'M NOT AS STRONG AS MOST OF THE CREW BECAUSE I'M NOT A PURE FANARIS.
ARE YOU ALL RIGHT, CHIEF?!
SORRY, CHIEF!
HUB BUB
HUB BUB
OH, IS THAT SO?
HE GOT BEATEN UP AGAIN!
WHY DID HE COME WITH US ANYWAY?
MU ASKED HIM TO.
HE'S GOOD IN THE ARENA AND EVEN LANDED A HIT ON MU...
...SO MU ACCEPTED HIS REQUEST TO COME.
SUPPOSEDLY, HE HAS A GOOD FRIEND IN MAGNO-SHUTATT.

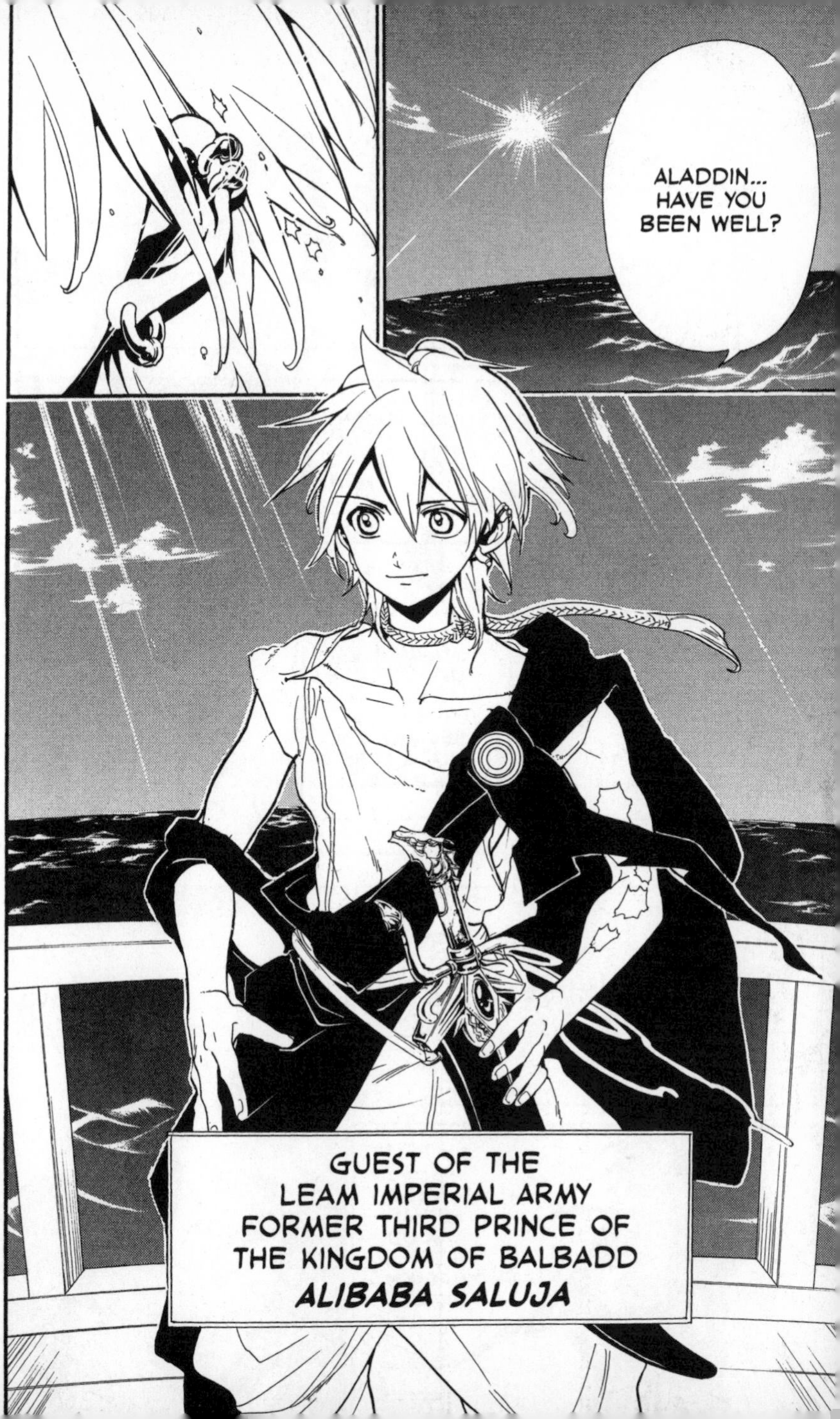
ALADDIN... HAVE YOU BEEN WELL?
GUEST OF THE LEAM IMPERIAL ARMY FORMER THIRD PRINCE OF THE KINGDOM OF BALBADD ALIBABA SALUJA

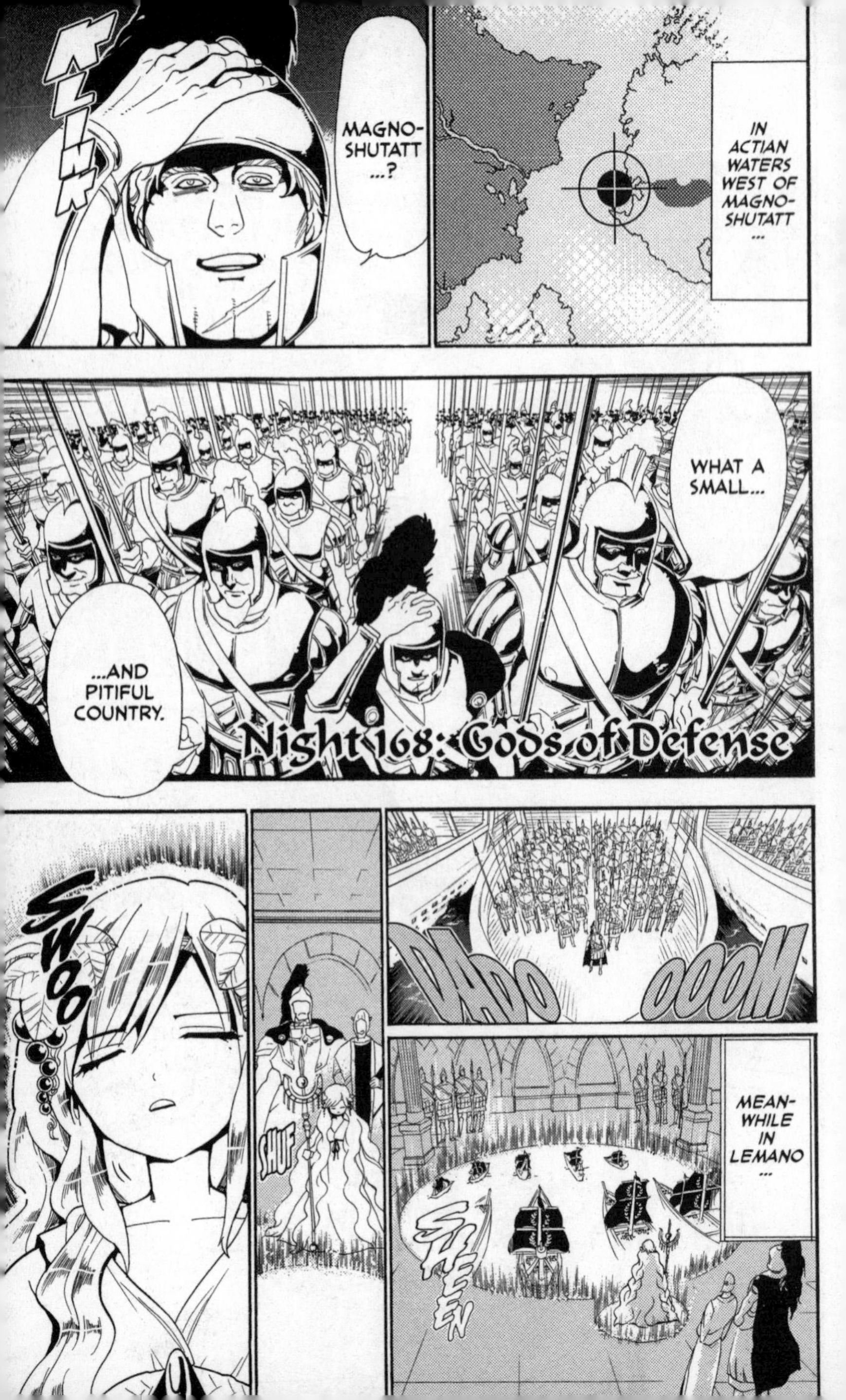
IN ACTIAN WATERS WEST OF MAGNO-SHUTATT...
KLINK
MAGNO-SHUTATT ...?
WHAT A SMALL...
...AND PITIFUL COUNTRY.
Night 168: Gods of Defense
DADOOOOM
MEAN-WHILE IN LEMANO ...
SHEEEN
SHUF
SWOO

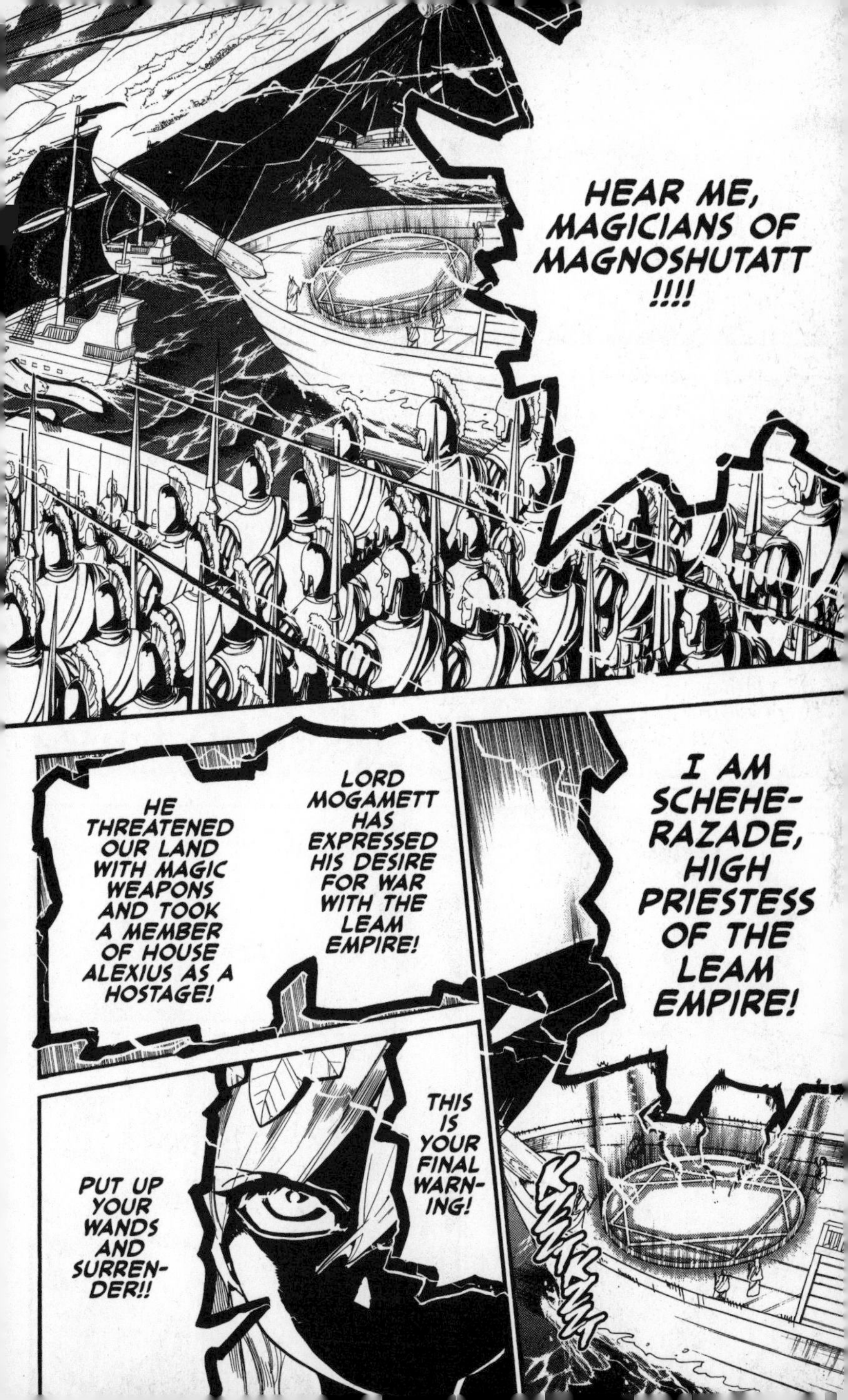
HEAR ME, MAGICIANS OF MAGNOSHUTATT!!!!
I AM SCHEHE-RAZADE, HIGH PRIESTESS OF THE LEAM EMPIRE!
LORD MOGAMETT HAS EXPRESSED HIS DESIRE FOR WAR WITH THE LEAM EMPIRE!
HE THREATENED OUR LAND WITH MAGIC WEAPONS AND TOOK A MEMBER OF HOUSE ALEXIUS AS A HOSTAGE!
THIS IS YOUR FINAL WARN-ING!
PUT UP YOUR WANDS AND SURREN-DER!!

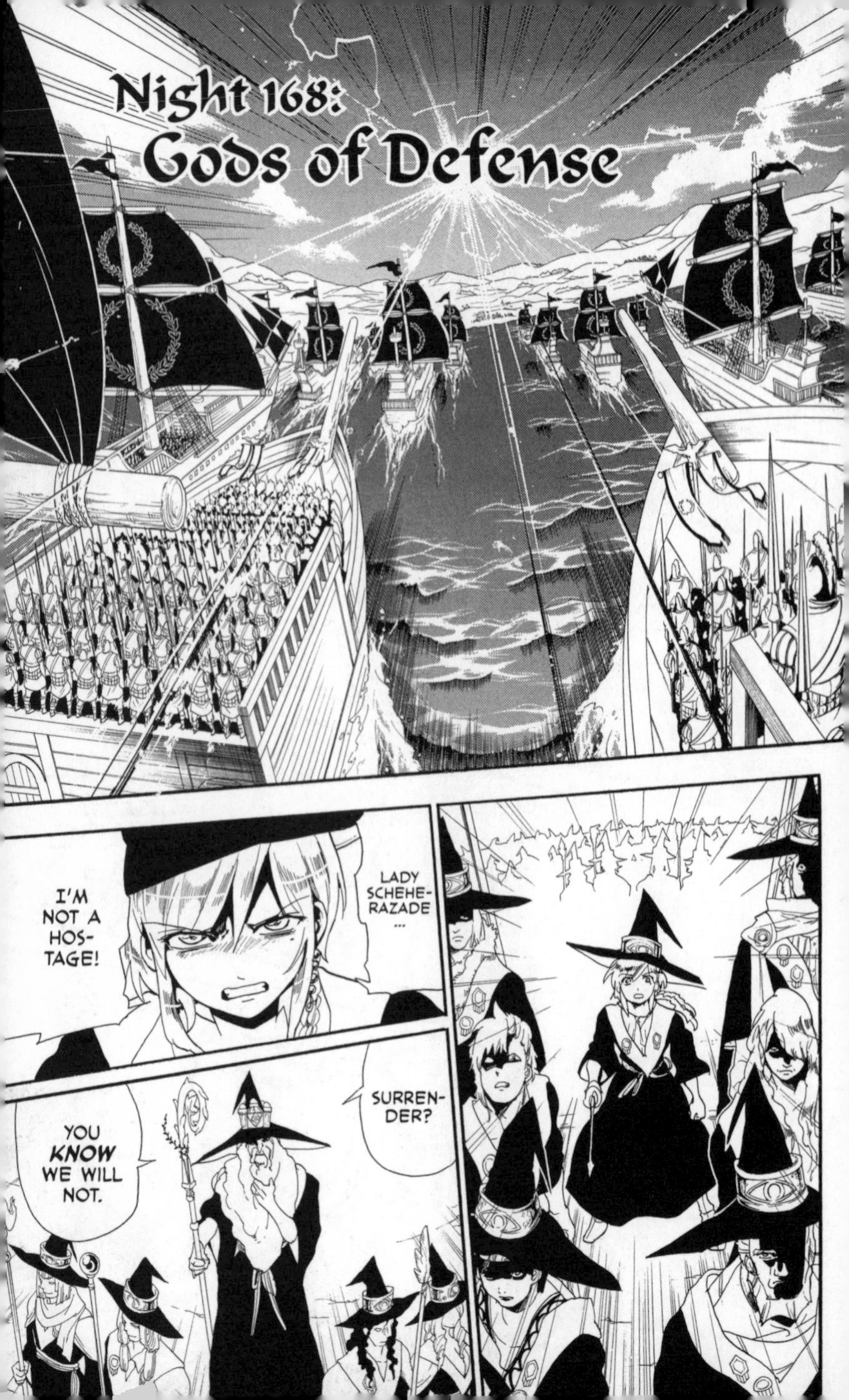
Night 168: Gods of Defense
LADY SCHEHERAZADE...
I'M NOT A HOSTAGE!
SURRENDER?
YOU KNOW WE WILL NOT.

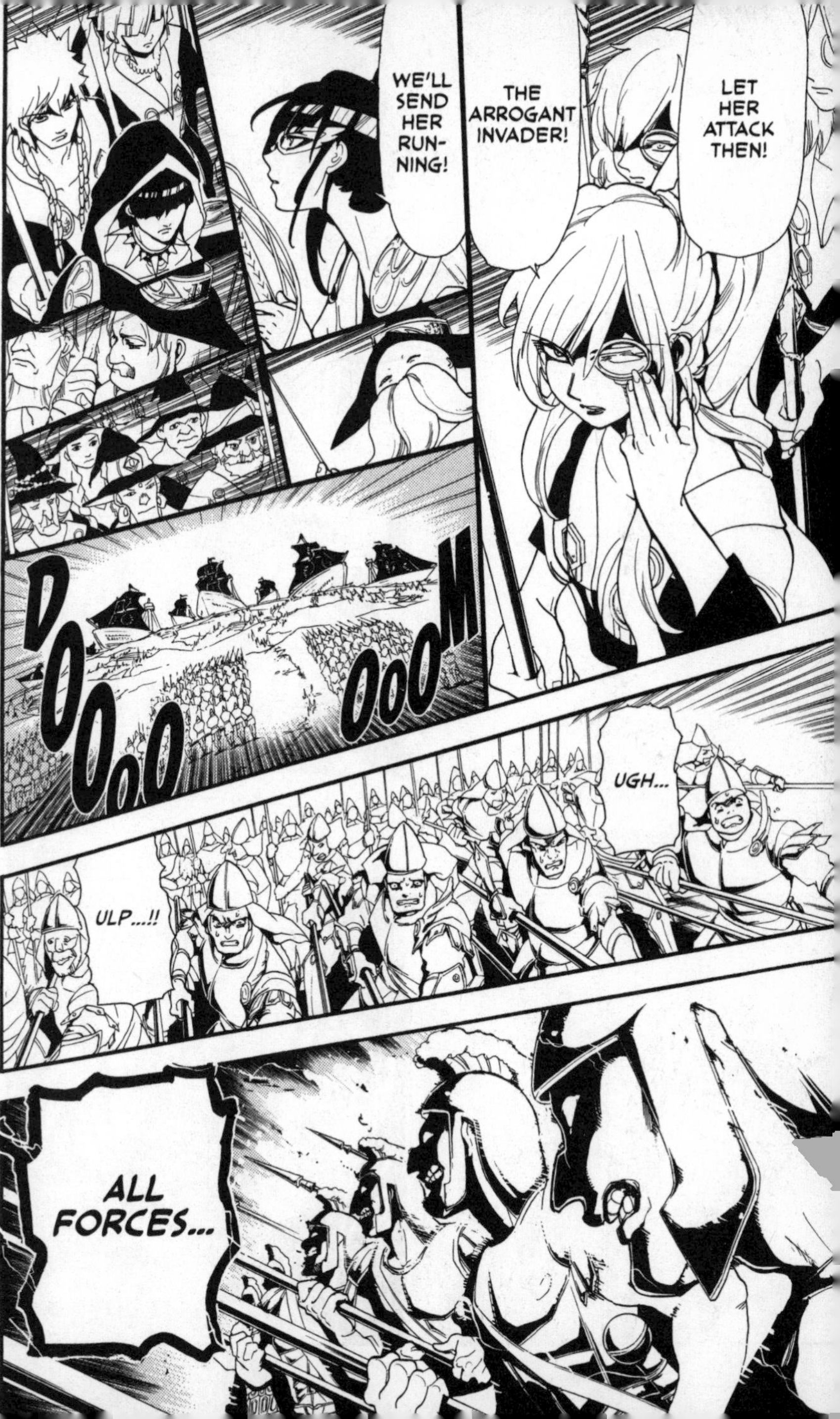
LET HER ATTACK THEN!
THE ARROGANT INVADER!
WE'LL SEND HER RUN-NING!
DOOOOOOOOM
UGH...
ULP...!!
ALL FORCES...

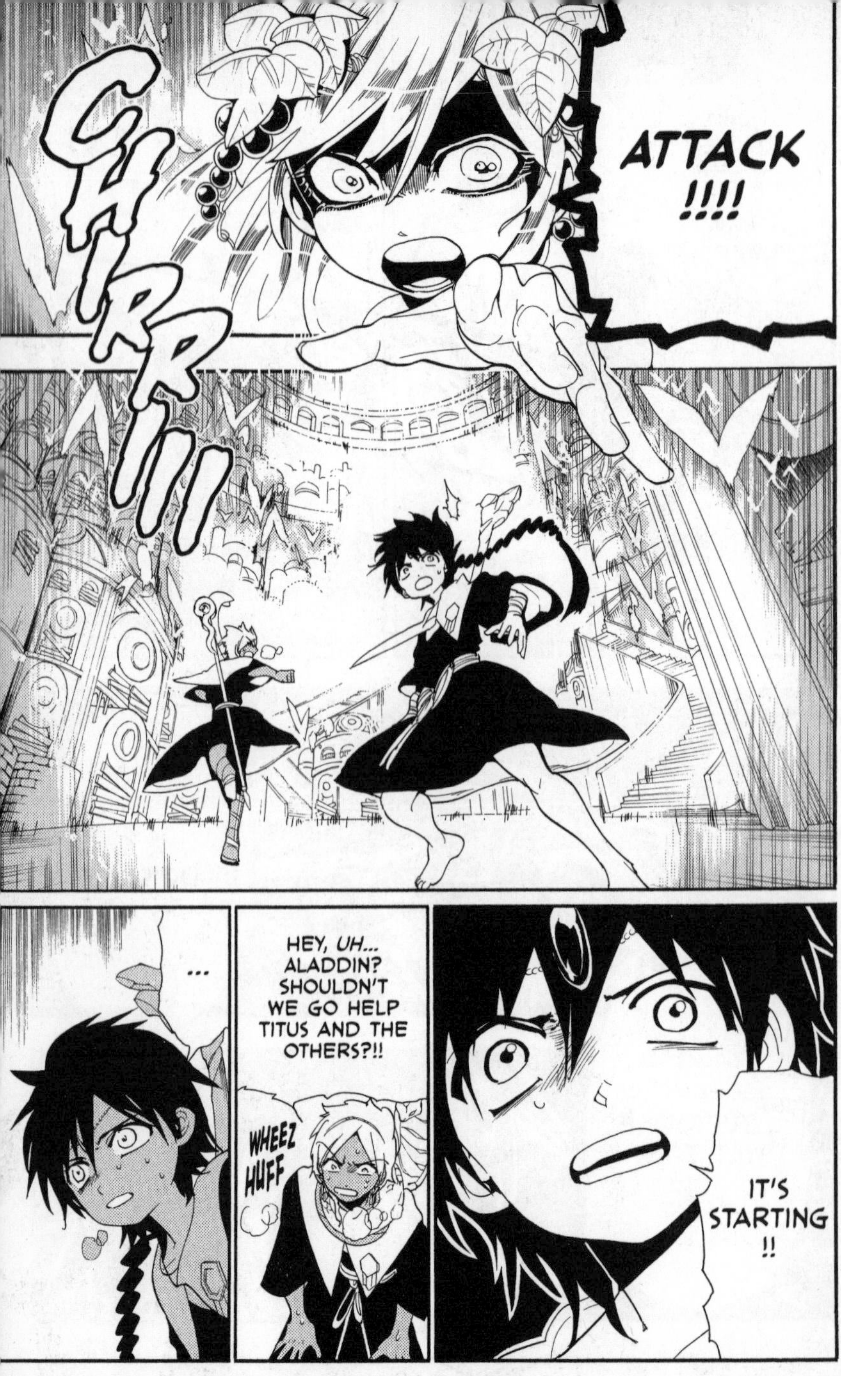
ATTACK !!!!
CHIRRIII
IT'S STARTING !!
HEY, UH... ALADDIN? SHOULDN'T WE GO HELP TITUS AND THE OTHERS?!!
WHEEZ HUFF
...

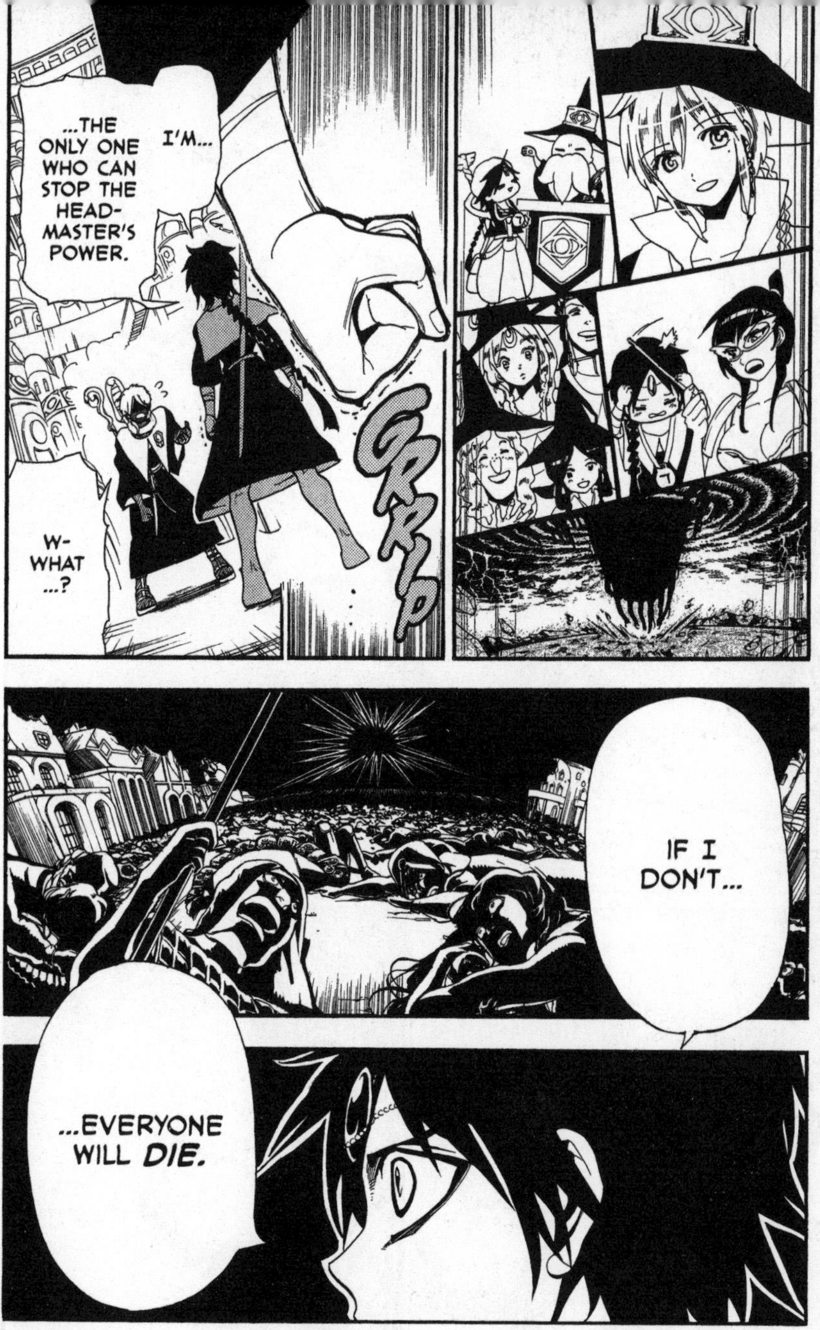
GRRIP
I'M...
...THE ONLY ONE WHO CAN STOP THE HEAD-MASTER'S POWER.
W-WHAT ...?
IF I DON'T...
...EVERYONE WILL *DIE.*

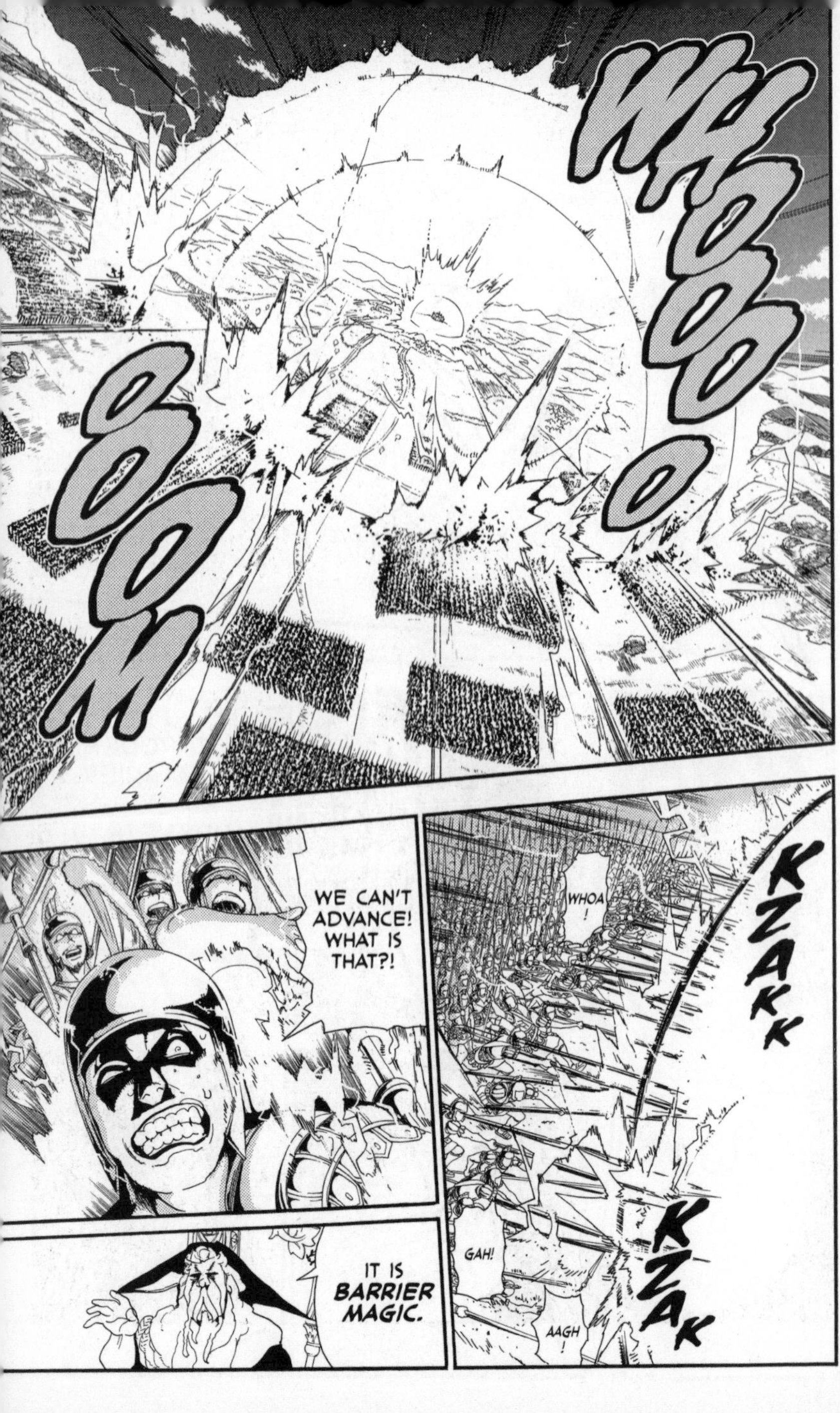
WHOOOOO
OOOM
KZAKK
WHOA!
KZAK
GAH!
AAGH!
WE CAN'T ADVANCE! WHAT IS THAT?!
IT IS **BARRIER MAGIC.**

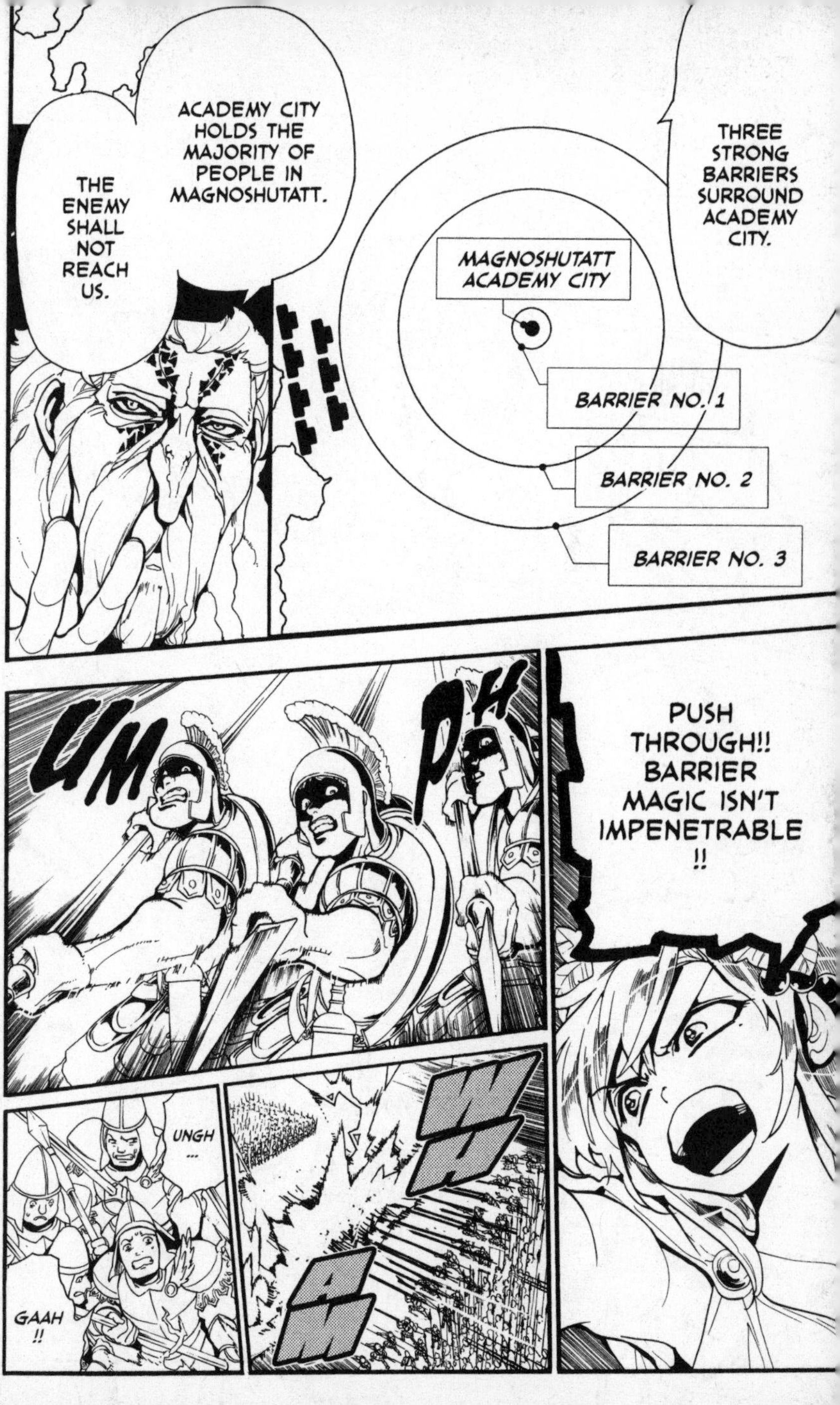
THREE STRONG BARRIERS SURROUND ACADEMY CITY.
MAGNOSHUTATT ACADEMY CITY
BARRIER NO. 1
BARRIER NO. 2
BARRIER NO. 3
ACADEMY CITY HOLDS THE MAJORITY OF PEOPLE IN MAGNOSHUTATT.
THE ENEMY SHALL NOT REACH US.
PUSH THROUGH!! BARRIER MAGIC ISN'T IMPENETRABLE !!
UMPH
WHAM
UNGH ...
GAAH !!

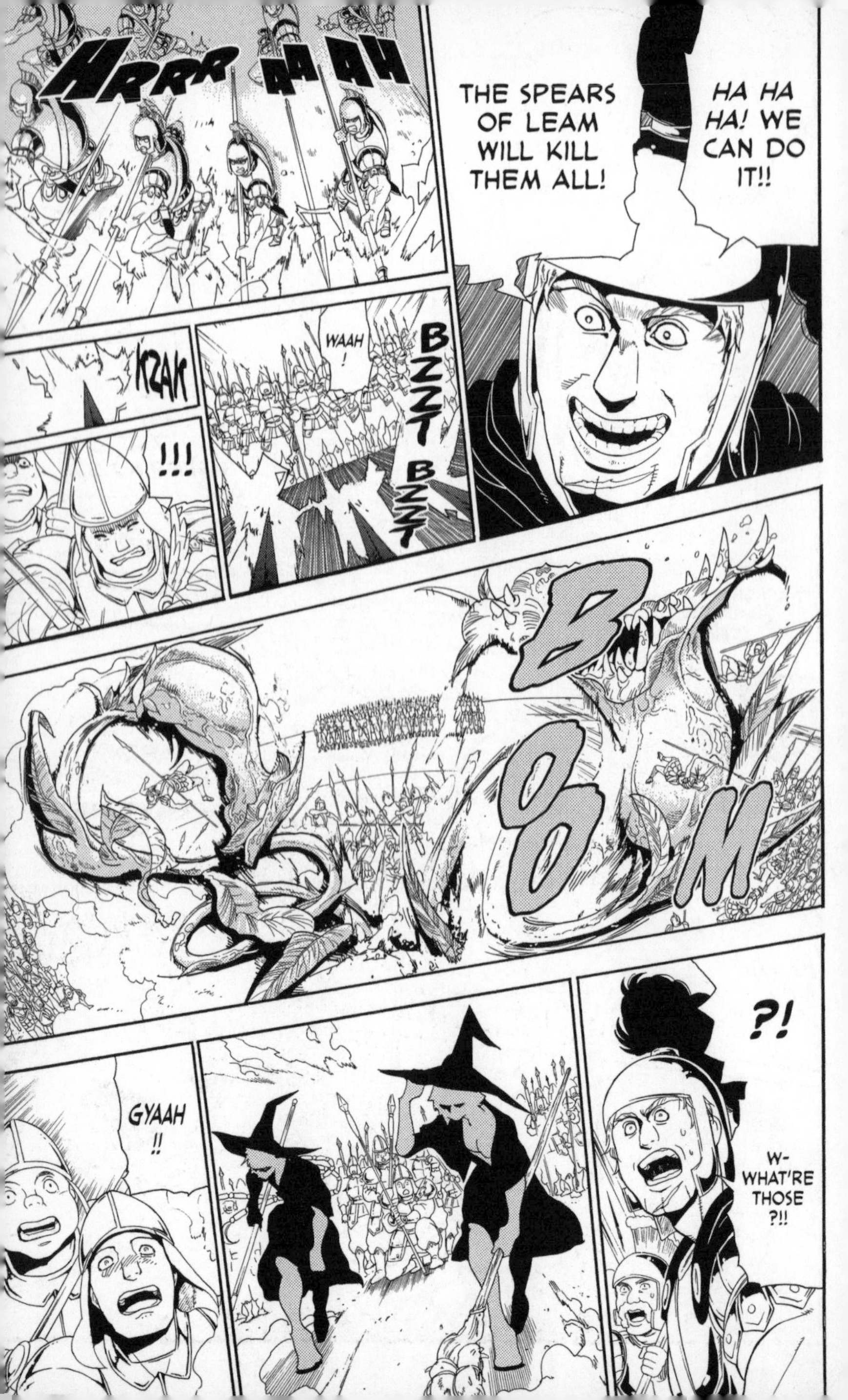
HA HA HA! WE CAN DO IT!!
THE SPEARS OF LEAM WILL KILL THEM ALL!
HRRR AAAH
WAAH!
BZZZT BZZZT
KZAK
!!!
BOOM
?!
W- WHAT'RE THOSE ?!!
GYAAH !!

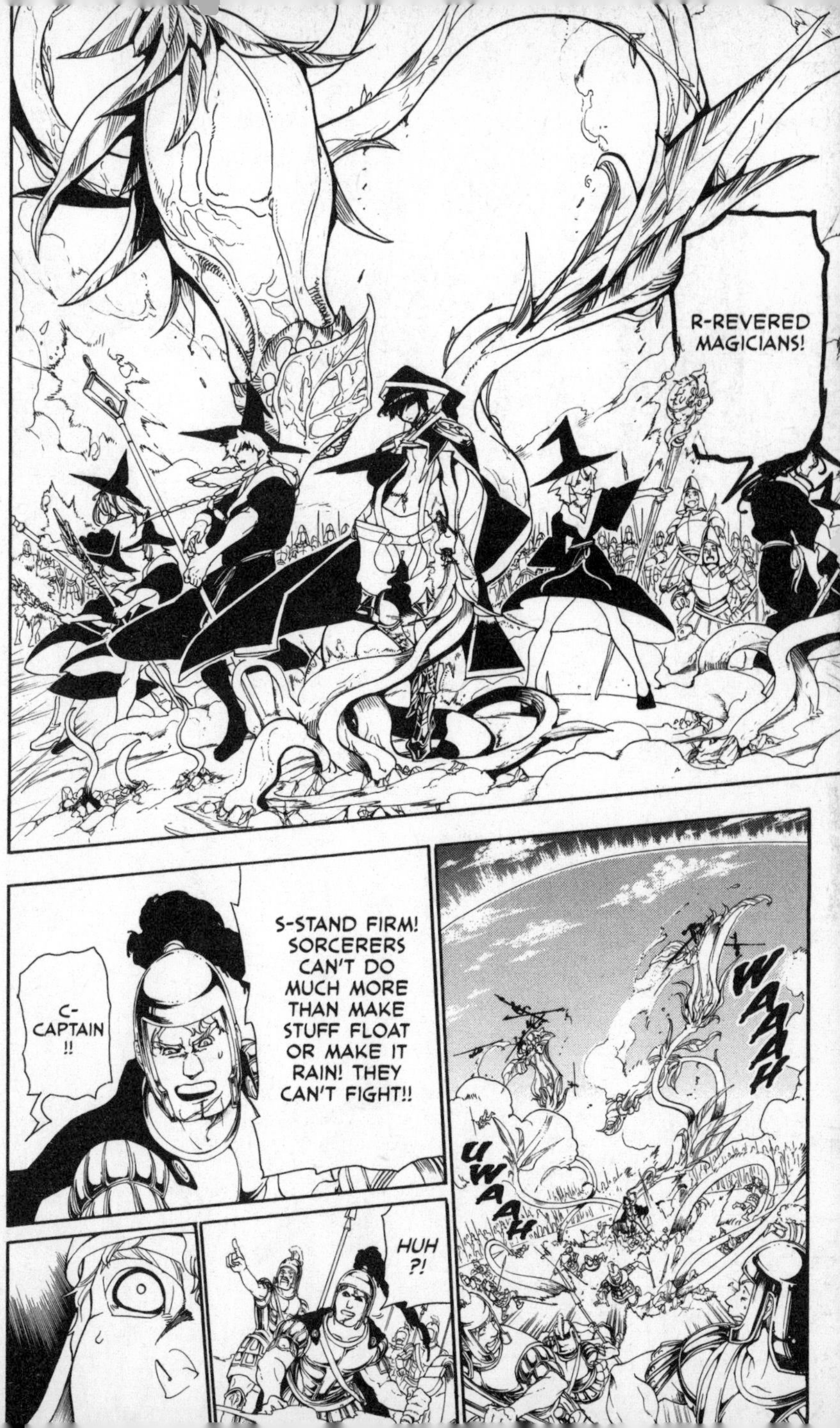
R-REVERED MAGICIANS!
WAAAH
UWAAAH
S-STAND FIRM! SORCERERS CAN'T DO MUCH MORE THAN MAKE STUFF FLOAT OR MAKE IT RAIN! THEY CAN'T FIGHT!!
C-CAPTAIN !!
HUH ?!

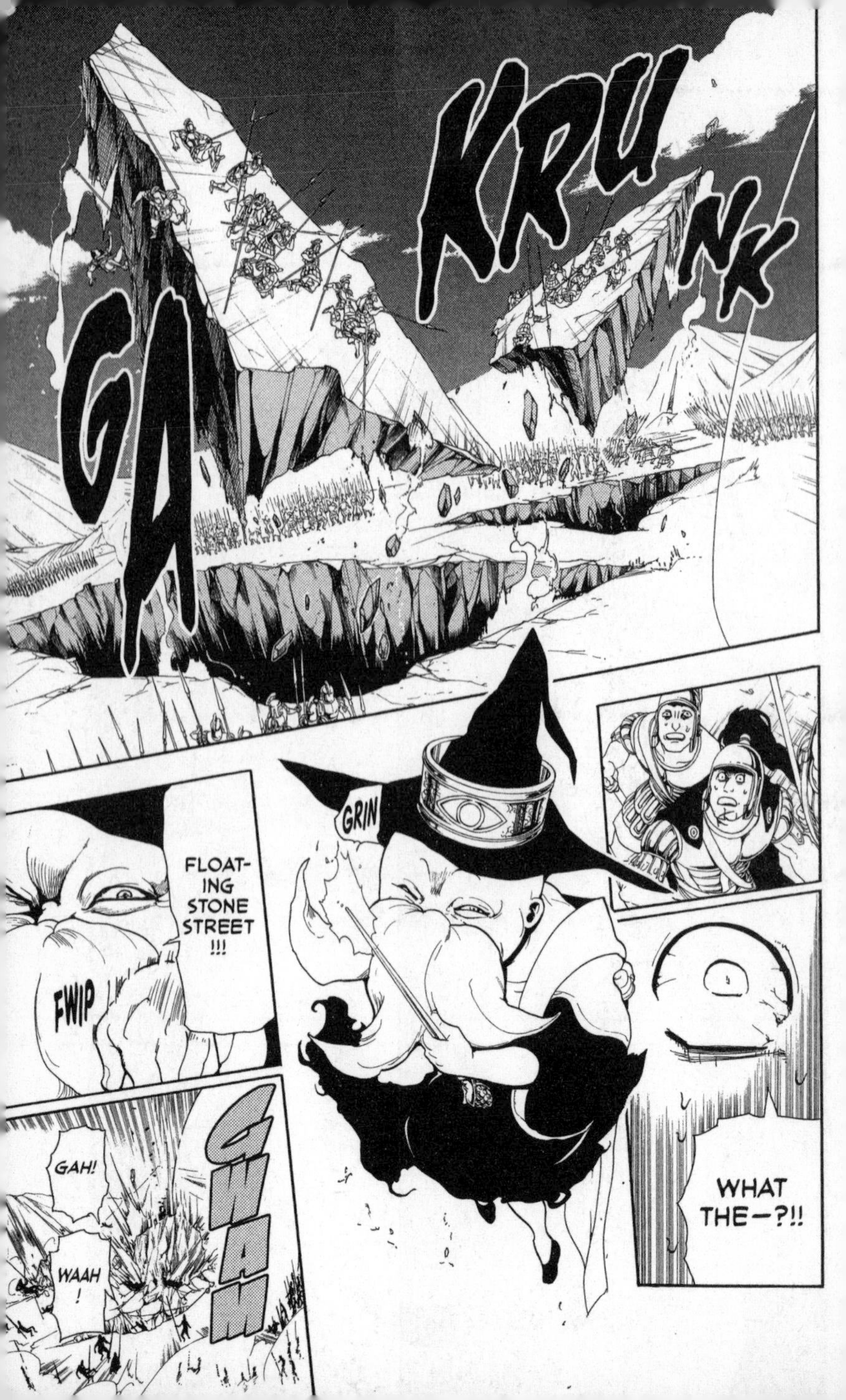
KRUNK
GA
GRIN
FLOAT-ING STONE STREET!!!
FWIP
WHAT THE—?!!
GWAM
GAH!
WAAH!

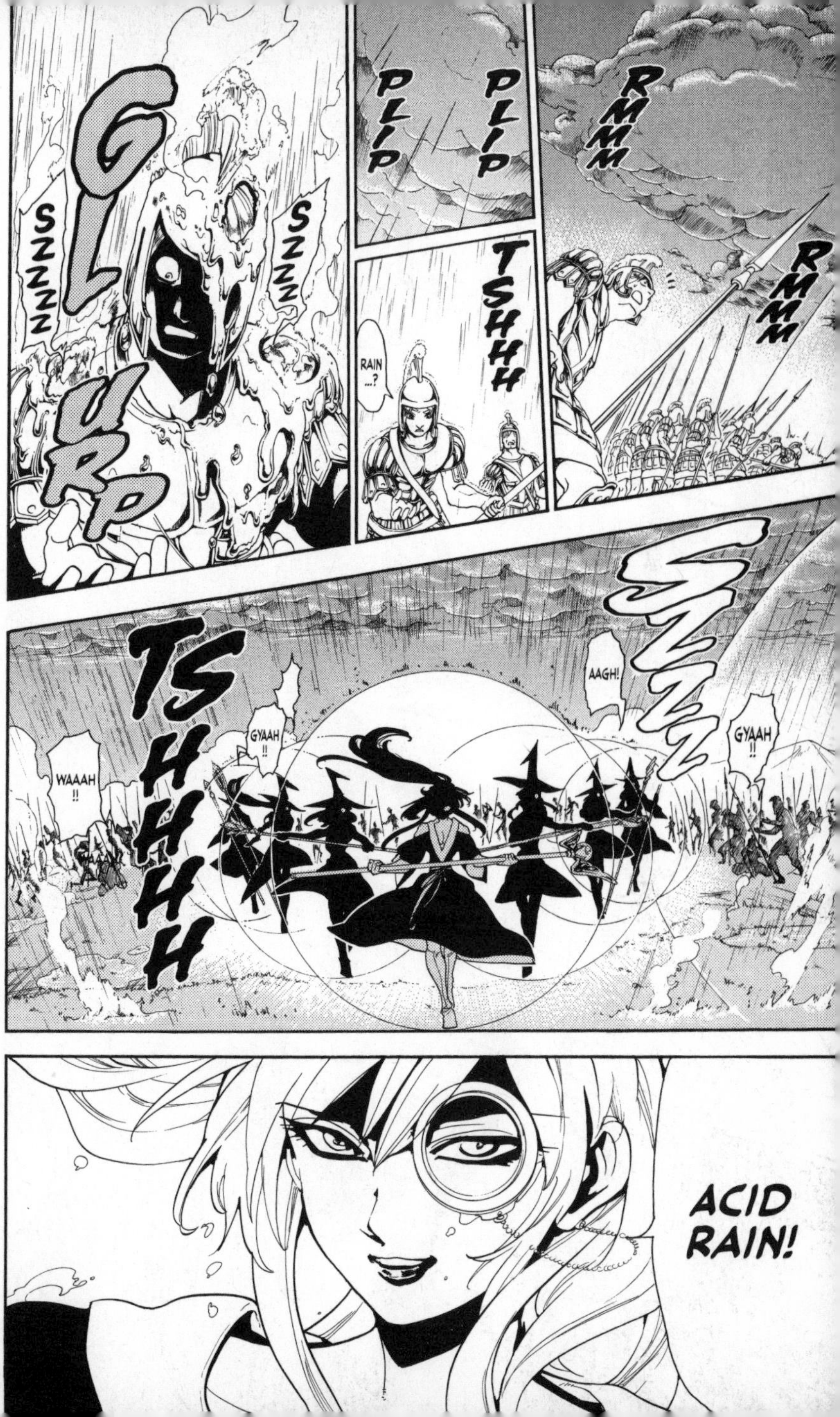
RMMM
RMMM
PLIP
PLIP
TSHHH
RAIN ...?
SZZZ
GLURP
SZZZZZ
GYAAH !!
AAGH!
GYAAH !!
WAAAH !!
TSHHHHH
ACID RAIN!

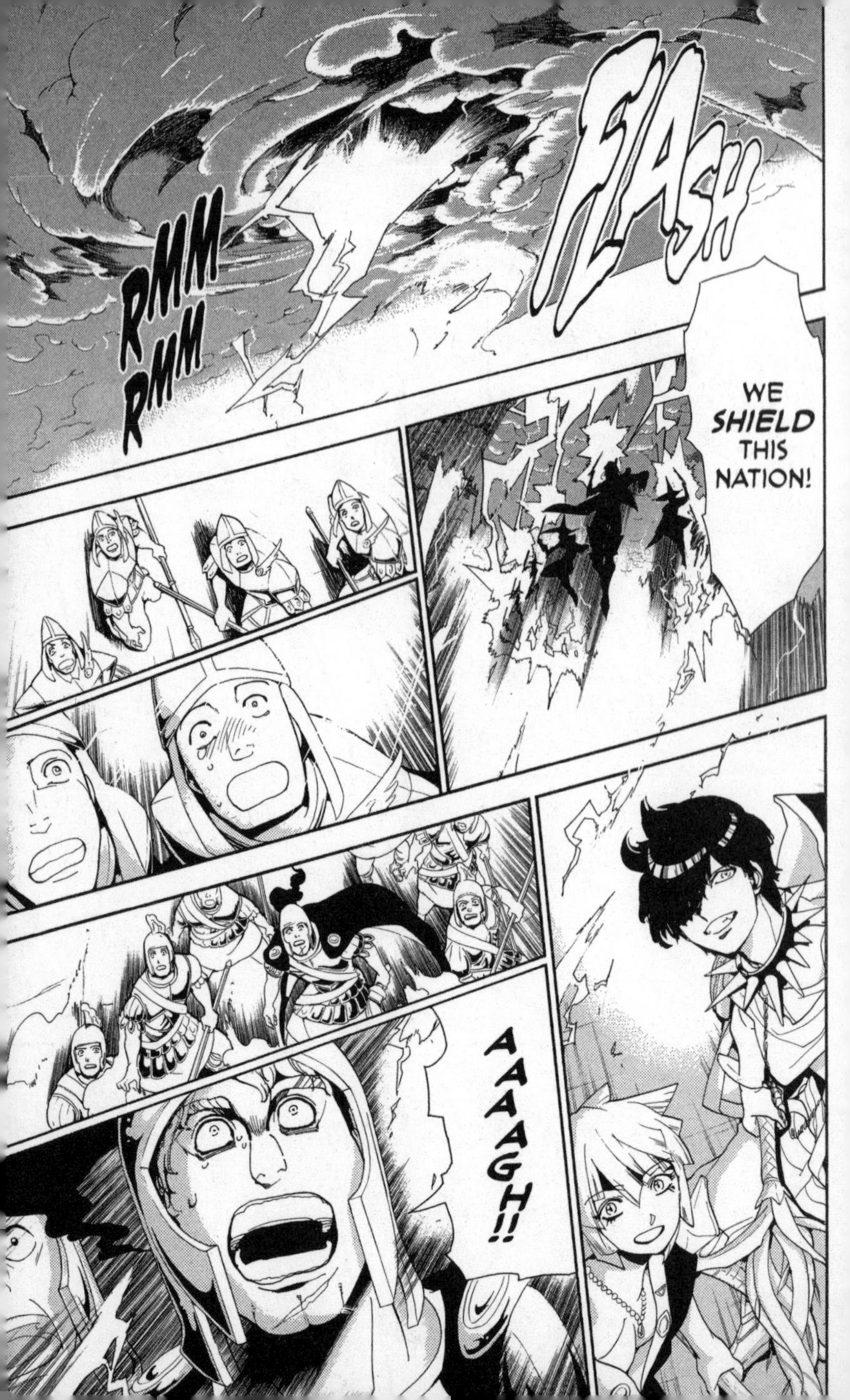
FLASH
RMM RMM
WE SHIELD THIS NATION!
AAAAGH!!

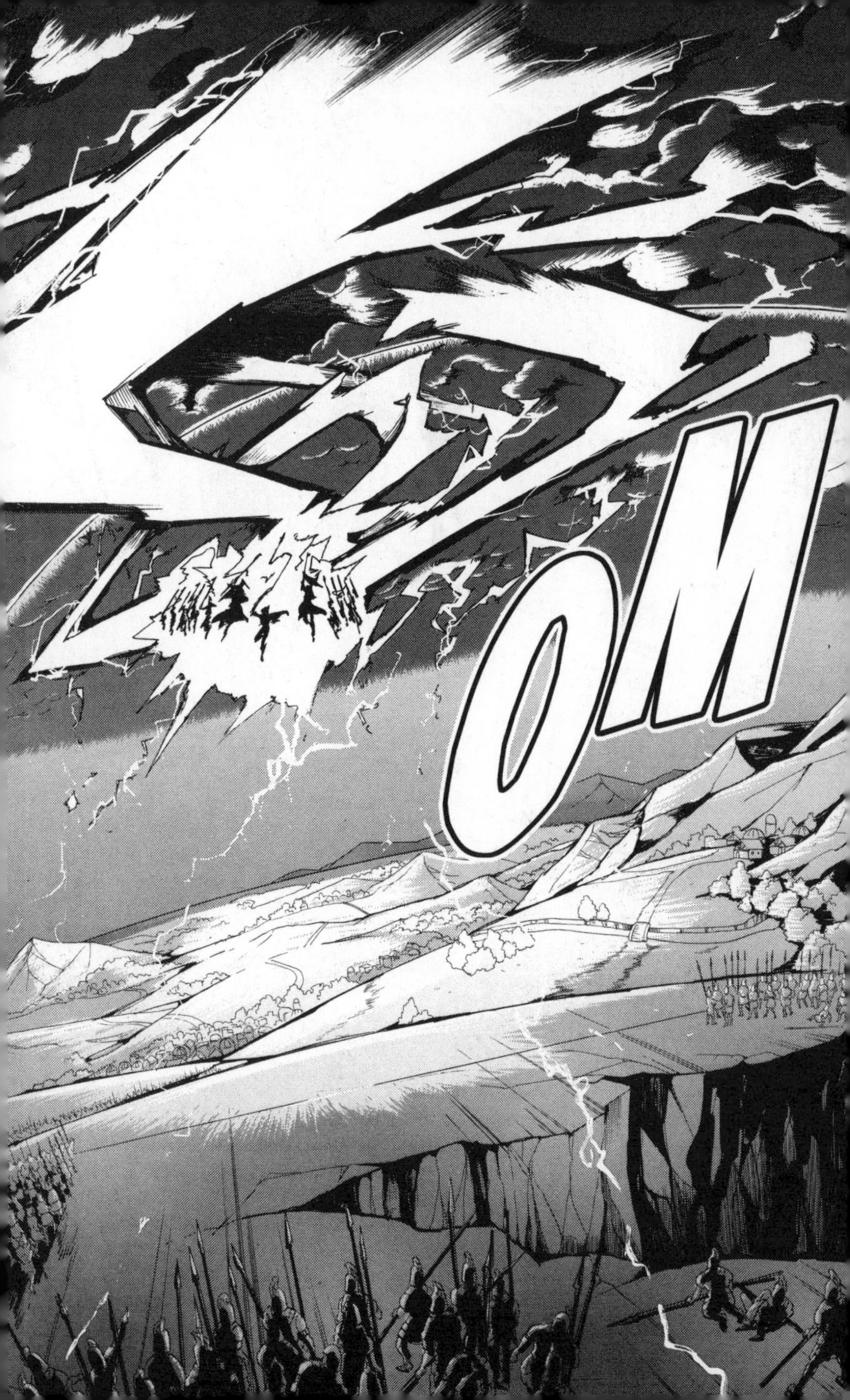
OM

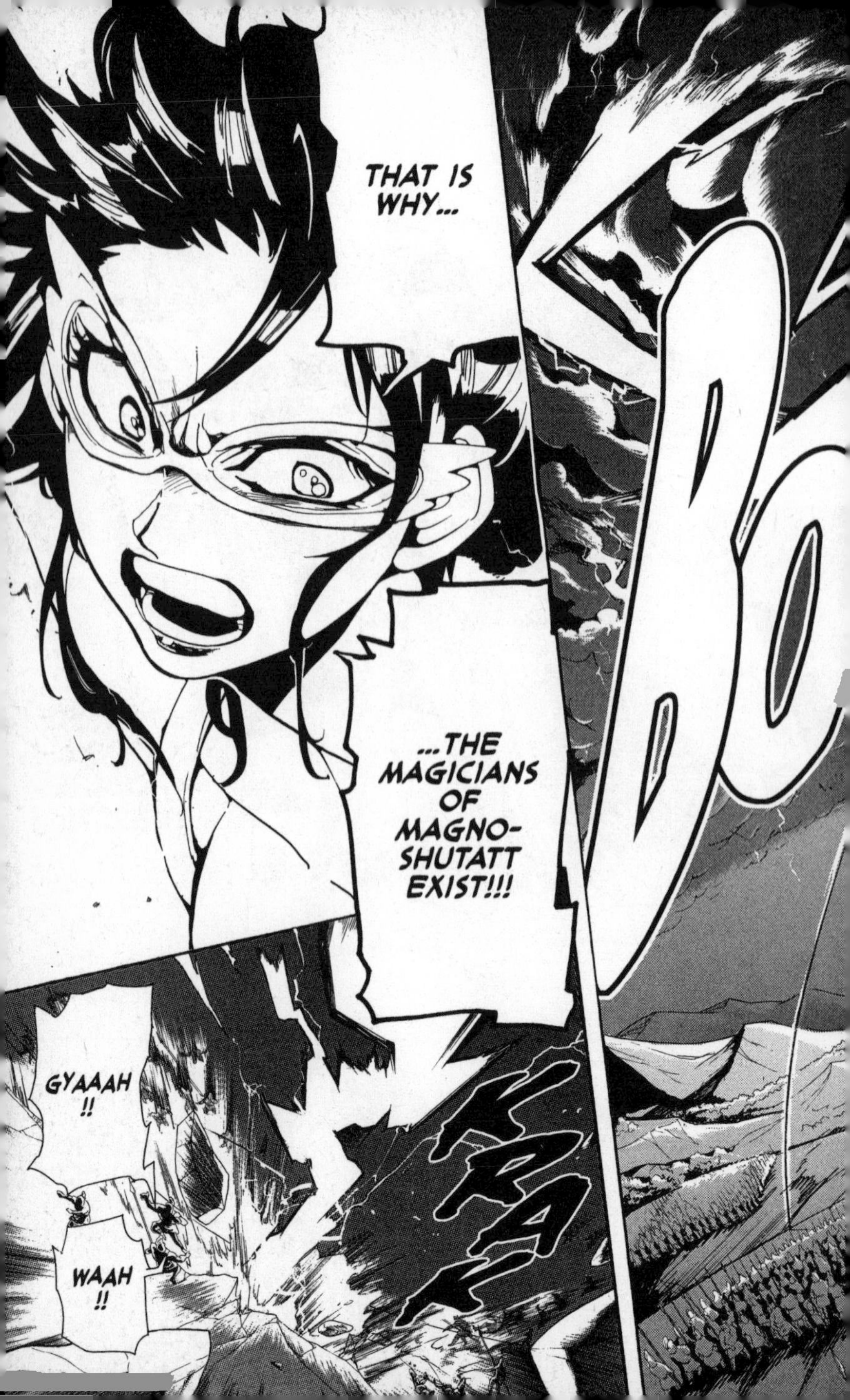
THAT IS WHY...
...THE MAGICIANS OF MAGNO-SHUTATT EXIST!!!
GYAAAH !!
WAAH !!

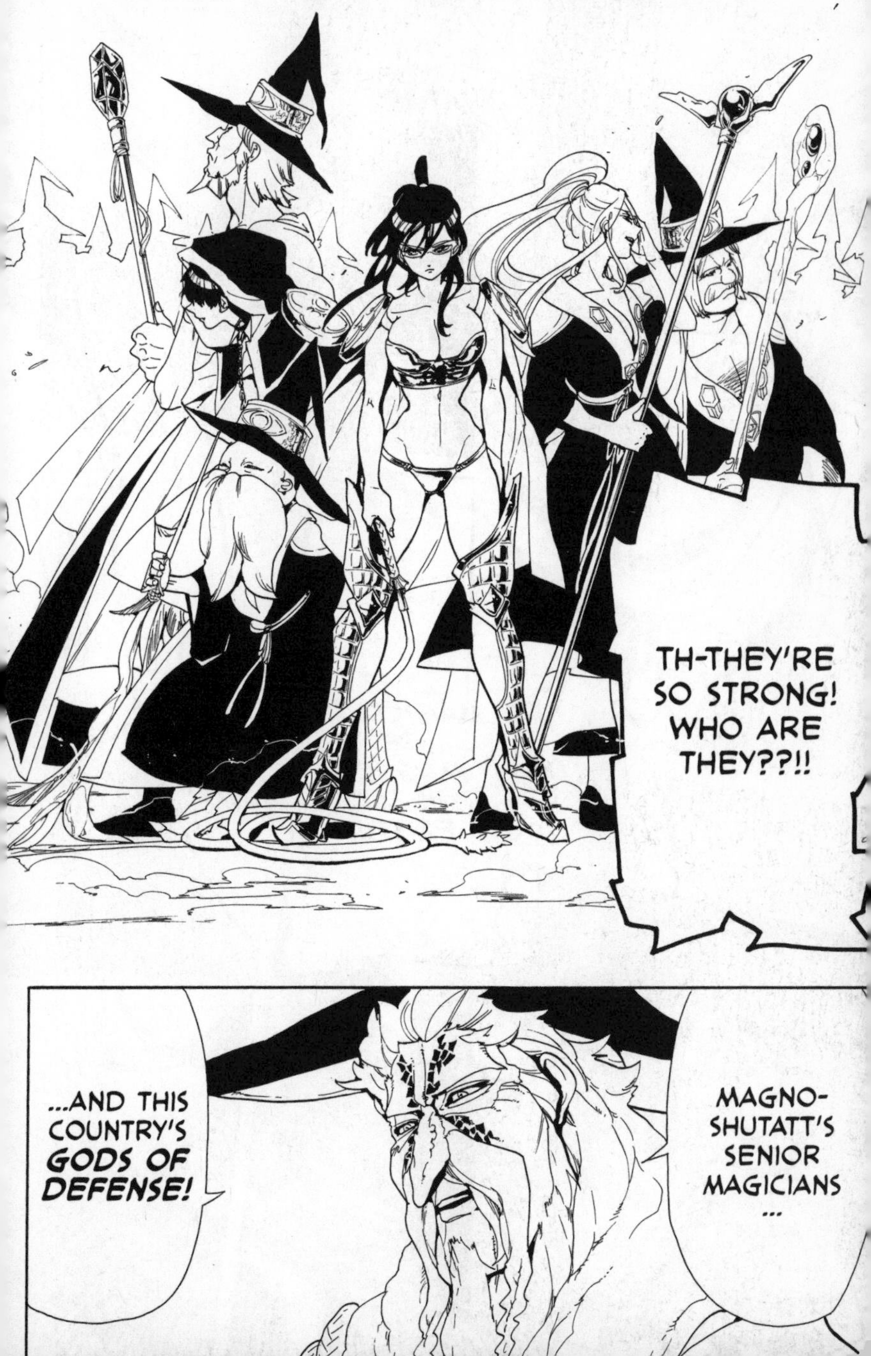
TH-THEY'RE SO STRONG! WHO ARE THEY??!!
MAGNO-SHUTATT'S SENIOR MAGICIANS ...
...AND THIS COUNTRY'S ***GODS OF DEFENSE!***

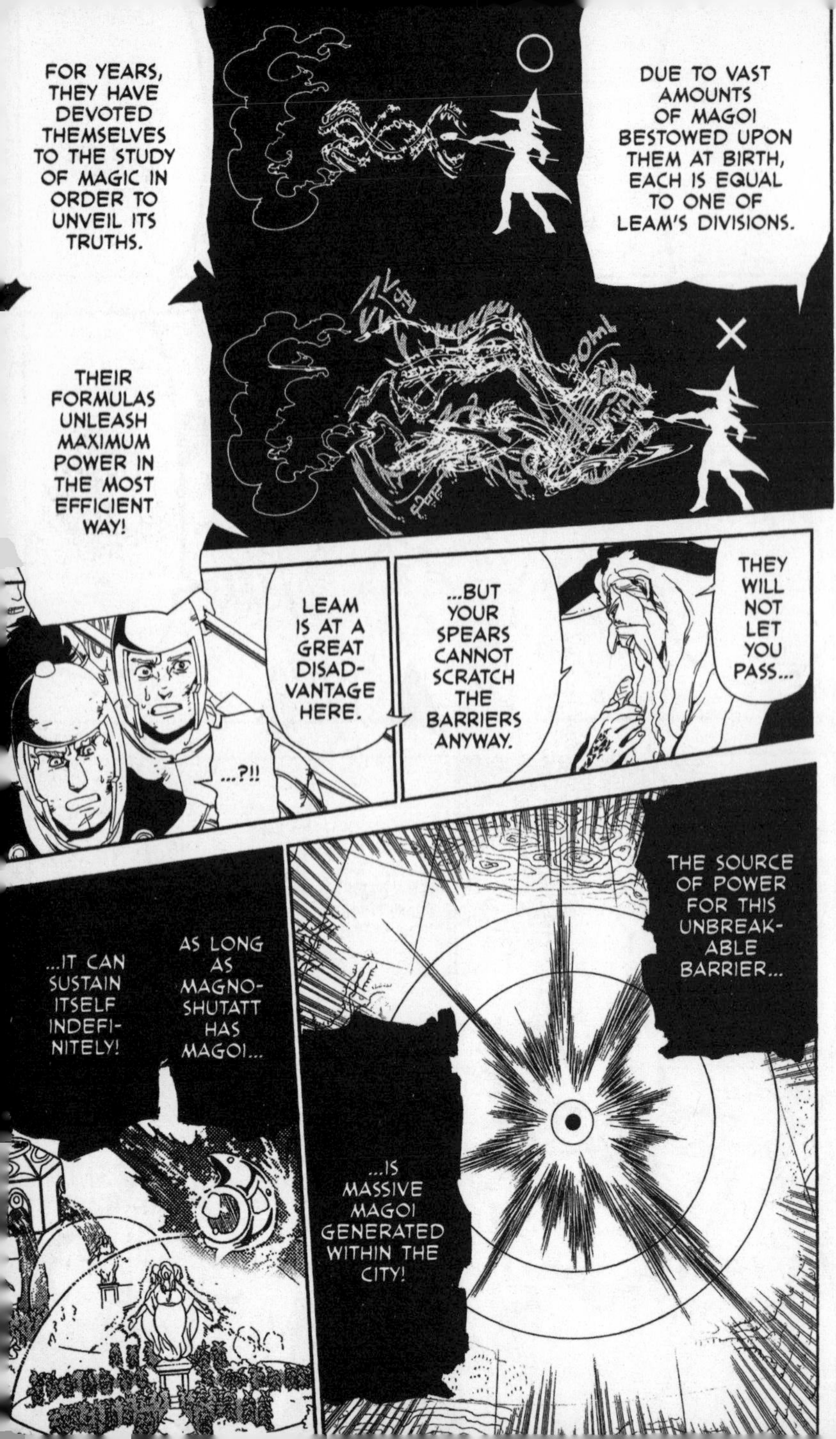
DUE TO VAST AMOUNTS OF MAGOI BESTOWED UPON THEM AT BIRTH, EACH IS EQUAL TO ONE OF LEAM'S DIVISIONS.
FOR YEARS, THEY HAVE DEVOTED THEMSELVES TO THE STUDY OF MAGIC IN ORDER TO UNVEIL ITS TRUTHS.
THEIR FORMULAS UNLEASH MAXIMUM POWER IN THE MOST EFFICIENT WAY!
THEY WILL NOT LET YOU PASS...
...BUT YOUR SPEARS CANNOT SCRATCH THE BARRIERS ANYWAY.
LEAM IS AT A GREAT DISAD-VANTAGE HERE.
...?!!
THE SOURCE OF POWER FOR THIS UNBREAK-ABLE BARRIER...
...IS MASSIVE MAGOI GENERATED WITHIN THE CITY!
AS LONG AS MAGNO-SHUTATT HAS MAGOI...
...IT CAN SUSTAIN ITSELF INDEFI-NITELY!

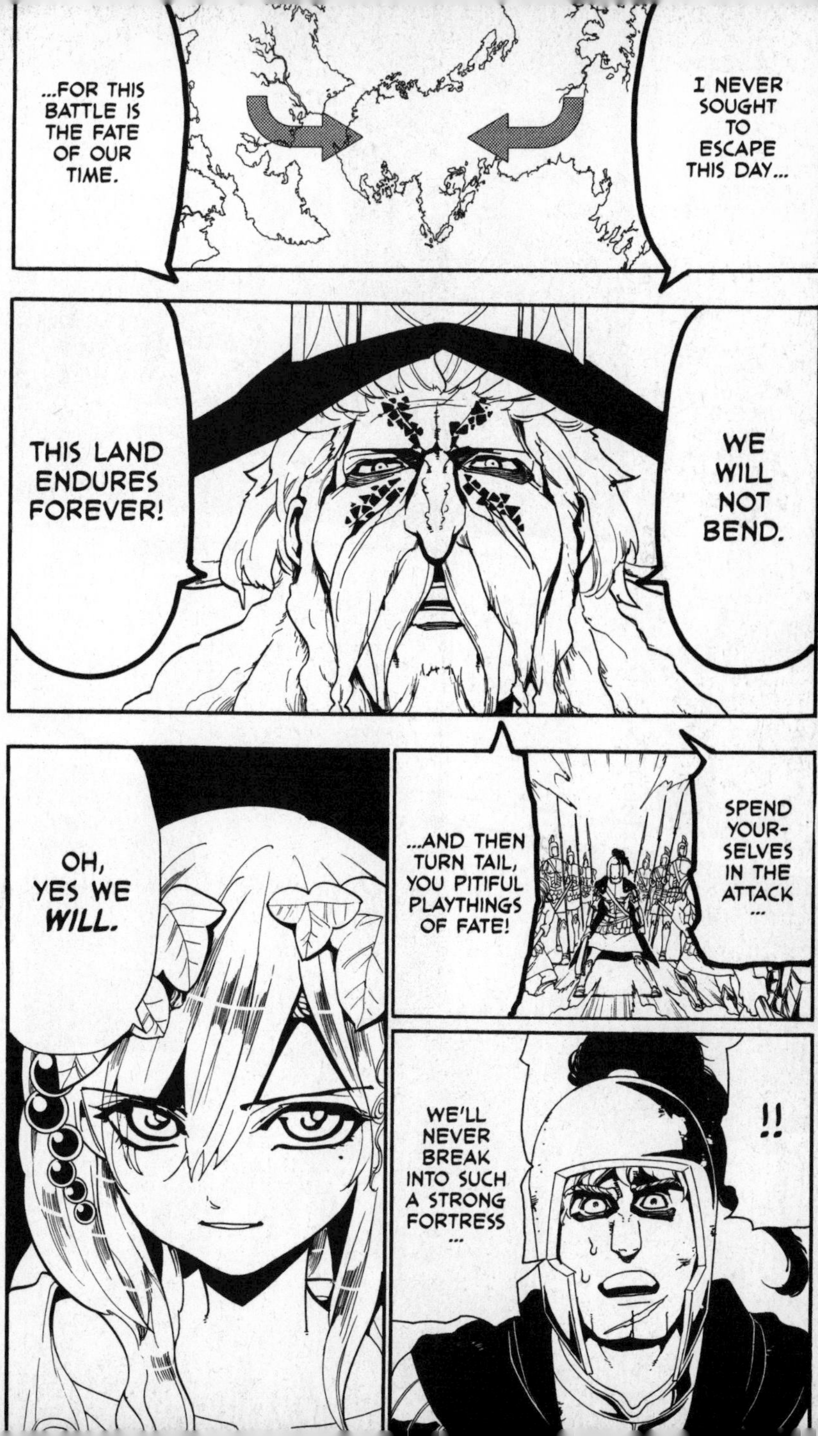
I NEVER SOUGHT TO ESCAPE THIS DAY...
...FOR THIS BATTLE IS THE FATE OF OUR TIME.
WE WILL NOT BEND.
THIS LAND ENDURES FOREVER!
SPEND YOUR-SELVES IN THE ATTACK ...
...AND THEN TURN TAIL, YOU PITIFUL PLAYTHINGS OF FATE!
!!
WE'LL NEVER BREAK INTO SUCH A STRONG FORTRESS ...
OH, YES WE *WILL.*

MAGI
The labyrinth of magic
17

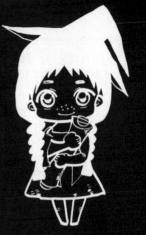

Staff

■ **Story & Art**

Shinobu Ohtaka

■ **Regular Assistants**

Tanimoto

Hiro Maizima

Yurika Isozaki

Tomo Niiya

Yuiko Akiyama

Megi

Aya Umoto

■ **Editor**
Kazuaki Ishibashi

■ **Sales & Promotion**
Shinichirou Todaka

Atsushi Chiku

■ **Designer**
Yasuo Shimura + Bay Bridge Studio

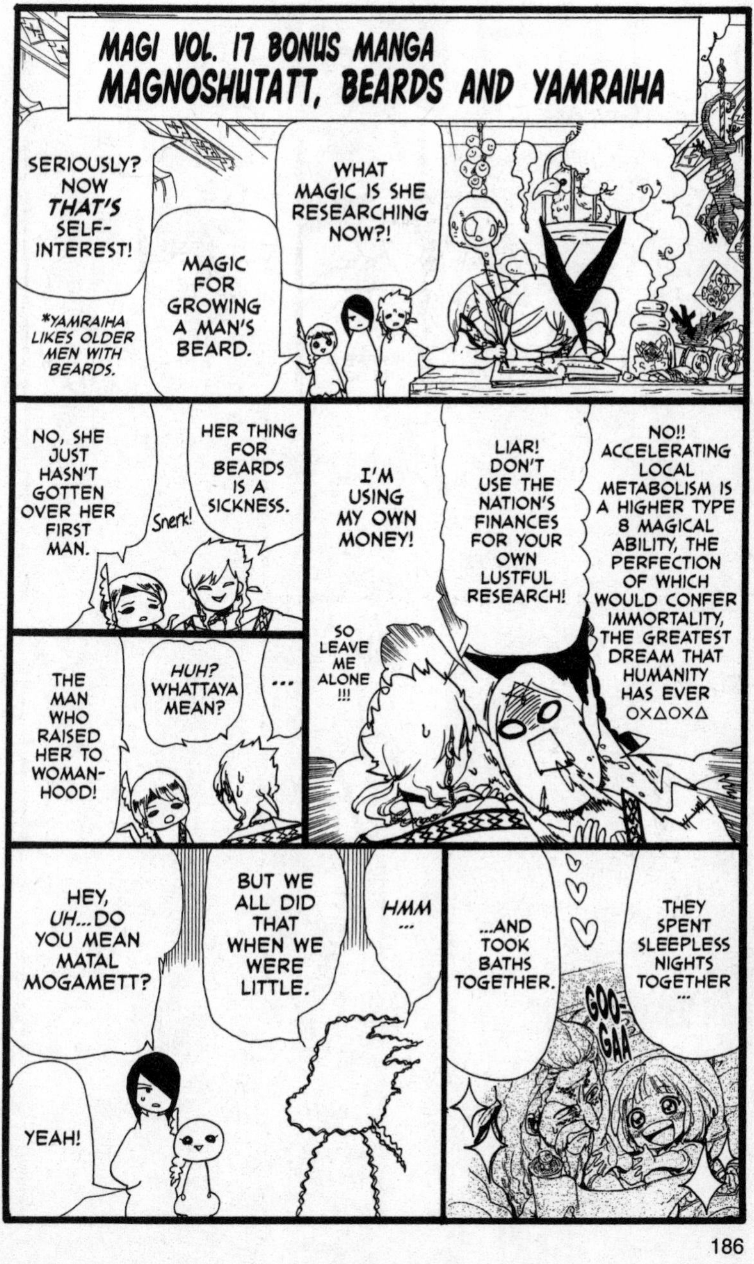
MAGI VOL. 17 BONUS MANGA
MAGNOSHUTATT, BEARDS AND YAMRAIHA
WHAT MAGIC IS SHE RESEARCHING NOW?!
MAGIC FOR GROWING A MAN'S BEARD.
SERIOUSLY? NOW *THAT'S* SELF-INTEREST!
*YAMRAIHA LIKES OLDER MEN WITH BEARDS.
NO!! ACCELERATING LOCAL METABOLISM IS A HIGHER TYPE 8 MAGICAL ABILITY, THE PERFECTION OF WHICH WOULD CONFER IMMORTALITY, THE GREATEST DREAM THAT HUMANITY HAS EVER ○×△○×△
LIAR! DON'T USE THE NATION'S FINANCES FOR YOUR OWN LUSTFUL RESEARCH!
I'M USING MY OWN MONEY!
SO LEAVE ME ALONE!!!
HER THING FOR BEARDS IS A SICKNESS.
Snerk!
NO, SHE JUST HASN'T GOTTEN OVER HER FIRST MAN.
...
HUH? WHATTAYA MEAN?
THE MAN WHO RAISED HER TO WOMANHOOD!
THEY SPENT SLEEPLESS NIGHTS TOGETHER...
...AND TOOK BATHS TOGETHER.
GOO-GAA
HMM...
BUT WE ALL DID THAT WHEN WE WERE LITTLE.
HEY, *UH*...DO YOU MEAN MATAL MOGAMETT?
YEAH!

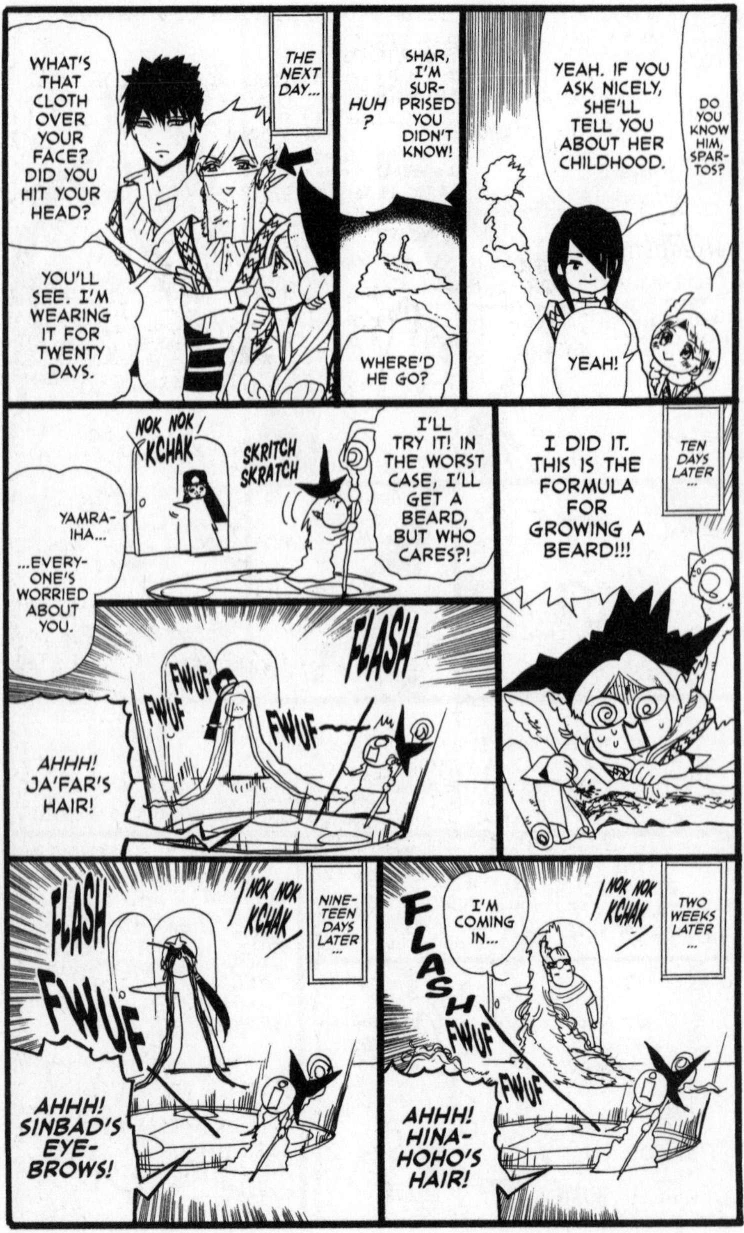
DO YOU KNOW HIM, SPARTOS?
YEAH. IF YOU ASK NICELY, SHE'LL TELL YOU ABOUT HER CHILDHOOD.
YEAH!
SHAR, I'M SURPRISED YOU DIDN'T KNOW!
HUH?
WHERE'D HE GO?
THE NEXT DAY...
WHAT'S THAT CLOTH OVER YOUR FACE? DID YOU HIT YOUR HEAD?
YOU'LL SEE. I'M WEARING IT FOR TWENTY DAYS.
TEN DAYS LATER...
I DID IT. THIS IS THE FORMULA FOR GROWING A BEARD!!!
I'LL TRY IT! IN THE WORST CASE, I'LL GET A BEARD, BUT WHO CARES?!
SKRITCH SKRATCH
NOK NOK KCHAK
YAMRAIHA...
...EVERYONE'S WORRIED ABOUT YOU.
FLASH
FWUF
FWUF
FWUF
AHHH! JA'FAR'S HAIR!
TWO WEEKS LATER...
NOK NOK KCHAK
I'M COMING IN...
FLASH
FWUF
FWUF
AHHH! HINAHOHO'S HAIR!
NINETEEN DAYS LATER...
NOK NOK KCHAK
FLASH
FWUF
AHHH! SINBAD'S EYEBROWS!

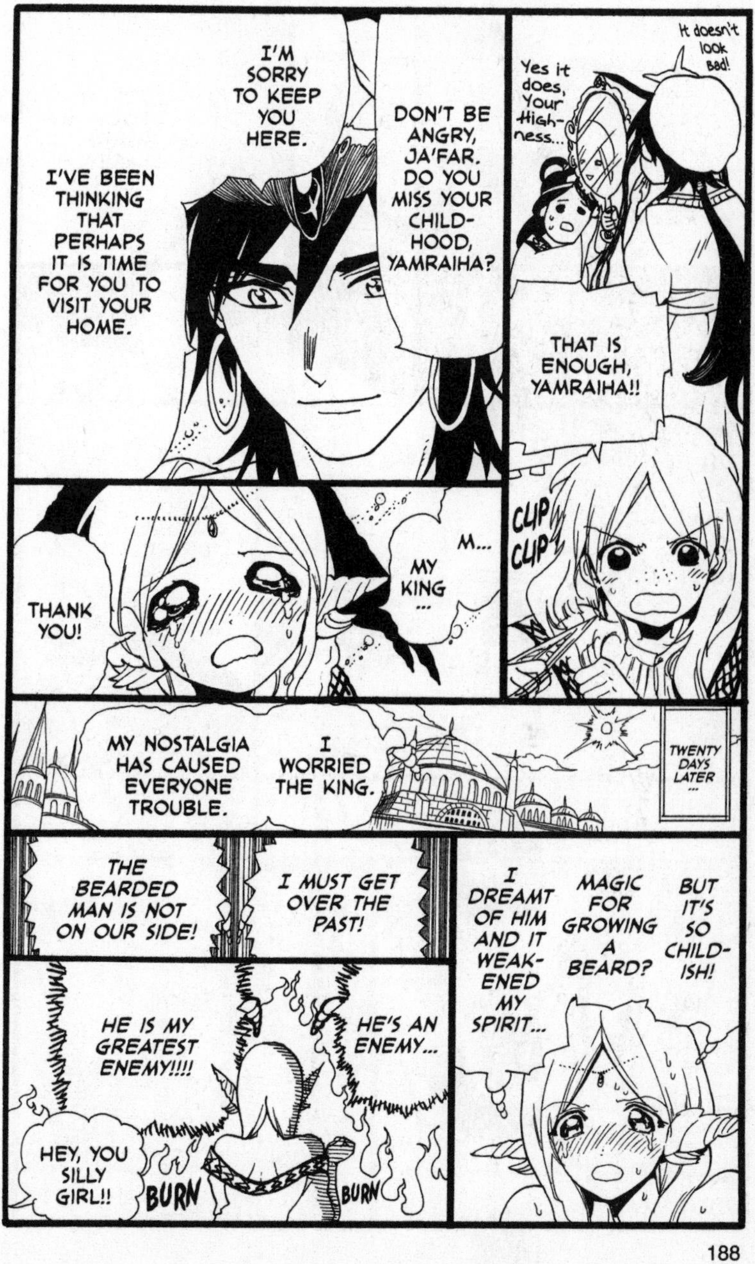
It doesn't look bad!
Yes it does, Your Highness...
THAT IS ENOUGH, YAMRAIHA!!
DON'T BE ANGRY, JA'FAR. DO YOU MISS YOUR CHILDHOOD, YAMRAIHA?
I'M SORRY TO KEEP YOU HERE.
I'VE BEEN THINKING THAT PERHAPS IT IS TIME FOR YOU TO VISIT YOUR HOME.
CLIP CLIP
M... MY KING...
THANK YOU!
TWENTY DAYS LATER...
I WORRIED THE KING.
MY NOSTALGIA HAS CAUSED EVERYONE TROUBLE.
BUT IT'S SO CHILDISH!
MAGIC FOR GROWING A BEARD?
I DREAMT OF HIM AND IT WEAKENED MY SPIRIT...
I MUST GET OVER THE PAST!
THE BEARDED MAN IS NOT ON OUR SIDE!
HE'S AN ENEMY...
HE IS MY GREATEST ENEMY!!!!
BURN
BURN
HEY, YOU SILLY GIRL!!

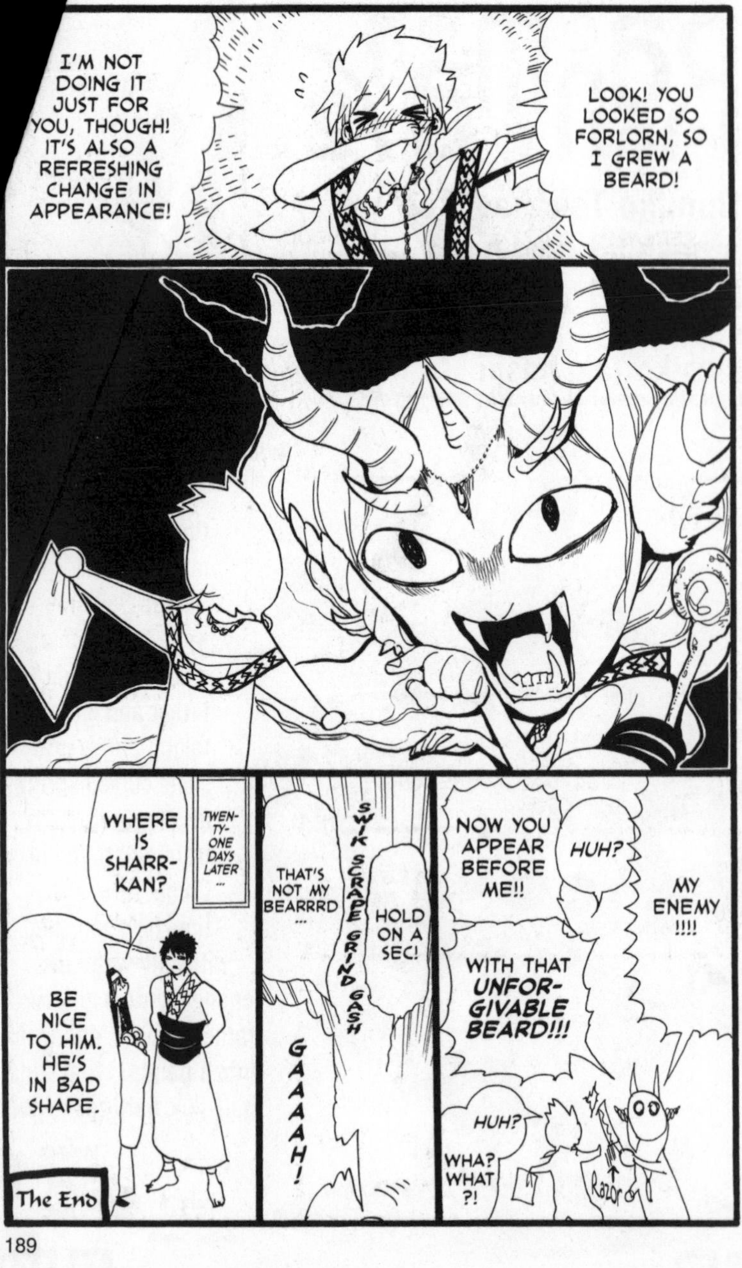
LOOK! YOU LOOKED SO FORLORN, SO I GREW A BEARD!
I'M NOT DOING IT JUST FOR YOU, THOUGH! IT'S ALSO A REFRESHING CHANGE IN APPEARANCE!
HUH?
MY ENEMY!!!!
NOW YOU APPEAR BEFORE ME!!
WITH THAT UNFORGIVABLE BEARD!!!
HUH?
Razor
WHA? WHAT?!
SWIK SCRAPE GRIND GASH
HOLD ON A SEC!
THAT'S NOT MY BEARRRD ...
GAAAAAH!
TWENTY-ONE DAYS LATER ...
WHERE IS SHARRKAN?
BE NICE TO HIM. HE'S IN BAD SHAPE.
The End

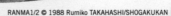

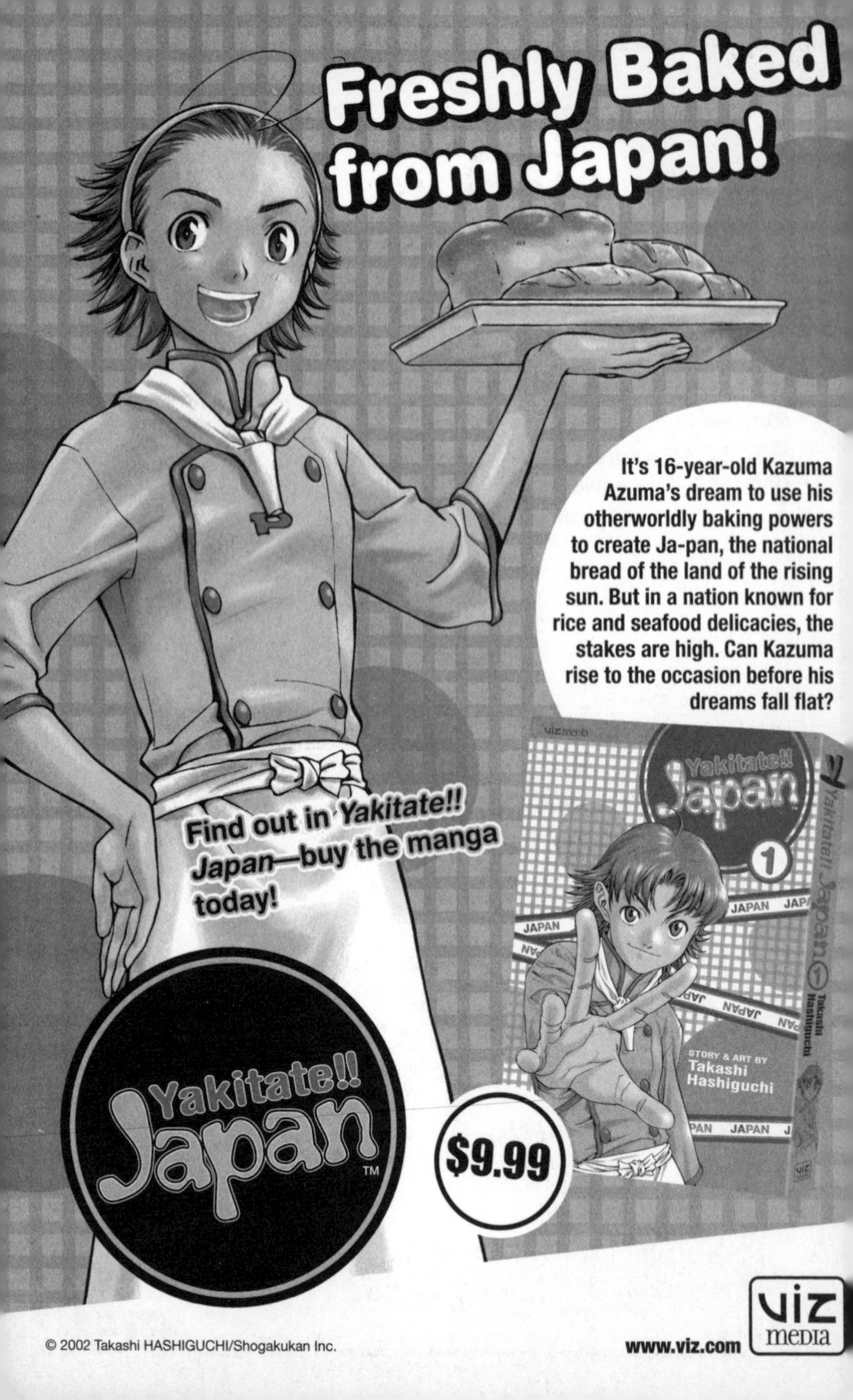
Freshly Baked from Japan!
It's 16-year-old Kazuma Azuma's dream to use his otherworldly baking powers to create Ja-pan, the national bread of the land of the rising sun. But in a nation known for rice and seafood delicacies, the stakes are high. Can Kazuma rise to the occasion before his dreams fall flat?
Find out in Yakitate!! Japan—buy the manga today!
Yakitate!! Japan TM
$9.99
Yakitate!! Japan 1
STORY & ART BY Takashi Hashiguchi
© 2002 Takashi HASHIGUCHI/Shogakukan Inc.
www.viz.com

You're reading the
WRONG WAY

◇◇◇◇◇◇◇◇◇◇◇◇◇◇◇◇◇◇◇◇◇◇◇◇◇◇◇◇◇◇◇

MAGI reads from right to left, starting in the upper-right corner. Japanese is read from **right** to **left**, meaning that action, sound effects, and word-balloon order are completely reversed from English order.

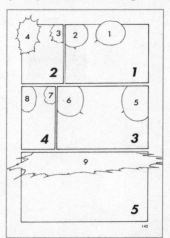

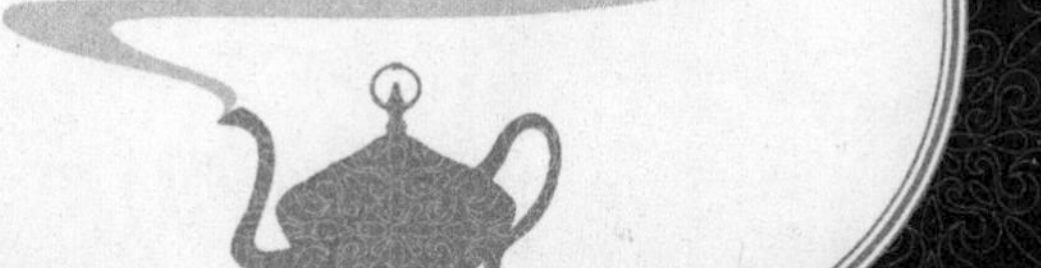